The Conflict of European and Eastern Algonkian Cultures

The Conflict of European and Eastern Algonkian Cultures

1504–1700

A STUDY IN CANADIAN CIVILIZATION

ALFRED

GOLDSWORTHY

BAILEY

Second Edition

UNIVERSITY OF TORONTO PRESS

Toronto and Buffalo

© University of Toronto Press 1969
Toronto and Buffalo
Printed in Canada
ISBN 0-8020-1506-9 (cloth)
ISBN 0-8020-6310-1 (paperback)
LC 78-434310
Reprinted in paperback 1976
First edition published by
New Brunswick Museum (Monograph Series no. 2)
Saint John, NB 1937

Lo! the poor Indian, whose untutor'd mind
Sees God in clouds, or hears him in the wind;
His soul, proud science never taught to stray
Far as the solar walk, or milky way;
Yet simple nature to his hope has giv'n,
Behind the cloud-topp'd hill, an humbler heav'n;
Some safer world in depth of woods embrac'd,
Some happier island in the wat'ry waste,
Where slaves once more their native land behold,
No fiends torment, no Christians thirst for gold.
To be, contents his natural desire,
He asks no angel's wing, no seraph's fire;
But thinks, admitted to that equal sky,
His faithful dog shall bear him company.

Pope, *An Essay on Man*, ll. 99–112

In loving memory of my mother
Ernestine Valiant Bailey
and of my father
Loring Woart Bailey, Jr.

Contents

Preface to the First Edition

As William Christie MacLeod has said, "Every frontier has two sides. Its movement forward or backward is the consequence of two sets of forces. To understand fully why one side advances, we must know something of why the other side retreats." The advance of French society into the New World cannot be explained in any terms except in those of the fur trade, for the prosecution of which the colony of New France existed, and from the proceeds of which it eked its economic subsistence. The Indian and his culture were the sine qua non of the fur trade in the first instance and of the social and religious development of New France in the second. From the contact of the Europeans and the Indians arose the inevitable conflict of their cultures which resulted in most cases in the obliteration of those of the Indian. Often the latter failed to survive the shock of the conflict, whereas in other cases he adapted himself to the new conditions which were imposed by the immigration of an alien race. This process is continuous throughout history and is present to some extent in our own society. On the other hand a fusion of Indian and European elements often occurred, with the result that a new culture which was neither European nor Indian was built up. For want of a better term it may be called "Canadian." This process has occurred with the immigration of every new cultural group into the Dominion, whether it be English, French, German, Ukrainian or Jewish. It is the purpose of this thesis to analyze the conflict, and to trace the fusion of Canadian culture in its initial stage; namely, that which occurred between the eastern Algonkians and the French traders in the sixteenth and seventeenth centuries. Although it was found more convenient to follow a topical arrangement, the chronological has been adhered to wherever it was possible. Only in treating of folk-tales has chronology been totally abandoned, and the chapter on that subject, on account of the nature of the material, stands somewhat apart from the remainder.

This work was submitted in 1934 as a thesis in conformity with the requirements for the degree of Doctor of Philosophy at the University of Toronto. Shortage of funds has necessitated the reduction of the length of the text for publication. Thus the chapter on the Laurentian Iroquois, published in part in the *Transactions* of the Royal Society of Canada, vol 27, section 2, 1933, the chapter on the conflict of English and Indian cultures in New England, and the concluding chapter on the conflict of cultures, have had to be eliminated. For the same reason it has been necessary to omit an index. Moreover, several chapters have been abbreviated.

The work has been much facilitated by the staffs of the University of Toronto Library and of the Public Archives of Canada; Mr. D. Jenness, Mr. Marius Barbeau, and Mr. W. J. Wintemberg, of the National Museum of Canada, have kindly given me their advice on various aspects of the problem; Dr. W. D. Lighthall graciously undertook to read the manuscript of the chapter dealing with the Iroquoian occupancy of the St. Lawrence Valley and to offer valuable suggestions; Dr. W. L. Holman gave me the benefit of his special knowledge of early diseases which elucidated many points which would otherwise have been totally obscure to me; Professor Chester Martin, Professor R. Flenley, and Professor G. W. Brown, of the Department of History, Dr. C. W. Jefferys, and others too numerous to mention, have displayed a kindly interest throughout. Dr. H. A. Innis has laid his wide and thorough knowledge of the Canadian fur trade at my disposal and has directed me to sources which I might not otherwise have known; but above all, I wish to acknowledge the painstaking care and the close and detailed supervision of Professor T. F. McIlwraith, under whose sympathetic direction the entire work was done. My debt to Dr. J. C. Webster, C.M.G., is very great, for without his interest and encouragement this work might not have been published. I am very much indebted to Dr. W. F. Ganong whose diligent reading, and invaluable criticism have led to the revision of several passages in the text. My wife has aided me greatly in preparing the manuscript for publication.

New Brunswick Museum, 1937   A.G.B.

NOTE TO THE SECOND EDITION

The text of the original edition has been reproduced by the offset process and is therefore that of the original printing. Some typographical errors which affect sense or spelling of proper names in a significant way have been listed in a section "Notes" at the back of the book. An asterisk in the margin of a text page indicates a note for the line opposite.

The author has provided a new introduction, entitled "Reappraisals" and an index has been added.

Reappraisals

The original edition of this work in 1937 was a publication of my doctoral dissertation three years after it had been presented. It was published by the New Brunswick Museum at the suggestion of Dr. Clarence Webster and Dr. W. F. Ganong and with the assistance of the former for which I renew my expression of gratitude made at the time. Because of the limitation of funds in those depression years, three chapters of the work as originally written were omitted from the published version: a chapter dealing with the relations of the English and the Indians in New England; a concluding chapter, which was afterwards published in the *Canadian Historical Review*,[1] and a chapter concerned with the effects of French contact with the Eastern Algonkian tribes on the ethnic revolution in the St. Lawrence Valley between the Cartier-Roberval period of 1534–42 and the return of the French to that area in the time of Champlain. Although a good deal of the substance of this chapter had already been published by the Royal Society of Canada,[2] its inclusion would have made more explicit the relevance to the present work of the peoples to whom I referred in 1933 as the Laurentian Iroquois.

I

In the thirty years that have elapsed since the publication of the first edition, scholars have continued to devote their attention to the problems there raised. Perhaps none has been so fully investigated as that of the origin and the ethnic and cultural affiliations and movements of the various Iroquoian peoples found at the beginning of historic times distributed over a wide area of northeastern North America, and elsewhere as well. It has been necessary to ask what bearing subsequent findings have had on the problem of the Laurentian Iroquois and whether in the light of these findings I should alter conclusions, or at least suppositions, to which I had earlier adhered. At that time the idea that the Iroquoian peoples had migrated into the northeast within comparatively recent times, displacing the prior occupants of Algonkian speech, appeared most likely in the light of what was then known. A. C. Parker's "migration" hypothesis, which was widely accepted, accounted for traits then thought to be of southern origin. According to this theory, these peoples had ascended the Ohio, bifurcating at the Detroit River, and perhaps again at Niagara, one branch moving north of the Great Lakes, and others, such as the Seneca and Cayuga, taking the more southerly route to their historic territories.[3] It was supposed that the extremity of the northern prong of the fork was represented by the Laurentian Iroquois. Quite in accord with this general view

1 "Social Revolution in Early Eastern Canada," *Canadian Historical Review*, XIX (September 1938), 264–76.

2 "The Significance of the Identity and Disappearance of the Laurentian Iroquois," Royal Society of Canada, *Transactions*, 3rd series, sec. 2, XXVII (1933), 97–108.

3 Arthur C. Parker, "The Origin of the Iroquois as suggested by their Archaeology," *American Anthropologist*, n.s., vol. XVIII (1916).

was the opinion that these Iroquoian peoples had in the latter part of the sixteenth century withdrawn into the interior under pressure from Algonkian-speaking hunters armed with iron weapons obtained from the French through the burgeoning fur trade.[4] They were variously supposed to have been Hurons, Mohawks, or Onondagas, or perhaps to have been affiliated with more than one of these groups. A theory supported by an earlier generation of scholars that the Iroquoian peoples had originated in the St. Lawrence had been almost universally abandoned, although this was not true of the related idea that, while Iroquoian, these St. Lawrence Indians may have been distinct from any of the historic tribes and confederacies of the seventeenth century.

The causes of their disappearance were less controversial. In 1603, Champlain found a party of Montagnais at Pointe des Allouettes, opposite Tadoussac, celebrating a victory over the Iroquois, won shortly before in the region of the Richelieu. H. A. Innis, in his history of the fur trade, gives other evidence that the Iroquois of the St. Lawrence had been driven out of the valley and gulf coast by Eastern Algonkian tribes.

The question then was not whether they had been forced to evacuate the St. Lawrence region, but who they were and where they went. Were they a separate and distinct Iroquoian group, the eastern van of the Hurons, the main body of the Mohawks or Onondagas, or a people or peoples closely related to the Lower Iroquois who withdrew from the St. Lawrence and merged with the latter in what is now the northeastern part of the state of New York? In my paper of 1933, I took the view that the people of Stadacona and their immediate neighbours were Mohawk, and that the Hochelagans, visited by Cartier in 1535 near the foot of Mount Royal, might have been Huron, but were more likely to have been Onondaga.

It was after I had arrived at these tentative conclusions that I chanced to find two quotations from seventeenth-century writings which appeared to bear them out. One of these was a Jesuit statement of 1644, referring to a "war – which had previously been so much to their [the Eastern Algonkians] advantage that they had become Master of their enemies' [the Iroquois] country, and had defeated them everywhere ...". It was particularly the second reference, however, that appeared to be conclusive. This was made in a memoir written in 1697 by Charles Aubert de La Chesnaye, and there are several reasons why it should not be lightly dismissed. Sir Thomas Chapais described La Chesnaye as having been "the most important Quebec trader" in 1664 on the eve of the arrival of Talon.[5] He had come to Canada in 1655 and had thus been in the country for the better part of half a century when he wrote the memoir referred to. As the chief agent in Canada for the Compagnie des Indes occidentales his contact with the Indian tribes was prolonged and intimate. In 1696, he prepared one of the most important memor-

---

4 Dr. W. N. Fenton has suggested additional reasons for the movement of the Iroquoian peoples out of the St. Lawrence Valley, including decimation by European diseases, their abandonment of defensible hilltop positions, and early frosts discouraging to agriculture. See his "Problems Arising from the Historic Northeastern Position of the Iroquois," in *Essays in Historical Anthropology of North America,* Smithsonian Miscellaneous Collections, vol. 100 (Washington: Smithsonian Institution, 1940), 175.

5 Thomas Chapais, *The Great Intendant: A Chronicle of Talon,* Chronicles of Canada, VI (Toronto, 1914), p. 65.

anda ever written on the commerce of New France. Three years before, he had been granted a patent of nobility by Louis XIV. It is clear from all that we know of him that his testimony must be treated with respect. This was that "... the true Algonquins possessed the land from Tadoussac as far as Quebec, and I have always thought that they came from the Saguenay; it was a tradition that they had driven the Iroquois from the site of Quebec and the neighbourhood which was their former home; they used to show us their towns and villages covered with wood newly sprung up. ..."[6] Here is undoubtedly the most authoritative seventeenth-century statement on this subject. " ... they used to show us ...," the author says, and his memory could carry him back to an earlier time in the history of the colony. It was the Algonkian-speaking Indians whose grandfathers and great-grandfathers had expelled the Iroquois who pointed out the remains of their towns and villages. These the old trader and public servant had seen with his own eyes. The statement is closer to the fact than any made during the colonial period. Students of the subject cannot afford not to take account of it. La Chesnaye would have known that the Hurons were an Iroquoian people, but he never would have referred to the Hurons as Iroquois. That term would have been used exclusively for the Five Nations of the League of the Iroquois, or one or more of them.

As is well known to students of the subject, La Chesnaye is not alone in identifying the former inhabitants of the St. Lawrence Valley as Iroquois, or in his testimony as to why they had vanished from this region in the previous century. Nicholas Perrot also wrote that "the country of the Iroquois was formerly the district of Montreal and Three Rivers. ..." Bacqueville de La Potherie also referred to the vicinity of Montreal and the upper St. Lawrence as former Iroquois territory.[7] Lafitau, Cadwallader Colden, Lewis H. Morgan, and W. M. Beauchamp also expressed this view. If later writers were influenced in their opinion by Perrot, it must have been because they regarded his statement as having been reasonably well founded.

In spite of the cogency of French opinion, and the not infrequent references in Micmac and Malecite tales to incidents of war between those tribes and the Mohawks, students of linguistics are generally at variance with the view that the Laurentian Iroquois were the ancestors of the Lower Iroquois or closely related to them. It is true that Father Cuoq, who established that the Laurentian Indians were Iroquoian, believed that the language of Cartier's vocabularies was Mohawk, but the results of later researches are not entirely in accord with this conclusion. Beauchamp made the proposal that Huron-Mohawk similarities were attributable to the long proximity of those peoples in the valley of the St. Lawrence. In 1940, Dr. W. N. Fenton, in the most comprehensive canvass of the subject up to that time, noted both the close linguistic affinity of the Mohawks and Oneidas and the probable affiliation of the Hochelagans with these tribes to the south.[8] By contrast the language of Stadacona, and presumably its immediate neighbours, is linked closely with Huron. The best-informed opinion appears not to have veered very

6 For further reference to this and the previous quotation from the Jesuit Relation of 1644, see Bailey, "Significance of Laurentian Iroquois" (note 2).

7 For the statements of Perrot and La Potherie see *The Indian Tribes of the Upper Mississippi Valley and Region of the Great Lakes,* Emma Helen Blair, ed., vol. 1 (Cleveland, 1911), p. 42.

8 Fenton, "Historic Northeastern Position of the Iroquois," pp. 176, 218.

far from this view. It was accepted as a possibility by the late Frank G. Speck,[9] and Mr. P. J. Robinson appears to have concluded that the language of the Cartier vocabularies was Huron. More suggestive still is Dr. Marius Barbeau's belief that two languages are there represented, with Huron predominating.[10] Lounsbury has carried these investigations a step further in concluding that, while there are some resemblances between Laurentian and Huron, the former represents a type of Iroquoian clearly distinct from those of the Five Nations.[11] He found closer affinity between Laurentian and Huron-Wyandot, Tuscarora, and Cherokee, than any of these with the tribes of the Iroquois League.

In a recent scholarly appraisal of the question of the identity of the Laurentian Iroquois, Professor Bruce G. Trigger of McGill University has made several cogent comments on the evidence of linguistics. He concludes that Laurentian has features in common with various northern Iroquoian languages but is identical with none of them.[12] "With only the immediate aim of considering the ethnic identity of the St. Lawrence Iroquois in mind," he continues, "the most important result of

9 Frank Gouldsmith Speck, *The Iroquois: A Study in Cultural Evolution*, Cranbrook Institute of Science, Bulletin 23 (2nd ed.; Bloomfield Hills, Michigan, 1955), p. 18. See also Percy J. Robinson, "The Huron Equivalents of Cartier's Second Vocabulary," Royal Society of Canada, *Transactions*, 3rd series, sec. 2, XLII (1948), 127–46.

10 Marius Barbeau, *The Language of Canada in the Voyages of Jacques Cartier (1534–1538)*, Contributions to Anthropology 1959, National Museum of Canada, Bulletin 173 (Ottawa, 1961), pp. 108–229. Dr. Barbeau expressed his belief that a minority of the words were Mohawk and that these were gleaned at Hochelaga, not Stadacona. It is hard to see what can be made of this supposition in view of the preponderance of archaeological opinion, mentioned below, that Hochelaga had strong Onondaga-Oneida affiliations. With such a confused question no clue should be neglected, even such a tenuous one as the close linguistic affinity of Mohawk with Oneida, and the archeological relationship of the Oneida and Hochelaga. Could the latter in fact have been an Oneida village? See Richard S. MacNeish, *Iroquois Pottery Types*, National Museum of Canada, Bulletin 124 (Ottawa, 1952), p. 71.

11 The question at the end of the foregoing note would appear to be answered in the negative by Dr. Lounsbury. See Floyd G. Lounsbury, "Iroquois-Cherokee Linguistic Relations" in W. N. Fenton and John Gulick, eds., *Symposium on Cherokee and Iroquois Culture*, Smithsonian Institution, Bureau of American Ethnology, Bulletin 180 (Washington, 1961), p. 17. "In the Iroquoian family a series of isoglosses can be drawn, largely but not entirely coinciding in their location, which oppose the outer languages (Cherokee, Laurentian, Huron-Wyandot and Tuscarora) against the inner or eastern languages (Five Nations languages, but especially the easternmost ones). These indicate a dialect cleavage within the proto-Iroquoian speech community."

Wright does not find archaeological interpretations in accord with Lounsbury's division between "outer" and "inner or eastern" languages. Specifically, he regards the Laurentian Iroquois as "a largely prehistoric manifestation of the Onondaga; ...." Here he is referring, surely, to the Hochelagan Laurentians, for whom archaeological evidence is available and also to related groups almost as far as Quebec; not to the people of Stadacona whose language is largely the basis for Lounsbury's classification of them as a separate Iroquoian people. As the Hochelagans and other upriver Laurentians were probably Onondaga, or Onondaga-Oneida, he thinks the term "Laurentian Iroquois" is redundant and should be discarded. So far as I am aware I first used the expression "Laurentian Iroquois." I think I coined it for the sake of convenience and brevity. I can see Dr. Wright's point as far as cultural classification is concerned, except that the Stadaconans and their neighbours, not being proved to be Onondaga or Oneida, must still be called something. We cannot call them Stadaconans because Stadacona was only one of a number of villages in the neighbourhood. I think therefore the term is still for historical purposes useful for them, and even for those farther up the river. The adjectival form "Laurentian" is preferable to using "St. Lawrence" adjectivally. On looking back on the use of the term I regret not having called these Indians the Laurentian Iroquoians, rather than the more restricted Laurentian Iroquois. See J. V. Wright, *The Ontario Iroquois Tradition*, National Museum of Canada, Bulletin 210 (Ottawa, 1966), pp. 4, 7.

12 Bruce G. Trigger, "Who Were the Laurentian Iroquois?" *Canadian Review of Sociology and Anthropology*, III (November 1966), 211. Here Professor Trigger gives a negative answer to the question asked at the end of note 10.

the linguistic work done is surely the failure to discover any notable similarities between the Laurentian language and either Onondaga or Oneida." He sees the evidence of linguistics and archaeology as being at variance, perhaps even, in the light of present knowledge, as irreconcilable.

The problem is complicated because, although we have significant evidence of an archaeological nature relating to Hochelaga and some neighbouring sites, our linguistic knowledge respecting that region is slight. With Stadacona and its neighbours the case is the reverse. It is most likely that the greater portion of Cartier's vocabularies derive from Stadacona, but what they tell us is unmatched by any knowledge derived from archaeological investigations. Generalizations are therefore difficult in spite of the remarkable achievements of the last half-century in the North American field. Many important features are shadowy in the extreme, often no less in late prehistoric times than in the earliest epochs, even the paleo-Indian. It is, however, unnecessary to discuss the entrance of man into the new world *via* Bering Strait and the migration routes over which he passed to the various parts of the western hemisphere where his remains and those of his cultures have been found. Subsequently, because of the dessication of the southwest, probably from around 7000 to 4000 BC, the makers of fluted points of the Folsom and Clovis types appear to have spread over the middle plains of North America, following extinct species of game, and to have occupied, however briefly, a wide area of the northeast, at least as far, according to some evidence, as Quaco Head, New Brunswick.[13] " ... present evidence from the Northeast," writes Dr. William A. Ritchie, "fails to connect, typologically, recognized paleo-Indian with Early Archaic assembleges, thus creating a probable hiatus of unascertained magnitude, prior to the established 3500 BC radio-carbon date for the latter."[14]

The duration of the Archaic culture is problematical and concerns us only as it bears upon the question of the relative validity of the two approaches that have been made to the problem of the origin and identity of the Laurentian Iroquois. On the one hand, there is the "migration" theory, given currency by A. C. Parker, and on the other the "in situ" theory which archaeological research has greatly strengthened over its rival. To the first I have already referred as having been favoured, within limits, in the paper of 1933: namely, that the Iroquoian peoples had migrated within relatively recent times into the northeast with their culture and language fully developed and identifiable as Iroquoian and, more specifically, that the Laurentian Indians had been a vanguard which in the sixteenth century withdrew to northern New York to form part of the Five Nations. Having hardly anything at all in common with this theory is the view that the ancestors of the Iroquoian peoples entered the area at a remote time, with their characteristic language and culture pattern unformed, and lacking many of the important elements of a later date by which their identity can be clearly recognized. We are confronted here with another gap in our knowledge, this time of the transition from the Archaic to the point at which archaeological evidence can be adduced in support of the "in situ" hypothesis.

13 William A. Ritchie, *Traces of Early Man in the Northeast,* New York State Museum and Science Service, Bulletin 358 (University of the State of New York, June, 1957), p. 8.

14 *Ibid.,* p. 14.

Much depends upon the interpretation that may be applied to the findings of Dr. William A. Ritchie and Dr. R. S. MacNeish who, both separately and in collaboration, have produced by far the most authoritative studies of the prehistory of New York and of the origins of the Iroquois.[15] Dr. Ritchie has pointed out how tenuous is the basis in material culture for a relationship between the Hopewellian and the Iroquoian. Dr. Byers speculates on the connection between the Lamoka group and the Kentucky Archaic, proffering the guess that the former might have introduced the Iroquoian language into the northeast, while cautioning that there is no proof that the Lamoka spoke ancestral Iroquoian or came from the south.[16] Dr. MacNeish has set forth in meticulous detail the evidence in support of a series of stages in the evolution of pottery types from the Point Penninsula through the Owasco, or variously, the Owascoid, and others designated, to those made by the historic Iroquois tribes of the seventeenth century. If the factual basis is sound, and it certainly appears to be, and if the culture as a whole could be assumed to have followed a process of change comparable to the pottery sequence, support would be given to the view that the Iroquois had achieved their culture pattern, with its essential traits, within their historic territories over a long *in situ* development. Unfortunately there is no certainty that the general culture of these peoples has followed a comparable and related sequence in such a way as to give a completely convincing clue to the ethnic affiliations involved. Thus on the basis of ceramics, Mohawk, in Dr. MacNeish's opinion, is more likely classed with certain Algonkian tribes than with such Iroquoian peoples as the Cayuga, Seneca, Erie, Neutral, and Huron.[17] Sequences may vary, as in the case of west central New York where Point Penninsula passes directly to Iroquois without an intermediate Owasco horizon.[18] Dr. Ritchie suspects Iroquois culture to be of composite origin, not simply a development from Owasco or a closely related forebear. He takes account of the effects of diffusion and raises questions concerning the validity of hypotheses in the light of radio-carbon dating.[19] Although Dr. Ritchie regards Dr. MacNeish's scheme of pottery development as too simplistic, he is a strong supporter of the latter's basic assumptions.[20] Whatever defects there may be in Dr. MacNeish's hypothesis they are probably confined to matters of detail. We are left therefore with the almost inevitable conclusion that the Five Nations had resided in northern New York from an early time, perhaps even antedating the beginning of the Christian era, and that those peoples found in the St. Lawrence Valley in Cartier's

15 See, for example, William A. Ritchie, *The Pre-Iroquoian Occupations of New York State,* Rochester Museum of Arts and Sciences, Rochester Museum Memoir 1 (Rochester, 1944), and Richard S. MacNeish, *Iroquois Pottery Types: A Technique for the Study of Iroquois Prehistory,* National Museum of Canada, Bulletin 124, Anthropological Series 31 (Ottawa, 1952).

16 Douglas S. Byers, "Second Comment on William A. Ritchie's 'Iroquois Archaeology and Settlement Patterns' " in Fenton and Gulick, eds:, *Symposium on Cherokee and Iroquois Culture,* p. 49.

17 MacNeish, *Iroquois Pottery Types,* p. 74.

18 William A. Ritchie, "Iroquois Archaeology and Settlement Patterns," in Fenton and Gulick, eds., *Symposium on Cherokee and Iroquois Culture,* p. 35. On the use of the terms "Owasco" and "Owascoid" with respect to Ontario sites, see J. V. Wright, *Ontario Iroquois Tradition,* pp. 94–5. The possibility of tracing the two Early Ontario Iroquois branches, Glen Meyer and Pickering, to a Middle Woodland base is envisaged. The whole of his chapter 6 is concerned with the relationships and sequences of which archaeological evidence, to date, is indicative.

19 *Ibid.,* pp. 31, 35.

20 *Ibid.,* p. 30.

time were an offshoot of one or more of them; or at least that this must be true for those who lived on the site and in the neighbourhood of the modern city of Montreal.

Dr. MacNeish, in his "possible reconstruction of Iroquois prehistory" postulates the presence of Point Penninsula culture, circa 400 BC to AD 600 over a wide area of northern New York and southern Ontario.[21] He shows the "earlier or transitional Iroquois" as having extended to Montreal and to the eastward, from c. AD 1100 and to have continued there on into the sixteenth century.[22] On archaeological grounds he identifies the dwellers in the Montreal area as Onondaga-Oneida, or closely affiliated to that group. This is the view I put forward in 1933. So little is known of the language of Hochelaga that one cannot say conclusively that the Onondaga-Oneida affiliation is contradicted on linguistic grounds. We must, however, regard the Hochelagans as having come in from northern New York rather than from the region to the north of Lake Ontario. We do not need to alter our view that they withdrew into their former home as a result of Eastern Algonkian pressure in the sixteenth century. Long residence in northerly areas, and in proximity to Algonkian-speaking hunters, might account for the seemingly northern shamanistic fraternities derived from earth-bound animals.[23] Dr. Fenton believed that possibly the blow-gun, and probably the eagle dance, were diffused to the Iroquois in the seventeenth and eighteenth centuries, and could no longer be regarded as evidence of southeastern origin. If his supposition were correct, the in situ hypothesis would gain strength without precluding necessarily the presence of an offshoot in the St. Lawrence Valley. Concerning the removal of these Indians, Dr. Ritchie has noted "the exodus of Iroquoian groups from the St. Lawrence Valley, sometime in the sixteenth century ..."[24] and Dr. MacNeish has spoken of the likelihood of the development of Onondaga culture in the region of Waterloo, New York with its gradual spread from there down the St. Lawrence almost to the city of Quebec.[25]

The conflict of evidence is far more acute with regard to Stadacona and neighbouring villages of which there were four to the eastward according to the Cartier narrative. We know that there were differences in material culture between Stadacona and Hochelaga but, as has been mentioned already, we have no archaeological evidence upon which to base a conclusion concerning the degree of cleavage between them, or for believing that the Stadaconans were not in fact Mohawks. Politically the Stadaconans appear to have been practically independent of Hochelaga. There was no political tie even with Achelacy, some thirty-two miles west of Stadacona (at the site of Portneuf). If the Stadaconans were Hurons as their language is said to indicate, the evidence from linguistics is in absolute contradiction with the view drawn from the statements of Aubert de La Chesnaye

21 MacNeish, *Iroquois Pottery Types*, p. 86.

22 *Ibid*. For further light on the possible affiliation of Hochelaga with the Onondaga-Oneida of eastern Ontario and New York State, see James F. Pendergast, *Three Prehistoric Iroquois Components in Eastern Ontario: The Salem, Grays Creek, and Beckstead Sites*, National Museum of Canada, Bulletin 208 (Ottawa, 1966).

23 Fenton, "Historic Northeastern Position of the Iroquois," pp. 164–5.

24 Ritchie, "Iroquois Archaeology and Settlement Patterns," p. 30.

25 MacNeish, *Iroquois Pottery Types*, p. 57.

and Perrot that they were Mohawks. A problem is thus created which probably cannot be resolved in the light of present knowledge.

One might accept with some measure of conviction the statement that these eastern Laurentians withdrew to Huronia, to confederate with other Hurons late in the sixteenth century. There is some evidence for such a westward movement of a part of the Huron people at about that time. Long residence in the northeast and possible intermarriage with the Eskimo might account for an Eskimo-like strain, cephalically, in some of the Hurons.[26] The Hurons and the Eastern Algonkians could have been enemies in the sixteenth century and allies in the changed circumstances of the seventeenth century when both were enemies of the Five Nations. The Stadaconan language might have been closely related to Huron without being identical with it, and one might lay more stress upon the opinion of the late Louis Allen than one was willing to do in 1933, namely that Cartier's vocabularies represented a separate Iroquoian language, rather closely related to Cherokee.[27] Acceptance of this view would not exclude the flight of the Stadaconans and their neighbours to join the Hurons as has been suggested. There is apparently no evidence of a linguistic nature to the effect that a significant body of these eastern Laurentians might have fled, not to the Hurons, but to the Mohawks, or even to the Onondaga or Oneida. That such a flight would have been necessary to square with the Perrot and La Chesnaye statements, and with the pattern of tribal alignments and affiliations of the time of Champlain, is clear enough. Unfortunately no reconciliation of the conflict of evidence is at present possible, and the question of the identity of the Stadaconans and their immediate neighbours must remain open, pending investigations of a more conclusive nature than have yet been undertaken.

II

Whoever the Laurentian Iroquois may have been, there was evident on their part, or at least on the part of the group residing at Stadacona, some hostility to the French, described as having resulted from the kidnapping by Cartier of Donnacona and other Indians from that place, and their removal to France. As has been several times noted, that group had vanished at the time of the opening of the second chapter in the story of French colonial enterprise. In 1603 Champlain found other Indians in occupation of the St. Lawrence and at war with the Lower Iroquois, particularly the Mohawks. Without committing myself precisely to any particular view as to the identity of Stadacona and its immediate neighbours, I have given reasons to believe that they were driven away by these other tribes found to be living there by Champlain in his day. As the French resorted increasingly to the fur trade in the last decades of the sixteenth century, such tribes as the Micmac and Montagnais, and less directly the Malecite (Etchemin), and Nascopi, found themselves in the path of the French advance, and thus exposed to all those cultural influences of Europe of which the French were the purveyors. The contact and interaction of the two peoples, European and Indian, took place during a period of prolonged war, and in circumstances that were of a very critical nature as far

26 Fenton, "Historic Northeastern Position of the Iroquois," pp. 176, 182–4.
27 Alfred G. Bailey, "Laurentian Iroquois," p. 99.

as the Indians were concerned. My original work attempted as comprehensively as possible to describe all these matters from the point of view of what might best be described as that of the ethnohistorian.

Of all the changes resulting from the contact, clash, and in some cases the fusion, of culture in this area of northeastern North America, none has received more attention than that of the nature, composition, and organization of the social group involved in the basic function of the pursuit of game upon which these peoples living there so largely subsisted at least in the autumn and winter months. The late F. G. Speck found widely distributed, and he fully described and annotated in a long series of trenchant papers, the institution of the family hunting territory. In his paper on land ownership among marginal hunting peoples, Speck described this family hunting group as composed of individuals united by blood or marriage, and maintaining the right to hunt, trap, or fish in well-defined, inherited districts.[28] He believed that this social unit, with the attributes that he observed it to have in the course of his fieldwork, and possessing and inheriting the territory referred to, had existed in ancient times and was evidence of a strong tendency towards an individual type of ownership, as contrasted with that of a collective or communal nature. Like the question of the Laurentian Iroquois, this view has given rise to an extended controversy which has probably not yet ended. As far as I am aware, Dr. Diamond Jenness was the first scholar to take a different view of the matter, in his *Indians of Canada* published in 1932.[29] Noting that "in eastern Canada individual families, or groups of two or three families very closely related, have possessed their private hunting-grounds within the territory occupied by the band since the early days of European settlement ..." he goes on to say that "it does not appear at all certain that this system of land tenure pre-dates the coming of Europeans... ." Dr. Jenness noted a similar partition of band into family territory among the Sekani; Jesuit testimony that they intended to locate each family of Montagnais in its own territory;[30] the Parry Island Ojibwa statement that hunting territories and maple groves still belonged to the entire band, and had never been partitioned among families. Finally there was Le Clercq's statement that the seventeenth-century Micmac practised distribution of territories to individuals for the hunting season. There is no evidence of individual or family inheritance of territories in any of these instances.

While Dr. Jenness' book was still in typescript he very kindly allowed me to read what he had written on the subject of hunting territories among primitive migratory peoples. I was able to add some evidence of band ownership in pre-Columbian times as well as additional indications of the reasons for the change from group to a more individual type of ownership as arising out of the changed condition of life consequent upon the contact with European intruders, more specifically through the fur trade.[31]

28 F. G. Speck, "Land Ownership among Hunting Peoples in Primitive America and the World's Marginal Areas," International Congress of Americanists, *Proceedings*, 1928, pp. 327-8.

29 National Museum of Canada, Bulletin 65 (Ottawa, 1932), p. 124.

30 Of course the effect of Jesuit intentions must not be exaggerated. In so far as they did influence the alleged change from band to family territories it would have been only one of a whole congeries of factors tending to bring about such a change.

31 See *infra*, chapter 8.

Although they made no reference to my work, Speck and Dr. Loren C. Eiseley took issue with Dr. Jenness' position on this question and proceeded to reaffirm the views which Speck had always held concerning it.[32] It is remarkable that alongside quite cogent arguments in support of their opinion, the authors should have included statements which indicate an imperfect acquaintance with relevant aspects of colonial history, and especially with such a fundamental factor as that of the fur trade as pursued by the French from the later years of the sixteenth century down to the moment of British conquest in 1759–60. The argument that the Indian could not have been influenced by conditions created by incoming Europeans because, as alleged, the fur trade did not become important until well on in the seventeenth century cannot fail to astonish anyone familiar with the early history of Canada.[33] The first century of intensive French interaction with the hunting tribes of the eastern seaboard and the St. Lawrence Valley would render completely irrelevant the statement that "family control cannot be traced to the sponsorship of the Hudson's Bay Company," and also the observation that the "occurrence of the family hunting group system among the Penobscot of Maine is still another instance of its prevalence beyond the pale of influence of the great company." No one, it seems safe to say, could ever have supposed that that remote business enterprise could have had anything to do with the Penobscot. When we pass from such irrelevancies to the emphasis which the authors place on Dr. Jenness' citation from Father Le Jeune, we must observe that Dr. Jenness' account rests upon a broader foundation of fact than the missionary's statement. Le Jeune's expression of Jesuit intentions should be taken into account, but, if omitted, Dr. Jenness' argument does not necessarily fall to the ground. The authors rightly draw attention to the ecological aspect of the problem, and to the fluidity and adjustable nature of institutions in varying circumstances, but they altogether omit the force of example of individualistic and competitive European institutions upon which my own work lays considerable stress.[34] They likewise discount the support given the latter approach by Dr. Julian H. Steward in his work on the economic and social basis of primitive bands.[35]

One of the most penetrating studies yet made of the family hunting territory is embodied in an article by John M. Cooper entitled "Is the Algonquian Family Hunting Ground System Pre-Columbian?"[36] He finds the individual rather than the family to be the real title-holder, although "land remains customarily in the family, passing down as a rule by donation or inheritance therein, and from this angle ... looks more like a group right. But on the other hand there is no rigid prohibition against alienation of land, at least by donation, to one not connected by blood or by marriage with the title-holder."[37] It may also be loaned for a season or two. "The right of land possession, use, and enjoyment ... appears definitely as something more than usufruct.[38] The band he regards as a "weak

32 Frank G. Speck and Loren C. Eiseley, "Significance of Hunting Territory Systems of the Algon-kian in Social Theory," *American Anthropologist*, n.s., XLI (1939), 269–80.

33 *Ibid.*, p. 270.

34 See *infra*, pp. 87–90.

35 In *Essays in Anthropology Presented to A. L. Kroeber* (University of California, 1936), pp. 331–50.

36 *American Anthropologist*, n.s., XLI (1939), 66–90.

37 *Ibid.*, p. 67.   38 *Ibid.*, p. 69.

and shifting thing,"[39] not possessed of the close cohesion ascribed to it in my work.[40] Yet the question is far from a simple one, for "sovereignty" is largely centred in the family, extended family, or kin group, and one wonders whether one might not sometimes be justified in speaking of band "sovereignty" where the family is very extended or the kin grouping large. Clearly allotment of hunting territories may take place within the group at the beginning of each hunting season, so that something may be said on both sides of the question, if I am not mistaken in my reading of Dr. Cooper's work.[41] Ownership in common was characteristic of those peoples who exploited the caribou, but the fur bearers were more efficiently taken by the individual than collectively. Nevertheless this circumstance would appear to have favoured "temporary non-inheritable tenure as in the allotment system" as readily as "permanent inheritable tenure as in the family hunting ground system... ."[42] I would not make as much as Dr. Cooper does of the family hunting territory being aboriginal because seemingly nearly coterminous with the coniferous area of Algonkian speech, until more is known of northern Athapaskan land tenure. As in the case of Speck and Eiseley referred to above, too much effort has been made to refute Le Jeune's plan mentioned in the Relation of 1635 as being influential in bringing about a process of individualization, when in fact, as is claimed in the present work, the whole force of the institutions and practices of the incoming society converged to bring about disintegrations and revisions in the native culture. Whatever his weaknesses, I think Le Clercq is a more reliable witness than Dr. Cooper would allow; but more damaging to the argument of those who support the more individualized type of tenure as aboriginal, is the failure to familiarize themselves sufficiently with the history of the early French fur-trading companies and missionary societies and the force of their impact upon the culture of the Eastern Algonkian peoples in the seventeenth century.

The results of the researches of Eleanor Leacock are at variance with those of Speck, and Eiseley, and in some respects of Cooper, and are in general accord with those of Jenness and myself. In her doctoral dissertation at Columbia presented in 1952 and entitled "The Montagnais 'Hunting Territory' and the Fur Trade," she found, in contrast to Cooper, that "What is involved is more properly a form of usufruct than 'true' ownership."[43] The products of the land were communally

39 *Ibid.*, p. 71.

40 See *infra*, p. 88 and p. 140.

41 J. M. Cooper, "Algonquian Family Hunting Ground System," p. 72. See also his statement on p. 83 concerning a great many peoples on the same level as the Northern Algonkians. It is often questioned "whether we are dealing with ownership in severalty or with band or tribal territorial sovereignty or with something intermediate between the two; ...."

42 *Ibid.*, p. 88. More recently, notes A. Irving Hallowell, in "The Size of Algonkian Hunting Territories: A Function of Ecological Adjustment," *American Anthropologist*, n.s., LI (1949), 35, Cooper "has expressed doubt about his own hypothesis," now stressing the ecological factor more than prehistoric culture sanctions, certainly, one would add, much more than the effects of European traits at work in the colonial milieu of the seventeenth century. Dr. Hallowell himself asks us (p. 36), and rightly, not to neglect "controlling factors" and "actual dynamics" of the hunting-territory system; rightly, but not at the expense of cultural determinants, as the inviolability of sacred cows in the midst of starvation should serve to remind us.

43 Eleanor Leacock, "The Montagnais 'Hunting Territory' and the Fur Trade," Columbia University, doctoral dissertation, 1952 [University Microfilms, Ann Arbor, Michigan, p. 8].

owned, and the idea of trespass did not exist except where sale of meat or fur was involved.[44] "The inescapable fact," she wrote, "is that the strength of individual land holding patterns characteristic of the western Montagnais decreases, not only northward toward the tundra where the Nascopi used to depend almost entirely upon the migratory caribou, but also *outward from the centre of the earliest and most intensive fur trade*" (italics in original).[45] In seeking to account for the changes claimed, she cites several of the points put forward in the present work, such as scarcity of game resulting from intensive killing of fur bearers with weapons of European origin, the desire of the French to deal with individuals rather than groups, and the effect of marriage between native women and white trappers.[46] She finds that Cooper sometimes fails to differentiate clearly between the family and the band as the owning group, and adds that "this is, after all, the point at issue."[47] What evidence has survived, and rational inference from that evidence, appears to her to invalidate the claim of Speck, Eiseley, and Cooper that the cases of the family hunting territory they cite are too early to have been a result of the impact of the fur trade. Disagreement with her view seems to the present writer to be fraught with difficulties, when considered in the light of all the elements of acculturation recorded in the present work. In a more recent work than that of Dr. Leacock, Edward S. Rogers has noted that the investigators of Grand Lake Victoria and Tête de Boule institutions "apparently delimited each man's territory without taking into account the communal nature of the hunting group. Speck listed three Misstassini brothers, "each with his own territory." "Nevertheless," adds Rogers, "these men hunted together."[48] Although Rogers appears to be in substantial agreement with the view taken by me in the present work,[49] he takes issue with me as to the existence of an allotment system at the time of contact.[50]

As the question of family hunting territories has reawakened an old controversy of the nineteenth century between "bourgeois" and Marxist ideologies,[51] I should like to say here that although I began the discussion of this subject, in the present dissertation, with a reference to Morgan's influence on Marx and Engels, and although my findings happened to accord more closely with those of the proponents of collectivism than with those who believe hunting territories were "privately" owned, it was never my purpose to try to sustain any particular ideological position. Although conscious of theoretical and social implications, my

44 *Ibid.*, p. 9.

45 *Ibid.*, p. 16.

46 *Ibid.*, p. 21.

47 *Ibid.*, p. 24.

48 Edward S. Rogers, *The Hunting Group–Hunting Territory Complex among the Mistassini Indians,* National Museum of Canada, Bulletin 195, Anthropological Series 63 (Ottawa, 1963), p. 55.

49 *Ibid.*, p. 74.

50 *Ibid.*, p. 83; I should add that in his admirable summary examination of previous theories in which he ranges (p. 86) "Stewart, Leacock, Jenness, and Bailey" on one side and "Cooper, Speck, and Eiseley" on the other, Rogers states that the "argument that the fur trade was responsible for the development of hunting groups and hunting territories is correct only in part." He believes "the changes which occurred in property concepts were of primary importance," and adds "Jenness and Bailey did not take these changes into account." The reader must decide for himself from a perusal of chapter 8 below whether this is indeed the case.

51 The reader's attention is directed to the article by Iu. P. Averkieva, "The Problem of Property in Contemporary American Ethnography," in *Soviet Anthropology and Sociology,* 1 (1962), 50–63.

concern was to present as accurately as possible the effects on the Eastern Algonkian tribes of the culture of the incoming Europeans and of the conditions which this movement of peoples created in the colony of New France in the sixteenth and seventeenth centuries. It would be reasonable to expect that ecological and aboriginal traits would be accountable for the nature of institutions in greater degree the more remote the peoples from the immediate proximity of the French. The possibility of diversity of origins and practice must always be considered. I see no reason to modify the view which I took over thirty years ago in the preparation of the present work, with respect to those groups exposed to intensive contact with the French. As far as the more remote groups in the northeast were concerned, this influence might have lessened in the last decades of the French régime as the trade moved west and when the settlements on the St. Lawrence became caught up in that larger drama, political as well as cultural, which was to decide the destiny of the northern half of the North American continent for a long time to come.

Before closing this new chapter which has been added to those of the earlier edition, and which must also serve as preface, I should like to express my appreciation of the help and encouragement given me by Miss Francess Halpenny and Mrs. A. M. Magee of the University of Toronto Press in bringing the work out, and, I hope, up to date, after so many years. And also I want to thank my friend and former student, Dr. William Spray, of the Department of History, St. Thomas University, for his kindness in making an index.

The Conflict of European and Eastern Algonkian Cultures

CHAPTER 1

THE ABORIGINAL POPULATION

With the melting of the glaciers and the gradual retreat of the ice which marked the close of the Pleistocene, scattered bands of nomads pushed their way into northeastern Asia in search of food. To what extent the lure of unknown lands contributed to the migration is impossible to say. The vanguards were doubtless forced onward by the pressure of kindred peoples in the rear whose increase responded to the milder conditions of the time. It is possible that they followed in the wake of the vast herds of bison, reindeer and other animals that found their way from Asia to Alaska by means of the land bridge that connected these areas in late Pleistocene times.[1] Although traces of man, such as worked flints, have been found in American preglacial deposits it is more probable that the full flood of the migration began at a later date.[2] No land bridge was necessary to the passage of man from one continent to the other. On a clear day the high coast of Alaska is easily discernable across the fifty miles of water that constitute Bering Strait, and the passage is facilitated by the Diomede Islands that lie midway between the two continents.[3] The migration continued until the whole of America was peopled south to Tierra del Fuego and east to Newfoundland.[4] It was not a conscious thrust upon the part of any one group to colonize a new area; it was rather an incident in the blind and fitful wanderings of diverse peoples of the same general stock which, doubtless, consumed many thousands of years, and which might have continued to the present day had not the European nations repeopled America and blocked the way for further advances from the northeast. Because of the high development which was reached by the autochthonous culture of middle America, and because of the great diversity of languages which were spoken by the American aborigines, fifty-six occurring north of Mexico alone, if for no other reasons, it has been concluded that the migration to America began not less than fifteen thousand years ago.

The Bering Strait theory has rivals which, at best, supplement rather than displace it. No amount of research has as yet revealed traces of the lost continent of Atlantis, and Professor Wiener's theory that the African negroes made frequent voyages to America in pre-Columbian times is offset by the fact that the American aborigines reveal no traces of admixture with this stock.[5] The land bridges between America and the Old World, that extended through Antarctica in the south and Greenland in the north, had sunk into the sea long before man made his appearance on the earth.[6] When Professor Elliot Smith postulates somewhat dogmatically that the civilization of middle America was

---

1. Jenness (1); 238.
2. Jenness (1); 236; Smith, G. E. 95. See also Goddard 262.
3. Jenness (1); 244 note.
4. Hrdlicka 44.
5. Jenness (1); 239.
6. Jenness (1); 238.

derived from that of Egypt, he is entering upon a course of speculation with which many eminent specialists in this field are not in accord.   Less tenuous is Rivet's theory that the many parallels between the grammatical structure of Melanesian and the Hokan group in California prove a derivation from the same linguistic stock.[7]   This linguistic theory appears more plausible when it is coordinated with the discovery of skulls, which in some ways resemble those of the Melanesian type, at Lagoa Santa, in Brazil, and in Southern California.   As geological opinion does not support the belief in a sunken continent in the Pacific, and as migrations by sea from Melanesia to America seem to be out of the question, it is more reasonable to suppose that the Melanesians and the Lagoa Santa people resulted from a division of the same race that occurred somewhere in Asia, and that the latter people found their way to America by way of Bering Strait.[8]

It is believed that the Eskimo of the Arctic areas of North America represent a recent, although not certainly the last, migration of a Mongoloid group into the western hemisphere,[9] and with the Lapps, Finns, and kindred peoples of Europe and Asia, they formed a sub-polar belt of Mongoloid peoples which was left incomplete by the gap between Scandinavia and Greenland, the people of these two areas having been unaware of each other's existence.   Also it has been suggested that the Siouans, the Iroquoians, and the Algonkians were among the earliest peoples to enter America.[10]   We are not, however, especially concerned here with speculations upon tribal migrations in pre-Columbian times, but rather with the nature of eastern Algonkian culture as it was when Europeans first encountered it upon the eastern Canadian littoral in the sixteenth century.

It is necessary at this point to distinguish between the terms "Algonkin" and "Algonkian".   The former was the name applied by the French explorers of the seventeenth century to a group who were so closely related to each other culturally and who acted with such concerted action in warfare that they might almost be considered to have constituted a tribe.   It is true that there were minor political cleavages between the Iroquet, to the west of Montreal Island, the Little Nation, of the lower Ottawa, the Island Algonkins, of Allumette Island, and kindred bands to the northward; but on the whole they may be treated as one group.   It was the Algonkins who gave their name to a linguistic stock which was widespread throughout North America and which may be designated by the adjectival form "Algonkian".   Those who spoke the Algonkian languages, extended within historic times from the foothills of the Rockies to Nova Scotia, and south, through New England, to the southern Atlantic states.   With respect to Canada they may be divided arbitrarily into central and eastern Algonkian, although the distinction between the two cannot be sharply drawn.   Although the Ojibwa and Cree of Ontario fall within the central group, the latter are almost indistinguishable in culture from the Miss-

7. Jenness (1); 240.
8. Jenness (1); 238-242.
9. Jenness (1); 248.
10. Jenness (1); 246; Theory of A. Hrdlicka, the origin and antiquity of the American Indian, Ann. Rep. of the Bd. of Regents, Smithsonian Institution, 1923, p. 493.

tassini Cree whose position above Lake Misstassini and on the Eastmain and Rupert Rivers warrants their inclusion in the eastern group.   These in turn merge with the Montagnais-Nascopi who inhabited the Province of Quebec and parts of the south Labrador coast.   Progressive research is revealing that even the distinction on the basis of culture between the Montagnais and Nascopi is an arbitrary one, although a geographical cleavage may be recognized in treatment. The Nascopi may be said to have comprised those bands who dwelt north of the height of land which separated the rivers which ran into the St. Lawrence from those which flowed into Hudson Bay and the Arctic waters. They occupied the coast, however, from Seven Islands eastward to the Strait of Belle Isle.   Under the term "Montagnais" may be grouped those bands which occupied the territory westward from Seven Islands to the headwaters of the St. Maurice, with the exception of a strip of territory along the north bank of the St. Lawrence which in the sixteenth century was occupied by the Laurentian Iroquois.   The Montagnais comprised the White Fish or Atticamegs of the St. Maurice, the Quebec and Tadoussac bands, the Porcupines and Squirrels of Lake St. John, the Papinachois from Escoumains to Manicouagan, the Betsiamites or Oumamiois from Manicouagan to Seven Islands, and several other groups of bands in the interior.   Unlike some of the Algonkins who had borrowed traits from the contiguous Iroquoian peoples, the Montagnais-Nascopi lived by hunting, fishing, and gathering, and did not practice agriculture. South of the St. Lawrence the Micmac, too, who occupied the whole of Nova Scotia, Prince Edward Island, Southern Newfoundland, and the gulf watershed of New Brunswick, lived entirely by hunting and fishing, although a myth concerning the origin of corn may indicate that they had at one time practised agriculture, as did their neighbours the Malecite or Etchemins of the St. John River valley.   Closely related to the Malecite were the Passamaquoddy of the of the St. Croix River, and the Penobscots of the river which now bears their name.   South of these were the Abenaki (the Tarenteens of the Puritans) who properly were the Canibas, the Norridgewalk of the Kennebec; but the name has been applied under the spelling "Wabanaki" to all the tribes from the Malecite in the northeast to the Sokokis and others in Maine and New Hampshire.   After King Philip's war in 1676 the remnants of several of the New England tribes amalgamated with the Abenaki or Wabanaki and fled to Canada for the protection of the French.   Of the New England tribes the Pequots of Connecticut, the Narragansetts of Rhode Island, the Wampanoags of Cape Cod, and the Massachusetts tribe, were representative.   Besides being hunting people, all of the New England tribes were agricultural and were known to the French in the early days as the Armouchiquois. At what moment all these eastern Algonkian tribes arrived in the territories which they occupied within historic times is extremely uncertain, because the chronology of pre-Columbian migrations is impossible to establish with any degree of certainty. Such were their positions when the western European nations effected contact with them by way of the Atlantic Ocean at the beginning of the sixteenth century.

CHAPTER 2

OCCASIONAL CONTACT ON THE GULF COAST

Independent of Trans-Atlantic enterprise was the cultural drift by way of India, China, Korea, Japan and Siberia, into northwestern America which gradually rendered the culture of the American Indian more complex and which brought it more into line with that of Asiatic peoples.[1] It was, however, a gradual process which worked no havoc in its passage which was in any way comparable to that resulting from the impact of European culture on the eastern seaboard.

The earliest voyages from Europe to America may never be unravelled from the skein of medieval legend, but the Norse Sagas bear the marks of authenticity, and it is probable that the Norsemen were the first to bridge the gap between Scandinavia and Greenland and to found the first White colony in America in about the year 1000 A.D. They seem, however, to have left no traces upon the culture of the aborigines, although a certain type of axe, the constellation which was known to the Eskimo as the Great Bear, and other traits, have been advanced by some scholars as evidence of this contact.[2] Charles G. Leland's theory of Norse influence upon Micmac mythology appears to have been based upon false analogies.[3] But direct contact with the Indians seems to be indicated, since the Skraelings of the Sagas may have been Algonkian, or proto-Algonkian, rather than Eskimo.[4] The occasional Norse, and possibly Irish, voyages may have persisted until 1347 A.D., but in 1409 A.D. the Norse settlement in Greenland was destroyed by the Eskimo, and contact with America ceased at least eighty-three years before the first voyage of Columbus.[5]

Other European peoples may not have been far behind the Norse and Irish wanderers. The Bretons are said to have shared in the Irish voyages, and, although fact and legend are here inseparable, the Pizigani map of 1367 A.D. suggestively depicts a Breton disaster in the region of 'les iles fantastiques'![6] Following the official recognition which was accorded to Columbus, several Western nations proclaimed prior discovery upon the basis of ill authenticated voyages. Among others, France claimed that her Norman and Breton seamen had been the first to reach America. Lescarbot quotes Guilliome Postel as having stated that America had been "regularly visited by the Gauls, and has been frequented for the last sixteen hundred years".[7] Although this assertion is doubtless completely without foundation, other claims cannot so easily be brushed aside. In 1514 A.D. it was stated that the French had for sixty years been accustomed to pay a tax on fish caught "tant en la cost de Bretaigne,

---

1. MacLeod (1); Chapter I. Barbeau (3); 403.
2. MacLeod (1); 12.
3. See chapter on mythology and folklore.
4. Babcock (1); 396; Gathorne Hardy 179, 193, 236-237.
5. This colony may have survived until later date. See Babcock (2); 63.
6. Babcock (2); 8. Beazley argues against St. Brandon's having reached America. v. 1; 230.
7. Lescarbot 24.

la Terre Neuvfe, Islande que ailleurs".[8]   It is difficult to know whether the
"sixty years" clause applies to Newfoundland as well as to the coast of Brittany, but la Roncière and.Harrisse appear to have considered it not beyond the
scope of reasonable possibility.[9]   On the other hand Justin Winsor and La
Roncière reject the Basque contention of having anticipated Columbus by one
hundred years.[10]   The Portugese were among the first to reach the coasts of
Acadia and Newfoundland, but whether they penetrated the Gulf of St. Lawrence is uncertain.   Their protagonists support their contention by pointing
to the supposed cucumbers and melons which were mentioned by Cartier.[11] The
first authenticated French voyage to the New World occurred in 1504 A.D. and
from this date onward a great many expeditions sailed from Norman and
Breton ports.[12]   Jean Denys of Honfleur is said to have explored the Gulf of
St. Lawrence in 1506,[13] although the occurrence of this voyage is not based
upon authentic evidence.   The Pensée set out from Dieppe in 1507.[14]   In his
voyage of 1508, Thomas Aubert, brought Micmacs or Beothuks back to
France, where they contributed to the models for a work in bas-relief which
is still preserved at the church of St. James in Dieppe.[15]   He is said to have
ascended the St. Lawrence to a distance of eighty leagues.

    The period of thirty years which intervened between the voyage of
1504 and that of Cartier in 1534 was one of intermittent, but nevertheless
frequent, contact with the Beothuk, and the eastern bands of Micmac and
Montagnais.   The Beothuk, who lived closer to the centre of the fisheries, were
probably the first to feel the impact of European civilization.[16]   On that part
of the Labrador coast which was frequented by the Montagnais Cartier encountered a vessel from La Rochelle in 1534,[17] and the Micmac, whom he met
in Prince Edward Island during his first voyage, showed by their behaviour
that they were already accustomed to the sight of Europeans.[18]   But the collision between aboriginal and European cultures cannot have been violent or
extensive before 1534 when the first voyage of Cartier marked the beginning
of a new period in which more than the edges of this first Canadian civilization
were skirted.   The Micmac and Montagnais were to develop the habit of
barter with Europeans, some of whom may occasionally have passed a winter
among the native bands.   They were gradually to become more aware of a
civilization that had little or nothing in common with their own; a more complex material culture; a specialized European conception of property of which
they had at first no notion; a society which was in general more various, but
in some respects less rigid than theirs; and a religion which, in its metaphysical
and especially in its social aspects, was completely alien to their comprehension.
With the advent of Cartier the period of occasional contact gave way to an era

8.   La Ronciere v. 3; 138.
9.   Harrisse.
10. Winsor (1); 70.
11. Winsor (1); 74.
12. Jesuit Relations v. 2; 39, 49, 201; MacLeod (1) 59.
13. Kohl 201.
14. Baxter 14.
15. Kohl 203, copy in Vitet, Histoire de Dieppe, 112; Jesuit Relations, v. 3, 39.
16. Biggar (2); 124, 125, 126, 132, 133. Hakluyt (2): 71. Ganong, C. K. 39.
        Biggar (1) 30.
17. Biggar (3);21.
18. Biggar (3); 42.

of almost steady infiltration of European traits into the cultural areas of the Atlantic provinces.

It is difficult, if not impossible, to form an idea of what the Indian thought of the European during the first period of encounter. It is difficult because, as we cannot transcend our own traditional processes, we are bound to read into the actual Indian view one that has been especially conditioned by our peculiar cultural background. That is, the subjective standpoint cannot be eliminated.[19]   Fortunately, however, we have a mythological statement of the Micmac experience which is not without value, although it represents an accretion from events which were doubtless spread over relatively long intervals of time.   The tale tells how a young woman, belonging to a Prince Edward Island band, dreamed that she saw floating in towards the land a small island decked with tall trees in which were living beings.   Standing on the island was a man clothed in rabbit skins.   When she awoke she consulted the shamans but they could make nothing of it.   Next morning the island was seen drifting towards the land, with trees and branches and bears crawling upon them.   The Micmacs seized their weapons, when, to their amazement, the bears were found to be men, some of whom lowered an extraordinary canoe and came ashore. The man clothed in rabbit skins was a priest who ministered to them.[20]

To Cartier, as he sailed along the low coast of Prince Edward Island, with its dark forests broken by meadows, the Indians who appeared unexpectedly in small fleets of canoes or afoot were wild and savage folk.   As their accoutrements were scant and rude the less evident aspects of their culture were estimated accordingly.   The European is so prone to appraise a man by the nature of his material possessions. Moreover, it is an almost universal tendency among people to regard those differing in culture from themselves as queer, sometimes ridiculous, and generally undesirable.   But contrarily, the Indians and the Europeans were interested in each other by virtue of their mutual strangeness, and each possessed something which was coveted by the other. The Indians wanted ironware and the Europeans wanted furs and especially information concerning the new land.

As early as 1534 the fur trade had become an incidental if slight accessory to the fishing industry.[21]   At Paspebiac Point, in Chaleur Bay, a group of Micmacs attracted Cartier's attention by exhibiting furs which they held up on sticks, and by making signs to the Bretons to come ashore.[22]   But in spite of their seeming friendliness, Cartier was wary of their great numbers, and he repelled their advances by shooting two small cannon over their heads and by scattering fire-lances among them.[23]   Clearly the strangers who controlled the thunder were heavily endowed with manito, but even the displeasure of the gods could not keep the Micmacs from the source of iron, for iron saved them from days of drudgery and enabled them to vanquish their enemies who were as yet armed only with stone, bone, and wood implements.   They re-

---

19. Spengler, v. 1; 30.
20. Rand (2); 225-226.   Also Ojibwa.   See P. Jones 27.
21. Biggar (3); 49.
22. Biggar (3); 49.   Also Murray 8.
23. Biggar (3); 49, 305.

turned on the following day and signified their desire to barter.[24]   This time Cartier was more venturesome.   There was a red cap for the chief, and knives, beads, and hatchets for others, all of whom gave furs in exchange.[25]   "The savages showed a marvellously great pleasure in possessing and obtaining these iron wares and other commodities, dancing and going through many ceremonies and throwing salt water over their heads with their hands."[26]   They bartered all their possessions and went away only to return with further store.   Some of the women advanced freely and rubbed the arms of the Bretons with their hands, doubtless thinking to gain strength thereby.   "And so much at ease did the savages feel in our presence that at length we bartered with them, hand to hand, for everything they possessed, so that nothing was left to them but their naked bodies; . . .".

Witnessing the repeated friendly gestures of the Micmac, Cartier began to see them as less savage than they had at first appeared.   His enthusiasm for their woodland territory soared under the mollifying influence of the warm July sun, and he considered that the natives "would be easy to convert to our holy faith".[27]

The Montagnais, too, shared with the Beothuk and Micmac the fruits, for good or ill, of the first impact.   While Cartier was returning along the north shore of the St. Lawrence, Indians from Natashquan boarded the vessels as freely as if they had been Frenchmen.   Their apparent confidence, when coupled with their statement that "the ships had all set sail from the (Grand) bay laden with fish," shows clearly that by 1534 fishing fleets had begun to penetrate beyond the Straits of Belle Isle.

24. Biggar (3); 52, 55.
25. Baxter 22.
26. Biggar (3), 53. Also Innis (1) 6.
27. Biggar (3); 56, 57.

CHAPTER 3

ACADIA AT THE TURN OF THE CENTURY

In the sixteenth century fishing was the preeminent industry of the
Terre Neuve. Due to primitive agricultural methods and the scarcity of meat
in Europe, codfish found a ready market and was available in large quantities.[1]
At some time during the third quarter of the century it was found that dry-
fishing was more economical than the green-fishing which had hitherto been
altogether practised. The new method of fishing reduced the outlay on such
commodities as salt and economized shipping.[2] Moreover, it led to a search
for harbours which were suitable for drying and which afforded ample supplies
of bait. With the development of dry-fishing three factors arose which stimulated voyages to the more remote areas of the coast and brought fresh bands
within the sphere of European influence. These were: the increasing scarcity
of timber available for staging, and the competition for better harbours between
the various national groups that frequented the Banks.[3] Basque and Portugese
whalers clashed with English and French fishermen in their attempt to control
the strategic points of the coast. The third factor was the growing importance
of the fur-trade. On the other hand there were two factors which opposed this
movement. First, the hostility of the Laurentian Iroquois to Europeans which
had been aroused by Cartier and others; and second, the distance of the cod
banks from the coast except at exceptional places such as Ile Percée. Moreover,
the coast was indented with harbours.[4] So that, as late as 1604 the fisheries
had not been extended beyond Canso, and in 1607 the members of De Monts'
expedition were not aware that there was good fishing beyond this point.[5]
Several times when Port Royal needed European supplies expeditions were fitted
out to go to Canso or Gaspé in search of fishermen. Cape Breton was still the
greatest area of contact between the European and the Micmac. At this time
the fur-trade was leading to the penetration of areas beyond the fisheries.

Although the manufacture of felt hats was under way in continental
Europe as early as 1456 it was not until the end of the sixteenth century that
hats of this variety became highly fashionable.[6] For "in the time of Jacques
Cartier beavers were held in no esteem; the hats made thereof are in use only
since that time; though the discovery thereof is not new, for in the ancient
privileges of the hat-makers of Paris, it is said that they are to make hats of
fine beaver. . ."[7] Cartier made no special reference to beaver, nor for that matter
to furs of any kind, but emphasized the wealth in fish and minerals.[8] But
during the last quarter of the century the fur-trade became of prime concern to
many European merchants. The fashion of wearing beaver hats spread rapidly
because only the most expensive hats were of beaver.[9] It is probable that the

1. Innis (1) 5.
2. Innis (1) 5.
3. Innis (1) 5.
4. Innis (1) 5.
5. Ganong, G. K. 52.
6. Unwin 131. Innis (1) 8.
7. Lescarbot v 3, 117.
8. Innis (1) 7-8.

bulk of the early trade was with the Montagnais who controlled the route to the interior by way of the Saguenay.   The fact that this was the only available route limited the early coastal trade.   Transportation facilities were meagre, the canoe being the chief vehicle, and the majority of the rivers of the gulf region were short, due to the proximity of the height of land to the coast.[10] Therefore, the Montagnais were largely dependent upon fishing, and trade was limited to the fishermen who frequented the harbours. Moreover, their population was sparce, and they were often absent from their coastal haunts for long periods.   Pont-Gravé made a voyage before 1600 in which no Indians were to be found at Tadoussac, and he had voyaged "as far as the three rivers, in search of savages, in order to trade with them".[11]   A large trade organization was further retarded by the fact that the commodity required considerable technical knowledge on the part of the purchaser, and the commodity itself was limited especially to beaver, although bear, marten, fox, rabbit and elk were among the articles of trade in the sixteenth century.[12]   The Indians themselves prized beaver above other animals, not only as a means of sustenance, but because "They wear no other clothes than a moose skin or a beaver robe which consists of five or six beaver skins sewed together."[13]   European contact had stimulated inter-tribal trade.   In 1603 Champlain encountered a band of Indians, possibly Montagnais, between Tadoussac and Gaspé who were on their way to barter arrows and moose flesh for beaver and marten with Etechemin, Algonkin, and other Montagnais bands.[14]   Trade was further constricted by rivalries among the Indians themselves.   Those tribes which, by their geographical advantage, acted as middlemen, resented attempts to destroy their monopoly position.   Moreover, European monopolies "attempted to control the price of beaver and to raise the prices of goods to the Indians. These factors tended to lessen the pressure of a complex civilization. . . . No monopoly or organization could withstand the demand of the Indian civilization of North America for European goods."[15]   Nevertheless monopolies were distinctly retarding factors.

On the other hand, states Dr. Innis, "heavy overhead costs incidental to the conduct of trade was an important cause of its rapid growth."[16]   Beaver was preeminently suited to the demands of the time, since "the heavy overhead cost of long voyages limited the trade to commodities which were highly valuable, to commodities demanded by the more advanced types of manufacturing processes of that period, and to commodities available on a large scale."[17]   "The trader encouraged the best hunters, exhorted the Indians to hunt beaver, and directed their fleets of canoes to the rendezvous.   Alliances were formed and wars were favoured to increase the supply of fur.   Goods were traded which would encourage the Indian to hunt beaver."[18]   The eastern Algonkians had effective methods of hunting.   The canoe, the pack-strap, knowledge of animal habits and of plants for food and medicine, and familiarity with the country,

---

9.   Innis (1) 9.
10.   Innis (1) 5-6.
11.   Champlain (2) 1, 48.
12.   Biggar (1) 31.
13.   Jesuit Relations 4, 203. Innis (1) 10.

enabled them to cover a wide territory and to secure furs in abundance.[19]   The rapid development of the trade was further dependent upon the Indian method of treating fur and upon the character of the felting process.   The Indians took the pelts when they were prime, and scraped and rubbed them with animal marrow.[20]   Each pelt was trimmed into a rectangular shape, and from five to eight were sewn together and worn with the fur next to the body.   When these were worn for fifteen or eighteen months the skin became greased, pliable and yellow, and the fur became downy.   Later known as "castor gras d'hiver", this type of fur was of the most value to the hat-makers as the guard hairs had largely disappeared and the fur was especially suitable for felting.[21]

As European technique in the manufacture of beaver hats improved, the number of workers and the demand for larger supplies of beaver pelts increased.   This necessitated a greater output of ironware and clothing materials for the trade.[22]   The American demand for European goods was persistent and cumulative.   Vast areas were involved and the rate of penetration was slow.[23] As late as the time of Champlain's expedition to the country of the Armouchiquois these Indians were still largely dependent upon the stone hatchets, "for they have no others except some few which they received from the savages on the coasts of La Cadie who obtained them in exchange for furs."[24]   Moreover, depreciation was rapid.   Iron implements were put to intensive work and were constantly wearing out when they were traded to more remote peoples. Among such nations as the Hurons iron implements were frequently destroyed at burial feasts.[25]

The displacement of stone, bone, wood, bark and antler by ironware caused a profound revolution in the economic life of the Atlantic littoral.   The standard of living was raised tremendously.   The division of labour between the sexes attained an unstable equilibrium, the regular round of economic pursuits which had been perfected by centuries of constant adaptation to the northern environment, became a monomania with iron as its fixation.   Evidence of the way in which it was received can be gleaned from the Port Royal narratives.   "One thing they have lacked up till now, which has been and still is the cause of their nakedness, the use of iron, without which all the handycrafts cease; and I believe," says Lescarbot, "that we should be very little more advanced than they if we had been deprived of this admirable invention. . . ."[26]

And again he says, "Our Indians, who do not till the ground, barter for them (fishing lines) with the French, as also for fishing hooks to bait for fish; . . ."[27]   And elsewhere, "for the (arrow) head, the savages who traffic

14.   Innis (1)   9.
15.   Innis (1)   13.
16.   Innis (1)   12.
17.   Innis (1)   12.
18.   Innis (1)   13.
19.   Innis (1)   16.
20.   Innis (1)   10.
21.   Innis (1)   10.
22.   Innis (1)   13.
23.   Innis (1)   14.
24.   Champlain (3) 66. Innis (1) 14. In the expedition against the Iroquois in 1615 only four or five of Champlain's Indians were acquainted with the handling of arms.
25.   Innis (1)   14.
26.   Lescarbot v. 1.   33.
27.   Lescarbot v. 3.   192.

with the Frenchmen attach thereto iron heads which are brought to them; . ."[28]
And Champlain, in speaking of the alleged mine in Acadia, says, "Monsieur
Preuert gaue the Sauages Wedges and Cizers, and other things necessarie to
draw out the said Myne; . . ."[29]   Evidences of an archeological nature which
have been unearthed in Acadia reveal iron axes, tomahawks, spearheads, knives,
kettles, metal pipes and glass beads.[30].

Other materials besides iron were in great demand.   Biard tells us how
the French lived, roved and hunted with the Indians without arms, fear or
danger.   These associations were partly through fishing, partly through fur-
trading, "For the Savages, who have neither, copper, iron, hemp, wool, vegetables, nor manufactured articles of any kind, resort to the French for them. . "[31]
And again, "They barter their skins of beaver, otter, deer, marten, seal, etc.,
for bread, peas, beans, prunes, tobacco, etc., kettles, hatchets, iron-arrow-points,
awls, puncheons, cloaks, blankets, and all other such commodities as the French
bring them."[32]   In 1604 Champlain made an expedition to the Indians of the
Penobscot or Kennebec who were then at war with the Micmac.   He said
that the Sieur de Monts desired to inhabit their territory and to teach them
agriculture "in order that they might not continue to lead so miserable a life
as they were doing".   Champlain prefaced the movement by presenting them
with "hatchets, paternosters, caps, knives and other little knickknacks. . . . .
All the rest of this day and the following night, until break of day, they did
nothing but dance, sing and make merry, after which we traded for a certain
number of beavers."[33]

Another article which was coveted greatly by the Indians of Acadia
was known as matachias, a word which, in Lescarbot's writings, signifies all
kinds of personal ornaments.[34]   It is possible that the term originally signified
wampum.   "Today they have no more of it; for they greatly use the Matachias
which are brought them from France. . . in Port Royal . . . the maids and
women make matachias with quills or bristles of the porcupine which they
dye. . . ."   The matachias of the Armouchiquois were esteemed very highly.
". . . and because they can get no great quantity of this by reason of the
continual wars of these two nations against one another, matachias are brought
unto them from France, made of small quills of glass mingled with tin or lead,
which are bartered with them by the fathom, for want of an ell; . . ."[35]

The trade in European materials which in the time of Lescarbot was
in full swing had been gathering in magnitude for at least two generations.
"Iron knives and axes, the steel and flint, with its great powers of carrying
fire everywhere, and coarse potteries and beads, must have begun already to
modify their habits.   The ancient arrow-maker must have ceased his art; the
son must have used an axe foreign to his father, and the squaw to ornament

28. Lescarbot v. 3. 191.
29. Champlain (2) v. 2. 225.
30. Piers 117.
31. Jesuit Relations 2 71.
32. Jesuit Relations 3 69.
33. Champlain (3) 50.
34. Lescarbot 3 157. W. L. Grant says the word is unknown in modern Micmac.
35. Lescarbot 3, 154-8.

her skins with French beads instead of small shells."[36]. Aboriginal artefacts tended to disappear and much of the craftsmanship must have become a lost art. But iron axes and hatchets rendered work more rapid and effective. Iron needles facilitated sewing where bone needles were used before,[37] and guns displacd bows and arrows.[38]

Lescarbot, Baird, and others, have borne witness to the fact that European foodstuffs and clothing materials supplemented ironware as important articles of trade . . . "of bread there is no talk from Newfoundland in the North until one come to the country of the Armouchiquois save such as they get by barter with Frenchmen, for whom they wait upon the sea-shore, sitting on their rumps like apes, as soon as the springtime comes, receiving in exchange for their skins—for they have no other merchandise—biscuits, beans, peas and meal."[39] "Our savages, Canadian, Souriquois, and others . . . . have only the tobacco of which we have spoken to warm their stomachs. . . "[40] Tobacco was the chief article in demand among the Micmac and Malecite which Europe could not then supply.[41] It is possible that it was cultivated by the Malecite to a certain degree, but the bulk of it was doubtless obtained from tribes farther to the south. This necessitated a degree of trade and friendly intercourse with the New England Indians.

Native furs tended to become displaced by European stuffs at the time of the Port Royal colony. "As for headgear, none of the savages have any, save that some of the nearer tribes truck their skins with Frenchmen for hats or caps; . . ."[42] And ". . . in Summer they often wear our capes, and in Winter our bed-blankets, which they improve with trimming and wear double. They are also quite willing to make use of our hats, shoes, caps, woolens and shirts, and of our linen to clean their infants, for we trade them all these commodities for their furs."[43]

The revolution in domestic pursuits which resulted from the displacement of native materials had a counterpart in the social and political sphere. Cartier's Indians were not great travellers beyond their own territories, nor did any of the natives spend their time in fruitless wanderings in pre-Columbian times to dangerous and mysterious regions beyond their view. In Cartier's words ". . . one could make one's way so far up the river that they had never heard of anyone reaching the end of it."[44] But the possession of iron accelerated work and gave more time for getting furs, and as the supply decreased they were continually led farther afield. Therefore, the Indians acquired a knowledge of the country beyond their own territories which weakened their distinctive traits, hastened diffusion, and created a general instability of life.[45] The search for furs led to an economical and political pressure on the tribes of the interior and was an important cause of the revival of inter-tribal warfare. "Wars between tribes, which with bows and arrows had not been strenuous,

36. Gilpin 261.
37. Innis (1) 15.
38. Innis (1) 16.
39. Lescarbot 3, 168.
40. Lescarbot (3) 177.
41. Ganong, C. K. 38.
42. Lescarbot 3, 133.
43. Jesuit Relations 3, 75, 77.
44. Biggar (3) 107.
45. Innis (1) 17.

conducted with guns were disastrous."[46]   As the colonists were leaving Port Royal in 1607 Membertou, the Micmac chief, returned from a war of revenge for the death of one of his own people. It is probable that fire-arms were first used here in inter-tribal war. Membertou and his men had them a year later. They were victorious, having killed twenty, and wounded ten or twelve.[47] At this time a law was passed forbidding the sale of fire-arms to the Indians.[48] It was ineffective, however, due to increasing competition in the trade, Indian demand, and international rivalry which created the necessity for strongly armed native allies. The hunt became more deadly when fire-arms and iron weapons supplanted the stone spear and arrow, with the result that the food supply became seriously diminished and the Indians were forced to rely more and more upon European foodstuffs.[49]

The new means of sustenance, together with the revival of warfare, and the time consumed in the hunt for furs, led to a decline in husbandry among the eastern Algonkians. "Our Souriquois formerly did the same (made earthen pots) and tilled the ground; but since the French bring them kettles, beans, biscuits, and other food, they are become slothful and make no more account of those exercises."[50] It is possible that Lescarbot was misled by Cartier's account of the Laurentian Iroquois into believing that the Micmac practised agriculture when he says, "The people of Canada and of Hochelaga . . . . also tilled the soil . . . and the land brought forth for them corn, beans, peas, melons, squash and cucumbers; but since their furs have been in request, and that in return for these they have had victuals without any further trouble, they have become lazy, as have also the Souriquois, who at the same date practiced tillage."[51]

European foods tended to unbalance the diet of the natives, causing and facilitating the spread of diseases, which resulted in a decline in the birth rate, and the depopulation of the adult members of eastern Algonkian society. Sometimes the European foods which were traded for furs were bad; at others poisons were used for nefarious purposes. Biard gives an account of this state of affairs in his relation of 1616:

> "They are astonished and often complain that, since the French mingle with and carry on trade with them, they are dying fast and the population is thinning out. For they assert that, before this association and intercourse, all their countries were very populous and they tell how one by one the different coasts, according as they have begun to traffic with us, have been more reduced by disease; adding, that why the Armouchiquois do not diminish in population is because they are not at all careless. Thereupon they often puzzle their brains, and sometimes think that the French poison them, which is not true; at other times that they give poisons to the wicked and vicious of their nation to help them vent their spite upon some one. This last supposition is

---

46. Innis (1) 18.
47. Ganong, C. K. 84.
48. Biggar (1) 88 Lescarbot 2, 368.
49. Ganong, C. K. 54, Denys 443, Thompson, D. 112-113, 199. Speaking of the Cree at the end of the 18th century he says—". . . When the arrival of the white people have changed all their weapons from stone to iron and steel, and added the fatal gun, every animal fell before the Indian . . . and thus their numbers soon became reduced." Innis (1) 4.
50. Lescarbot 3, 195. Not certain that Micmac practised agriculture.
51. Lescarbot 3, 250. Leclercq 212, also refers to tobacco and corn among the Gaspesian Micmac in former times.

not without foundation; for we have seen them have some arsenic and sublimate which they say they bought from certain French Surgeons, in order to kill whomsoever they wished, and boasted that they had already experimented upon a captive, who (they said) died the day after taking it. Others complain that the merchandise is often counterfeited, and that peas, beans, prunes, bread, and other things that are spoiled are sold them; and that it is that which corrupts the body and gives rise to the dysentery and other diseases which always attack them in Autumn. This theory is likewise not offered without citing instances, for which they have often been upon the point of breaking with us, and making war upon us. Indeed there would be need of providing against these detestible murders by some suitable remedy if one could be found.

Nevertheless the principal cause of all these deaths and diseases is not what they say it is, but it is something to their shame; in the Summer time, when our ships come, they never stop gorging themselves excessively during weeks with various kinds of food not suitable to the inactivity of their lives; they get drunk, not only on wine but on brandy; so it is no wonder that they are obliged to endure some gripes of the stomach in the following Autumn. . . .

. . . if they stay, their stores would soon be consumed; so they go somewhere else until the time of famine. Such are the only guards they leave. For in truth this is not a nation of thieves. Would to God that the Christians who go among them would not set them a bad example in this respect. But as it is now, if a certain Savage is suspected of having stolen anything he will immediately throw this fine defense in your teeth, **We are not thieves, like you. . . .**" [52]

Thus, mismanagement of affairs on the economic plane had repercussions in the political sphere which were detrimental to the welfare of both sides of the frontier. The personal element in turn affected the economic and social relations of the two groups. French opinion of Micmac short-comings was balanced by Micmac apprehension of the vices and frailties of the French. Because each group considered itself superior, each could treat the other as an equal. Nevertheless centrifugal forces were often operative beneath the surface:

"With all their vices, they are exceedingly vainglorious: they think they are better, more valiant and more ingenious than the French; and, what is difficult to believe, richer then we are. They consider themselves, I say, braver than we are,boasting that they have killed Basques and Malouins, and that they do a great deal of harm to the ships, and that no one has ever resented it, insinuating that it was from a lack of courage. They consider themselves better than the French; "For," they say, "you are always fighting and quarreling among yourselves; we live peaceably. You are envious and are all the time slandering each other; you are thieves and deceivers; you are covetous and are neither generous nor kind; as for us, if we have a morsel of bread we share it with our neighbor."

. . . Also they . . . consider themselves more ingenious, inasmuch as they see us admire some of their productions as the work of people so rude and ignorant; lacking intelligence, they bestow very little admiration upon what we show them, although much more worthy of being admired. Hence they regard themselves as being much richer than we are, although they are poor and wretched in the extreme.

Cacagous, of whom I have already spoken, is quite gracious when he is a little elated about something; to show his kindly feelings toward the French he boasts of his willingness to go and see the king, and to take him a present of a hundred beaver skins, proudly suggesting (and counts) that in so doing he will make him richer than all his predecessors. They get this idea from the extreme covetousness and eagerness which our people display to obtain their beaver skins." [53]

---

52. Jesuit Relations 3, 105-109.
53. Jesuit Relations (1) 173-177.

On the whole, however, political relations between the French and the Eastern Algonkians were extremely amicable. Montagnais and Micmac had experienced a century of contact. The Malecite had a Breton colony in their midst in 1612 and probably earlier,[54] and when Champlain encountered the Indians of the Penobscot in 1604, they "withdrew on one side and greatly enjoyed seeing us, as it was the first time they had seen Christians."[55] The Montagnais, whom Pont-Gravé had taken to France in one of his voyages prior to 1603, were more favourably impressed with Europe than Tainoagny and Domagaya had been, for on their return they "reckoned up the faire Castels, Palaces, Houses, and people which they had seen, and our manner of living."[56] More were eager to visit France in 1603, for "one of the Sagamos of the Mountayners . . . . gaue his Sonne to Monsieur du Pont to carrie him into France . . . . praying him to vse him well, and to let him see that, which the other two Sauages have seene which we had brought backe againe. . . . Monsieur de Preuert in like manner brought home foure Sauages, one man which is of the South Coast (Acadia), one woman and two children of the Canadians."[57] According to Lescarbot the Micmac were not as trustful as the Montagnais in this respect: "And when the question is raised of asking them for some of their children—I speak of the Souriquois in whose land we dwelt—in order to bring them into France, and show it to them, they will not give them; and if any one of them yields, presents, and great promises must be made him, or hostages given."[58]   And again, "This Oagimont has a very comely daughter of about eleven years of age, whom M. de Poutrincourt desired to take with him, and asked for her several times in order to present her to the Queen, promising him that he should never lack corn or ought else; but the chief has never been willing to accede thereto."[59]

Nevertheless "of foreign nations, the French are almost the only people they admit to their harbours, for the sake of disposing of their beaver skins and other peltries, in exchange for necessary clothing and utensils."[60]   To the Montagnais ". . . there was no nation in the world to which they wished more good, than to the French."[61]   When Poutrincourt returned to Port Royal in 1610 it was "impossible to describe the joy with which these poor people (Micmac) received the Sieur and his company.   And, in truth, there was still greater reason for this joy, since they had lost all hope of ever again seeing the French live among them. They had had some experience of our kind treatment when we were there, and seeing themselves deprived of it, they wept bitterly when we left them three years ago. . . . When Sieur de Poutrincourt arrived there, he found his buildings entire, the Savages (as these people have been called up to the present) not having touched them in any way, even the furniture remaining as we had left it.   Anxious about their old friends, they asked

54. Jesuit Relations 2, 27.
55. Champlain (3) 49. He may of course have been mistaken.
56. Champlain (2) v. 2, 157.
57. Champlain (2) v. 2 229.
58. Lescarbot 3, 87.
59. Lescarbot 2, 360.
60. Jesuit Relations 2, 201.
61. Champlain (2) v. 2, 158.

how they were all getting along, calling each individual by his name, and asking why such and such a one had not come back.   This shows the great amiability of these people, who, having seen in us only the most humane qualities, never flee from us, as they do from the Spaniard in this whole new world."[62]   The tie was strengthened by Poutrincourt's unselfish and liberal policy towards the Micmacs.[63]

Purely social relations between the Europeans and the natives which were partly determined by economic factors, partly by considerations of a purely personal nature, coloured the attitude of the natives towards the Europeans.   Sexual relations with the native women sometimes worked to the detriment of French imperial and commercial interests.   Poutrincourt encountered a ship from St. Malo at the mouth of the St. John.   Complaint "was made to him by a captain of the savages, that one of the crew of the said ship had stolen away his wife and was abusing her . . . . the guilty one . . . . escaped, however, in a shallop, and went off with the Savages, prejudicing them against the French. . . ."[64]   It is said that the Micmac maidens were modest and bashful; the men modest and insulted when some foolish Frenchman dared to meddle with their women.   "Once when a certain madcap took such liberties, they came and told our captain that he should look out for his men, informing him that anyone who attempted to do that again would not stand much of a chance, that they would kill him on the spot."[65]   Lescarbot, with a quaint pragmatism, asserts, "As for the maidens who are willing, if any man has abused them, they will tell it at the first occasion, and therefore it is dangerous to dally with them; for one ought not to mix Christian blood with infidel. . . ."[66]   The austere morals and upright characters of such men as Biard and Champlain must have exerted a restraining influence upon the frailer colonists and traders of the gulf coast.   In one instance Biard says, "We have also succeeded in reclaiming a certain young man of great courage and hope who . . . has roamed about for a whole year with the Savages, adopting their ways and dress—not without suspicion, too, of something worse."[67]   The Eskimo, who were less tractible than the Eastern Algonkians, became the implacable enemies of the French "and do us a great deal of harm.   This warfare was begun (as they say) when certain Basques tried to commit a wicked outrage.   However, they paid well for their cursed incontinence, but not only they, for on their account both the St. Malo people and many others suffered, and still suffer a great deal every year. . . There are only three tribes which are on terms of friendship with us, the Montaguets, the Souriquois, and the Eteminquois."[68]

The arguments of the Jesuits were weakened by the bad examples set by their own countrymen with respect to sexual morality.   Monogomy was preached to the Algonkians while the Bretons, Normans, and Basques, entered upon a wide-spread course of promiscuity with the native women.   It is therefore not surprising if the talk of Christian continence fell largely on deaf ears.

---

62. Jesuit Relations (1) 67-69.   64. Jesuit Relations 1, 67.
63. Jesuit Relations 1, 157.   65. Jesuit Relations 3, 103.

Biard says that Membertou remained monogomous because he realized better than the other sagamos that many evils arose from the quarreling of wives, and the children of rival wives.   In reality a single wife's burden of labour was often too great for one individual to withstand, and she would often welcome another woman as a fellow worker rather than despise her as a rival.[69]

Concerning sexual relations with the Indians, Lescarbot stated that he "never saw amongst them any immodest gesture or look. . . ." which he attributed purely to their nakedness.[70]   Indeed, it seems that the pastime which today might be classed under the term "fondling", or more colloquially "necking", was unknown among the aborigines of North America.   Sagard is authority for the Hurons, and Lescarbot for the Micmacs.[71]   "But our savages were, in my opinion, brutal before the arrival of the French in their territories; for they had not the Knowledge of this sweet honey (kiss) which lovers suck from the lips of their mistresses, when they begin to bill and coo, and to prepare nature to lay their offerings of love on the altar of the Cyprian queen."   These observations led Lescarbot to question the statement of Cartier "that there are meeting houses and, as it were, colleges, wherein the girls are prostituted, until they marry; and that widows do not remarry. . . ."[72]   Speaking elsewhere of Cartier's remark, he says,

> ". . . among our Souriquois no such thing is known; not that these savages have any great regard for continence and virginity, but they do not think to do evil in corrupting it; but whether by frequentation with the French or otherwise, the maids are ashamed to be unchaste in public; and if it happen that they abandon themselves to anyone it is in secret. . . . The maidens of Brasil have the same liberty as those of Canada to prostitute themselves as soon as they are able. Indeed, the fathers act as their pandars, and think it an honour to give them to the men of these parts, in order to have children of their blood . . . and we see, to our great hurt that God has severely punished this vice by the pox, which was brought by the Spaniards from Naples, and by them transmitted to the French, a disease which before the discovery of those lands was unknown in Europe."[73]

Each group being economically indispensable to the other at this time, a state of social equality was apparent in the day-to-day life of the Atlantic area.   That the Indians felt this is evident from the words of a Micmac chief which are recorded by Biard: "having heard M. de Pourtrincourt say that the King was young and unmarried: "Perhaps," said he, "I may let him marry my daughter; but according to the usages and customs of the country, the King must give me some handsome presents; namely four or five barrels of bread, three of peas or beans, one of tobacco, four or five cloaks worth one hundred

66. Lescarbot 3, 167.
67. Jesuit Relations 2, 101.
68. Jesuit Relations 3, 69.
69. Jesuit Relations 2, 229.
70. Lescarbot 3, 164.
71. Sagard 111. Lescarbot 3, 208.
72. Lescarbot 2, 179.
73. Lescarbot 3, 162-3. A form of syphilis was said to have been brought by Columbus from Hispaniola. It may have been unknown in North America. If so, it was introduced by the English, French and Dutch in the 16th and 17th centuries. On the other hand it may have been known in the old world in medieval and ancient times. See chapter on Disease.

sous apiece, bows, arrows, harpoons, and other similar articles."[74]   On the other hand, apart from such serious proposals, both groups were given to banter and friendly deceptions which were meaningless in themselves but which illustrate the temper of the social relations.   As the Indians were inquisitive "some of our men made them believe that French women have beards on their chins, and have left them in that good opinion, so that they were very desirous to see some of them and their manner of dress."[75]   The Indian children were more timid than their elders at this time, since Biard saw "one of our little boys make a Savage, a foot taller than himself, fly before him;. . . ."[76]

There appears to have been a sprinkling of marriages which were legal to the French as well as to the Indians among the illicit relations which were recorded, and although ". . . . there was more or less intermarriage between these settlers and this tribe (Micmac) which more firmly cemented the bonds between them,"[77] it was doubtless negligible at this period.   Nevertheless miscegenation was an important feature of the contact of races which became frequent at the time of the founding of Port Royal.   The Bretons and Basques, more than other European people seem to have exerted the widest influence upon the Malecite and the Micmac.   Malouidit, meaning those of St. Malo, was at a later date the name given to the metis among the Malecite, "because the greater part of their fathers came from St. Malo."   Likewise the grain which was introduced among them was known as "Maloumenal".[78]   The measurements of living Malecite and Micmac "now unquestionably mixed with French-Canadian blood" show physical types which are predominently dolychocephalic, yet with considerable brachycephalic elements which are perhaps due in part to European admixture.[79]   On the other hand, the immediate results of miscegenation with the native women may be summarized as fivefold. First, sexual relations were salient in the spread of disease among the native populations.   Second, the Indian men were deprived of potential wives by the excess of males who were now competing successfully with them in the art of love.   The resulting jealousy tended from time to time to disrupt the friendly relations between native and immigrant.   Conversely, the desire of the women for foreign mates led to the despising of their own men.   Fourth, the dislocation in the proportion of the sexes to each other led, doubtless, to despair, perhaps suicide, and, in general, to a highly unsettled state of existence for the excess Indian males; unless, of course, the higher mortality rate, resulting from the use of fire-arms, restored the balance.   And fifth, the marriage ties of French and Indians must have been greatly strengthened by the presence of offspring.   There appears to be no evidence to indicate the precise status of these offspring at this time; but no doubt it exerted a modifying influence on the culture of both groups.

A discussion of biological changes in the native stock will be deferred

---

74.   Jesuit Relations 1, 177.
75.   Lescarbot 3, 141.
76.   Jesuit Relations 3, 93.
77.   Piers 100. See Dionne on sexual relations in Brazil (1) 97.
78.   Jack (1) 197.
79.   Dixon (4) 408.

until a later chapter.   Suffice it to say here that contemporary accounts appear to indicate that the population of the Atlantic littoral declined rapidly during the latter years of the sixteenth century.   Membertou said that he had seen Indians as thick as the hairs on his head.   "It is maintained that they have thus diminished since the French have begun to frequent their country. . ."[80] To the unbalancing of the diet and the introduction of a new set of diseases against which they had no immunity, which have already been noted, may be added bad living conditions as a cause of the fall of the birth rate and of an increase in mortality.   Periods of war followed by terms of idleness and drunkenness in the vermin-ridden encampments undermined constitutions and resulted in a decline of physical resistence.   Moreover, new kinds of vermin not only helped to consume the food supply, but acted as carriers of the new diseases.   "The savages had no knowledge of these animals (rats) before our coming; but in our time they have been beset by them, since from our fort they went even to their lodges, a distance of over four hundred paces, to eat or suck their fish oils."[81]

The economic and social life is indicated to some extent by the changes which occurred in the eastern Algonkian languages in the sixteenth century. "Now to return to our savages; although by traffic with them, many of our Frenchmen understand them, yet they have also a language of their own, known only to themselves; which makes me doubt my statement that the language which was in Canada in the time of Jacques Cartier is no more in use;[82] though for the sake of convenience they speak to us in a language more familiar to us, with which much Basque is mixed; not that they care greatly to learn our languages, for there are some of them who say that they do not come to seek after us; but by long frequentation they cannot but retain some few words."[83]   For example, the people of the gulf coast adapted the word "bacalos", meaning cod-fish, from the Basque term "bacaillos", although their own name for the cod was "apégé".[84]   "Indeed, they have been so long frequented by the Basques that the language of the coast tribes is half Basque." Although doubtless a gross exaggeration, Lescarbot's statement is some indication of the extent of contact at this time.   Sometimes a word was introduced into the native tongue for which there was no Algonkian equivalent.   Thus, a change in manners is apparent from the statement that ". . . . our savages have no salutation on departure, save indeed adieu, which they have learned from us."[85]   But the first things which the Indians learned from the Europeans were vile and insulting words; "and you will often hear the women Savages (who otherwise are very timid and modest) hurl vulgar, vile, and shameless epithets at our people, in the French language."   Biard asserts that they did not know the meaning of the words but their outbursts evoked laughter and amusement from the French.[86]   It seems probable that they did know the

80. Jesuit Relations 1, 177.
81. Lescarbot 3, 227. This is the common house rat.
82. Lescarbot 3, 114-115.
83. Lescarbot 3, 125.
84. Lescarbot 2, 24. Called today Pejook.
85. Lescarbot 3, 207. Rand (1) gives adu as 'farewell,' and adeawiktak as 'to bid
        him farewell.'
86. Jesuit Relations 2, 9.

meaning of these terms since tribes such as the Montagnais used the names of the private parts in friendly banter and apparently with a non-European sense of the obscene.

The barrier of language which confronted the first missionaries was one of the chief obstacles to christianization. Biard was forced to make a thousand gesticulations and signs to express his ideas because he did not know the Micmac tongue.[87] And the Indians "often ridiculed, instead of teaching us, and sometimes palmed off on us indecent words, which we went about innocently preaching for beautiful sentences from the gospels." Moreover, it was difficult to translate ideas the expression of which had no counterpart in the Micmac tongue. Biard believed that abstract concepts and their expressions did not exist because he thought that the Indians had "no definite religion, magistracy, or government, liberal or mechanical arts, commercial or civil life, they have no words to describe things which they have never seen or even conceived."[88] Thus, he asserted that Indian conceptions were limited to sensible and material things; that there was nothing abstract, internal or spiritual, such as wisdom, fidelity, mercy, gratitude, piety, holy, blessed, angel, grace, mystery, sacrament, temptation, faith, law, prudence, subjection or authority. It is true that Micmac was probably weak in abstractions, because the Indian's method of thinking was different from the European's. His system was one of percepts rather than one of concepts. Thus, although Biard could discover no word for justice, the Indians "love justice and hate violence and robbery".[89] Thinking in particulars rather than in universals they could recognize and love a just man or a just act without having to trouble themselves with the abstraction. As a matter of fact, however, they were not so deficient as Biard seems to have believed. In the nineteenth century Rand found all the above concepts in Micmac, except subjection, piety and gratitude, although verbs to subject, to reverence, and to thank are given.[90] The Micmac words for angel and sacrament are, of course, derived from their French or English equivalents. The missionaries were doubtless handicapped by their error in translating French metaphorical words into the sometimes literal expressions of Micmac. Membertou took literally "Give us this day our daily bread" when he said "if I did not ask him for anything but bread, I would be without moose-meat or fish".[91]

Scarcely less important as an obstacle to conversion was the failure of the French to acquaint themselves with the fact that there was a religion of any kind among the eastern Algonkians. Speaking of the Indians of Massachusetts, Champlain says "I suppose that they are not different in this respect from our savages, the Souriquois and Canadians, who worship neither the moon nor the sun, nor anything else, and pray no more than the beasts."[92] And Lescarbot proposed the Lockean theory that their minds were "like to a bare canvas, which is ready to receive whatever colour one will give to it. . . . . This is why our savages of New France will be found ready to receive the Christian doctrine. . . . ."[93] "If they do not know God, at least they do not blaspheme

87. Jesuit Relations 2, 11.
88. Jesuit Relations 2 9-11.
89. Jesuit Relations 2, 11, 73; 3, 197.
90. Rand (1).
91. Jesuit Relations 1, 165-167.
92. Champlain (3) 96.
93. Lescarbot 3, 91.

him, as the greater number of Christians do", reveals the narrow vision of the time.[94]

On the other hand, the Indians were impressed by the external trappings of Catholicism. Young Indians who were not yet Christians would carry candles, bells and holy water, and march in good order in funeral processions. "Thus they become accustomed to act as Christians. . ." and the way is paved through their aesthetic senses to a real conversion.[95]

Moreover the discernment of certain material benefits on the part of the Indians worked in favour of the missionaries. They sometimes saw their fellows cured of illness by means of European magic. On one occasion a bone, taken from the relics of St. Lawrence, was placed on the sick man, and vows being said for him, he straightway improved.[96] At another time ". . . a sick man was lying, who had already been ill three months, whose recovery had been despaired of. . He was completely bathed in cold perspiration, an almost certain sign of death, since a heavy fever had taken possession of him . . . the Father had held out a cross to him to be repeatedly kissed, and had left it hanging about his neck. . . But the next day . . that sick man, yesterday at the point of death, came on board in a state of health, and, joyfully and reverently displaying the cross, went to Father Biard, and testifying with great delight of his recovery, ascribed it to the power of the Holy Cross."[97] Some of these cures are not so remarkable when it is remembered that when the shamans had pronounced a malady to be mortal, the sick refrained from eating, and their relatives threw water on them to hasten the end. When Membertou fell sick, his children, though nominally Christians, were prepared to exercise this rite. Poutrincourt induced him to eat some food and he recovered. ". . . today he tells this story with great satisfaction, and very aptly points out how God has thereby mercifully exposed the malice and deceipt of their aoutmoins."[98] Indeed, with the growing successes of the French ". . . this lying race of prophets have lost must of their authority since the coming of the French and now universally complain that their Devils have lost much of their powers. . ."[99] Ineffectual as European therapeutics in the seventeenth century must have been, it is probable that they were sometimes made use of by the eastern Algonkians. The complexity of European culture was relatively great. The native shaman was often confronted by situations which were completely alien to his experience and with which he was therefore unable to cope. His failure to do so, together with the scorn that was heaped on his head by the missionaries, cost him his prestige, and made him a steadfast and cunning opponent of the new faith. To him the sign of the cross was a potent gesture, but it was no more awful than the printed page. "This it is which all who have written of them say that the savages most wonder at, to see that by a piece of paper I make known my will from one end of the world to the other; and they thought that there was enchantment in the paper."[100]

Sometimes it was necessary to force the Micmacs to conform to the new

94. Jesuit Relations 1, 93.
95. Jesuit Relations 2, 53.
96. Jesuit Relations 2, 19.
97. Jesuit Relations 2, 281.

98. Jesuit Relations 1, 169.
99. Jesuit Relations 2, 77.
100. Lescarbot 3-128.

order. Reverence for the dead is deeply seated in the breasts of every people and may be considered as one of the main springs of the religious impulse. "It happened that Martin was stricken a week after his baptism with the disease (dysentry) and died thereof. . . . In his last moments he requested that when he died he should be buried with the Christians. There was some trouble about this. For the Savages having still some reverence for the burial places of their fathers and friends, wished to take him to Cape Sable, forty league distant from the Port. On the other hand, the Sieur wished to have him buried according to his request. Thereupon a dispute arose, and the Savages, seizing their bows and arrows, wanted to take away the corpse. But the Sieur placed a dozen arquebusiers under arms, who carried it off without resistence. . . When this was done they were all given some bread, and went away happy."[101]

It is no wonder that the process of conversion was extremely slow. Messire Jesse Flesche had, in his zeal, sprinkled the water of conversion upon a hundred Micmacs in 1610, but he knew nothing of their language and their instruction was negligible. When Biard arrived at St. John he was astonished to find that the unbaptized knew as much as the five who had been baptized. Some did not know their baptismal names when asked. They did not know what Christians were. When asked whether they had received baptism, they answered, "Yes, the Patriarch has made us like the Normans."[102] "They accepted baptism as a sort of sacred pledge of friendship and alliance with the French." Of Christianity they knew nothing. As the legend has it:

> When the priests first came "most all the Indians were witches. Some were willing to be christened, some were unwilling. They asked the priest. "What is Christening for?" . . . "If you are not christened, you are lost for good." . . . "Lost, in the woods?" . . . "No, in hell." . . . "Where is hell?" . . . "Black place, fire there burns the soul." . . . "How do you go there, by road?" . . . "No, your soul goes there." . . . "Where is my soul?" . . . "You might sicken and die. After you die you might see your soul." . . . "How can a soul go out from the birch-bark cover around the dead body, tightly bound?" . . . "You should dig a hole and put the dead in it." . . . "That would be even harder to get out of, couldn't go anywhere then." . . . "Yes, you could go to Heaven." . . . "Heaven? what is Heaven?" . . . "Nice band (of music) in Heaven, nice berries there." . . . "How go there?" . . . "If you do not fight, do not talk bad, you can go there. If you murder, steal, you will go to Hell, for your sin." . . . "Sin? what is sin?" They knew nothing. [103]

In spite of their lack of understanding, they were none the less eager to be initiated into the French tribe. Bertrand, in his "Lettre Missive" says that twenty were baptized "with as much enthusiasm, fervour and zeal for Religion as would have been evinced by a person who had been instructed in it for three or four years."[104] But Biard noted scarcely any change after baptism. "The same savagery and the same manners, or but little different, the same customs, ceremonies, usages, fashions and vices remain, at least as far as can be learned. . . ."[105] Sometimes the Indians reproached the Jesuits when, after baptism, they

101. Jesuit Relations 2, 149-151.
102. Jesuit Relations 1, 163; Jesuit Relations 2, 89.
103. Parsons (1) 90.
104. Jesuit Relations (1) 121.
105. Jesuit Relations 1, 165.

were asked to renounce polygamy and to live as Christians.   They said that the French were wicked to try to make them believe that they should agree to conditions that they had never understood, or been able to understand.[106] As long as they were in good health they did not readily submit to the rules of the Christian faith, "which to their ideas are a little too harsh"; but they were amenable to fear, and Hell, when painted in seventeenth century terms, was a sufficient stimulus, so that "already there has become deeply seated in the minds of the Canadians the belief that those who die without Baptism are consigned to eternal torments. . ."[107]

On the whole, the period prior to 1613 was one of breaking new ground and becoming accustomed to the Indian mind, rather than of substantial accomplishment on the part of the missionaries.   The barrier of language, the sometimes bad conduct of the traders, the hostility and jealousy of the native shamans, the deeply-seated religious beliefs and practices, and the traditions of their ancestors, together with the different mental categories of two so widely divergent cultures as those of the eastern Algonkian and the western European, conspired to minimize and dissipate the religious zeal and the moral example of the first missionaries.

Hitherto the influence of French upon Indian culture has been stressed, although the opposite tendency was discernable with respect to the fur trade, and to social and political relations.   Apart from these data, already given, the culture of the eastern Algonkians influenced that of the French both in Canada and in France. These influences were of two kinds; first, those involved in the borrowing of native materials; and second, those which ensued from the observation of alien cultures and which resulted in an examination of conscience on the part of the French humanistic intelligentsia in the sixteenth century.

The breadth of the Atlantic separated the French in Acadia from their cultural base in France and diminished the intensity of the complex European civilization in its relation to the native cultures.   The Indian food supply had, therefore, at times, considerable survival value for the French.   On one occasion they were saved from starvation by presents of elk meat, birds, fish and bread.[108]   At another time Poutrincourt sent some of his men to live with the Indians on account of the scarcity of food.[109]   Concerning the first Acadian mollusc culture in 1604 Lescarbot is quoted as having said, "There is a little chapel, built after the fashion of the savages, at the foot of which there is such a store of mussels as is wonderful. . . I believe that Monsieur De Monts' people did not forget to choose and take the biggest. . ."[110]   The Jerusalem artichoke was among the Indian roots which contributed to the food supply of the colonists.[111]   The French were not always so successful.   Once, when searching for the Chiquebi, or (Manioc?) potato, they found that the Indians had preceded them and that scarcely a day's supply remained.[112]   That these

---

106. Jesuit Relations 3, 149.
107. Jesuit Relations 2, 277.
108. Jesuit Relations 2, 263.
109. Jesuit Relations 3, 185.
110. Ganong (3) 16.
111. Jesuit Relations 2. 169. Called helianthus tuberosus.
112. Jesuit Relations 2, 245. See note 77.

roots were not entirely distasteful to the French is evident from the fact that they were sometimes imported into France. "We brought some of these roots (Indian potato) to France which had increased so much that today all the gardens are full of them. . ."[113]

Likewise the popularity of tobacco became very great at the beginning of the seventeenth century. "Certain Frenchmen are so bewitched with it that, to inhale its fumes, they would sell their shirts."[114] And, referring to the Micmac, Lescarbot says, "Our savages also plant great store of tobacco. . . . And our Frenchmen who have frequented them are for the most part so bewitched with this drunkenness of tobacco, that they can no more be without it than without meat or drink, and upon it they spend good money."[115] But that it was not yet popular in France seems to be evident from Champlain's explanation.[116]

Not only in woodcraft and canoemanship were the French the pupils of the Indians,[117] but also in superstitions which, though scouted by the humanist, Lescarbot, were credited by some who had a more medieval caste of mind. Speaking of the Gougou of Gaspé, Prevert of St. Malo told Champlain that "he passed so near the haunt of this terrible beast that he and all those on board his vessel heard strange hissings from the noise she made, and that the savages with him told him it was the same creature. . . ." Even Champlain himself held "that this is the dwelling place of some devil that torments them in the manner described,"[118] for which view he was ridiculed by Lescarbot.

In France the influence of the contact upon the lower strata of society was scarcely negligible. Between the times of Cartier and Champlain Norman maidens were decked with furs brought from the Indians of America, and the illiterate mind of the peasants[119] must have stirred and fired at the exotic visions conjured up by tales of feathered savages and strange and unfamiliar beasts that roamed the great undiscovered wilderness. Their mythology may have been enriched by tales of the Gougou of Gaspé, but they were not ready to modify their conventional attitudes. As against this, the triumph of the humanistic scholars awaited only the support of concrete examples. These were forthcoming in the narratives of voyages to strange lands. Even the Jesuit Biard could say that "in Paris we cannot sleep without having the doors well bolted; but there we close them against the wind only, and sleep no less securely for keeping them open."[120] Here were a people who did not make thieves of themselves for the love of property. Through his knowledge of the Micmac, Lescarbot could see many of the social ills with which civilized society was beset.[121] "And if only through considerations of humanity, and because these people of whom we shall treat are men like ourselves, we have reason to be roused with the desire of understanding their modes of life, and

---

113. Lescarbot 3, 254.
114. Jesuit Relations 3, 117.
115. Lescarbot 3, 252. Micmac tobacco, probably nicotiana rustica occasionally grown by French in Nova Scotia today. See LeClercq 515.
116. Champlain (2) 2, 168.
117. Jesuit Relations 1, 171, 159; Ganong C. K. 75.
118. Champlain (2) 2, 227.
119. Winsor (2) 313.
120. Jesuit Relations 4, 85.
121. Lescarbot 3, 189.

their customs . . . For they have courage, fidelity, generosity, and humanity, and their hospitality is so innate and praiseworthy that they receive among them every man who is not an enemy. There are not simpletons like many people over here (Europe); they speak with much judgment and good sense; . . . . So that if we commonly call them Savages, the word is abusive and unmerited. . . . ."[122]

Although ideas of this nature crept into France during the latter half of the sixteenth century the process was necessarily slow. For sixteen years after Cartier and Roberval had finished their work, the French public knew only the "Bref Recit" and the scant narrative of Jean Alfonse,[123] and "sixty-four years passed after this famous voyage before Cartier's own countrymen could read an account of it in their own tongue."[124] So that at the beginning of the seventeenth century Cartier's voyage to the rapids of the St. Lawrence was unknown, and Champlain thought himself the discoverer of this place.[125] But of some significance was the fact that savants of the stamp of Rabelais were conversant with the explorations of their time. Rabelais was a careful student of Cartier's voyages and he sends Pantagruel upon a journey to the Gulf of St. Lawrence.[126] The extraordinary voyage in French literature received a great impetus from geographical discovery which strengthened the belief in ethical relativity among the humanists, and which, by comparison with the alien cultures outlined in the narratives, gave the European satirist a whip with which to scourge his own society.[127] Perhaps more than any other, Montaigne found the American Indian a yard-stick with which to measure European civilization in the sixteenth century. His conversation with a Brazilian at Rouen in 1563 rendered more definite his concept of the noble savage and of the golden age of innocence from which European man had degenerated.[128] He says, "Nous les pouvons donc bien appeller barbares, eu esgard aux regles de la raison; mais non pas eu esgard a nous, qui les surpassons en toute sorte de barbarie. . . . Ce que nous voyons par experience en ces nations la surpasse non seulement toutes les peinctures de quoy la poesie a embelly l'aage dore, et toutes ses inventions a feindre une heureuse condition d'hommes, mais encores la conception et le desir mesme de la philosophie." The concept of "le bon sauvage" about which the "philosophes" of the eighteenth century such as Rousseau, Voltaire, Diderot, and others weaved their ideology, had its roots in the essays of Montaigne.[129] Thus, contact with the American Indians, not the least important of which were the eastern Algonkians, which was officially promoted for the political and commercial aggrandizement of the French monarchy, was a remote precursor of the French Revolution.

---

122. Lescarbot 1, 31-33.
123. Winsor (2) 303.
124. Biggar (1) Preface 1.
125. Lescarbot 2, 111. Belleforest in L'Histoire universelle du monde, Paris 1570, does not mention it. He was however in many respects grossly inaccurate.
126. In the fourth book, A. Lefranc, Les navigations de Pentagruel. Smith, W. F. Rabelais and his writings, p. 185. Biggar (3) 222.
127. Atkinson, G. The extraordinary voyage in French literature before 1700.
128. Dionne (1) 100; Villey, P. Les sources et les evolutions des Essais de Montaigne, 1908, v. 2, 156, 510; Montaigne, Essays, translated by E. J. Trechmann with intro. by J. M. Robertson, Lond. 1927, v. 1, p. 202-215.
129. Atkinson, G. Relations de voyage, p. 10. See also Chinard, G. L'exotisme americain dans la litterature francaise au 16e siecle, Paris, 1910. See also pp. 63-81, Le bon sauvage.

CHAPTER 4

THE EASTERN ALGONKIANS AND THE BALANCE OF POWER

In the preceding chapter we traced the development of French enterprise in Acadia from its inception to the destruction of Port Royal in 1613 by the English pirate, Argall. Meanwhile in 1608 Champlain had selected Quebec for the site of his headquarters in the New World both on account of its protected position and its central location with respect to the northern fur-bearing areas. The French were at this time concerned with the task of gaining control of the trade routes to the interior by forming alliances with the tribes situated along these routes and by eradicating inter-tribal jealousies which were often marked by hostilities prejudicial to French interests. It will be seen that the balance of power was held by the tribes which served as middlemen between the French and the northern interior and that these sought by every means at their command to maintain their positions as such. As the demand for furs increased and as the frontiers of the fur-trade receded the French made frequent attempts, which were not always at first successful, to penetrate the areas controlled by the middlemen. These attempts rendered the impact between the European and the native cultures severe and led to the manifold disasters which befell the aboriginal populations which will be outlined in succeeding chapters.

Sometimes the middlemen, such as the Hurons, were almost exterminated by the Iroquois whose rising imperialism, which resulted from their access to supplies of European weapons through the medium of the Dutch, threatened the very existence of the French colony on the St. Lawrence throughout the greater part of the seventeenth century. Mention will be made of the French attempts to divert the fur-trade from the Dutch and to conciliate or cripple the Iroquois. Much was to be feared also from the growing power of the English colonies on the Atlantic seaboard whose interest in the trade was not inconsiderable. In the course of this rivalry it was found to be of interest to both peoples to cement an alliance with the Abenaki whose territory lay on the border of those claimed by the French and the English, and whose position may be likened somewhat to that of a buffer state. Inverting the order of subjects outlined for consideration in this chapter let us begin by tracing the main outlines of the struggle between the French and the English to secure the good will and alliance of the Abenaki.

Verazzano had encountered these Indians in 1524 and he was alleged to have said that the Bretons had made contact with them before his time. It is said that they were not again visited until 1605, in which year Weymouth discovered the Penobscot, made prisoners of several of the inhabitants, and thereby earned the enmity of these people.[1] Weymouth's expedition was followed by many others. In 1607 when some of the prisoners were returned, communications were established with the English who sold them brandy for

---

1. Maurault 72-74.

the first time, and it is said that a chief submitted to the English crown in the name of his people.   But throughout the ensuing year the Indians were ill-treated, and the English, in fear of their menacing gestures, abandoned their fort.   When Hudson tried to effect a landing at the Penobscot in 1609 he was chased away by the inhabitants.[2]

After the destruction of Port Royal the English did not occupy Acadia for fear of the Indians, and it was not until 1623 and 1624 that posts at Piscataqua River, and at Casco Bay were established.   Trade was then carried on with more amicable relations than at any other time.   Between 1613 and 1626 the Abenaki had little contact with Europeans.   In the latter year the Pemaquid trading post was founded, but the English made no attempt to colonize the area.[3] The Narantsouak or Norridgewock Abenaki, known also as the Canibas, which was a variant of Kennebec, were driven up the Kennebec river by the white men. The English established the settlement of Kousinak near here in 1629 where they carried on an extensive trade in peltries for a time.   But trouble with the Indians diminished and eventually destroyed the trade.[4] This and most other Maine posts were abandoned probably before King Philip's war in 1675.

From the beginning the French had been more successful in treating with the Indians of Maine than had the English.   Champlain had quickly made himself efficient in the art of forest diplomacy, and French interests generally coincided more closely with those of the Indians.   Moreover, during the first quarter of the seventeenth century, when the English were bungling Indian affairs, the French did not come into close contact with the Abenaki of the Kennebec.   To the eastward the feud between La Tour and d'Aulnay caused a rupture between the Penobscots and the Etchemins who were led against each other by these warring factions.   This enmity, which lasted for several years, did not involve the Indians of the Kennebec.[5] As late as 1640 the Capuchins were engaged in missionary work on the Penobscot, but the Canibas, the largest of the Abenaki groups, were probably not visited.   During the 'thirties and 'forties the English corrupted them with liquor in the prosecution of the fur-trade.[6]

It is possible that the supply of furs in the Abenaki country failed to meet the growing demand made by the English fur traders after the founding of Massachusetts Bay, for in 1637 a party of Abenaki arrived at Quebec with the intention of proceeding to Three Rivers to exchange wampum for the beaver of the Algonkins who traded there. Not only did the Montagnais object to this diversion of trade but "it is not for the good of Messieurs the Associates; for those barbarians come to carry off the Beavers of these countries, to take them elsewhere", i.e., to the English.[7] In spite of Montagnais and French efforts to stop them the Abenaki continued upon their way.   They declared that they had come to aid their allies in war and that it was not their purpose to trade.   Nevertheless their cabins were searched and their arquebuses were

2. Maurault 76-80.
3. Maurault 102-106; Moloney, 32-36.
4. Jesuit Relations 36, 238.

5. Maurault 164.
6. Maurault 102-108.
7. Jesuit Relations 12, 187-189.

confiscated.   This act was not a violation of customary procedure.   It is probable that inter-tribal rivalry in the trade of the seventeenth century sharpened the sense of property among the eastern Algonkians.   At any rate, the Montagnais had a custom that "When other nations arrive in their country, they would not dare pass beyond without permission from the Captain of the place; if they did, their canoes would be broken to pieces.   This permission to pass on is asked for with presents in hand; if these presents are not accepted by the Chief . . . he tells them he has stopped the way, . . At these words they have to turn back, or run the risk of war."[8]

Contact with the people of the St. Lawrence Valley was, however, at this time very infrequent. Some Montagnais Christians preached to the Abenaki in the country of the latter in 1643, "but those people have no acquaintance or commerce with any one else, except with some English who are wont to go there; . . . " Likewise a Montagnais missionary knew nothing of the English, for when he went to an English settlement "He took them for Frenchmen,—the Savages do not yet know how to distinguish the Europeans, either by nation or by religion."[9]   Some time later, however, two Abenaki arrived at Quebec to request that a missionary be sent to their country.[10]

Other peoples also began to find their way to Quebec for the first time since the French occupation.   A Socoki warrior, a neighbour of the Abenaki to the westward, had been made a prisoner by the Algonkins and tortured by them.   When he was brought to Sillery in 1643 he was treated kindly by the French and the Montagnais and was sent back to Saco "in order to show the affection of the French and Savages for him", in spite of the fact that the Island Algonkins are said to have remained intractible and treacherous.[11]   The Algonkian peoples had not yet attained the Iroquoian idea of forming a league for protection against common enemies and often fought with each other. Such was the case when, in 1646, the Etchemins went to war with the Gaspé Micmac, although both were at the time nominally allied to the French.[12]

In the middle of the century the policies of the missionaries and the fur-traders seem to have been at variance with respect to the Abenaki.   The traders feared that if the Abenaki became frequent visitors to Quebec they would tend to divert the trade to the English.   So that when thirty Abenaki arrived at Quebec in July, 1649, "they are notified that they are not to come again, and that their goods will be plundered if they return."[13]   On the other hand the Jesuits made overtures to the Abenaki.   Father Dreuillettes visited twelve or thirteen villages on the Kennebec and along that part of the Acadian coast which was occupied by the English.   Everywhere he was "received like an Angel descended from Heaven".[14]   In 1651 he wrote to Governor Winthrop asserting that the Mohawks were planning to massacre the Abenaki who had been for many years allied to the Canadian Christians.   He asked for aid on behalf of the French and Abenaki separately in accordance with the French

8. Jesuit Relations 12, 189.
9. Jesuit Relations 24, 61-63.
10. Jesuit Relations 28, 215.
11. Jesuit Relations 24, 185, 191-193.

12. Jesuit Relations 28, 205.
13. Jesuit Relations 34. 57.
14. Jesuit Relations 37, 257.

policy of treating the tribes as sovereign powers, but in his negotiations with Plymouth he referred to the Abenaki as subjects of that colony who by virtue of this fact merited protection from the Iroquois.[15]   Plymouth "has the Proprietorship of Koussinoc (formerly Abenaki territory, now Augusta, Maine) and for its rights of lordship takes the sixth part of what accrues from the trade."[16]   The Dutch were asked by Plymouth to stop the trade in arms to the Iroquois, and to aid the English in attacking them.   The Boston government assured Dreuillettes that all the colonies would be urged to move against the Iroquois, and the merchants led the priest to believe that they would undertake private expeditions if the state should take no action.

It is clear that the officials of New England adopted a conciliatory attitude toward Dreuillettes because they perceived the influence which he already exerted over the warlike Abenaki.   When, in 1652, an English servant to one of the traders accused the Jesuit of speaking ill of the English, the Indians protested that this was not the case, that the Father was of their nation, that he had been adopted as a fellow countryman, and was the wisest of captains.   Whoever attacked him attacked all the Abenaki.   Confronted by this situation, the English reprimanded the servant and stated that the confidence which the Indians had in Dreuillettes would foster good feeling between the English, French and Indians in this part of the country.[17]   They never carried out their declared intentions, however, of joining the French in a war against the Iroquois.   It is said that French efforts to secure their aid in this project caused the failure of the alliance of the colonies which had been proposed in 1647 by the English.[18]   The Indians themselves were possessed of no illusion concerning the friendship of the English during the negotiations at Plymouth and Boston; for Noel Negabamat, the Christian chief of Sillery, had said in 1651, "The Englishman replies not; he has no good thoughts for us.   This grieves me much; we see ourselves dying and being exterminated every day."[19]

By the middle of the century most of the eastern tribes were beginning to be convinced that they could not expect what they considered as justice at the hands of the English, and that their only hope of survival lay in presenting a united front to the usurpers of their territories. Ambassadors from the Sokoki, representing four villages of that tribe, appeared at Plymouth in 1651 to promise aid to the Abenaki,[20] and in the following year the French succeeded in cementing an alliance between the Sokoki and the Algonkins, who had, for some years past, carried on an intermittent war with each other.   Algonkin prisoners were detained in the land of the Sokoki, and warriors belonging to the latter tribe were beaten, mutilated, and burnt with brands at Sillery in 1652 by Algonkins who were enraged by successive Iroquois victories.   But a general council of the tribes granted them their lives, and it was stipulated that an alliance would be formed if the Sokoki delivered the Algonkin prisoners at Sillery. In 1653 ambassadors arrived, bringing peace, and the tribes declared

15. Dreuillettes. Jesuit Relations 36, 79.
16. Jesuit Relations 36, 99.
17. Jesuit Relations 38, 31.

18. Eastman 20.
19. Jesuit Relations 37, 77.
20. Jesuit Relations 36, 101.

themselves to be formally allied.[21]   By this means the Sokoki hoped to be delivered from the annual wampum tribute which they were compelled to pay to the Iroquois, and the Sillery Indians were glad to receive the cooperation of the Sokoki in protecting the beaver hunt in the vicinity of Quebec from hostile inroads.[22]

The French were beginning to resent the encroachments of the English no less than were the Indians.   The Relation for 1659 presents the situation succinctly:

> "The English have usurped all the Eastern coast from Canceau to New England, and have left to the French that which extends towards the North; the principal points of the latter are called Miscou, Rigibouctou and Cape Breton. The district of Miscou is the most populous and the best disposed, and contains most Christians. It comprises the Savages of Gaspé, of Miraimachy, and of Nepigigouit. Richibouctou is a beautiful river, and important for its trade with the Savages of the river St. John." [23]

Thus it is seen that French trade was centred in northeastern Acadia in that area which was farthest from English intrusion.   That it was only a matter of time before the English would have control of the whole of Acadia was suggested at a later date by Lahontan, who wrote:

> "To be plain, the knowledge I have of that Country, makes me forfee that the English will be mafters of it fome time or other. . . . They have already begun to ruine the Commerce that the French had with the Savages, and in a fhort time, they'll encompafs its intire Deftruction. The French they will prize their Goods too high, though they are not fo good as thofe of the Englifh, and yet the Englifh fell their Commodities cheaper." [24]

As far as actual prices were concerned the English had an economic advantage over the French.   But the temperament, the religious beliefs, and the larger economic interests of the expanding commonwealths impelled the English to ride rough-shod over those tribes that stood in their way. Events in the 'sixties were shaping towards that last great fight for existence on the part of the New England tribes, known as King Philip's war.   For our present purpose the remainder of the century will be devoted to two subjects.   First, the struggle of the Abenaki to maintain their position on the Atlantic seaboard, and their failure and subsequent migration to the St. Lawrence watershed; and second, the inroads made by the Penobscots, the Etchemins, and the Micmac, at the connivance, and sometimes with the active cooperation, of the French, upon the frontier settlements of New England.

In 1676 one hundred and fifty Abenaki arrived at Sillery from New England to seek refuge from the war.   Others, among whom were several Sokoki, were to be found at Three Rivers.[25]   In Maine their compatriots were fighting tooth and nail to drive the English back.   Casco was attacked, the English fled in terror from the Kennebec, and many were killed. On November 13th the Abenaki made a treaty with the English at Boston but the peace was

21. Jesuit Relations 40, 197.
22. Jesuit Relations 36, 105.
23. Jesuit Relations 45, 59.

24. Lahontan 3, 326.
25. Jesuit Relations 60, 135.

short lived for in 1677 further aggressions were made upon the New England frontier.[26]   The Abenaki obliged the English colony of Sagadahock to pay them tribute, but a fierce battle ensued in which the English cavalry won the day.   This was followed by another in which a thousand Abenaki and Sokoki were slain, and many fled to the Penobscot, Acadia and Canada.   Those who came to Canada brought a great quantity of peltries to the French, to whom they also supplied the canoes which were necessary to the fur-trade.   But the migration was not an unmixed blessing for these people, for from a country fertile in corn, fish and animals, where they had a good and cheap market for their goods with the English, they had come to Sillery which was "devue de toutes les commoditez de la vie, et il n'y a plus de terres bonnes a semer du bled d'Inde, outre que les Francois vendent fort cher leurs marchandises aux Sauvages."[28]   From 1681 to 1684 great numbers of Abenaki migrated to Sillery,[29] so that soon the villages of Sillery and Sault de la Chaudière comprised three hundred families,[30] and another settlement sprang up on the banks of the St. Francis River.[31]   The remaining Abenaki were invited to settle on the St. Francis and to march with the French against the Iroquois.[32]   By 1687 there were seven hundred Abenaki at Sillery alone, and in that year Father Bigot, the superior of the mission, made a journey to New England to induce more to come.[33]   In 1688 de Menneval wrote concerning conditions in the Atlantic settlements:

> "Il y en a deux nations differentes entre la rivière de Pentagouit et celles de quinnibiqui, les cannibas en petit nombre vers Pentagouit et les abenaquis beaucoup plus nombreux vers quinnibiqui; ils sont asses affectionnes aux francois et hayssent naturellement les Anglais, mais comme on ne fait rien pour eux et qu'au contraire les Anglais les visitent, leurs font des presens de temps en temps et leur fournissent les choses dont ils ont besoing a très bon marche, et mesme a perte aux depens du Roy, cela fera à la fin qu'ils les gagneront tout a fait et en pouroient dans la suitte avier des avantages contre les Francoises. Ils paroissent asses portes a la prière et a se faire instruire dans la religion et sy on y establissoit une mission comme celle du Sillery pres de Quebec cela pouvait estre utile dans la suite pour le service du Roy et de la religion, mais il faudrait quelque depense pour cela." [34]

Besides the three villages in Canada another was founded in 1698 at Naurakamig in Maine to provide a suitable location for teaching the Indians agriculture.[35]   The mission was maintained at Sillery until 1699 when the land which had been ceded in trust for the Indians, was retroceded to the Jesuits.   In 1700 all the scattered villages were collected at St. Francois du Lac, Yamaska County, Quebec.[36]

Meanwhile in Acadia the struggle for supremacy became more intense.

---

26. Murdoch 1, 154.27 Maurault 171
28. Collection de manuscripts relatifs, 1, 272-273.
29. Jesuit Relations 62, 25, 109; 63, 67.
30. Lahontan 48-90.
31. Maurault 275.
32. Jesuit Relations 63, 57.
33. Eastman 242.
34. Series C 11 D—(1) 1.
35. Jesuit Relations 65, 87, note 10.
36. Lahontan 1, 48, 49.

Castin led the Penobscots against the English in 1687 in revenge for the pillage of Pentagouet by Andros,[37] and two years later the Indians took Pemaquid, incited, it is said, by the Jesuit, Thury.[38]   The English trader had reduced the Indians to a state of debt peonage, so that when the post fell, "They bid him order his book of accounts to be brought, and to cross out all the Indians' debts. . ."[39]   The French officers from Canada sometimes donned Indian dress and fought along side of their dark-skinned allies,[40] but more often they merely supplied materials as an incentive and as a means to carry on the war.[41] A letter written by M. de Lagny, dated at Paris, 21st. Feb., 1690, leaves no doubt as to the source of powder and arms used by the Abenaki and kindred peoples.[42] Moreover, Denonville, writing in 1690, outlined the success which the Indians were having in their attacks on the English posts:

> "En partans de Canada j'ay lesse une très grande disposition a atirer au Christianisme la plus grande partie des sauvages abenaquis que abitent les bois du voisinage de Baston. Pour cela il faut les atirer a la mission nouvellement etablie pres Quebec sous le nom de St. fransois de Sales; je l'ay vue en peu de temps au nombres de six cents ames venues du voisinage de Baston. Je l'ay laisse en etat de l'augmenter beaucoup si elle est protegée; J'y fait quelque depense qui n'y a pas esté inutile. La bonne intelligence que j'ay eu avec ces sauvages par les soins des Jesuites et sourtout des deux Peres Bigots freres a fait le . . . de toutes les ataques qu'ils ont fait sur l'anglois cet este ausquels ils ont enlevé saise forts outre celui de Pemacit ou ils y avait vimt pieces de canons ils leur ont tué plus de deux cents hommes avec des presans de hardes, de poudre et de plomb ou les maintiendra aisement dans nos interais. Ils seront tres utiles à la colonie francoise surtout si on les engage a se venir etablir dans la nouvelle mission de St. francois de Sales qu'ils faut soutenir avec soin et fortifier le vilage car sans doute les anglais pouront les envoyer ataquer par les Iroquois. . . ."[43]

And in the following year Champigny wrote to the Minister:

> "Les sauvages de l'Acadia ont envoyé icy en hiver plusieurs de leurs gens qui nous ont raporté que les anglais les avoient fort solicitez de se rendre a eux, les assurant qu'ils s'etoient rendus maistres de Quebec, mais qu'au lieu de les croire et d'ecouter leurs propositions ils n'avoient pas cesse de leur faire la guerre et mesme qu'ils leur avoient pris une barque chargée de marchandises . . . M. de Frontenac a fair donner de la poudre et des balles aux sauvages pour en porter a leurs nations afin de les exciter a continuer la guerre, il s'est engage de leur envoyer quelques canots pour leur en porter avec d'autres munitions, je suis bien persuade que cela ne peut estre que tres utile, ces sauvages nous estans fort atachez et ennemis irreconciliables des anglois a cause d'une trahison qu'ils leurs ont faite . . . massacrant une nombre considerable de leurs gens qui estoient allez parmis eux de bon foy. . . ."[44]

In 1692 he urged the home government to continue to send a good supply of presents to incite the Indians to destroy the English settlements in Acadia:

---

37. Murdoch 1, 175.
38. Murdoch 1, 177.
39. Gyles 16.
40. Murdoch 1, 184-5.
41. Collection de manuscrits relatifs.
42. Murdoch 1, 193.
43. C 11 A 11, Denonville, 1690.
44. C 11 A 11, Champigny to the Minister, 1691.

"Les sauvages de l'acadie meritans bien de n'estre pas oubliez, Nous vous prions de leur procurer l'année prochaine les mesmes graces que le Roy leur a accordé celle cy, En leur envoyant les presens contenus dans un estat cy joint pour leur donner moyen de continuer la guerre et les exciter de nouveau à detruire les anglais à quoi ils reussissent fort bien comme vous le verrez. . . ." [45]

On the other hand the English were making determined, if somewhat bungling efforts to establish peace with the border tribes, and there is evidence that the Indians themselves were tiring of the war.[46]   In 1693 the English built a fort at Saco, and in spite of the opposition of Thury, the Indians made a treaty with them, at the same time giving hostages.[47]   But in 1694 the captain of Pemaquid violated a flag of truce displayed by a party of Indians and thereby destroyed their conciliatory attitude.   Villieu, a French official in Acadia, went to Nashwaak and Penobscot to confer with the Abenaki in order to keep them loyal to the French, and with Micmac, Malecite and Abenaki support he fell upon Dover, New Hampshire, killing a hundred and four, taking twenty seven prisoners and scalping a girl.[48]   On the 20th May, 1695, a party of fifty canoes arrived at Pemaquid and a truce of thirty days was agreed upon.   When the Indian delegates met the English commissioners the latter refused to negotiate a treaty until all English prisoners were given up, although they refused to surrender those Abenaki who were languishing in Boston.[49] In 1696 the French gave the Indians 4,000 livres worth of presents to attack Pemaquid, and the commander of that post hauled down his flag on the conditions demanded by the French; namely, that the French and Indian prisoners in Boston should be exchanged for the garrison of the fort who should be guaranteed against the fury of the Indians.   The Abenaki had some cause to be enraged, for when the fort was taken, "within was found a Canibat Indian in irons, half dead.   It took the good father nearly two hours to file off the fetters of this poor captive, . . Among papers of the governor, a recent order was found, received from Boston, directing him to hang this Indian."[50]

On the 10th July, 1697, Governor Villebon of Acadia dispatched a party of Micmac from Nashwaak with powder, lead and rations to raid any English encampments along the coast that might be available for plunder. "These savages departed in good disposition and with the intention of giving no quarter to the enemy places where they should pass; and I gave them 100 lbs. powder and 500 lbs. lead, *for hunting on the sea shore* in going to Pentagouet. . ."   They killed some English and burned one alive in revenge for the killing of a chief.   The Malecite and the Penobscot Indians were also involved in this expedition.[51]

At this time the English authorities attempted to check the zeal of the Abenaki through engaging French intervention, and a correspondence was entered upon with a view to effecting this purpose.   But on the 21st September,

---

45. C 11 A 12, Champigny, 1692.
46. Murdoch 1, 200-201.
47. Murdoch 1, 210.
48. Murdoch 1, 211.   Collection de manuscrits relatifs v. 2, 135-143.
49. Murdoch 1, 217.
50. Murdoch 1, 219.
51. Murdoch 1, 235.

1698, Frontenac wrote to the governor of New York declaring that the English could not expect the Abenaki to cease their raids on the settlements while their fellows were detained as prisoners at Boston.[52]   In 1699 the English were still trying to induce the Abenaki to drive away the Jesuits and replace them with ministers of their own.   But these Indians refused to break their alliance with the French, asserting "that the English must quit their country; that they would never suffer them to settle there. . . ."[53]

The English trader, Nelson, wrote a letter to the Board of Trade on the 24th September, 1696, in which he summarized the situation in Acadia and on the New England border:

> "The English colonies depend on improving the lands, etc. The French of Canada, on their trade of furs and peltry with the Indians; consequently their whole contrivance is to maintain their interest and reputation with the Indians, which has been much augmented by that late foolish and unhappy expedition from New England by Sr. W. Phips, as also for want of due care of settlement in the countrie of Nova Scotia, after the taking of Port Royal." [54]

He might have added that the French had succeeded in outwitting the English in forest diplomacy, and that, in the course of their social relations, the English had gradually goaded the Abenaki into a state of uncompromising war.

2.

Those tribes in the northeastern area, of which the main artery of trade was the Saguenay, dwelt under economic and social conditions very different from those of the Abenaki.   They were not wedged between two expanding imperial units whose basic economy differed in kind to the extent which marked the French and English colonial enterprises.   Moreover, during the first half of the century, they were isolated enough to escape annihilation by the Iroquois, whereas the Abenaki were exposed to disintegrating influences from three sources.   On the other hand, after Champlain established communications with the Hurons and Algonkins, they tended to be left behind in the scramble for European materials which characterized the expanding fur-trade throughout the period.   The establishment of the Ottawa route to the interior lightened the impact of European civilization upon these tribes but left them at a disadvantage in that their technical equipment remained upon a more elementary level.

At the time of the founding of Quebec, however, the Saguenay was still the main trade route to the northern interior, which was inhabited by the upper Montagnais, and beyond them by the Misstassini Cree, in which beaver was plentiful.   But the territories of those Montagnais bands which extended from Tadoussac to Quebec were probably early denuded of beaver, since trade

---

52.   Documents relating to colonial history of New York, v. 403.
53.   Jesuit Relations 65, 95-97.
54.   Murdoch 1, 203.

with these peoples extended back to the time of Cartier.   It has been suggested that the possession of European materials enabled them, after the middle of the sixteenth century, to expel the Mohawks and Onondagas from the St. Lawrence Valley.   Therefore, by the end of the first decade of the seventeenth century their chief function had become that of middlemen between the French and those bands who dwelt farther inland. Moreover, they preserved this seemingly advantageous position with jealous care.   In 1608 Champlain wrote:

> "This is the region to which our savages go with the merchandise we give them in exchange for their furs, such as beaver, marten, lynx, and otter which are found there in large numbers and which they bring to our ships. These northern tribes tell our Indians that they see the salt sea. . . . I have often desired to explore it, but have been unable to do so without the natives, who have been unwilling that I or any of our people should go with them." [55]

During the next three decades, while French imperialism was circumventing the waters of the upper Ottawa and the Georgian Bay, the Sillery and Tadoussac Montagnais continued to guard their harbours from the inroads of more outlying bands who dwelt to the eastward towards the land of the Nascopi.   In 1635 a woman was baptized at Sillery who

> "told me that the people of her nation were called ouperigone ouaouakhi, that they dwelt further back in the interior, below Tadoussac, and on the same side; that they could descend through the river from their country to the great river saint Lawrence; that her countrymen had no commerce with the Europeans; 'that is why,' she said, 'they use hatchets made of stone'; that they have Deer and Beavers in abundance, but very few Elk; that they speak the Montagnais language, and that they would certainly come and trade with the French, were it not that the Savages of Tadoussac try to kill them when they encounter them." [56]

Nevertheless the emergence of the Hurons as middlemen in the Ottawa trade together with the decline of beaver in the lower St. Lawrence area reduced the Montagnais peoples to a lower standard of living and forced them to lean more heavily upon the French for support.[57]   Those Montagnais and Algonkins who were accustomed to spend a large part of the year in and about Quebec began in 1643 to lose their economic independence, which was augmented by the benevolent charities of the missionaries and others.[58]   We observe at this time the incipient move towards the degradation of the reserve system in Canada. Moreover, disease, famine and war supplemented economic dependence in disintegrating the native cultures.   In 1644 fear of the Iroquois kept the Montagnais from hunting south of the St. Lawrence where the best hunting was to be found.   One party escaped the Iroquois but returned with nothing to eat but the cords of their snow-shoes.   The aged and infirm, who would otherwise have perished, were kept alive at Sillery to the number of forty by the French.[59]   However, trade continued at Tadoussac, although it was inconsiderable when compared with that of the Ottawa; and when the Jesuits

55. Champlain (1) v. 18-19.
56. Jesuit Relations 8, 41.
57. Innis (1) 24.
58. Jesuit Relations 23, 313.
59. Jesuit Relations 25, 105-111.
60. Jesuit Relations 21, 91.

tried in 1640 to induce the Tadoussac Montagnais to move to Quebec they refused on the ground that "it was important to them not to withdraw from Tadoussac."[60]   The Quebec Montagnais, who used wampum to some extent, carried on a small trade with their compatriots at Tadoussac.[61]

When they were not excluded, more distant peoples kept coming to this port year by year.   In 1640 the missionary "saw some young men of the Sagné here, who had never seen any Frenchmen; they were much astonished to hear me speak their own language."   When the Tadoussac Indians said that the priest was their relative they could not believe it "for our beards put a difference, almost essential, so to speak, between a European and a Savage."[62] The Betsiamite people, who dwelt east of Tadoussac towards the territory of the Eskimo, were still "insignificant nations of whom we know little".[63]   The new bands who were beginning to arrive in 1643 for the first time were generally from the interior,[64] although some of these refused to come down to Tadoussac on account of the disease that was rampant there in the 'forties.[65]

It is not improbable that many were deterred also by fear of the Iroquois who were beginning to appear in the St. Lawrence Valley in ever-increasing numbers, and who had waged an intermittent war since long before the French establishment at Quebec.   French influence exerted against torturing Iroquois prisoners at Sillery and Three Rivers in 1645 paved the way for the first peace in many years between the Iroquois and their enemies, the Hurons, Algonkins, Montagnais, the Atticamegs, who were a western group of the Montagnais, the Sokoki and the Abenaki.[66]   But the peace was short-lived. With the mid-century extension of Iroquois imperialism which effected the dispersal of the Hurons and the destruction of the Ottawa river trade, the Saguenay again became the road to the northern interior, which was occupied by the Cree and the Ojibwa, instead of the St. Maurice and the Ottawa.[67]   In May, 1646, when the latter route was still open, there were only ten cabins of Indians at Tadoussac, and only five casks of beaver and one hundred and fifty-one moose skins were traded.[68]   But in October, 1650, the merchants "intend to attract the Savages thither and then carry on a good trade in Beavers".   A journey up the Saguenay was undertaken "to make arrangements with the Savages, and cast the hook for this trade. . . . they brought back about 300 . . . . . Beavers."[69]   The Tadoussac Indians, who had formerly barred the way to the interior tribes, now invited the French to come to convert them. Moreover, distant peoples were welcomed at the port in this year.   The Papinachois and Betsiamites, who dwelt towards Anticosti, began to come to Tadoussac.   The Jesuits attributed this change to the growth of Christian spirit; to a shift in the trade routes; and to the desire on the part of the Tadoussac Indians, who had been depleted by war and disease, to swell their ranks to meet the Iroquois raiders.[70]   The latter were accustomed to ambush isolated hunting parties.   In 1652, when the Jesuit, Buteux, and a large part

61. Jesuit Relations 18, 111.
62. Jesuit Relations 21, 99.
63. Jesuit Relations 18, 227-229.
64. Jesuit Relations 26 103.
65. Jesuit Relations 33, 29.

66. Jesuit Relations 27, 245.
67. Jesuit Relations 45, 233.
68. Jesuit Relations 28, 201.
69. Jesuit Relations 35, 59.
70. Jesuit Relations 35, 275.

of his flock were killed, the remnant fled to Tadoussac for refuge, making a journey of a hundred leagues through the forest to that place.[71]   In the same year the Sillery Indians did not dare to pursue their usual hunt and extreme want prevailed at that settlement.[72] In July 1653, the Micmacs, the Etchemins, and the Montagnais, undertook a campaign with not unqualified success against the Iroquois,[73] but shortly afterwards another peace caused a mometary lull in military activity.   The French were extending their tentacles towards those tribes who dwelt beyond the country of the dispersed Hurons, and they in their turn were finding their way to the French settlements.   Under cover of the peace some of the more distant of the central Algonkian tribes made journeys to Sillery.[74] "Those tribes have as yet never seen a single European; they still use stone hatchets and they cook their meat in long vessels made of bark, which serve them as kettles, just as was formerly the custom among our Savages. They have no iron tools, all their implements being of bone, wood or stone."[75]   In 1653 the first news of the Winnebago and their Algonkian neighbours were received by the French.

Nevertheless in 1657 the Iroquois found it profitable to disperse the Kepatawanejach, Outabitibek and Ouakwiechiwek, bands of Montagnais on the upper waters of the Saguenay.[76] The cessation of hostilities in 1658 merely presaged a renewed burst of violence on the part of the Iroquois.   In 1659 they carried the war east to Tadoussac.[77]   In June, 1661, this settlement was burned and destroyed, and the total population, numbering over a hundred, was forced to seek refuge at Quebec.   A race ensued between the French and the Iroquois to reach outlying bands.   Father Bailloquet visited seven or eight peoples who dwelt a hundred and sixty leagues northeast of Quebec, among whom were the Papinachois, the Betsiamites, the "Nation of the bare Mountains" and the Oumamiouek.[78]   Up to this time Lake St. John had been the limit of French penetration in the northern interior, but in 1661 Menard reached Necouba, which lay near the height of land half way between Tadoussac and Hudson Bay.[79]   This was "a place noted for a Market that is held there every year, to which all the Savages from the surrounding country resort for the purpose of conducting their peltry traffic."[80]   Here sixty natives greeted the French.

At the same time the Porcupine Montagnais of Lake St. John were ravaged by the Iroquois, and the "Squirrel nation" to the east of Necouba was destroyed.[81] In 1662 Necouba itself was laid waste. It had never been visited by the Iroquois before, and the inhabitants, not expecting attack, were unarmed.   It was the avowed purpose of the Iroquois to raid the territory from this point northward to Hudson Bay.[82] Throughout the following year many of these northern peoples sought refuge at Quebec.   The remnant of the Sillery colony, which moved into the capital, was augmented by three or four hundred

71. Jesuit Relations 37, 203.
72. Jesuit Relations 37, 147.
73. Jesuit Relations 38, 179.
74. Jesuit Relations 41, 181-183.
75. Jesuit Relations 41, 183-185.
76. Jesuit Relations 45, 233.

77. Jesuit Relations 45, 107.
78. Jesuit Relations 47, 61.
79. Jesuit Relations 46 275.
80. Jesuit Relations 46, 275.
81. Jesuit Relations 46, 285-287.
82. Jesuit Relations 47, 151-153.

Algonkins, and Micmac and Montagnais bands were among the refugees. Many of the latter had never seen the French before.[83]   Although the Sillery Algonkians, armed with javelins, hatchets and arquebuses, scored a victory over the Iroquois in 1663,[84] it did not prevent them from invading the territories of the Papinachois at Isle Verte and driving away all the moose so that virtual starvation ensued.[85]   But conditions here, as elsewhere, improved for a time after the punitive expeditions of Tracy and Courcelles in 1665 and 1666, so that, in 1668, two hundred and fifty-six persons, besides the Indians of Sillery and Tadoussac, went to the land of the Papinachois to trade.[86]

In this year, however, an event occurred which was destined to impair seriously French interests in the northern interior.   With the establishment of Charles Fort on Rupert's River, the English began to cut into the French monopoly of the territory lying east and south of Hudson Bay.[87]   It has been stated that the dispersal of the Hurons in 1649 favoured those peoples who traded along the Saguenay route, but that these again suffered when the French succeeded in establishing relations with the central Algonkians, such as the Ottawas, who lived on the rivers and lakes which lay beyond the old territories of the Hurons.   Now French trade began to suffer in the whole northern area from English competition on the Bay; but the Indians were immediately thrown into a more favourable economic setting by virtue of this competition, for from the English "goods were obtained on a large scale, and, with access by sea, at much more favourable rates."[88]

Three times previously the French had tried to penetrate the country of the Misstassini Cree in their endeavours to reach Hudson Bay by land, but each time they had failed.[89]   Now, in 1671, Father Albanel determined to push through to the Bay by way of the Saguenay.   Opposition was still strong and the Tadoussac Indians opposed his intention, although guides, after much persuasion, finally offered their services.   Later, however, they opposed his passage by every means in their power.[90]   But in spite of the opposition he reached Lake St. John where bands, who had previously been dispersed by the Iroquois and their fear of smallpox, were now gathering under the protection of the Iroquois peace.   Among them were Misstassini Cree who possessed a hatchet and tobacco which had been obtained from the English on Hudson Bay.[91]   Albanel encountered further opposition when he reached the height of land by Paslistaskau.   Here a Cree stopped him with a harangue: "Black Gown, stay here; our old man, the master of this country, must be notified of thy arrival."   He wished the Jesuit to purchase his passage because "The rivers are to them what fields are to the French, ..."[92]   It is probable also that he did not want Albanel to proceed at all, but he did not have recourse to violent means, and when Albanel met the head man of the district he declaimed: "abandon the plan of carrying on commerce with the Europeans who are trading toward the North sea, among whom prayer is not offered to

---

83. Jesuit Relations 48, 61.
84. Jesuit Relations 48, 99.
85. Jesuit Relations 48, 285.
86. Jesuit Relations 52, 219.
87. Innis (1) 123.

88. Innis (1) 45.
89. Jesuit Relations 56, 213.
90. Jesuit Relations 56, 151.
91. Jesuit Relations 56, 155.
92. Jesuit Relations 56, 171.

God; and resume your old route to lake St. John, where you will always find some black gown to instruct and baptize you."[93]   The missionary continued to Nemiskau lake, which he described as having formerly been a flourishing trade centre north of lake Misstassini.   Its population had been dispersed or killed by the Iroquois seven or eight years before and it had not since been repeopled.[94].   When he arrived at the shore of the Bay he made the observation that "under pretext of favouring the Nation with whom they were wont to trade, these people were likely to take umbrage at our visit and our claims, our purpose not being clear to them."[95]   However, he explained to the bands, the names of which he has enumerated in the Relation,[96] that it was the French who had given them peace with the Iroquois for the five previous years, and that he had come not to trade with them but to convert them.   In answer a chief stated that his young men would bear his thanks to lake St. John during the course of the next year.   And while on his return journey by way of the Minahigouskat, the Jesuit "planted the standard of our mighty and invincible monarch on that river, to serve as a safeguard to all those Tribes against all the Iroquois nations."[97]   Here he encountered two hundred Misstassini Cree who "promised that they would repair to lake Saint John the next Spring, to receive instructions and baptism."[98]

It is probable that, in spite of Albanel's mission, the French were not in any large degree successful in retaining the northern trade, in view of the fact that the Indians had access to cheaper goods through the English.   The Jesuit Nouvel, writing to the governor, 29th May, 1673, summed up the economic situation of the colony.   The establishment of the English on Hudson Bay, and the proximity of the Iroquois, with whom the "Missisakis", a central Algonkian tribe, went on their winter hunt, was prejudicial to the interests of the colony.   These people had never up to that time showed any disposition to embrace Christianity.   The English, by their great liberality, were making an impression on the savages around lake Superior.   Des Groseilliers and the English were beginning to draw the central Algonkian peoples to Hudson Bay.[99]   On the other hand, in 1674, "a portion of the Mistassin left . . . . for Quebec, to present their respects to Monsieur de Frontenac. . . . They also intend to crave his protection against the Iroquois."[100]

Throughout the closing decades of the century a trade, which was still worthy of prosecution, was carried on by the French in the lower St. Lawrence areas.   Seven Islands was in 1674 an important centre of the trade with the Betsiamites and kindred peoples.   Here a great concourse of Indians habitually collected.[101]   But the Nascopi were still beyond the pale of European influence:

"Those who are farther down than the 7 Islands are less sociable, for they have never associated with the french or Europeans. They have, however, gentle natures. Notwithstanding this, they destroyed a European ship; that in consequence of a quarrel after drinking, and

---

93.   Jesuit Relations 56, 177.
94.   Jesuit Relations 56, 183.
95.   Jesuit Relations 56, 191.
96.   Jesuit Relations 56, 203.
97.   Jesuit Relations 56, 209.

98.   Jesuit Relations 56, 209.
99.   CIIA, v. 4. pp. 3-4.
100.   Jesuit Relations 59, 45.
101.   Jesuit Relations 59, 49.

the defeat of some of their people, whom the Europeans had first attacked and killed." [102]

Other tribes, however, were being brought into closer alignment by the force
of changed economic conditions.   The Betsiamites had some years before been
at war with the Gaspé Micmac.   In 1677 the Etchemins and the Micmac were
gathered at Rivière du Loup to the number of four or five hundred.   Two
hundred of these were Micmac, although these tribes "do not love each other
much, and have no close relations with each other." [103]   In 1678 Chicoutimi
was a trade and mission centre for the Misstassini, Etchemins, Abenaki, Papinachois, Outabitibecs, Algonkins, and other Montagnais. [104]

It was to the interest of the French that they should bring about an
alignment of the tribes and establish greater control over this area.   For here,
as well as on Hudson Bay, was there a leakage in the fur-trade.   On the 18th
October, 1684, it was alleged by de Courville, a trader at Tadoussac, that the
Papinachois were accustomed at this time to travel over to the south shore and
thence to Boston, to trade furs with the English, besides with the French at
Pentagouet, on the St. John, and at Isle Percée.   It was said that only the
salmon and the seal fisheries remained at Tadoussac and along the Papinachois
coast, which these people exploited as a means to obtain arms, ammunition
and other merchandise, from the French settlers. [105]   Moreover, the rivalry between traders and the ill-treatment of the Indians was causing a disorganization
of the trade in Acadia, [106] which was still profitable in the time of Denys, [107]
although it "is not so good there as formerly". [108]   It is probable that the medley
of tribes at Chicoutimi in 1678, of which we have just spoken, was the result
of a decline in beavers in Acadia and the lower St. Lawrence areas.

3.

Throughout the period with which we are dealing the St. Maurice
was subject to the same vagaries of fortune as was the Saguenay route, and
although it was perhaps the least important of the three principal highways
to the interior, some consideration of Three Rivers and its tributary area is
necessary to an understanding of the position of the eastern Algonkians in the
balance of power.   Early in the century Three Rivers became a rallying ground
for those Algonkin groups which inhabited the lower Ottawa, which went
under the names of the Iroquet, La Petite Nation, and the Island Algonkins,
and which were, together with the Montagnais, the Hurons, the Etchemins,
and others, the object of a jealousy and a hatred on the part of the Iroquois
which extended back to the time of Cartier's sojourn on the St. Lawrence.

Three Rivers was frequently the terminus of the Algonkin fleets trading

---

102.   Jesuit Relations 59, 57.   Uncertain whether Eskimo or Nascopi.
103.   Jesuit Relations 60, 271.
104.   Jesuit Relations 61, 85-87.
105.   Collection des manuscrits relatifs v. 1, 327-328.
106.   Murdoch 1, 165.
107.   Denys 105.
108.   Denys 219.

from the Ottawa and the upper St. Maurice.   Here, in 1633, they invited the French to establish a settlement.   Champlain, whose influence with the Algonkins was probably greater than that of any other European, had accused them of wanting to go to the English, but to the invitation he replied, "When that great house shall be built, then our young people will marry your daughters, and we shall be one people."[109]   Four years later a fort was built which served to protect the traders from the fury of the Iroquois.

Besides their trade with the Hurons and various central Algonkian tribes, the Algonkins had before 1640 established a commercial intercourse with the Outakwamiwek who dwelt towards the height of land, and who may have been a northern Montagnais, a southern branch of the Misstassini, or a southwestern Nascopi band.   These, in turn, traded with the Papinachois.[110] This commerce along the St. Maurice led to French contact with a new group who lived on the upper waters of that river.   These were the Atticameg or White Fish Indians who seem to have constituted the most westerly subdivision of the Montagnais peoples.   They first made their appearance when the fort was built in 1637, and throughout subsequent decades they served as middlemen between the French and the Hurons when the Ottawa route was unsafe.[111]

These Atticamegs were an unwarlike, amenable people, who were slow to involve themselves in the intricacies of the new civilization.   While other bands were accustomed to camp with their families about the French settlements, the men-folk of the Atticamegs would make a quick descent of the St. Maurice, trade diffidently, but in a friendly manner, with the French, and vanish into the depths of the forest, only to repeat the behaviour in the following year.   But the missionaries were anxious to make them more accessible to the benefits of Holy Church, and, in 1640, efforts were made to induce them to a sedentary life, not however together with the Algonkins at Three Rivers "because they were of different natures and language."[112]   It was decided to settle them at a place which was one day's journey up the St. Maurice.

But success was not immediate, and it was not until two years later that the Atticamegs, as a composite group, agreed to visit Three Rivers, Sillery and Quebec, on the invitation of the Montagnais Christians.   This time, contrary to their usual practice, entire households were brought in 13 canoes that bore sixty persons in all.   The Christians taxed themselves to supply the newcomers with eels and corn, and into some of the latter was instilled a frame of mind which was not hostile to the propaganda of the missionaries.[113]   The contact served to strengthen the trade relations between the French and the bands that dwelt beyond the upper waters of the St. Maurice.   In 1650 the Indians of Three Rivers were prosecuting a trade with the Outaoukotwemiwek "who scarcely ever go down to the French settlements", but with whom an influx of European materials preceded personal contact.[115]

109. Jesuit Relations 5, 205, 211.
110. Jesuit Relations 18, 115.
111. Jesuit Relations 9, 115.   See note 20.
112. Jesuit Relations 18, 113.
113. Jesuit Relations 24, 67-71.
115. Jesuit Relations 35, 239, 241.

The French had no sooner penetrated the territories of the Atticamegs than the Iroquois, hard upon their heels, executed an invasion, forcing these Indians to seek refuge at Three Rivers before they had time to collect their furs "which are the money wherewith they buy their clothes, and most of their food, from the French."[116]   Charity compelled the Indians to hunt for food to keep their women and children from starvation, but Three Rivers was one of the most exposed points to Iroquois attacks,[117] and so great were their devastations of the St. Lawrence Valley between Montreal and Quebec that the French found it necessary to increase the arms of their Indian allies.[118]   But in spite of this measure the Indians who traded on the Ottawa route either feared to come down to the French settlements or were intercepted by the Iroquois. Trade had formerly amounted to two or three thousand livres worth of beaver skins per annum, but in 1652 "the warehouse at Montreal has not bought a single beaver skin from the Savages".   At Three Rivers what revenue remained was used to fortify the place, and extreme poverty prevailed at Quebec. These facts indicate that the dispersal of the Hurons had·wrought havoc with the economic life of the colony, that the volume of trade which flowed into the warehouses of the French by way of the St. Maurice and the Saguenay was not great enough at this time to meet the heavy overhead costs entailed, and that the tribes which occupied these rivers were beginning to be subjected to a hostility similar to that borne by the Ottawa middlemen.[119]

Nevertheless some trading continued to be done with the Atticamegs. In 1657 a party of French and Indians ascended the Batiscan and returned laden with beaver skins.[120] On July 19, 1659, twelve Atticameg canoes arrived at Three Rivers with a good supply of furs, while preparations were being made to go to Outawak.[121]   On August 1st Three Rivers received a fleet of thirty three canoes from the Atticamegs, the Piskatangs, and the Mississagas. The latter had gone from the Sault by an inland route which passed through the Atticameg country.   The journey had taken them five months.[122]

We have seen that these and other commercial activities in the northern interior provoked the Iroquois to fresh acts of violence, and that in 1660 the colony was on the verge of destruction.[123]   In the following year thirty Atticamegs and two French were killed in a single skirmish above Three Rivers, and the ensuing months witnessed the virtual extermination of the tribe, which was completed a few years later by the smallpox.[124]   In 1663, after repeated advice from the colonial officials, Louis XIV's government commenced military expenditures which resulted in the establishment of forts at Three Rivers, Quebec, and on the Richelieu.[125]   Tracy and Courcelles chastized the Iroquois, relations were established with the Ottawas and other central Algonkian and Siouan peoples in the 'seventies and 'eighties, so that the trade of the St. Maurice subsequently dwindled into relative insignificance.

---

116.   Jesuit Relations 37, 71; 36, 147.
117.   Jesuit Relations 36, 195.
118.   Jesuit Relations 38, 61.
119.   Jesuit Relations 40, 211.
120.   Jesuit Relations 43, 51.

121.   Jesuit Relations 45, 105.
122.   Jesuit Relations 45, 105.
123.   Jesuit Relations 46, 221.
124.   Jesuit Relations 9, 115. Note 20.

4.

The Algonkins and other tribes who lived on the Ottawa and its tributary waters to the westward were marginal to the area under consideration in this paper and therefore will not concern us to the same extent as the eastern peoples.   It has been seen, however, that events on the Ottawa, and in the country of the Hurons and central Algonkians, influenced the vagaries of the economic, social and political life of the eastern tribes, and that these aspects of life cannot be considered without involving the variations in the larger scene. During the first quarter of the century the direct route of the Ottawa was open to the passage of Montagnais, Algonkin, Huron and French traders.[125]   It was the continuous purpose of the Iroquois, particularly of the lower Iroquois, to break this monopoly, either by destroying the Indian allies of the French, or by disrupting the alliances between those tribes, as they attempted to do between the Montagnais and the Hurons in 1635, in order to divert the trade from the French to the Dutch by bringing the Hurons into line with themselves.[126]   But earlier than the Hurons, the Algonkin peoples were middlemen and therefore held the balance of power.   After the decline of beaver in their own areas they attempted to make themselves the carriers by exacting a toll on the Hurons who attempted to descend by the Ottawa route.[127]   "Their design was to get all the merchandise from the Hurons at a very low price, in order afterwards to come themselves and trade it, with either the French or the English."[128] The Iroquet, and Petite Nation Algonkins on the lower reaches of the river, were soon dispersed by the Iroquois.   We have seen that many of them fled to Three Rivers, Sillery, Quebec and Tadoussac.   This movement contributed to the break-down of cultures that had flourished in isolation. The island Algonkins alone resisted the disintegrating influences of war, disease, drunkenness, and Christianity, fighting the advances of all comers with such success, ephemeral though it was, that they have been branded as treacherous, vindictive, warlike, and unsociable, by the historians of the period.

Their resistence to Christianity was one aspect of their attempt to maintain their place as middlemen in the trade,[129] as it was also a fight against social disintegration and decay. Throughout the 'thirties some measure of success attended their efforts,[130] but by 1643 they were "nearly all ruined and reduced to nothing."   Nevertheless they were still proud and hindered the conversion of the Hurons and central Algonkians.[131]   In 1654 Paul Tessouat, formerly the chief of the Island Algonkins and great opponent of the French, died, it is said, in Christian humility. The date marks the end of the Island Algonkins as a major economic and political force in the history of New France.   By 1658 they were "running the risk of total destruction. . . . For the Iroquois is playing his last stake, having left his country in order to go and exterminate them".[132]

---

125. Innis (1) 20.
126. Jesuit Relations 8, 59-61.
127. Innis (1) 25.
128. Jesuit Relations 5, 239-241.

129. Jesuit Relations 24, 209-215.
130. Jesuit Relations 9, 275.
131. Jesuit Relations 23, 303.
132. Jesuit Relations 44, 219.

But long before this occurred the Hurons superceded the Algonkins as middlemen on the Ottawa.   Their status as agriculturists gave them an abundant supply of corn which enabled them to make the long journeys that were necessitated by the nature of the fur-trade.[133] Their advantageous position, however, was not maintained for long, since their destruction followed, in 1649, that of the Algonkins, and the Ottawa route was ruined by the concentration of the Iroquois on Montreal throughout the succeeding decade.[134] Although the Hurons continued for some time to be carriers they had to compete with the Iroquois in this respect after the middle of the century.

It has already been stated that the French never contemplated the destruction of the Iroquois, which would have caused the allies of the French to become their enemies if they had no more need for French protection.   It was felt that the better policy was merely to weaken the Iroquois by occasional punitive expeditions.[135]   Moreover, frequent attempts were made to attract the Five Nations to Montreal and Quebec.   The "Brandy Parliament" which met at Quebec on October 10th, 1678, was concerned principally with the Iroquois trade.   Formerly, when trade had depended entirely upon the Ottawa and northeastern tribes, brandy had been used, not to attract, but to exploit, the Indians.   Now, with the destruction of the Hurons and the growing Iroquois imperialism which resulted in the invasion of the northern hunting areas, they became the principal traders.   Brandy was the only French article which cost little and bought much.   In other wares the English and Dutch had the advantage.[136]   The memoirs of the period are full of references to cheap English goods. In 1685 Denonville wrote "Les Anglois donnent leurs poudres a bien meilleur marché que les Francois, ce qui faict que les sauvages les vont chercher chez aulx et leure portent leurs castors."[137]   Occasionally, however, cheaper goods supplemented military demonstrations in throwing the balance of power into the hands of the French.   On July 10th, 1673, Father Garnier wrote from the Seneca country to the governor, stating that peace had been made

> "with all the nations with whom M. de Courcelles had gone down to make war, the King having taken them under his protection; it has been recommended to all their young bloods not to turn their arms in this direction. . . . They will willingly bring their furs to Montreal if goods are cheaper than at Orange where they are dearer this year. They wish also that the French should live among them, especially those who are the most useful, such as blacksmiths and armourers. . . ." [138]

The clash of economic and political interests in North America eventually led to the disruption of the Iroquois state.   A split between the upper and lower Iroquois, which resulted from the fur-trade, has been noted as early as 1654,[139] but in general, except for occasional intervals of armed peace, the energy of the

---

133. Innis (1) 23.
134. Jesuit Relations 36 165.
135. Lahontan v. 1, 391.
136. Eastman 195-96, 137.
137. Collection des manuscrits relatifs v. 1, p. 347.
138. C 11 A v. 4, p. 9.
139. Jesuit Relations 41, 201.

Five Nations was directed towards breaking the power of the French.   Such a peace followed the expeditions of Tracy and Courcelles, so that in 1667

> "The Savages, our allies, no longer fearing that they will be surprised on the road, come in quest of us from all directions, from a distance of five and six hundred leagues, . . . either to reestablish their trade, interrupted by the wars; or to open new commercial dealings, as some very remote tribes claim to do, who had never before made their appearance here, and who came last summer for that purpose." [140]

But the peace was not of long duration.   By 1681 control of the fur-trade had passed from the Hurons to the Ottawas who also had fled westward to escape from the Iroquois.[141]   In 1683 the Ottawas supplied two thirds of the beaver which was sent to France in that year.   De La Barre declared that the Iroquois were determined to destroy the Ottawas, in order to secure the trade to the Dutch instead of to the French, who, for their part, did not encourage peace between the Iroquois and the Ottawas.[142]   But whatever the conditions were that prevailed along the western routes the eastern Algonkians generally suffered.   When the Ottawa was open, the tribes on the Saguenay and the St. Maurice could not secure employment as fur carriers.   When it was closed, the Iroquois extended their invasions into the areas occupied by those who would otherwise have benefited.   With the introduction of European cultural traits the supply of beaver in the areas occupied by the eastern Algonkians early tended to become depleted, so that when the occupation of carrier was denied them, their position became a sorry one.   The loss of economic independence which resulted from these conditions, was made worse by a decline in the demand for beaver in the European market, due to a change in styles and other factors, during the closing years of the seventeenth century.[143] In 1699 Diereville wrote, "Beaver hunting is the most valuable to the Savages, although the price of it has been diminished for some time."[144]   Throughout the eighteenth century the French continued to cultivate what remained of the eastern Algonkians for military reasons, but even missionary effort waned, and their day, except for such isolated peoples as the Nascopi and some of the Misstassini Cree, was definitely over.

---

140. Jesuit Relations 51, 169.
141. Innis (1) 43, 49.
142. Innis (1) 51.
143. See Innis, chap. 3.
144. Diereville 73.

CHAPTER 5

THE DISPLACEMENT OF MATERIALS

1.

The supply of European materials doubtless seldom exceeded the demand which was made by the Indians, even by those whose favourable position as middlemen in the fur-trade gave them ready access to the wares of the Old World. Superiority of their material culture secured to the French the durable friendship of the first tribes whom they encountered, with the exception of the Laurentian Iroquois, and enabled them to establish settlements on the continent under the most favourable auspices. This superiority offset the limited supply as a factor in the rapid displacement of native materials, since ".... the effect of a migrating people upon those among whom they settle is proportional to the degree of superiority of the immigrant culture, and . . . the greater be the superiority of the introduced culture, the smaller need be the number of its introducers. . . . It is the recognition of the superiority of the material objects and arts which precedes and makes possible the acceptance of other elements of an introduced culture. . . It is the knife and the hatchet. . . but above all . . . the fire-arms of the European which impress the man of rude culture and lead him to regard their possessors as beings of a higher order than himself."[1]

Omitting abstract observations on the relative inferiority and superiority of Indian and European material culture, each of which was sufficient unto itself, having been built up to meet its special environment by the slow and arduous process of adaptation, the fact remains that the Europeans brought implements and utensils which the Indian could use to the greatest advantage in the prosecution of his own economic life. European cutting tools were keener and more durable than those of the natives. European containers were stronger, capable of undergoing greater wear and more easily transported than the Algonkian. It was, therefore, an obvious desire on the part of the Indian to obtain those articles by which his own crafts could be carried out more rapidly and easily. Hence, the native utensils and implements were cast aside.

The effects of the influx of European materials upon the native life were far-reaching. The old handicrafts fell into disuse and the skilful technique required to fashion implements of stone became to a large extent a lost art. It is probable that the division of labour between the sexes was thrown out of kilter, in that man's labour was changed more than woman's. In warfare, hunting and manufacturing, the use of iron, where only stone had been used before, accelerated the pace and left a greater degree of leisure for the men. Just as the axe was by far the most important implement employed by the men,

---

1. Bartlett 477-478.

so the kettle was probably the most revolutionary article which came within the sphere of the woman.   Insofar as it was the wife who made such things as clothing and snowshoes it is probable that her work was less disturbed than was that of her husband.   This will become more abundantly clear as the outline proceeds.

But no treatment of primitive economics could be complete without some consideration of the religious factor, however brief it may be. The reasons for which the Indians regarded the wares of the Europeans as superior to their own will become more completely evident when we come to treat specifically of the clash of cultures in the religious sphere.   It will serve our purpose here if we bear in mind the fact that the efficacy of an implement, for example, was determined by factors which operated from beyond the material world.   That is, there were in the primitive cosmogony what we would call a set of extra-physical forces which exerted a continuous and comprehensive influence over the furniture of this world, and the relative potencies of these mystical forces were equated with the relative superiority of the materials which they controlled or with which they were interpenetrated.   In New France an iron knife was superior to a stone knife because it possessed a more concentrated supply of mysterious power.   The Europeans who made the iron implements were superior to the Indians for the same reason.[2]   A warrior always made his own weapons and when he died they were buried with him because he needed them in the land of the dead for the same purposes as he had employed them in life. If those who had survived him had not placed the implements within the grave he would have heaped calamity upon their heads.   This belief caused a continual drain upon the supply of material possessions which were obtained from the Europeans in the early days of the fur-trade.   In 1608 Champlain noted that ". . . when a man or woman dies, they make a grave, into which they put everything they own, such as kettles, furs, hatchets, bows, arrows, skins and other things."[3] This custom persisted for many years in spite of the efforts of the missionaries to extirpate it, and as late as 1681 they found it necessary to coerce the Abenaki of Sillery in this respect.   "They no longer change Cabins at the death of a person, as they used to; and I make them give in public the articles Left by the Savages when they die."[4]   The discontinuance of this practice coincided with the process of disintegration in the religious life of the aborigines, but at first material objects constituted an integral part of the cosmos as they conceived it.   That European materials were especially efficacious was exemplified by the fact that a Montagnais in 1634 used iron in a magic rite to cause the death of a man a hundred miles away.[5]   Although we will treat of the displacement of Indian materials in our own terms of relative utility and degree of superiority we should try to keep in the back of our minds an apprehension of the native world-view.

European material objects found their way into the hands of the

---

2. Compare Levy-Bruhl 334.
3. Champlain (1) v. 49.
4. Jesuit Relations 62, 39.
5. Jesuit Relations 6, 197.

Indians by several means, such as theft, salvage, pillage, donation and exchange. Stealing was rare although it was not entirely unknown among the eastern Algonkians. Salvage was prevalent throughout the sea coast areas, although it was necessarily sporadic. Even the Eskimo who roamed over the coasts which abutted those inhabited by the Micmac obtained much of their iron in this way. "The iron which they find near the stages of the cod-fishers serves them to make arrowheads, knives, cleavers and other tools, which they themselves skilfully devise, without forge or hammers."[6] Sometimes, especially in Acadia and New England ,the Malecite, Canibas and other Abenaki, resorted to pillage in the course of their numerous wars. A letter of 1689 records the sacking of two forts in Maine which resulted in the acquisition of European goods in this way."[7] Sometimes when a band of French went astray in the forest the Micmac knew how to bargain for what they required, such as blankets, corn, flour, powder, lead and guns.[8]

Frequently the Indians received materials as gifts which the missionaries donated for the purpose of instilling in them a frame of mind which was amenable to Christianity and which would serve as tangible mementos of the aggressive Faith, or which the traders bestowed for commercial, and the officials for political, reasons. During the early decades of the seventeenth century it was customary for the Montagnais to exchange presents freely with each other. The French, whose possessions were coveted generally, were not always willing to accede to the demands of this custom, and their failure to assume the polity of the natives in this respect sometimes caused ructions of a minor order. The French noted the reserve with which they were treated by the Montagnais at Quebec in 1634, and on enquiry they discovered that because they did not treat the Indians as brothers, that is, because they did not exchange presents with them, they in turn were treated as foreigners. Liquor and gunpowder were greatly prized by the natives at this time.[9]

In 1637 the Jesuits presented to the Montagnais children at Quebec iron arrow-points, knives, rings, awls, needles and other trinkets as a reward for their knowledge of the catechism.[10]. At Tadoussac in 1642 the priest invited the bands from the upper Saguenay to visit the port every year, accompanying his words with presents—awls to pierce their ears so that they might not resist his words and tobacco with which to burn their old customs and adopt better ones.[11] At Sillery in 1643 "The reward for catechism was a knife, or a piece of bread, at other times a chaplet,—sometimes a cap, or an axe, for the tallest and most intelligent; it is an excellent opportunity for relieving the misery of these poor peoples."[12] In the same year a Montagnais band took with it on a hunting expedition a crucifix, a rosary, tapers and a paper calendar to insure abstinence from meat on festival days.[13] In 1676 a priest wrote from Quebec'

6. Jesuit Relations 45, 69.
7. Collection des manuscrits relatifs v. 1, p. 465.
8. LeClercq (2) 172-173.
9. Jesuit Relations 6, 257-259.
10. Jesuit Relations 11, 227.
11. Jesuit Relations 22, 237.
12. Jesuit Relations 23 311.
13. Jesuit Relations 26, 115.

"One must be provided in this country with medals, small crucifixes a finger in length, or smaller still; small brass crosses and brass
rings, also some in which there is the figure of some saint, or the face
of Jesus Christ or the Blessed Virgin; wooden rosaries, very black and
very thick, which they wear hanging from the neck or about the
head; . . ." [14]

Mirrors, knives, and needles were presented by LeClercq to the Micmac Christians on his departure from their country in 1680.[15]

But by far the greatest volume of European materials which the Indians
possessed were acquired through trade, something of which has already been
said in dealing with the eastern Algonkians in the balance of power. In some
areas the native shell beads or wampum became a medium of exchange after the
advent of the white people. The not infrequent references to "porcelain" in
the Jesuit Relations testify to the fact that its use was not unknown among
the Montagnais and kindred peoples.[16] It is impossible to prove that wampum
was used as a medium of exchange in pre-Columbian times, although the
worked variety was limited in supply and it was in constant demand for
ornamental and probably religious purposes.[17] It was, then, a commodity
rather than a medium of exchange and only became so because the European
materials were valued by the Indian even more highly. The early commercial
transactions between Europeans and Indians in which wampum was used really
partook of the nature of barter.

Usually, throughout the northeast, pelts were bartered directly for
European wares. In this connection the Relation of 1634 quotes a Montagnais
statement: " 'The Beaver does everything perfectly well, it makes kettles,
hatchets, swords, knives, bread; and in short, it makes everything.' He was
making sport of us Europeans, who have such a fondness for the skin of this
animal. . . . My host said to me one day. . . . 'The English have no sense;
they give us twenty knives like this for one Beaver skin.' "[18] After the monopoly passed to the One Hundred Associates in 1627 the volume of European
materials used in the Tadoussac trade became restricted. Nevertheless the
Indians received by this means "cloaks, blankets, nightcaps, hats, shirts, sheets,
hatchets, iron arrow heads, bodkins, swords, picks to break the ice in winter,[19]
knives, kettles, prunes, raisins, Indian corn, peas, crackers or sea biscuits, and
tobacco," in exchange for the hides of moose, lynx, otter, martens, badgers
and muskrats, "but they deal principally in Beavers, in which they find their
greatest profit."[20] Lahontan cites the types of articles which were exchanged
with the Indians for pelts in the 'eighties as short light muskets, powder, ball
and cut lead, or small shot, axes, knives and sheaths, sword blades for darts,
kettles, shoemakers' awls, fish hooks, flint stones, blue serge caps, common
Brittany linen shirts, short coarse woollen stockings, Brazil tobacco, coarse
white thread for nets, coloured sewing thread, pack thread, vermillion, needles,

14. Jesuit Relations 60, 137.
15. LeClercq (2) 307.
16. Jesuit Relations 7, 217; 8, 259.
17. Holmes 234.
18. Jesuit Relations 6, 297-299.
19. These probably supplanted the black stone ice picks, such as have been found
        at Tadoussac by W. J. Wintenburg.
20. Jesuit Relations 4, 207.

Venice beads, "Some Iron Heads for Arrows, but few of 'em," a small quantity
of soap, and a few sabres or cutlasses. "Brandy goes off incomparably well."[21]
Much the same type of articles were current throughout the next decade. A
memoir of 27th September, 1692, lists a number of articles which were sent
to the Abenaki-Penobscot at that time, as 30 light muskets, 20 carbines, 24
pistols, 24 bayonets, 2,000 lbs. powder, 400 lbs. lead, 400 lbs. of balls, 700
lbs. of duck shot, 16 quarts of flour, 16 quarts of eau de vie; also blue serge,
hats, stockings, shirts, blankets, tobacco, prunes, knives, lines, and swords,
etc.[22]   A list for 1693 affords a comparison between the goods traded to the
Malecite, Micmac and Canibas, as follows:

	Malecite	Micmac	Canibas
Powder	575 lbs.	500	1100
Muskets	10	2	21
Shirts	13	12	32
Stockings	1 pair	12	5
Blankets	1	12	3
Shot	500 lbs.	600	2100
Bar lead	100	100	520

Each received goods in proportion not only to the needs of the Indians themselves but also to those of the French who proposed, as we have seen in the
preceding chapter, to use the Canibas as a bulwark against English expansion
in Acadia. It is seen from the chart that for this reason the Canibas received
arms and ammunition which were, perhaps, out of proportion to their numbers.[23]

2.

Although the greatest number of European articles among the Indians
may be counted as having been acquired by trade, there were certain groups of
materials that were confined to one or more methods of acquisition, such as the
articles of a religious nature which were donated for purposes of proselytization
or the weapons which were furnished to the Abenaki for political reasons.
Although trade accounted for the greatest volume the methods of acquisition
were not always coincident with the classes of materials acquired, the most
important of which may be classed under the headings of implements and
utensils, food, clothing, dwellings, and transportation.

Of these the implements and utensils were not the least revolutionary.
Metal weapons, which were speedily acquired, might, if the ramifications were
pursued, be seen to have had a transforming influence upon every aspect of life.
During the Kirke regime the Montagnais had access to iron ware, and after the
restoration of New France in 1632 they resumed commercial relations with the
French. LeJeune says that "they asked me for a knife, and I gave them one;

---

21. Lahontan 1, 377-378.   22. Murdoch 2, 73.   23. Murdoch 2, 129.

they asked me for some string to tie to an iron arrow-head or dart, with barbed teeth.   They throw these darts against the Beavers. . ."[24]   Shortly afterwards the missionary's knife was borrowed to bleed the sick.[25]   In 1634 the Montagnais possessed iron-pointed harpoons, and an iron blade, fastened to whale bone, was used in hunting beavers.[26]   We saw that the Micmac were the recipients of iron implements at an early date.   In the seventeenth century the flow continued fitfully.   Denys says, "Since the French have come to these parts, and they have been given arrow heads of iron, they no longer use any others. . ."[27]   Bone knives "served them in place of knives of iron and steel, the use of which we have since introduced among them."[28]   And elsewhere:

> "But they practice still all the same methods of hunting, with this difference, however, that in place of arming their arrows and spears with the bones of animals, pointed and sharpened, they arm them today with iron, which is made expressly for sale to them. Their spears now are made with a sword fixed at the end of a shaft of seven or eight feet in length. These they use in winter, when there is snow, to spear the Moose, or for fishing Salmon, Trout, and Beaver. They are also furnished with iron harpoons. . ."[29]

And again:

> "With respect to the hunting of the Beaver in winter, they do that the same as they did formerly, though they have nevertheless now a greater advantage with their arrows and harpoons armed with iron than they had with the others which they used in old times, and of which they have totally abandoned the use."[30]

Although the bow and the iron-pointed arrow were common among the Montagnais of both Quebec and Three Rivers in the early 'thirties, fire-arms were used but rarely,[31] although some of them were armed with arquebuses in 1633[32]   These seem to have been all obtained from the English during the period of the Kirkes.[33]   "Since they have come into possession of fire arms, through their traffic with the English, they have become fair huntsmen, some of them shooting very well.   My host is one of their best musketeers; I have seen him kill Bustards, Ducks and Snipes; but their powder is very soon exhausted." . . . . "As to their fishing, they use nets as we do, which they get in trade from the French and Hurons."[34]   In 1637 swords, shields, hatchets, knives, and poles, were among the weapons in use among the Montagnais and the Hurons,[35] and in the same year a party of twelve Abenaki arrived at Quebec, three of their number having arquebuses.[36]   By 1640 they were becoming common among both Christians and pagans at Quebec,[37] and the Tadoussac Montagnais were using pistols.[38]   In 1644 a resuscitated chief at this post gave presents of his sword, dagger and pistol to warriors.[39]   At Three Rivers "there were some who had arquebuses. . . ."[40] and by 1648 they were said to have been numerous.[41]   But by 1643 the authorities began to exercise greater care

24. Jesuit Relations 5, 61.
25. Jesuit Relations 5, 143.
26. Jesuit Relations 6, 309-311.
27. Denys 117.
28. Denys 401.
29. Denys 442-443.
30. Denys 443.
31. Jesuit Relations 8, 45.
32. Jesuit Relations 5, 137.
33. Jesuit Relations 7, 73.
34. Jesuit Relations 6, 309.
35. Jesuit Relations 12, 201.
36. Jesuit Relations 12, 189.
37. Jesuit Relations 18, 101-5.
38. Jesuit Relations 20, 191.
39. Jesuit Relations 26, 163.
40. Jesuit Relations 24, 205.
41. Jesuit Relations 32, 283.

in the distribution of arms. "The use of arquebuses, refused to the Infidels by Monsieur the Governor, and granted to the Christian Neophytes, is a powerful attraction to win them; it seems that our Lord intends to use this means in order to render Christianity acceptable in these regions."[42]   Moreover, the Christians were less likely to change their political colour, whereas the pagans were uncertain, and even the allegiance of the Christian Iroquois at a later date was not well defined, so that restrictive measures continued to be made throughout the century.[43]

In spite of this the arquebus continued to be a frequent article of trade. When peace was concluded with the Iroquois in 1645 the Sillery Indians "replied by a fine salvo of musketry. . ."[44] The Tadoussac Indians were receiving presents of powder, indicating fire-arms, in 1646.   And among the presents given to the Algonkians and Hurons at Quebec in 1658 were: to the Algonkians, 12 livres wt. of powder and 30 of lead, 12 swords, and two guns; and to the Hurons, 12 swords, 200 iron arrow-heads, and 12 hatchets.[45]   In 1650 traders went up the St. Maurice to the Outaoukotwemiwek "who scarcely ever go down to the French settlements", with arms for defense and to sell.   One of the first articles acquired by the Atticamegs was a French drum for ceremonial purposes, and in 1651, when the Jesuit Buteux visited these people in their own territory, they did not greet him with a salvo, not because they were unable for "we have plenty of fire-arms, powder, and shot", but because they were at prayers.[46]   By 1663 most of the Indians of the St. Lawrence watershed were skilled in the use of muskets.[47]   In 1661 distant bands towards the height of land, at Necouba, and elsewhere possessed quantities of fire-arms,[48] and of the Indians north of lake St. John in 1671 Albanel says, ". . . of lead and powder, hatchets and knives, swords and muskets, they had no lack."[49]   Arms and ammunition were the only commodities which Jolliet, the seigneur of Anticosti and Mingan, mentioned in 1679 as having been traded with the Papinachois for seal skins and other furs.[50]   The Micmac, who had been the earliest recipients of European materials, made an almost complete substitution of the musket for the bow and arrow in the seventeenth century.

"The musket is used by them more than all other weapons, in their hunting in spring, summer and autumn, both for animals and birds. With an arrow they killed only one Wild Goose; but with the shot of a gun they kill five or six of them. With the arrow it was necessary to approach the animal closely; with the gun they kill the animal from a distance with a bullet or two." [51]

In the time of Chrestien LeClercq the Eskimo were using guns in their wars with the Micmac, although bows and arrows still predominated.[52]

42.   Jesuit Relations 25, 27.
43.   See for example C 11 A, V. 4 Oct. 29, 1674.
44.   Jesuit Relations 27, 273.
45.   Jesuit Relations 44, 105.
46.   Jesuit Relations 24, 85; 37-37.
47.   Boucher 64.
48.   Jesuit Relations 46, 277.
49.   Jesuit Relations 56, 161.
50.   Lahontan v. 1 224, 305.
51.   Denys 443.
52.   LeClercq (2), 268.

Those people, on the other hand, whose territories were removed from the trade routes were slower to receive the benefits of the superior imported materials.   Among these were the Betsiamites.   It is said that thirteen muskets were given to them in 1646 by the Micmac at the conclusion of the war between them,[53] but in 1652 they were said to have been very poor, to have been without fire-arms, and to have dwelt inland for fear of the Micmac who were again at war with them. [54] And as late as 1670, "They do not yet use fire-arms, but are very skilful in shooting with the bow.   When they have a string to fish with they think themselves very rich."[55]   Also the Malecite were generally behind their neighbours, the Micmac and the Penobscots, in the acquisition of European wares, although their military position gave them some distinction in the eyes of the French.[56]

The French supply of arms to the Algonkians was probably a direct result of the Dutch supply to the Iroquois.   The unfortunate Hurons had received adequate arms too late to withstand the Iroquois power.   The French found that warfare and the growing competition in the trade necessitated more powerful native allies.   Occasionally the Montagnais received arquebuses from Iroquois prisoners, and it is probable that by 1647 all Iroquois raiding parties on the lower St. Lawrence were armed in this way,[57] although some bows and arrows are referred to as late as 1653.   Wicker armour and shields did not fall into disuse immediately after the introduction of fire-arms as is sometimes supposed.   Wooden corselets, stitched and interlaced with sticks, and wooden shields, were in use among the Indians of Three Rivers in 1643, and the Mohawks were, in 1645, still using shields which they carried on their backs.[59]

Nevertheless the supply never equalled the demand and certain peoples found it increasingly difficult to secure arms as the fur frontier advanced beyond their territories.   LeClercq says that Micmac children used bows and arrows for killing birds,[60] and Diereville mentions beaver traps as being effective and cheaper than powder and lead in 1699.[61]   Moreover, the arms which they did receive were not always of the highest quality.   The Indians claimed that the French sold bad wares, that the muskets were continually bursting and maiming them, after they had paid high prices for them.[62]   Villebon wrote to the minister in 1695 concerning the evil consequences which resulted from selling poor arms to the Indians at Pentagouet:

> "Un sauvage de Pentagouet en a esté estropie et mort deux jours apres ce qui les a fait beaucoup murmurer et a presque empeche le partie de guerre qu'ils avoient forme. . . ." [63]

Lahontan puts into the mouth of Adario an overdrawn, though probably not entirely false, summary of the situation: for beaver skins

---

53. Jesuit Relations 30, 143.
54. Jesuit Relations 37, 235.
55. Jesuit Relations 53, 89.
56. See Gyles for the state of the Malecite in the last decades of the century; 8, 19.
57. Jesuit Relations 27, 233; 32, 33.
59. Jesuit Relations 24, 205; 27, 299.
60. LeClercq 92.
61. Diereville 74.
62. Lahontan v. 2, 422.
63. C 11 D 2-(2).

> "by a mighty piece of Friendship, they give us in exchange Fufees, that burft and Lame many of our Warriors, Axes that break in the cutting of a Shrub, Knives that turn Blunt, and Lofe their Edge in the cutting of a Citron; Thread which is half Rotten, and fo very bad that our Nets are worn out as foon as they are made; and Kettles fo thin and flight, that the very weight of Water makes the Bottoms fall out." [64]

The use of domestic utensils and implements also wrought radical changes in the habits of the Indians, much of whose time had in pre-Columbian times been spent in the manufacture of these articles by relatively tedious processes.   The most important domestic article acquired from the Europeans was the kettle, which was in use, together with the knife and the axe, among the Micmac when Denys first arrived in Acadia.[65]   "They have abandoned," he says, "all their own utensils, whether because of the trouble they had as well to make as to use them, or because of the facility of obtaining from us. . . . the things which seem to them invaluable. . . . . Above everything the kettle has always seemed to them, and seems still, the most valuable article they can obtain from us."[66]   He makes what seem to be the only known references to the cumbersome Micmac kettles which were made from the bowls of trees:

> "The axes, the kettles, the knives, and everything that is supplied them, is much more convenient and portable than those which they had in former times, when they were forced to go to camp near their grotesque kettles, in place of which today they are free to go camp where they wish. One can say that in those times the immovable kettles were the chief regulators of their lives, since they were able to live only in places where these were." [67]

And again: for making dwellings and cooking food

> "they have good axes, knives more convenient for their work, and kettles easy to carry. This is a great convenience for them, as they are not obliged to go to the places where were their kettles of wood, of which one never sees any at present, as they have entirely abandoned the use of them." [68]

The importance of these kettles, which were washed only when first acquired,[69] was accentuated by the fact that the Micmac did not employ "either tablecloths, napkins, tables, dishes, plates or forks."[70]

Being more isolated from European influences, their neighbours, the Malecite, acquired an adequate supply of kettles and other utensils at a later date.   In 1690 kettles were used together with bark dishes, guns, hatchets, and looking-glasses, and although corn was shelled from the cob with clam shells due to the scarcity of knives, yet kettles were used for boiling the corn.   But when a Malecite lost or left his kettle behind he boiled his food by placing hot stones in a bark dish.[71]

In 1633 the Montagnais, who sometimes lost or broke their kettles resorted to the same custom, but those living within the French settlements soon acquired all the articles customary to a French peasant household,[72] such

64. Lahontan 2, 576.
65. Denys 399.
66. Denys 440-441.
67. Denys 442-443.
68. Denys 406.
69. LeClercq (2), 121.
70. LeClercq (2), 120.
71. Gyles 21, 45, 48.
72. Jesuit Relations 5, 97; 7, 45.

as dishes and furniture, and in the 'fifties the Atticamegs and other outlying Montagnais bands added the kettles to the sum of their domestic possessions.[73]

To the consideration of weapons, and domestic articles in general, a note may be added upon the change in fire-making apparatus which was due to the contact.   Flint, steel, and tinder, which were carried in a pouch that was elsewhere called a strike-a-light, superceded wooden drills to some extent in the seventeenth century.[74]   In the 'thirties metallic stones were supplanted by flint and steel among the Montagnais, which were supplemented by matches of twisted hemp cords, or splinters of wood tipped with sulphur.   The tinder box was also adopted.[75]   In 1634 Lejeune wrote, "I brought a french fuse with me, and five or six matches.   They were astonished at the ease with which I could light a fire."[76]   However, these things were not in general use at this time, and as late as 1690, if a Malecite lost fire, he could make it by twirling a stick with the end in a socket of another stick held between his knees.[77]

3.

In treating of the eastern Algonkians in the balance of power we noted that the acquisition of European weapons, the demand of the European market for furs, and the compulsion with which the Indians supplied furs for the things which they needed in return, depleted the game upon which the Indians were dependent for food in the St. Lawrence and Atlantic areas at an early date.   The extinction of the moose in Cape Breton was an early phenomenon.[78]   On Miscou Island prior to 1647 ".... there were formerly Elks, but they have all been exterminated."[79]   It is true that the cannibalism of a party of Micmacs, who killed and ate a boy in 1635 who had been left among them by the Basques, may not have been prompted by hunger, but cannibalism was resorted to in 1680 during a season of starvation.[80]   And the famine at Miscou in 1644 may have been due to a lack of snow to obstruct the animals, not to a depletion of game; nevertheless, game was scarce on the Nepisiquit in 1645.[81]   There were only a few porcupines, and "They were compelled to eat their dogs, their skins, and their shoes," although later they killed enough to eat.   With respect to the beaver, "Few in a house are saved; they would take all.   The disposition of the Indians is not to spare the little ones any more than the big ones."[82] The frequency with which the Gaspé Micmac were accustomed to hunt up the Saguenay in the third quarter of the century was probably due to a diminution of game in their own territories.

A similar condition prevailed among the Montagnais after the Kirke

73. Jesuit Relations 37, 55.
74. Hough 579.
75. Jesuit Relations 12, 72.
76. Jesuit Relations 6, 217.
77. Jesuit Relations 12, 211-213; Gyles 48.
78. Ganong, C. K. 53.
79. Jesuit Relations 32, 35.
80. Jesuit Relations 8, 29; LeClercq (2), 113.
81. Jesuit Relations 32, 41; 28, 27.
82. Denys 432.

occupation in 1629. Lalement intended to winter with a Montagnais band, but he says, "I was compelled to return 11 days later; for as they could not find enough for themselves to eat, they were compelled to come back to the French."[83] In 1635 plans were afoot to make the Montagnais sedentary in order that they might cultivate the soil and avoid starvation. and in order that the beaver should multiply. It was feared that they would exterminate the species around Quebec, as had already occurred among the Hurons.[84] In the same year the native population at Three Rivers was at the edge of starvation, although elk were still plentiful in 1636, for "not since ten years have the Savages killed so many Elk as they have this winter, the snow being in exactly the condition they desired for hunting them."[85] Settlement at Three Rivers was also planned since "there is now scarcely any more game in the neighbourhood of the French."[86] Some years later in the mountains of Notre Dame, near Matane, game was scarce in spite of favourable snow conditions, and in the same region in 1662 ". . . Providence . . . does not always choose to work a miracle in order to transport moose, as it did of old in sending a shower of quails. . . . Only rugged, wild, and inaccessible regions are sought, because there the wild animals are more easily found."[87] During the dispersal by the Iroquois of the bands about lake St John it was stated in 1671 that game had increased, whereas among the Betsiamites, who received fire-arms later than the other Montagnais, there were moose, and caribou, but very few beavers. Among the Malecite famines were avoided by extensive consumption of shell fish.[88]

With the decline in the food resources of the country the eastern Algonkians lost a measure of self-reliance and became increasingly dependent upon Europe for their supplies. These were chiefly vegetables, or vegetable products, since there were few cattle in the colony, and those that were were "very seldom slaughtered."[89] Champlain gave bread and peas to his Montagnais allies in 1609, and in the 'thirties "they get from our people galette, or sea biscuit, bread, prunes, peas, roots, figs and the like."[90] When LeJeune wintered with the Montagnais he gave them a barrel of sea biscuit, a sack of flour, Indian corn, prunes, parsnips and wine. "It was the expectation of this food which made them wish to have a Frenchman with them."[91] And of the famine at Three Rivers in 1635 the Relation says, "Now these comings and goings of famished Savages lasted almost all winter; we usually made a little feast of peas and boiled flour for all the new bands, and I have seen certain ones among them eat more than eight bowlfuls of this before leaving the place."[92]

On the other hand European condiments were generally unpalatable to the Indian and were therefore adopted more slowly. Although it was said that the Quebec Montagnais were learning to salt their food in 1633, they were

83. Jesuit Relations 4, 213.
84. Jesuit Relations 8, 51.
85. Jesuit Relations 9, 71.
86. Jesuit Relations 12, 163.
87. Jesuit Relations 47, 167.
88. Murdoch 1, 240.
89. Jesuit Relations 22, 175.
90. Champlain (1), 105-106; Jesuit Relations 6, 273.
91. Jesuit Relations 7, 71.
92. Jesuit Relations 8, 33.

still eating dried and smoked meat without bread or salt in 1646, and two years later the Jesuit found that they cooked their peas and corn without butter, vinegar, meat, fat, oil, salt, bread or wine, to his dissatisfaction.[93]   But by 1658 "Intercommunication causes the palates of some Frenchmen to adapt themselves to smoked flesh, and those of some Savages to salted food. . . . ." But ". . . I have never seen a Savage that did not abhor Dutch cheese, radishes, spices, mustard, and similar condiments."[94]

With the introduction of European foodstuffs went a change in the manner of eating among those Indians who dwelt in and about Quebec.[95]   In 1636 the Montagnais children "became so accustomed to our food and our clothes, that they will have a horror of the Savages and their filth."   In 1646 the Montagnais at Tadoussac were aping French manners:

> ". . . they begin to imagine that, in order to be good Christians, they ought to live altogether in the French fashion; and upon this thought, they act the polite . . . they make a cabin apart, in which to take their meals; they set up tables; they make the men eat together, and the women separately; and as they had remarked that the French did not eat all that was offered them, those who serve at Table did not give the leisure, especially to the women, to take a sufficient meal." [96]

It had hitherto been a sacred duty to eat all that had been provided. The "festin a tout manger" fell into disuse with the decline in native religious practices.

Among those peoples who dwelt farther from the settlements similar though less complete changes occurred.   Among the Micmac, however, the conditions that prevailed at the end of the sixteenth century continued throughout the seventeenth.[97]   But it was not until after 1647 that the Porcupines and other peoples about lake St. John were given the opportunity of developing a taste for imported foods.[98]   The supply to the Malecite was intermittent and even at the end of the century aboriginal foods prevailed, although flour, prunes, and other wares were not unknown.[99]   All the eastern Algonkian tribes acquired a preference for Brazilian tobacco over the native-grown variety and large quantities of it were imported from France.   In 1676 an impost of ten percent ad valorem was laid upon it, thus, the buying power being equal, reducing the consumption.[100]   The changed food of the Indians had the effect of unbalancing the diet and promoting diseases, possibly lactary troubles and infantile disorders, which resulted in a higher infant mortality.[101]

In order to lessen the toll made by the Indians on European foodstuffs the French made frequent but on the whole unsuccessful attempts to render the hunting Indians sedentary and to teach them the art of agriculture in order that they might become self-supporting.   The New England Indians cultivated maize and other vegetables, and the Abenaki, Penobscot and Malecite practised

93.   Jesuit Relations   5, 103; 29, 75; 32, 265.
94.   Jesuit Relations   44, 279.
95.   Jesuit Relations   5, 101.
96.   Jesuit Relations   29, 127.
97.   LeClercq   (2), 111, 112.
98.   Jesuit Relations   31, 253.
99.   Gyles 46.
100.   Lahontan   1, 373.
101.   Compare Pitt-Rivers 56.

agriculture to a less extent, as did also the Algonkins,[102] but the Micmac, Montagnais, Nascopi, and Misstassini Cree were entirely without this resource. The Micmac believed that their ancestors had cultivated corn and tobacco but "the negligence of their ancestors, they say, deprived them today of all these conveniences so useful and so essential to the nation as a whole."[103]   It was not suggested that the scramble for furs was the cause of this change.   As for the Montagnais, "This tribe does not occupy itself in tilling the soil; there are only three or four families who have cleared two or three acres, where they sow Indian corn, and they have been doing this for only a short time."[104] In 1633 it was proposed to engage men to clear and cultivate the land, and to teach agriculture to the Indians, and to establish a seminary for boys and girls. More French settlers were needed to set an example, and to keep the Indians, particularly those of Tadoussac, from losing heart.[105]   But "you will instruct them today, tomorrow hunger snatches your hearers away, forcing them to go and seek their food in the rivers and woods."   Moreover, some of those who became sedentary lost their adroitness in the hunt and were jeered at by their relatives.   But the depletion of their food resources and the fear of the Iroquois forced the Indians at a later date to cluster about the French settlements and to engage in agriculture in a desultory manner.

But not all of the eastern peoples were entirely dependent upon game, and European foods, for, besides wild berries, some of the tribes had a minor resource in the sugar maple.   Although the Algonkins lacked the maple sugar industry, it was practised by the Montagnais, Micmac, Malecite, Abenaki and others.[106]   There has been some dispute as to whether the manufacture of sugar originated from the ingenuity of European settlers, or whether it was aboriginal.   A certain seventeenth century writer declared that the Indians practised "this art longer than any now living among them can remember,"[107] and both Mr. A. F. Chamberlain and Mr. D. Jenness do not question that this was so.[108] But Father LeClercq, quoting Sagard on the use of maple sap among the Hurons, fails to mention the process of reducing it to sugar, and Chamberlain, although supporting his belief on the testimony of Rasle, who knew the Indians at first hand in the eighteenth century, mentioned Mohican and Menomini legends in which reference is made to maple sap, but none to sugar.[109]   It is significant, as Dr. W. F. Ganong has asserted, that sap is frequently referred to in the earlier records, which however say nothing of so remarkable a phenomenon as sugar.   It is his contention that the eastern Algonkians could not, by placing hot stones in their bark containers, arrive at a sufficient degree of heat and maintain it for a sufficient length of time to reduce the sap to sugar,

---

102. Jenness 276.
103. LeClercq (2), 213.
104. Jesuit Relations 4, 195.
105. Jesuit Relations 6, 145 seq.
106. Jenness 2, 76; although Jenness says the Montagnais did not have sugar industry LeJeune (Jesuit Relations 6, 273 note 24) mentions Michtan or maple from which these people obtained sweet juice. See also Ganong (3), 225.
107. Chamberlain (11), 382.
108. Jenness 44.
109. LeClercq (1) 1, 208; Chamberlain (10) 39. Dr. Ganong has drawn attention to the fact that Thevet, in a work published in 1558, and based in part on conversations with Cartier, seems to say that the value of maple sap was first discovered accidentally by the French in Canada. See "Crucial Maps," etc. Trans., R.S.C., 3rd series, sect. 2, vol XXX, 1936, p. 127.

and, although he believes that the use of sap was aboriginal, he submits that
the degree of heat necessary for sugar could not have been attained until the
European had furnished the Indians with metal kettles.[110]   And certainly Henshaw's reproduction of Lafitau's sketch shows that "For the kettles employed
in boiling the sap the Indians are evidently indebted to the French trader; . ."
But Dr. Ganong's thesis is less tenable in the face of the fact that certain of
the eastern Indians possessed pottery, and of the additional fact that the Iroquois were accustomed to freeze the sap in broad shallow vessels, thus separating
the water from the sugar.[111]   Moreover, although Dr. Ganong suggests that
no sugar was manufactured before 1675, there is a reference to this process
among the Ojibwa in the year 1668.[112]   At this time the French made it better
than the Indian women "from whom they have learned how to make it."[113]
By 1684 the French had begun to refine it and to turn it to much advantage.[114]
LeClercq speaks of the use of the maple among the Micmac:

> "As to the water of the maple which is the sap of that same tree,
> it is equally delicious to French and Indians, who take their fill
> of it in spring. It is true also that it is very pleasing and abundant in
> Gaspesia, for, through a very little opening which is made with an axe
> in a maple, ten to a dozen half-gallons may run out. A thing which
> has seemed to me very remarkable in the maple water is this, that if,
> by virtue of boiling, it is reduced to a third, it becomes a real syrup,
> which hardens to something like sugar, and takes on a reddish colour.
> It is formed into little loaves which are sent to France as a curiosity,
> and which in actual use serve very often as a substitute for French
> sugar."[115]

On the other hand Lahontan says, "Tis but few of the inhabitants that have
the patience to make Maple-Water . . . so there's ſcarcely anybody but Children that give themſelves the trouble of gaſhing theſe Trees."[116]

The change from aboriginal to European clothing was less complete
and generally secondary in importance to implements, utensils, and food, for
reasons which shall appear below.   When Denys first went to Acadia in the
'thirties he says that European clothing was not prevalent.[117]   As we observed
in an earlier chapter, hats were among the first articles of clothing to appeal
to the natives, although they never wore hats or caps until they were traded
from the French.[118]   The fact that the Micmac usually went bare-headed in
1699 may be indicative of the decline in the fur-trade at that time.[119]   Moreover, even in the 'eighties other European garments were by no means universal,
for "although some of our Indians now make their garments from blankets,
cloaks, coats, and from cloths that are brought from France, it is nevertheless
certain that . . . . the Indians clothed themselves only in skins . . . . in
which indeed, many of these people are clothed even to the present day."[120]

---

110.   LeClercq (1) 122-123 Editor's Note.
111.   Henshaw 344.
112.   Decouvertes et etablissement 3, 510.
113.   Henshaw 343.
114.   Chamberlain (11) 49.
115.   LeClercq (2), 122.
116.   Lahontan 1, 366-367.
117.   Denys 407.
118.   LeClercq (2) 98, but Jenness (1) 73 says Micmac and Malecite wore caps in
       winter.
119.   Diereville 97.
120.   LeClercq (2) 93.

The dress of the European was often unsuited to forest life and was found irksome to the native, so that ". . . . it is

> not possible to persuade them to dress in the French fashion, and there is nothing so grotesque as to see one of our Indian women dressed either in the common fashion or as a lady. . . . They say that they cannot make themselves like this dress, and that it would be impossible for them to walk or to work freely with the clothes of our Frenchwomen." [121]

The European dress, however, had a decorative value which made it popular among the more sedentary individuals. The Christians of Miscou in 1647 abandoned canoe-building on Sunday and donned their finest clothes, and their love of finery was such that a certain old man was "never willing to appear in any ceremony, whether public or private, except with a cap, a pair of embroidered gloves, and a rosary. . ."[123] But the Indian, although he sometimes adopted European dress, usually at first failed to apprehend the proprieties that accompanied it, and in consequence he often wore odd gadgets, such as boat-pulleys and keys, as ornaments.[124]

Similar phenomena were to be observed among the Montagnais. "Now that they trade with the French for caps, blankets, clothes, and shirts, there are many who use them; but their shirts are as white and as greasy as dish cloths, for they never wash them."[125] As among the Micmac shirts were worn over all other garments, probably for the sake of compactness in moving through the bush. But in 1632 dress was mostly aboriginal, and even caps were infrequent, although throughout succeeding decades imported garments bulked more largely as a result of gifts and trade.[126] In 1634 LeJeune noted the presence of French hats, and a woman's dress at this time consisted of a long skirt, hooded cloak, great coat, blanket, or skins tied together. The men wore one stocking of leather and one of cloth, and "just now they are cutting up their old coverings or blankets, with which to make sleeves or stockings." Sleeves were still removable as in pre-European times.[127] The Montagnais vied with the Micmac in their lack of apprehension of the proprieties of European dress:

> "Since they have had intercourse with our Europeans, they are more motley than the Swiss. I have seen a little six-year-old girl dressed in the great coat of her father, who was a large man; yet no Tailor was needed to adjust it to her size, for it was gathered around her body and tied like a bunch of faggots. One has a red hood, another a green one, and another a gray, all made . . . best suited to their convenience. Another will wear a hat with the brim cut off, if it happens to be too broad." [128]

Nightcaps, which the Montagnais begged at the store, were worn in the day time, and hats for men and women were worn by both sexes.[129]

---

121. LeClercq (2) 94.
123. LeClercq (2) 247.
124. Jesuit Relations 44, 291.
125. Jesuit Relations 5, 25; Collection de manuscrits relatifs 1 100.
126. Jesuit Relations 28, 243.
127. Jesuit Relations 7, 9-11.
128. Marie de L'I. 32; Jesuit Relations 44, 289.
129. Jesuit Relations 44.

> "It is true that those who mingle with us most often are beginning to make a distinction in their headdresses, the men choosing our hats or riding-caps, and the women our red wollen night-caps; . . . But they are not so particular that a woman will not use a riding-cap, and a man a night-cap, in the very middle of the day. . . In new France, a woman's dress is not improper for a man."

Whereas to go without breeches was ridiculous and offensive to the French, it was advantageous from the native point of view:

> "You will see Savages dressed in French attire, with worsted stockings and a cloak, but without any breeches; while before and behind are seen two large shirt-flaps hanging down below the cloak. This offends the French, and makes them laugh, but would not cause a Savage to lose his gravity in the slightest degree. That fashion seems all the more tasteful in their eyes because they regard our breeches as an encumbrance, although they sometimes wear these as a bit of finery, or in fun." [130]

Although it was said that, in the 'forties, most of the Christian Indians at Sillery were dressed in French clothes, the Relation of 1669 seems to belie it, since at this time "was introduced something very different from the ordinary solemnities;" the new chief "was clothed entirely in French dress, and instead of the tall head-dress . . . the wife . . . put on . . . a cap adorned with a very handsome tuft of fathers." [131]

For ceremonial purposes European clothes were deemed fitting by the Montagnais.   On the occasion of the birth of the Dauphin "six suits of clothing truly royal" were given to an Indian in France.   "They were entirely of cloth of gold, velvet, satin, silk plush, scarlet and everything else in keeping." These were eventually distributed to the Christians at Quebec. [132]   At a Christian marriage in 1640 the bride was dressed by the French ladies and the men were clad in the king's gifts.   The pagan women, seeing girls married "arrayed in the small treasures of the country which they greatly valued," did not hesitate to express their envy. [133]   But it was said that only the young, and therefore more adaptable, Indians approved of the French fashions. [134]

Occasionally it was felt that all this finery was unbecoming to Christians as in the case of an Abenaki woman in 1681, who, as the priest says, "begged me to have a dress with a border of gold braid changed for a plain one for her."   Moreover, with conversion to Christianity and the adoption of monastic dress went a relatively exaggerated growth of modesty and a new sense of the sinfulness of the flesh.   The girls of the Ursuline convent were "so- modest that, if one of them had her throat even a little uncovered, the others tell her that she will drive away her good angel. This is now so accepted among them that, to warn a girl to keep within the bounds of decorum, they say to her, "Be careful that your good angel does not leave you;" and the girl to whom this remark is made looks herself over, to see that there is nothing unseemly." [135]

Those who frequented the port of Tadoussac imitated the French in

---

130. Jesuit Relations 44, 295.
131. Jesuit Relations 16, 91; 52, 225.
132. Jesuit Relations 15, 223; 227.
133. Jesuit Relations 18, 127-129.
134. Lahontan 2, 425.
135. Jesuit Relations 19, 51.

dress as in other respects.   A chief in a handsome coat under a scarlet cloak was noted in 1636, and ten years later "They were . . . . dressed for the most part in french style, a shirt of white Holland linen, a neckband of lace, and a Scarlet Cloak."[136]   But those farther up the Saguenay and in other outlying regions retained the native costume on account of its superiority in forest life, as did those even of Sillery, Lorette, the Madeleine, and the Mountain missions when they were on hunting or war expeditions.[137]   In the Betsiamites country "the woods are very hard to pass through, on account of the density of the trees, although these are very small; all french clothes are torn in them.   On this account, the savages wear nothing but skins, because, the forests being very dense, the hunters in less than a Day, tear all the stuffs that the french Sell them."[138]   In 1674 the Betsiamites of Seven Islands "could not hunt there, if they were not entirely clad in skins instead of our stuffs, which would be quickly torn to pieces."[139]

On the whole, the introduction of European clothing was definitely less revolutionary than that of food and implements.   It is true, however, that in those areas where fur-bearing animals declined most rapidly greater dependence was had upon imported stuffs, and that the natives suffered from a lack of both indigenous and foreign clothing when the fur-trade declined, as in the case of some of the Abenaki of St. Francois de Sales in 1684.[140]   But although it did not always displace the native apparel it did, in general, affect the styles of native clothes to a large extent.   The cloak became the broad-skirted seventeenth century coat; and the French hats, shirts and trousers which have been mentioned above must have had some modifying influence.   And in 1696 a certain Micmac band "had to pay so dear for everything that, although they were free from drunkenness, they were but scantily clothed, after having killed five hundred moose this winter."[141]

It is difficult to gauge the influence of European clothing upon the health of the Indians.   In a cold climate like that of eastern Canada the superior article of clothing would have been that which possessed the greater protective property, and it is well known to this day that no cloth ever manufactured by a European has equalled the fur of the Indian as a protection against the inclement weather.   Moreover it is possible that skins absorb sweat better than wool, and in this respect the native material was perhaps more sanitary.   In the warmer climate of the Pacific Islands, Mr. Pitt-Rivers has found that "European clothes are the most effective promoters of skin disease, and of influenza, colds, coughs, and the pulminary ailments that afflict races first brought into contact with civilization."[142]   For this reason he concurs with the Rev. W. J. Durrad to the effect that "of all the evil customs introduced by civilization, the wearing of clothes is probably the greatest."   It is certain, as we shall see, that pulmonary troubles were rampant among the eastern Algonkians in the seventeenth century.

---

136.   Jesuit Relations   9, 227; 28, 205.
137.   Eastman 174.
138.   Jesuit Relations 59,   59.
139.   Jesuit Relations 59,   51.

140.   Jesuit Relations 63,   87.
141.   Murdoch 1, 217.
142.   Pitt-Rivers 58.

5.

When the missionaries went with the Montagnais on their winter hunting expeditions to live as they lived, they found that the native dwellings were draughty and cold, affording little protection, that to keep warm near the fire was to become uncomfortably hot and to be blinded by the ubiquitous smoke, that filth was the order of the day and night, and that to know extreme hunger and thirst were normal experiences. It was for these reasons that LeJeune asked "When they find themselves in comfortable beds, well fed, well lodged, well cared-for, do you doubt that this miracle of charity will win their hearts?"[144]   Sometimes those who were more adaptable built themselves french houses, as in the case of LaNasse, who in 1633 built a house of boards with a hatchet and nails from an old boat. In 1638 two families were so pleased with their new house at Sillery that, wherever they went they said that the Jesuits "wished to revive their nation which was rapidly dying out."[145]   In 1643, besides the bark cabins, there were four french houses. "The principal advantages of these houses are the little lofts in which they bestow their possessions, and their little belongings, which formerly became scattered and lost for want of a place in which to keep them."[146] French dishes and furniture, and European methods of sanitation were being employed.[147]   In the hospital court at Quebec the French built cabins for the Indians with boards, nails and rafters, but they failed to make a smoke hole in the roof so that they were rendered useless.[148]   On the other hand when a cabin was erected for a sick woman in 1643 it was "quite in the Savage fashion. She hung all around it robes of Beaver, and of Moose, wholly new and finely embroidered." In 1644 those who had been made sedentary had stone houses, while the others had merely bark.[149]

Whereas blankets were used by the Sillery Indians for beds as well as for clothes, they were used as coverings for the medicine lodges and for ordinary dwellings by the wandering Indians, such as the Porcupine people of lake St. John.[150]

Among the settled Indians the lock was, perhaps, the most significant innovation, not so much in itself as an article of utility, as much as a symbol of the new order of society that was struggling into being. In pre-European times the native dwelling was always open to the stranger who happened by. In a collective, if not communal, life the sense of property was elementary and stealing was rare or entirely absent. It is true that weapons and implements were personally owned, but the religious aspect of the relationship between a man and his effects was strong enough to deter any who were tempted to violate the usages of the group. Moreover, unlike European society the sexes were not

---

144. Jesuit Relations 9, 101.
145. Jesuit Relations 14, 217.
146. Jesuit Relations 23, 307.
147. Jesuit Relations 12, 173; 24, 59.
148. Jesuit Relations 35, 33.
149. Marie de l'I. 29.
150. Jesuit Relations 6, 163; 18, 123; 37, 219.

segregated in adolescence and a degree of promiscuity prevailed.   But with the growth of the European mores segregation and monastic seclusion became common.   The girls at Sillery were sometimes locked in at night for protection against visiting male friends, and property in articles of trade became more highly prized.   The first bark chapel erected at Tadoussac, in 1640, was furnished with a board door and padlock.

On rare occasions the Micmac also were known to build cabins "approaching the shape of our buildings," and at Miscou in 1646 there were sixteen persons settled in two houses "built in the French fashion."[151]   But as a general thing those who were not habitués of the settlement showed no desire for the dwellings which LeJeune had considered so far superior to their own wretched cabins.   The Micmac had "also no less repugnance to building houses and palaces like ours.   They ridicule and laugh at the most sumptuous and magnificent of our buildings."[152]   It has been argued that unsanitary native dwellings and domestic habits have been a cause of the decline in population which is so noticable in those areas which have been visited by European culture.   Mr. Pitt-Rivers has suggested that, as far as the Pacific Islands are concerned, this is not the case; but that rather the adoption of European dwellings, with their bad ventilation and airtight roof and walls, by native peoples may be a secondary cause of their decline.[153] With respect to the eastern Algonkians in the sevententh century the evidence is not sufficient for corroboration.

6.

Of the least importance was the influence of European means of transportation upon those of the aborigines, who themselves had developed methods upon which the European could not improve and which he readily adopted as the best suited to the need of traversing wide stretches of forest on foot in winter or of navigating the rapid streams and rivers that led to the fur-bearing interior.   It was consequently only among coastal people such as the Montagnais and the Micmac, who found it necessary to make short sea voyages, that any influence was discernible.   In 1634 the Montagnais band, with whom LeJeune wintered, were making use of a shallop which was furnished with a sail, besides their bark canoes.[154]   And on one occasion a blanket was used as a sail to propel an ice-floe at Tadoussac.[155]

Among the Micmac shallops were in use in 1659,[156] and in Denys' time canoes were only used for river travel.   All had boats for the sea, some of which were bought from the fishermen, but most of which were taken when

151.   Jesuit Relations 24, 149; 30, 127.
152.   LeClercq (2) 99, 103-104.
153.   Pitt-Rivers 56.
154.   Jesuit Relations 7, 85; At Tadoussac at the present time heavy boats of wood are made in the shape of Montagnais canoes. They can be paddled, rowed or sailed. They represent a complete fusion of European and Indian traits in one unit.
155.   Jesuit Relations 33, 37.
156.   Jesuit Relations 45, 67.

they were left by the French during their voyages to France.[157] "These Shallops they buy of the French who frequent their shores, . . . and they handle them as skilfully as our most courageous and active Sailors of France. They made a little Bridge of wood to enable them to embark dryshod in these Shallops, which are held for them ready launched." These were propelled by oars, as well as sails,[158] which were sometimes made of bark or moose skin when cloth was not obtainable.[159]

None of the eastern Algonkians used their dogs to haul their toboggans, and they either employed the tump-line or loaded their effects on the toboggans and hauled them themselves. The Montagnais adopted the dog-sled in later times, and from the French borrowed the dog-harness with shafts and tandem traces.[160] This apparatus was doubtless transposed from the horse-drawn vehicle. Although oxen were used to draw sleds in 1663, it was not until 1665 that the first horses arrived in Canada. The Indians who first saw them were "astonished that the Moose of France . . . . were so tractible and so obedient to man's every wish."

157. Denys 196, 340.
158. Jesuit Relations 47, 223,229.

159. Denys 422.
160. Speck (3) 279.

CHAPTER 6

DRUNKENNESS AND REGULATION

It has been suggested that, in the Pacific Islands, the use of European alcohol has not only not been a cause of depopulation, but has borne no co-ordinated relationship with the phenomenal decrease in native populations.[1] But in New France, in the face of overwhelming evidence to the contrary, one would hesitate to make a similar assertion, even when one treats the Jesuit Relations with reserve as being missionary propaganda, since the Jesuit testimony is corroborated from other sources, notably the records of the official failure to control the liquor situation, and the fact of the decline and of the dispersion, or possibly the extinction, of the Sillery Algonkins and Montagnais. "All the Indians in contact with Europeans become drunkards, and this does great harm to our converts, for of many who were good Christians several have fallen away,"[2] is a mild summary of the situation in the seventeeth century.

Although the Kirkes had been accused of first trading brandy to the eastern Algonkians, we have already witnessed its use in Acadia at the turn of the century, and Champlain had forbidden the trade on pain of fine and corporal punishment. And the Indians had said "Keep your wine and your brandy in prison. It is your drinks which do all the ill, and not we Indians."[3] Nevertheless drunkenness had reached frightful proportions among the Montagnais by 1634.[4] "There was a time when they had a horror of our European drinks; but they have now become so fond of these, that they would sell themselves to get them."[5] Orphans were many "for they die in great numbers since they are addicted to drinking wine and brandy. . . . ."[6] To stem the evil regulations were drawn up in 1636. Intoxicated Indians were to declare who had sold them liquor and the culprits were to be fined. If they refused to tell they were to be forbidden entry to French houses. If they were admitted, both French and Indians were to be punished.[7] For an infringement of these restrictions a Frenchman was fined fifty francs, but the guilty Indian promised to remunerate him in peltries.

Although in 1642 the Micmac had said "Write to France, and tell the Captains to send ships here, and not to send us any more of those poisons that destroy us. . ."[8], two years later liquor was said to be the scourge of the Miscou mission.[9] Moreover, the Micmac were the source of much drunkenness among the Montagnais. "Some Savages from that quarter (Acadia) have brought barrels full of brandy to Tadoussac; from Tadoussac they have come to Quebec, and this year have caused the greatest disorder among the Savages."[10] The Basques, who were still frequenting the waters of the St. Lawrence above

---

1. Pitt-Rivers 54, 69.
2. Boucher 61.
3. Eastman 28-29.
4. Jesuit Relations 6 251-253.
5. Jesuit Relations 6, 275.
6. Jesuit Relations 6, 239.
7. Jesuit Relations 9, 203-205.
8. Jesuit Relations 22, 241.
9. Jesuit Relations 28, 37.
10. Jesuit Relations 22, 43; 24-143.

Tadoussac, added to the disorder by their trade in wine.[11]   Up to 1646 the priests at Sillery had taken upon themselves the task of punishing Indian transgressions, "But the irregularities which the vessels usually occasion by their liquors, cause us to abandon this charity, and to refer to the Justice of the country the punishment of the too frequent cases of drunkenness, while they are anchored in our ports."[12]   When some of the Indians found that they were the special objects of this justice they declared, "They make us take the discipline when we get drunk, and they say nothing to the French."   In consequence the governor had some French placed on the wooden horse "exposed to a frightful Northeast wind."[13]   On the other hand the Indians were sometimes only too ready to punish themselves, and on more than one occasion they asked permission to beat themselves with whips.[14]

But the disorders became so violent that, on the advice of the Jesuits, His Majesty's council of state, on March 7, 1657, forbade the liquor trade on pain of fine for the first offence and whipping and banishment for the second. As the enforcement of the regulations was difficult, the council authorized an attorney to arrest drunken Indians and compel them to name the French vendors.[15]   On the 9th December of the same year "a tavern was set up at three rivers, at which wine was sold to the savages, . . . two pots for a winter beaver, and one pot for a summer beaver . . . but, as disorderly acts were not stopped by this device, complaints were raised against that tavern. . . The Conclusion was that it must not be continued. Nevertheless, it was continued."[16]

On 5th May, 1660, Bishop Laval issued a bill of excommunication against all those who were found selling liquor to the Indians, because "il met tout ce christianisme dans un peril evident d'une ruine totale, . . ."[17]   For the severity of this action he gave five reasons.   The Indians were selling all the proceeds of the chase for liquor with the consequence that their families were naked and starving.   Some, to obtain brandy, sold their own children into servitude.   Drunken children assaulted and injured their parents.   Men used brandy as a philter to make girls drunk in order to seduce them, and quarrels and murders were prosecuted with impunity.[18]   Following Laval's decree of excommunication, one Nicholas Vvil was shot on 7th October, 1661, and one La Violette on the 11th. On the 10th another was flogged for trading brandy to the Indians.[19]

For a short time the repression of the liquor traffic was effective, but when Mezy broke with Laval the disorders recommenced.   The ecclesiastical authorities were to be thwarted in their design of eradicating the trade in brandy for the remainder of the century by the continuous pressure of the state, the officials of which believed that the economic subsistence of the colony depended upon it as an essential feature of the fur-trade.   For twenty years Colbert opposed the stand of the church on this question.   He declared that

11. Jesuit Relations 27, 149.
12. Jesuit Relations 29, 81.
13. Jesuit Relations 27 119.
14. Jesuit Relations 29, 77-79.
15. Eastman 78-79.
16. Jesuit Relations 43, 77.
17. Mandements des eveques 14-15.
18. Jesuit Relations 46, 103-105.
19. Jesuit Relations 46 187.

the suppression of the traffic was causing the Algonkians to go to the English and Dutch where they were given rum for their furs and where they were schooled in the faith of the heretics.   But as liquor in New France had never been successfully suppressed the act of suppression could hardly be responsible for a commercial understanding with France's enemies.[20]   Laval called up all the resources of his keen brain to refute the arguments of French officialdom. The council of state had adduced a set of arguments in favour of the liquor traffic, condemning the bishop for his acts of excommunication.   There was no precedent for making a reserve case of drunkenness in any country in which people were addicted to it.   When crime resulted from drunkenness royal judges were appointed to punish it.   If what was a sin in Canada was not so elsewhere, people's minds would become confused on the rules of the church.   The crimes which were caused by the Indians becoming drunk were not sufficiently heinous to be made a reserve case by the priests.   And lastly, the commerce brought the Indians to the French and gave them a chance for conversion instead of their going to the Dutch and the English.   Without the commerce in eau-de-vie the trade would be diverted.   To the first of these Laval responded that the Indians had an inordinate desire for liquor and in consequence were not to be treated as other races.   To the second, there was no reason why the church should not support the state in preventing crime.   To the next, if the disorders were as great among all peoples as they were among the Indians the rule would be the same all over the world.   To the next, every mortal sin which causes the ruin of religion might be treated as a reserve case.   Besides, the priests lived with the Indians in the woods, and were the best judges, sometimes the only witnesses, of crimes.   And to the last, wherever drunkenness had existed there had been little hope of conversion.   For this reason it had been necessary to abandon the Gaspé and the lower Algonkian missions.   The Indians would not go to the Dutch and English because four hundred Iroquois had come to live with the French, coming from a wet to a comparatively dry community. Liquor did not bring the Indians to the French and conduce to a stronger alliance, because the French made the Indians drunk and cheated them of their furs.   The Dutch got the trade because they gave cheaper goods.   Therefore, they got the best furs and the French got the left-overs for brandy.   In any case the Iroquois were the only people who trafficked with the Dutch and the English, and this was not because of liquor but because of the proximity of their territories.[21]

The government, however, refused to concede the reason of Laval's arguments.   In January, 1662, the governor issued permits to sell liquor to the Indians.   On 24th February, 1662, the decree of excommunication was renewed on account of disorders of great violence.[22] In 1663 the Jesuits declared that the excessive drunkenness had ruined their missions.[23]   On September 28th, 1663, the sovereign council took more drastic action.   All persons were prohibited from selling any kind of liquor to the Indians under any pretext.

---

20. Eastman 79-81.
21. Mandements des eveques 149.
22. Mandements des eveques 42.
23. Jugements et deliberations, 1 8-9.

A fine of three hundred livres was set for the first offence, and banishment or the lash for repetitions, on the ground that the Indians "enclins al'yvrongnerie mesprisant les loix du Christianisme, s'adonnoient a toutes sortes de vices, et abandonnoient l'exercice de la chasse, par lequel seulement cette colonie a subsiste jusqu'a ce jour; . . ."[23]   But instead of the specified three hundred livres, a certain Gilles Esnard was fined only fifty livres in November of that same year for selling liquor to the Indians.[24]   On April 24th, 1664, the sovereign council provided that any one might arrest a drunken Indian and force him to disclose the name of his "bootlegger".[25]   On September 3rd the judge of Three Rivers was ordered to inform and proceed against vendors of intoxicating liquors.[26]

The governor, Argenson, had allowed a liquor store to be opened at Three Rivers on condition that the lessee should pay fourteen hundred livres towards the building of the parish church.   As a result the inhabitants of Three Rivers drew an act of assembly calling for the absolute suppression because of abuses which had developed under cover of the permit to sell beer and bouillon to the Indians.   The sovereign council was favourable, and on April 29th, 1665, prohibited the lodging of Indians in homes, because under pretense of hospitality there were some who made a practice of hiding their baggage for several days in order to exploit them more thoroughly.   Dissension, however, rendered the order ineffective.[27]   Murders, violence, and other disorders continued, so that on December 6th, 1666, the council ordered the prohibition of trade in brandy by anyone, to any Indian, under any pretext, on pain of arbitrary fine or corporal punishment for the first offence, and three hours on the "wooden horse" for the second, etc.[28]   In spite of the ordinances the peace of the north shore from Montreal to Quebec continued to be disrupted by murder and rape, especially at Three Rivers, Cap de la Madeleine, and Champlain.   The Indians, remaining drunk for several months on end, were unable to hunt.   They traded all their pelts for liquor to the detriment of the legitimate traders.   They were, therefore, unable to pay their debts for lead, powder and clothing.[29]   On 20th June, 1667, fines for vendors were set at from fifty to two hundred livres, and serious offenders were to receive one month's imprisonment with fifteen days exposure on the wooden horse for one hour a day, with the name of the crime appended to public view.   Indians were to be fined fifty livres, or, if they had no money or pelts, they were to receive imprisonment and exposure as in the case of the French.[30]   In the following year the council found that the Indians at Montreal, Three Rivers and elsewhere were perpetually drunk and in the worst disorder.[31]

On November 10th, 1668, the government completely reversed its policy on the liquor traffic.   Louis XIV was not to be outdone by his Spanish

24. Jugements et deliberations, 1 64.
25. Jugements et deliberations, 1 181.
26. Jugements et deliberations, 1 274.
27. Jugements et deliberations, 1 340; Eastman 80.
28. Jugements et deliberations, 1 368.
29. Jugements et deliberations, 1 474 seq; Eastman 124-125.
30. Jugements et deliberations, 1 406-408.
31. Eastman 125.

rival in the New World and he was doubtless anxious to imitate the policy of Spain in treating the Indians of Mexico and elsewhere as full-fledged Spanish citizens, subject to no disabilties on account of their native origin.   He was not aware of the real effect of hispanization upon the natives of the Spanish domains.   All he knew was the hearsay of the Spanish court, when that court itself was not fully aware of the miscarriage of its policy.   Accordingly the council decided to further the process of assimilation by allowing all the inhabitants of New France to sell any kind of liquor to the Indians without restriction.   By this means trade was to be diverted from the English.   If Indians became drunk they were to be placed in the pillory for two hours and fined two beaver skins.   The French found drinking with the Indians were to be subject to the same penalty.   For the time being the clergy maintained an ominous silence.[32]

In the same year Talon founded a brewery in order to substitute beer for brandy to decrease the use of intoxicating drinks "which occasion great lawlessness here; that can be obviated by using this other drink, which is very wholesome and not injurious."[33]   It was estimated that 100,000 livres were spent yearly for wine and brandy.[34]   At Tadoussac conditions showed a temporary improvement:

> "The excellent Regulation that has been imposed upon Tadoussac all this past Winter, where no outbreak has been seen in this respect, has been followed by an advantageous Traffic; and it has been proved by experience that the great means of rendering the French and the Savages rich in their mutual commerce is to exclude from it all trading in drink. . ."[35]

That the improvement here and elsewhere in the colony was only temporary was soon to be made evident.   In 1672 and 1673 there were some Montagnais, Algonkins, Mohicans and Sokoki at the mission of la Prairie de la Magdeleine, which was predominately Iroquoian and which was said to be a stronghold against drunkenness.   Whereas "Brandy has ruined the Algonquin Missions" due to "The insatiable avarice of the French. ."[36]   Although the Brandy Parliament of 1678 had pointed to Sillery as a model village, Father Beschefer wrote in 1683 that the Algonkian mission had been reduced by drunkenness to a few wretched fragments who were scattered in the woods."[37]

> "Sillery is the home of the Algonquins, where they formerly had one of the most flourishing missions in Canada; but drunkenness caused such disastrous ravages among them that there is only a wretched remnant of that nation, scattered through the woods and in places where—as they no longer have any missionaries to reproach them for their misconduct—They can indulge in this vice with greater freedom." [38]

Conditions were equally if not more deplorable among the Micmac.

---

32. Jugements et deliberations, 1 534; Eastman 127-128.
33. Jesuit Relations 51, 173.
34. Eastman 122-123.
35. Jesuit Relations 51, 269.
36. Jesuit Relations 58, 75; Eastman 181.
37. Eastman 226.
38. Jesuit Relations 62, 259.

Bishop St.-Vallier declared that brandy had killed all the old men and great numbers of the young people among the cross-bearer Micmac.[39]   LeClercq said that the French made the Indians drunk and cheated them in the trade.   They perpetrated a further fraud by diluting the liquor with water.   The Indians were made to sell all their household goods to obtain brandy.   The French seduced and practised indecency with the native women who were made drunk for the purpose.   The liquor made the Indians kill each other and destroy their own property and that of the French.[40]   The most sordid picture of all is painted by Denys, and it is recommended to any who have any doubts concerning the degrading influence which liquor had upon every aspect of the native life.   The Indians were trading themselves into destitution.   Fraud in trade, the wholesale seduction of women by the fishermen, the promotion of disease and civil strife, the disintegration of the group spirit and the loss of the will to live, all resulted from the deliberate debauching of the Micmac with wine and brandy.   The Jesuits had been forced to abandon the mission.[41] Conditions were almost equally bad among the Malecite in 1690, who ". . . . when they came in from hunting, they would be drunk and fight for several days and nights together, till they had spent most of their skins in wine and brandy, which was brought to the village by a Frenchman. . . ."[42]

Drunkenness became more prevalent in the Indian villages which were remote from the settled area around Quebec, Three Rivers, and Montreal.   It was found that the inhabitants were neglecting agriculture to carry liquor into the woods to meet the Indians and engage in an illicit trade, so that on June 26th, 1669, this was prohibited.[43]   That the fine and chastisement were not persuasive is seen from the repetition of this enactment on May 12th, 1678, and on October 31st, 1678, the council registered an ordinance of the King against the French going into the woods to trade at the Indian settlements.[44] Although cases of enforcement are on record,[45] the king found it necessary to issue a further ordinance on May 24th, 1679, forbidding brandy to be carried to the Indian villages,[46] with fines of one hundred livres for the first offence, three hundred for the second, and corporal punishment for the third, although the Indians could obtain brandy in the French settlements in retail or whole-sale quantities, which seems to indicate that the illicit trade, which was injuring the economic welfare of the colony, was aimed at, and not the sale of brandy to the Indians, since Louis XIV still favoured a policy of assimilation.[47] This policy continued to bear evil fruits.   The Indians themselves had set up taverns on the St. Lawrence which Frontenac found it necessary to suppress. He also forbade the French to sell liquor to the Indians for the clothes which they were wearing, or their guns and ammunition.[48]

---

39. LeClercq (2) 189. Note 2.
40. LeClercq (2) 253-258.
41. Denys 444-450.
42. Gyles 34.
43. Jugements et deliberations 1 558.
44. Eastman 189; Jugements et deliberations 2, 256.
45. Jugements et deliberations 2 343.
46. Edits, ordnances royaux, 1 235.
47. Eastman 198-199.
48. Eastman 183.

We have seen that at about this time the Abenaki began their migrations from their home in what is now the state of Maine to Sillery where they replaced the dispersed and decimated Montagnais and Algonkins. One of their reasons was, allegedly, to escape from the English rum trade at the New England posts. Unfortunately they found conditions no better on the St. Lawrence.[49] They found that ". . . the french are as wicked as the English. They get drunk here, as we do in Acadia."[50] Those who remained in Acadia, overwhelmed with debts and persecuted by unscrupulous creditors, sometimes went over to the English.[51] Those at Sillery went to the Jesuit Bigot to beg him to prevent the French from selling them excessive quantities of liquor, and:

> "when several of them went to a merchant in quebek to sell some furs, and when the merchant offered each of them a glass of brandy, not one of them would take it. I am careful, however, not to regard as a sin in them the act of taking a few Drinks of brandy or of wine, which they sometimes do while eating in the houses of the french. . . ."[52]

In spite of the ordinances which provided for the imprisonment of intoxicated Indians "no heed was paid to those orders, and most of the savages who became drunk escaped from Quebek without being taken."[53] As an act of suppression Bigot instituted at Sillery in 1685 "the Holy pillage". From every Indian found intoxicated were to be taken "some petty effects belonging to his cabin, in order that the effects so taken might Serve to pay the Archers who would come to put that drunken Savage in prison."[54] He displayed, however, an understanding of the native psychology. "While I was issuing all the orders against drunkenness, I allowed more diversion and dancing in the mission than I would have permitted at other times; this I did to make them swallow the pill more easily. . ."[55]

In 1688 Denonville wrote to the minister that liquor was causing the ruin of the colony. Twenty years before, two thousand Indians, all enemies of the Iroquois, had lived in the French settlements. Now scarcely thirty could be gathered together. He attributed the cause to brandy. He himself had seen so many die from its effects. He recommended the complete prohibition of sale to the Indians. On this the intendant, Champigny, was in complete accord.[56] The evidence from Canada and Acadia in 1689 supported the truth of his observations. The population was declining rapidly and the birth rate was decreased:

> "De la sont venus tant de maladies incurables et mortelles qui ont altere leur temperament et leur bonne constitution naturelle, et qui ont faict mourir un sy grand nombre de Sauvages les uns a la fleur de leur aage et les aultres en langeur avant la vieillesse. On en a vu devenir fous; quelques uns ont egorge, roti et mange leurs enfans; d'aultres se sont tuez par le fer, le poison ou par le feu." [57]

---

49. Jesuit Relations 63, 117.
50. Jesuit Relations 63, 131.
51. Eastman 245.
52. Jesuit Relations 62, 129.
53. Jesuit Relations 63, 103.
54. Jesuit Relations 63, 105.
55. Jesuit Relations 63, 115.
56. Eastman 247-248.
57. Collection de manuscrits relatifs 1, 542-533.

The Jesuits sounded a warning note in a series of trenchant memoirs:

". . . Si le Roy ne fait garder ses ordonnances et celles du conseil de
Kebec sur le sujet de l'yvrognerie des sauvages, ils periront, ils con-
tinueront de commetre d'horribles crimes, ils abandonneront la colonie
a qui d'ailleurs ils sont tres utiles en paix par la chasse, mais particu-
larement en geurre contre nos ennemys qu eux seuls seuvent atteindre
dans les bois, ils perdront la foy qu'ils ont recue au bapteme, et ceux
qui ne sont pas encore chretien seront dans l'impossibilite de se
convertir. . . ."[58]

An anonymous memoir of 1693 declared that the bodies of dead Indians were
to be found in the rivers and woods with barrels of brandy beside them.
Drunken Indians had set fire to the houses of settlers in revenge against some
who had "gloried in having debauched with their brandy more than two
hundred Indian women or girls. . ."   In the previous year " 'savage men
and women, drunken and naked, dragged each other into the streets, where in
the sight and to the great scandal of everybody, they did publicly, like brute
beasts, things shameful and infamous . . . that decency does not permit' the
author to relate."[59]   A dark picture of social conditions at this time is painted:

". . . la nation des Algonquins autrefois si considerable y si formidable
aux Iroquois est destruitte et anneantie par les eaux de vie que les
francais leurs ont donne. . . . de la nation seule des Algonquins que
leur nombre et leur courage rendoient redoutable a nos ennemis on en
compte sans parler des autres plus de deux mille que l'eau de vie a
exterminez. . . .
Toutes les femmes enceintes addonnees a l'yvrogneurie ou avortent ou
se font avorter ou causent la mort a leurs enfans soit en les jettant dans
le feu, ou dans les eaux, ou les meurtrissant contre terre; soit aussi
parceque leur lait sclarit ou se corrompt par le frequent usage de l'eau
de vie n'en ayant pas d'autre a leur donner. . . . Je revois rien des
parricides, des yncestes, des voils, des prostitutions, et de mille autres
infames et brutalitez detestables ou ils se plongent, et qui sont les fruits
ordinaires de cette boisson, par le moyen de la quelle plusieurs de ceux
qui la vendent ayant fait perdre la pudeur avec la raison aux femmes,
ils les—corrompent les ayant enyvrees; d'ou viennent les divorces des
mariages, les dissentions a dans les familles, le libertinage des grands
et, des petits, et une pauvrete si extreme qu'il ne reste a ces yvrognes
et yvrognesses ni hardes, ni haches mesme pour couper du bois, ni
chaudiere, ni bled, ni aucune des choses necessaires pour la vie ou pour
la chasse; tout de qui leur apartinoit ayant reste couverts en eau de vie
au profit de ceux que pour pescher plus aisement, comme l'on dit, en
eau trouble, les depouillent de tout en cet estat pour tres peu d'eau de
vie abusant de leur yvresse pour faire un frauduleux commerce dont les
sauvages ne conviedroient pas s'ils croient en leur bon sens.

To the end of the century the Indians disclaimed responsibility for
deeds which they committed while in a state of intoxication.   A memoir of
1693 observes:

". . . il arrive souvent qu'un sauvage qui voudra du mal a un autre
faira semblant d'etre yvre pout le tuer ou pour violer une femme, et
apres leur yvresse, il direct tranquillement qu'ils n'avaient point
d'esprit, quand ils ont fait cela, y les voyla plainnement justifies."[60]

When they were actually drunk they were not responsible according to their
own world-view.   It will be remembered that in the primitive cosmogony

58. CI1A 12, 1692.
59. Eastman 274-275; C11A 12, 2, 1693; Memoir on liquor among the Indians.
60. C11A 12, 2, 1693.

the distinction between material and immaterial is not sharply drawn, and that every object in nature is the abode of supernatural or mysterious power in varying degrees. In another category were the supernatural agents who themselves were efficacious in varying degrees of potency. Brandy was the embodiment, or was the medium through which an evil supernatural agent worked. When an Indian drank brandy he was temporarily inhabited by this agent who was responsible for his acts.

To the end of the century the government continued to enact ineffectual ordinances against drunkenness. For example, on January 12th, 1699, it was decreed that Indians who became drunk should suffer imprisonment and a fine of two "castors gras"; and that the vendors should be fined twenty livres for the first offence, forty for the second, and sixty for the third.[61] For economic reasons the spirit was seldom behind the letter of the law, and in conclusion, Eastman says, "Clearly, the immediate profits from the fur-trade were greater when brandy was used as an article of barter, inasmuch as it rendered possible a scandalous exploitation of the Indian."[62] On the other hand, it stripped the French of indispensible native allies when the hour of crisis came.

To the end of the century the ecclesiastics, vanned by the Jesuit cohorts, fought the liquor traffic to the last ditch, and it must be admitted that, from the point of view of the Christian ethic, their attitude was the only justifiable one. From the scientific viewpoint it is probably true to say that liquor was one of the chief causes of the decline and approximate extinction of the native populations.

61. Jugements et déliberations 4, 256.
62. Eastman 291.

CHAPTER 7

DISEASE AND TREATMENT

1.

"When the French reached Canada they found that the Indians were possessed of a knowledge of medicine and surgery that was in some ways the equal of their own. In their application of the medicinal properties of the vegetable kingdom the Indians were probably superior to the French physicians. They had remedies for each and every occasion, expectorants, emetics, purgatives, astringents, even emenagogues and abortificients. . . . Their system of medicine was an unwritten one that was handed down from generation to generation and, in spite of the manifold defects of such a system, was surprisingly complete. In the hands of the women of the tribe was placed the treatment and care of the sick."[1] Thus does Dr. Heagerty relate the accessories of the European, which were very poor and not to be judged by present standards, and American cultures with respect to the treatment of disease. The Montagnais and the Abenaki measured up favourably with the English and the French in their knowledge of what, to the contemporary scientific mind, may be termed natural causes, but the category of natural causes was one that could not have been recognized by the native mind which perceived supernatural inter-penetration, or perhaps identity, with the physical environment. It is certain, therefore, that no sharp division separated the habit of mind which led to the use of medicinal herbs from that which had recourse to incantation and exorcism, these two being necessarily involved in the same process. The sweat-lodge and the emetic were more than supplemented by the special knowledge of the native witch-doctor. "If they happen to fall into a sickness . . . . the aoutmoin blows, with exorcisms, upon the part afflicted, licks it and sucks it; if that is not enough he bleeds the patient, opening the flesh with the point of a knife or other instrument." "Concerning wounds, the aoutmoins of our Souriquois and of their neighbours lick and suck them, using a beaver's kidney, of which they put a slice upon the wound, and so it heals itself."[2]

The early travellers found that certain ailments which were current among Europeans of the time were absent from native society, of which palsy, dropsy, gout, rheumatism, stone, gravel, gall, colic and asthma were notable.[3] The diseases from which they suffered were few in number, "and there is little doubt that the infectious diseases, such as measles, scarlet fever, diphtheria, chicken-pox, small-pox, typhus, typhoid, malaria, and yellow fever, as well as the venereal diseases, and possibly tuberculosis, were importations."[4] They could cope with the diseases which they knew, with the exception perhaps of

---

1. Heagerty 1, 268. For Micmac and Montagnais medicines see (Speck (16) 313-317.
2. Lescarbot 3, 185-186.
3. Lahontan 2, 418; LeClercq (2) 241.
4. Heagerty 1, 270.

scurvy, but when they became infected with diseases of the white man "their system of medicine broke down."[5]   Accordingly, recourse was sometimes had to European remedies when the diseases suffered were recognized as importations from Europe, as was often the case.   In 1633 the Montagnais, as a group, were opposed to the application of French remedies, although certain individuals were found to be more adaptable, and ointments from the European pharmacopoeia were used on occasions.[6]   In 1640 the mother superior of the hospital at Quebec declared that the Indians had "no difficulty in taking our medicines, nor in having themselves bled",[7] and in the following year:

> "We have received and helped in our Hospital sixty-seven sick Savages, and one Frenchman; we have maintained, during the winter, the poor and the infirm who were not able to follow their tribesmen to the hunt; seven persons have been baptized in our house, and only four of our sick ones have passed away to the other life. . . ." [8]

In 1642 over four hundred and fifty medicines were dispensed, which exhausted the supply at the hospital.[9]   On the other hand Lahontan says that the Indians were in general opposed to the use of French medicines in his day.[10]

2.

All of those bands which frequented the French settlements in the seventeenth century, including the Sillery, Tadoussac, and upper Saguenay Montagnais, Atticamegs, Algonkins, Abenaki and Hurons were treated by the hospital sisters for those diseases with which they could not cope.[11]   Of all these diseases which ravaged the Europeans scurvy alone was indigenous.   It was also prevalent among the natives, but could not have been severe, since they would otherwise have long before been terribly depleted by this means.   It was fostered by the salt meat diet of the sea-faring French who lacked the fresh vegetables which contained vitamins necessary to health.   When these could be obtained they were found valuable to both peoples.   The remedy with which the Laurentian Iroquois had saved Cartier's crew from destruction in the previous century was not known to the eastern Algonkians who could do nothing in this respect for the early Quebec, and the St. Croix and Port Royal colonies.   Scurvy or "mal de terre" ravaged Three Rivers in 1634 and 1635, and the Miscou colony in 1637 where both the French and the Micmac were victims.[12]   At Miscou it ceased only after 1643, having carried off priests and traders in alarming numbers.[13]   But it continued at intervals throughout the century to effect considerable havoc.   At Quebec in 1643 a woman suffered from a disease of the legs which was characterized by festering sores, filthy and

5.   Heagerty 1, 269.
6.   Jesuit Relations 9, 193; 32, 279.
7.   Jesuit Relations 19, 21.
8.   Jesuit Relations 20 243.
9.   Jesuit Relations 22, 173.
10.   Lahontan 2, 470.
11.   Jesuit Relations 24, 161.
12.   Heagerty 1, 11-12; Jesuit Relations 12, 265.
13.   Jesuit Relations 32, 39.

evil-smelling.[14]   It is usually difficult for the laymen to diagnose diseases from random symptoms mentioned in books, but there is some reason to believe that scurvy was responsible for the above cases.   Dr. Heagerty is authority for the statement that scurvy was the disease which ravaged Richibucto and Chedabucto in 1659 and 1661, which resulted in many deaths.   The only symptom recorded is the breaking of an internal abscess.[15]

Of all the imported diseases syphilis was perhaps the earliest which was communicated to the north American Indian.   Controversy has raged around the problem of its indigenousness.   Even if it originated in Haiti in the form which it took in "the golden age of the pox" the difficulties of transportation and the known slowness with which cultural traits were diffused throughout aboriginal America would scarcely have militated against its spread to north America.   In Havelock Ellis's opinion, "it scarcely even yet seems certain that what Spaniards brought back from America was really a disease absolutely new to the Old World, and not a more virulent form of an old disease of which the manifestation had become benign."[16]   It even seems uncertain whether it was syphilis or yaws with which Columbus' men were infected; and syphilis may have been rampant in the east as early as the Crusades.   The increased contacts through trade with Asia which were frequent at the time of the discovery of America may have accounted for the outbreak at the Siege of Naples.   If the Indians were previously without it, it may account in a large measure for the depopulation that resulted from contact with the Europeans in the Colonial era.   On this point Dr. Knott has said that "a more destructive type of venereal disease tends to develop from inoculation with the virus derived from an individual of a remoter race. . . ."[17]   It is, therefore, astonishing that it does not bulk larger in the accounts of early travellers.   However, we have observed that it was introduced early.   Some of Cartier's crew suffered from syphilis in 1536, and the Indians "suffered from gonorrhoea which they undoubtedly acquired from the whites. . . ."[18]   LeJeune refers to the ailments of a certain medicine-man of the Montagnais in 1634 who suffered from pains in the loins which were attributed to licentiousness, and the context might appear to indicate syphilis.[19]   Lahontan declared that venereal diseases were common on the upper Mississippi in his day,[20] and Kalm referred to the prevalence of syphilis in New France during the declining years of the French regime.   It is, therefore, not strange that the "mal de la baie St. Paul" which has been identified as syphilis, became epidemic on the St. Lawrence in the third quarter of the eighteenth century.[21]

Less mystery surrounds the history of small-pox among the eastern Algonkians.   Although the exact point of origin is not known the Indians were well aware that it was an importation from Europe.   It raged from 1616

---

14.   Jesuit Relations 24, 177.
15.   Heagerty 1, 12; Jesuit Relations 47, 63.
16.   Ellis, H. 6, 321; also Williams.
17.   Knott 8, 21-22.
18.   Heagerty 1, 270.
19.   Jesuit Relations 6, 169.
20.   Lahontan 2, 465-466.
21.   Heagerty 131 seq.

to 1620 and thousands were carried off in the area between Cape Cod and the Mississippi.[22]   The small-pox which afflicted the Montagnais at Quebec in 1635 was characterized by fever, pox, blindness and diarrhoea.   Wherever the priests went the disease broke out.[23]   Blindness and emaciation were symptoms among the Montagnais in 1636, and three years later the disease broke out afresh, having been brought from the Abenaki country by a returning party of Island Algonkins.   Although four families came to settle at Sillery LeJeune sent them away so that they would not contract small-pox.   Thus disease retarded the transition from a nomadic to a sedentary life.[24]   The disease was virulent and the toll of life was heavy.   Cases were recorded in which the bones, hollowed with putrifaction, pierced the skin, and the sores were large and deep.[25]   By 1645 the epidemic had abated.   "Disease would soon have killed all, had it continued to rage as furiously as we have seen it do."[26]   Even so, it all but exterminated the Attimegs in 1661 who were already greatly reduced by Iroquois bullets.

The most destructive of all the small-pox epidemics broke out at Tadoussac in the winter of 1669-70.   Midst cold and hunger, two hundred and fifty persons died of the Montagnais, Algonkins, Papinachois, and Micmac, from Sillery to Tadoussac.   One shipload "all resembled Monsters rather than human beings, their bodies were so hideous, emaciated, and full of corruption."[27]   Whereas from a thousand to twelve hundred Indians had formerly frequented Tadoussac scarcely a hundred remained in the summer of 1670. It is said that six score had died at Tadoussac alone.[28]   Across the St. Lawrence at Ile Verte, theriac, described as a sovereign remedy, was administered to "living skeletons and bodies all disfigured. . . ."[29]   Nearby the missionary was forced to "live in a place infected with a horrible stench" while caring for a band of Micmacs.   The French rendered efficient service

> "by the assiduous attentions which they bestowed upon our sick Savages . . . in attending them, dressing their sores . . . burying them after their death . . . I have seen some of them with an admirable courage and zeal, load the dead bodies upon boats in the icy waters; and then unloading them, carry them on their shoulders, although the putrid matter ran from all parts upon their garments and cloaks."

That the French possessed a certain immunity may be gathered from the fact that, although one was slightly ill "none of them have experienced any injury".   The Father was attacked but recovered.

Of the Abenaki at Sillery in 1682 the Relation declared that nearly all had been attacked by small-pox, but adds that "Not many persons have died This year in the mission."[30]   In 1684, at the instigation of LeClercq, a Micmac migration was made to Sillery, but "God has granted the favour to most of these Gaspesians to die at Sillery this year, some time after having arrived there."[31]

---

22. Heagerty 1, 57-58.
23. Heagerty 1, 20.
24. Jesuit Relations 16, 101-103.
25. Jesuit Relations 19, 17.
26. Jesuit Relations 27, 171.

27. Jesuit Relations 53, 69.
28. Jesuit Relations 53, 77.
29. Jesuit Relations 53, 71-75.
30. Jesuit Relations 62, 145.
31. Jesuit Relations 63, 69-71.

Although Acadia had long been a fruitful soil for European diseases the small-pox encompassed great destruction in the last decade of the century. Great numbers of Penobscots and Malecite died in the regions of Pentagouet and Meductic.[32]   Gyles, who was a prisoner among the Malecite at this time, describes the epidemic that afflicted his band.   The diseased person would bleed at the mouth and nose, turn blue in spots, and die in two or three hours.   More than a hundred died among his immediate people.   It caused the Indians to scatter and they were not reunited when he left them in 1698[33].

Although small-pox was perhaps the most lethal of all diseases that afflicted the eastern Algonkians it had sturdy companions in arms.   In 1634 many were attacked by scrofula, or tuberculosis, the symptoms of which were sores full of pus, covered with a horrible looking crust. which attacked the ears, neck and arm-pits.[34]   Of the sick among the Montagnais in 1637 "nearly all die of consumption, becoming so thin that they are nothing but skin and bone. . . ."[35]   One of these, a woman, was stricken with paralysis and rawness of the loins.[36]   Another, the son of a sorcerer, having developed "a most horrible scrofulous affection near the ear, we were afraid he would give the disease to the little boys we have in our House, and so we refused him.   Monsieur Grand . . . has this child's sores dressed, and dresses them himself."[37] Pleurisy and consumption, which were perhaps induced by the wearing of European clothing, attacked the Christian Indians at Sillery in 1639.   In 1644 an Indian was found to be suffering from an abcess in the head, worms issuing from the ears, rotting flesh, limbs falling away piecemeal, accompanied by great pain.[38]   Ten years later at Tadoussac a child with a scrofulous neck and throat eaten away, was noted.[39]   Again, what appears to have been tuberculosis was recorded at Quebec in 1658.[40] Lahontan declared that consumption resulted from the use of brandy which had been adulterated in France.[41]   Moreover, after 1659, when the Saint Andre was stricken while on its way to New France, typhus became as frequent in the colony as the arrival of the king's ships from the Old World.[42] Typhus may have been the epidemic which raged at Tadoussac in 1661, and which Menard declared was hitherto unknown, and which swept away all those whom it attacked.   Death was accompanied by violent convulsions and contortions of the limbs.[43]   Other diseases of a minor nature, such as dropsy, were not infrequent results of the contact with European culture.[44]

---

32. Heagerty 1, 20.
33. Gyles 34.
34. Jesuit Relations 6, 263.
35. Jesuit Relations 12, 7; Burns, Coleman, Hirsch and Maher.
36. Jesuit Relations 11, 111.
37. Jesuit Relations 7, 301.
38. Jesuit Relations 25, 215.
39. Jesuit Relations 41, 195.
40. Jesuit Relations 44, 267.
41. Lahontan 2, 465-466.
42. Heagerty   1, 107-108.
43. Jesuit Relations 46, 255.
44. Jesuit Relations 22, 157-159.

3.

The view has already been submitted that the primitive is not aware of the theory of natural causation which was brought to its fruition in the scientific minds of the nineteenth century.   Events are ascribed to supernatural imminence.   For instance, disease was the result of occult power which may have been loosed by the breaking of a tabu.   The efficiency of therapeutics resulted from the fact that they were the instruments of opposing supernatural powers.[45]   If a Micmac suffered from stomach trouble a sorcerer would blow upon his stomach, accompanying his act by appropriate incantations.   If he were not cured it was because "the Devil is there inside of the sick man, tormenting and preventing him from getting well."[46]   When in 1633 the Jesuits remonstrated with a shaman for treating a fevered child with blowing, and beating of drums, recommending rest instead, he remonstrated, "That is very good for you people; but, for us, it is thus that we cure our sick."[47]

Of one thing the Indians were certain: the virulent diseases from which they suffered were the direct result of contact with the Europeans.   Moreover, it was useless for the priests to say that baptism was not the cause of the abnormally high death rate.   They were baptized and they were dying.   Moreover, the priests were notorious wizards.   The priests might not even be aware of their baleful influence, and they might deny it in good faith, but the denial would be worthless to the Indian mind.   The rite brought down the wrath of supernatural beings upon them.[48]   To the scientist this view may appear puerile in the extreme, but how different was it from the view of disease which was held by contemporary Europeans?   The supernatural element was invoked as an explanation in each case.   To the European events in this world were the result of the will of God.   The Jesuits sometimes asserted that God sent the diseases to punish the Indians and thereby strengthened their belief that evil manitou was being set upon them by the magic of the invaders.[49]   In their zeal for saving souls, they were apathetic towards the physical death of the Indians.   "The joy that one feels when he has baptized a Savage who dies soon afterwards, and flies directly to Heaven to become an Angel, certainly is a joy that surpasses anything that can be imagined."[50]   Given the Jesuit theology, this sentiment was valid and ethical.   The discrepancy was due to the fact that the Indians felt physical well-being, with reservations, to be the greatest good.   Their purpose was to increase this well-being by incantation and preserve it by tabu.   But the incantation of the shaman may have been closer in form to the prayer of the Jesuit than at first it might appear.[51]

Although their belief in the power of the white man's God remained

---

45.   Compare Levy-Bruhl 35-37.
46.   Jesuit Relations 3, 119-123. See also Jesuit Relations 6, 175 for Montagnais belief that disease is the result of a she-manito who gets inside and feeds on the flesh.
47.   Jesuit Relations 5, 237.
48.   Levy-Bruhl 45; Jesuit Relations 7, 277.
49.   Jesuit Relations 63, 89.
50.   Jesuit Relations 8, 169.
51.   Sir James Fraser makes a sharp distinction between magic and religion.

constant, the Indians varied in regarding it as benevolent or injurious. In 1635 the Montagnais accused the Jesuits of having killed one of their number by having given him a statue of Jesus, after which he died.[52]   On the other hand, since the Jesuits were free from the current diseases, a Montagnais shaman recommended to a sick man the wearing of black stockings like those worn by the Black Robe in order to be cured.   This the manitou had told him.[53]   In 1637 the Montagnais children thought that anything obtained from the French was a cure for illness. "You will see them coming to ask us for prunes, because they have a sore foot or hand."[54]   At Quebec in 1646 several Indians were cured by wearing European religious relics, in the efficacy of which the French also believed.[55]   It was, therefore, not strange that "These nations persuade themselves that they die almost entirely through charms; and hence, measuring us by the same standard, they think and believe we are greater sorcerers than they themselves."[56]   In 1635 the Montagnais explained the assault of the Hurons upon a band of French by saying that those "who, falling ill with a certain epidemic which last autumn afflicted all those Nations, believed that this malady was caused by the French, and it was this which made them treat the French in this way; . . ."[57]   As the sorcerers were ridiculed by the priests, and as the imported diseases grew in dimension, they were discredited, having been thought to have lost power over the manitou.[58]   The Indians at Three Rivers in 1636 believed that "what gives life to us, gives death to them", since "as we do not readily bestow these sacred waters except upon those who we see are not going to abuse them, on account of their proximity to death, these Barbarians for a while had this idea that Baptism was fatal to them."[59]   In the following year some Montagnais expressed the belief that the deaths among the northern tribes were due to the trade in French articles with the Nipissings.[60]   Again, to the argument that intemperance was the cause of their decline, they countered, ". . . . it is not those drinks that take away our lives, but your writings; for since you have described our country, our rivers, our lands, and our woods, we are all dying, which did not happen until you came here."[61]   At another time a Basque had written their names on paper and thereby had taken away their souls.[62]   The principle of sympathetic magic is also seen from the belief that the native medicines were of no avail when the priests knew that they were being used.[63]

Among the Montagnais and certain of the Algonkins the belief that baptism was the cause of death persisted throughout the period.   The Jesuits found that at Three Rivers in 1639 "The persecution against us is again commencing; the small-pox or some other similar disease unknown to me, having broken out among the Savages, the Devil makes them say that we are the cause of this contagion."[64]   "Since we pray", said the Indians, "we see by experience that death carries us off everywhere."[65]   In 1647 a sorcerer of Tadoussac heard

---

52. Jesuit Relations 9, 195.
53. Jesuit Relations 9, 113.
54. Jesuit Relations 12, 141.
55. Jesuit Relations 29, 197-199.
56. Jesuit Relations 12, 87.
57. Jesuit Relations 8, 43.
58. Jesuit Relations 12, 7-9.

59. Jesuit Relations 8, 251-253.
60. Jesuit Relations 11, 197.
61. Jesuit Relations 9, 207.
62. Jesuit Relations 11, 195.
63. Jesuit Relations 24, 31.
64. Jesuit Relations 16, 53.
65. Jesuit Relations 16, 39.

a manitou say, "that the Faith and prayer brought death to most of those who embraced it. . . . . He said that it was not the God of the believers who governed the Earth, especially their countries,.......that it was he who ruled the Savages; . ." Immediately after baptism a child became covered with sores.[66] The missionary found the northern tribes at Tadoussac unfriendly, and he attributed their coldness to the belief that baptism had caused the great epidemic of the previous winter. This belief somtimes kept the bands from coming to the posts with their furs and thus retarded the expedition of trade. The Betsiamites, who dwelt farther down the St. Lawrence, held the same view.[67]

On the other hand, the Iroquet Algonkins came to Three Rivers in 1647 to receive instruction. Knowing that the diseases were European in origin, they believed that European rites were necessary to cure them.[68] A similar anxiety to receive baptism was displayed by the pagan Micmac at Miscou in 1645.[69] But of all the eastern Algonkian tribes the Abenaki were the most steadfast in their adherence to the methods of the French. Their friendship for the French may have been induced by their hostility towards the English, or, with respect to the treatment of disease, it may have resulted from fortuitous circumstances. At any rate in 1647 an abandoned sorcerer recovered from his illness after he had been baptized.[70] On another occasion an Abenaki, who was with a Malecite party, declared that to sing and breathe on a sick member of the group was useless for only God could cure him.[71] Unlike the Malecite and the northeastern Indians the Abenakis believed that God had cured them miraculously of many diseases since the faith had been introduced. The faithful resisted the sorcerers who wished to cure by invocations. They redoubled their prayers on this account and were cured. Although great numbers of the Abenaki died at Sillery in 1681 they did not heed the assertions of the pagans that prayer was the cause.[72]

4.

Mr. Pitt-Rivers has contended that "no native races have been extinguished by violence, starvation, and civilized drink and diseases, whatever the extent to which their numbers have been reduced by these means . . . neither the incidence nor the morality of diseases whether endemic or epidemic are any indication of the growth or decline tendencies in a population. The incidence of endemic diseases is invariably far higher among civilized and dense populations than among savages. Epidemic diseases, especially when newly introduced, sometimes sweep away a large proportion of the population, but if the settled tendency of the population is to increase rather than decrease, the survivors, unless entirely new factors supervene, must continue the upward trend at the same rate of increase."[73] The eradication of disease, hygenic improvements,

66. Jesuit Relations 31, 243-245.
67. Jesuit Relations 31, 159.
68. Jesuit Relations 31, 281-283.
69. Jesuit Relations 28, 31.
70. Jesuit Relations 31, 197.
71. Jesuit Relations 32, 221.
72. Jesuit Relations 62, 39.
73. Pitt-Rivers 54-55.

and immunization would not correlate with greater survival capacity.   Instead of immunization "a total substitution of population takes place" when the stock does survive.[74]

Although the Abenaki said in 1646 "that a malady which caused vomiting of blood had destroyed a good part of their nation," they seem to have survived to the present time in a more numerous coherent group than most of the eastern Algonkians.   The inference from the proposition of Mr. Pitt-Rivers is that their adaptibility has resulted from a substitution of stock. On the other hand "it is said that they are dying in such numbers in the countries farther up, that the dogs eat the corpses that cannot be buried"; and the Atticamegs, at least, appear not to have survived the ordeal of war and disease, although the remnants may have sought refuge with other bands.   Moreover, by 1650 the Sillery colony was said to have been reduced to little more than widows and orphans.   And at Tadoussac in 1646 "There were reckoned, formerly, on the shores of this port, three hundred warriors or effective hunters, who made with their families about twelve or fifteen hundred souls. . . . . humbled by diseases which have almost entirely exterminated it . . . Jesus Christ . . . seems to wish to repeople this tribe with a goodly number of Savages who land there from various places. . . ."[75]   Here we have a substitution of stock, not from within the community, but from without.   But a great deal may be said for the theory of immunity.   Epidemics of small-pox were rife in Europe in the seventeenth century, whereas "All the French born in the country were attacked by the contagion, as well as the Savages.   Those who came from . . . France were exempt from it, except two or three, already naturalized to the air of this region."[76]

It seems probable that disease was in itself a cause of decline to the point of extinction, and together with the introduction from without of implements and utensils, food, clothing and liquor, it reacted upon the secondary mores in such a way as to break the morale of the people by the disintegration of the immaterial aspects of life, resulting in a loss of the will to live.

---

74. Pitt-Rivers 8. Mr. Pitt-Rivers does not tell us how it is possible for a substitution of stock to take place without involving immunization. One would have supposed the substitutes to have survived on account of their immunity.
75. Jesuit Relations 29, 123-125.
76. Jesuit Relations 19, 9-11.

CHAPTER 8

POLITICAL MODIFICATION

1.

When Lewis H. Morgan, working in the influence of the evolutionary thought of the nineteenth century, made his famous enunciation that human society evolved from "savagery, through barbarism, to civilization", the communist economists, under the leadership of Frederick Engels, seized upon it to support their contention that a period of communal ownership of property, concomitant with a state of sexual promiscuity, had preceded individual ownership and the individualistic family.[1] Although Morgan's schematic method is now generally rejected by anthropologists, particularly those of the extreme wing of the diffusionist school, there is some reason to believe that individual ownership of real property was unknown among the eastern Algonkians prior to the conflict with the culture of the European immigrants.[2] Just as in American agricultural communities where "there is an annual allotment of fields to the households of the group", so in the non-agricultural areas of the eastern Algonkians the same characteristics of communal ownership of land existed to the same degree.[3] Lahontan confirms this statement in speaking of the hunting Indians in general:

> ". . . they agree among themselves, as they are Travelling, to allot each Family a certain compafs of Ground, so when they arrive at the place they divide themfelves into **Tribes**. Each Hunter fixes his Houfe in the Center of that Ground which is his Diftrict. . . . There are eight or ten Hunters in each Cottage, who have four or five Lakes for their fhare. . . . But above all they are fo Juft, that they would choofe rather to die for Hunger than to struggle out of the Bounds alloted them, or to steal the Beafts that are taken in their Neighbours Traps." [4]

Although this statement seems to indicate that the property right of the family after allotment was religiously respected, it is modified by another which Lahontan makes elsewhere:

> "The Savages are utter strangers to diftinctions of Property, for what belongs to one is equally anothers. If any one of them be in danger at the Beaver hunting the reft fly to his Affiftance without being fo much as ask'd. If his fufee burfts they are ready to offer him their own. . . . Money is in ufe with none of them but those that are Chriftians, who live in the Suburbs of our Towns." [5]

The inordinate love of the French for their material possessions contrasted strongly with the attitude of the Montagnais and sometimes irritated the latter, threatening disruption of the friendship between the two peoples.[6] For the Montagnais' impulse to share was deeply rooted enough to cause the scene at

---

1. Engels, Origin of the family.
2. Grinnell.
3. Wissler 184.
4. Lahontan 2, 481.

5. Lahontan 1, 420.
6. Jesuit Relations 5, 171.
7. Jesuit Relations 20, 249.

the hospital in 1640 in which sick Indians shared the medicines given them by the French irrespective of the diseases from which they suffered.[7] The impulse was common to the area. Of the Papinachois it was said, ". . . their goods are held almost in common".[8] This, of course, did not extend to personal articles, such as clothing, weapons, utensils; or immaterial possessions, such, perhaps, as the right to sing certain songs, and it was therefore not surprising that the Montagnais and the Micmac had a great horror of theft.[9]

But with respect to the food supply and the land that went with it, the spirit of mutual helpfulness appears to have prevailed. The Tadoussac Montagnais were accustomed to hunt in bands, and those of Lake St. John broke up into "bands", each going to winter in its own district.[10] Each Atticameg band assembled in its own district "on certain days of the year; and, although they have their own limits, if any one advances upon the lands, or rather into the woods, of his neighbors, that occurs without quarrel, without dispute, without jealousy."[11] Among the Micmac, where the semi-annual allotment of territories, before the fall and winter hunts, was practised, the restriction against trespass was more severe than among the Atticamegs:

> "It is the right of the head of the nation . . . to distribute the places of hunting to each individual. It is not permitted to any Indian to overstep the bounds and limits of the region which shall have been assigned him in the assemblies of the elders. These are held in autumn and in spring expressly to make this assignment." [12]

Although the tribe is not specified, the practice of selecting hunting territories seems to have prevailed as late as 1723:

> "The principle of the Indians is to mark off the hunting ground selected by them by blazing the trees with their crests, so that they may never encroach on each other. When the hunting season comes, each family pitches its tent in the neighborhood of its chosen district." [13]

Here it is definitely specified that the family, and not a larger kinship group, was the unit receiving allotment. It is possible that at an earlier date a larger group was involved.

Dr. Speck, in his closely analytical studies of eastern Algonkian society, gives us an exact picture of the institution of the hunting territory as it exists today. In general the family hunting group is a kinship group composed of individuals united by blood or marriage, maintaining the right to hunt, trap, or fish, in certain inherited districts bounded by rivers, lakes or other natural landmarks. The group is known by a family name and the territories are patrilineally inherited. Trespass, though rare, is punishable. Thus a community of land together with common economic interest strengthens the kinship group.[14] This institution formerly prevailed at least as far south as New

---

8. Jesuit Relations 49, 55. Similar practice among the Micmac. See LeClercq (2) 117.
9. Jesuit Relations 63, 253; There is some reason to believe that Malecite recognized ownership of songs. See Mechling (1).
10. Jesuit Relations 37, 187; 59, 29.
11. Jesuit Relations 31, 209.
12. LeClercq (2) 237.
13. Innis (1) appendix A.
14. Speck (14) 327-328.

England.[15]   We are told that the Montagnais band is composed of a more
or less stable number of families, that they travel together as a horde and come
out to trade at definite rendezvous on the coast.   In some places the boundaries
of the territories are somewhat fixed, in others the hunter disregards territorial
limits and follows his game where he wishes. At present patrilineal inheritance
prevails.[16]   Among the Micmac the families are large and form local groups,
possessing emblems.   They consist of husband, wife and children, and other
relatives left to his support, such as grandparents, aunts, uncles, and even relatives by marriage. These family groups are associated with definitely recognized
hunting territories which are inherited as among the Montagnais.[17]   The
boundaries of the territories are not strictly recognized as elsewhere, for example, among the Penobscot, and the family group is capable of some elasticity.[18]
Among the Malecite and the Penobscot boundaries were more respected and the
local groups were more definitely associated with the prevailing food animal
from which they took their names.[19] Trespass upon Algonkin family territories
is occasionally punishable by death, but more often by conjuring against the
life or health of the offender.[20]   Permission to pass through the family territory is obtainable, and a temporary exchange of hunting privileges between
families sometimes occurs. Reciprocal hunting privileges are entertained between
the Misstassini and the Nichicun bands, and patrilineal inheritance prevails as
elsewhere, although among the former matrilineal descent is not unknown.[21]

In what respect do the present family hunting territories differ from
those of pre-European times?   Apart from the fact that the bands were at that
time larger than they are today, having been subject to reduction by war,
liquor, disease, and the economic and social disruption of the group life, the
main point of difference lies in the fact that whereas formerly ownership was
vested in the band whose territories were semi-annually allotted, today ownership is vested in each individual family whose territory is patrilineally inherited.
At this point the question of terminology becomes of more than passing
interest.   In his "Primitive Society", Lowie employs "communism" as a term
to express ownership to the exclusion of all personal rights, which, as he says,
probably never occurs.   He admits the frequent occurrence of joint-ownership,
which may be termed also "communal ownership" when the parties to joint-
ownership constitute the community.   Among the eastern Algonkians the
band, owning the land conjointly, constituted the community.   There might,
therefore, be some justification for designating pre-European eastern Algonkian
ownership of land as communal.   Lowie uses Speck's data to support the main
thesis of his book; that is, that the biological family is the oldest and most
universal social unit, more basic than the clan or the band.   But surely it is a
case of relative importance with respect to function.   In our society the family
is based on monogamy in law, and property, including children, is largely
subject to individual ownership.   But with the Montagnais the sense of group

15. Speck (9) 292.
16. Speck (3) 277-280.
17. Speck (1) 130, 96, 90.
18. Speck (1) 94, 130.

19. Speck (3) 283-285; Speck (11) 9-13.
20. Speck (8) 4-8.
21. Speck (18) 458-461.

solidarity was great, the ownership of land and the food supply were vested in the band, although seasonally leased to individuals for obvious economic reasons, and children were the charge of the whole band.[22]   Although Lowie's instance cited from the practice of the Crow appears to justify his somewhat fine distinction between legal communism and the feeling of communal solidarity, as expressed in mutual hospitality and the custom of sharing the food supply, surely, where there is no written law, the two tend to be one and the same in function, as the above quotations from Lahontan seem to indicate.[23]

2

Some of the forces which brought about the change from group to individual ownership of hunting territories may be indicated from the conditions which prevailed among the eastern Algonkians throughout the seventeenth century.   In the first place the organization of the fur-trade tended to dissolve the solidarity of formerly distinctive groups,[24] which had, in pre-European times been self-subsistent.   They now became dependent upon an external source for many of the articles with which they had supplied themselves, such as weapons, implements for domestic use, utensils, and to a less degree, food and clothing.   A greater amount of travel, which resulted from the recession of the fur frontier and necessitated longer journeys to the interior, together with the increased activity of a people who were becoming more and more dependent upon trade as a source for their materials, brought formerly isolated bands into closer and more frequent contact with each other, and with the French at the posts which placed a new emphasis upon land-ownership, and tended to obliterate their distinctive traits.   Moreover, the growing need for European wares necessitated a more extensive killing of the beaver and other fur-bearing animals than had formerly been needed for food and clothing. With the scarcity of game resulting from this need, together with the substitution of the more destructive fire-arms for the bow and arrow, the club, and the spear, the bands were forced to split into families, since the diminishing food supply in any one area was not sufficient for the subsistence of a large band.   In the 'thirties LeJeune had accompanied a fairly large Montagnais band to its winter quarters.   In 1668 the Indians of the Saguenay "are obliged to scatter here and there, in order not to injure one another by their proximity in hunting."[25] Under these conditions the need for more effective conservation of game became acute and was urged by the Jesuits.[26]   "It is not easy to combine systematic trapping with band ownership, because all members of the band are not equally interested in every section of the country or in the conservation of the fur-bearing animals there.   The man who knows of a good beaver river will leave a few animals to propagate and go back the next year; but if he never expects to go back he will kill all the beaver, and not leave

22. Jesuit Relations 6, 255.
23. Lowie 206-213.
24. Innis (1) 17-18.

25. Jesuit Relations 51, 271.
26. Jesuit Relations 8, 57.

them for some one else."[27]   Added to this, the French were always desirous of dealing with individuals rather than with groups, the members of which were not thought by them to be responsible for each other's actions.   More-ever, the actual pelts were owned by individuals.   Thus, personal ownership might by easy transference have been extended to the hunting lands.   Added to this, the change from band to family ownership was partly due to the influence of white trappers who married native women and occupied trapping areas without consulting the bands.[28]

Concurrent but often at variance with the interests of the French fur-traders were those of the Jesuits who desired to render the hunting Indians sedentary and civilized in order that they might be the more easily converted, and whose influence was great in destroying the group solidarity of the eastern Algonkian bands.   South of the St. Lawrence their achievement in this respect was slow.   Although a small settlement of Micmac was centered at Miscou in 1642 the tribe as a whole was still generally nomadic.[29]   And Nepisiquit could boast of only two families of fifteen persons in 1646.[30]   In LeClercq's time the plan to settle the Indians "in order that we might humanize these peoples, settle them with us, employ them at the cultivation of the land, bring them into submission to our laws and customs" was still in prospect.[31] Whereas settlements were relatively more successful at Quebec, in Acadia fishing and trading occupied the French exclusively, the visits of missionaries were infrequent, and the Indians were kept to their hunting, all of which retarded settlement.   Nevertheless, Richard Denys, writing to the Marquis de Seignelay in 1689 concerning the settlements in Baye Chaleur, gave more imposing figures:

> "Il a fixe deux villages de sauvages pres de ses habitations, l'un dans la baye des chaleurs de 60 familles, et d'environs 400 ames, l'autre . . . de 80 cabanes ou familles de 500 ames; ainsy sa concession est peuplee de 103 francois et de 900 sauvages a qui il fournit toutes leurs necessites temporelles et spirituelles aiant toujours entretenu a ses depens des religieux ou des prestres." [32]

The Jesuits who had dedicated themselves to the Malecite mission expressed the hope in 1677 "that the Fields that have been offered them for the cultiva-tion of Indian corn" and the chapel would induce them to become stationary,[33] but at the end of the period Villebon declared that the Indians of the St. John could not be induced to give up their lands and settle in one spot.[34]   The Penobscot and the Malecite, together with closely related peoples, had lived in villages and had cultivated the soil when first encountered by Europeans, but in the seventeenth century they lost their sedentary habit to some extent, under the influnce of the French who induced them to revert more to hunting in the interest of the fur-trade.[35]   On the other hand those Abenaki who

27. Statement of Mr. D. Jenness.
28. Jenness (1) 121; Note: Miscegenation will be dealt with in the following chapter.
29. Jesuit Relations 22, 239.
30. Jesuit Relations 28, 213.
31. LeClercq (2) 304-305.
32. CllD 2-(1).
33. Jesuit Relations 60 269.
34. Murdoch 1, 244.
35. Lahontan 1, 227; Editor's note.

migrated to Quebec became perhaps the most successful agriculturists of all the eastern Algonkians, on account of their previous adaptation to this occupation.[36]

At the beginning of the period more success was attained among the Montagnais of the most immediate area although the traders threatened to drive the neophytes from the proposed settlement in fear that they would relinquish hunting and thereby ruin trade.[37] But after the return of the colony to France in 1632 the Jesuits renewed their efforts to range the Indians under their protection.[38] The solidarity of the bands, and the individual's fear that if he embraced Christianity he would incur the displeasure and derision of his fellows, called for a policy by which the mass resistance of the bands could be broken. "Now it will be so arranged that, in the course of time, each family of our Montagnais, if they become located, will take its own territory for hunting without following in the tracks of its neighbours. . . . ."[39] The Jesuits were to see that the transition from group to individual hunting should be made.

In 1636 efforts were made to civilize the Montagnais by educating them in the habits of the French. Girls were to be reared as Christians, to be given dowries and married to the French, or to be kept as domestics and dressed in the French manner. Already those in domestic service "care no more for the Savages than if they did not belong to their nation."[40] Already the Montagnais children mocked the un-Europeanized Indians and became "so accustomed to our food and clothes, that they will have a horror of the Savages and their filth."[41] This process continued until the Quebec band was extinct, or decimated and scattered, and was complete by the middle of the century.

The Jesuits hoped to break the wandering habits of the Montagnais by bringing them into closer contact with the sedentary Hurons at Quebec.[42] To this end two families were settled at Sillery in 1638 who were to form a nucleus for a larger colony. As proximity to the French at this time promised greater security certain Atticamegs, Porcupines and Island Algonkins, wished to be counted among the number of settlers. When the adults asked whether their children should be ejected after their deaths they were told that among the French the property of the parents was inherited by the children.[43] When the founder of the Sillery colony died in 1639 the Indians were told that six workmen should always be kept for them. "They could not understand how this could be done, nor why these workmen could not at once take the money he left for them, nor how a dead man could make living men work; for they know not what it is to have rents and revenues."[44] The growing individualism was immediately discernable when two converts renounced their relationship with one of their number who had given himself over to drunkenness. "This is an act fit to astonish all those who know the

36. Jesuit Relations 62, 123-125.
37. Eastman 114-115.
38. Jesuit Relations 8, 15.
39. Jesuit Relations 8, 57.
40. Jesuit Relations 9, 103-105.
41. Jesuit Relations 9, 107.
42. Jesuit Relations 12, 79.
43. Jesuit Relations 14, 211.
44. Jesuit Relations 15, 233.

customs of the Savages, who cannot endure that any one should touch their kinsmen; . . ."[45]

Sillery gradually increased in size during the 'forties; from a hundred and sixty-seven in 1645 to two hundred in 1647 when fifteen arpents of land were cleared but not yet entirely under cultivation.[46]   In 1651 the Company of New France granted the seigneury of Sillery, which was to be under the control of the Jesuits, to the Indians who were to enjoy equal civil rights and commercial privileges with the French.[47]   Among those who became Christians and settled at Sillery the old sentiments of group solidarity were broken, since all Christians considered themselves as brothers.   Thus conversion cut across the old divisions between Hurons and Algonkians, Montagnais and Micmac, destroyed the solidarity of the ancient tribes and created a new one.[48] But the uprooting of the old habits together with the high mortality from war, disease and drunkenness, which resulted from economic and religious penetration, destroyed the Sillery colony, and by 1699, the place being deserted, the land was transferred to the Jesuits.[49]

The Jesuits encountered greater difficulty in their attempt to convert and render sedentary the Indians who were accustomed to frequent the post at Three Rivers than they had at the more protected Sillery.   Three Rivers served as a terminus for the fur-fleets of the Algonkin middlemen of the Ottawa river valley.   Conspicuous among these were the Island Algonkins who, on account of their key position in the trade, and as particular objects of Iroquois fury, were warlike and intractable.   In 1636 public opinion was still strong enough to preserve the group spirit, and individuals, in fear of being mocked by their people, generally rejected conversion unless they were dying.[50]   In 1639 an Algonkin declared, "Some of my people cast upon me the reproach that I am becoming a Frenchman, that I am leaving my own nation; and I answer them that I am neither Frenchmen nor savage. . . "[51]   One of the Island Algonkins was suspected of an alliance with the French to make them die.   They spied on him and dishonoured him by exclusion from their banquets.   To appease God's anger against his people and to draw down His mercy he chastized his body with thorns.[52]   The case illustrates the impossibility of conforming to two diametrically opposed moralities at one and the same time.   Ten years later the solidarity of the Christian group at Three Rivers was disintegrated by the presence of a floating population of pagan Hurons, Algonkins and Atticamegs, and it seems that Jesuit efforts at this point can scarcely have been successful, although during the 'fifties when the Iroquois menace was at its height the Indians were more ready for close affiliation with the French.   We have already seen that Three Rivers dwindled in importance after the founding of Montreal and after the western trade routes were established, which led to contact with the Ottawas during the last quarter of the century.

---

45.   Jesuit Relations 20, 151.
46.   Jesuit Relations 27, 121; 28, 185; 30, 155.
47.   Eastman 115-116.
48.   Jesuit Relations 37, 149; 46, 67.

49.   Eastman 164.
50.   Jesuit Relations 9, 41-43.
51.   Jesuit Relations 16, 115.
52.   Jesuit Relations 16, 125-129.

3.

A distinctive aspect of the new society was that which involved a change in the status of individuals and classes of individuals. In primitive times the band was composed of families who were more or less closely related. All heads of families enjoyed an equality in economic and political status which was in marked contrast to contemporary European society. It is true that prisoners taken in war, if not at once killed, served as slaves to the free and equal members of the band,[53] but it is probable that they were sometimes adopted into the band, as they often were among Iroquoian peoples, whence their state of slavery ceased. If they remained as slaves they were not inherited but were freed on the death of their master.[54] It has been stated that the Algonkians, who were great gamblers, sometimes reduced themselves to slavery by this means, but the instance cited by MacLeod may have been a result of the economic condition inherent in the fur-trade although it is not beyond doubt that this occurred in pre-European times.[55] Because material possessions were not highly prized, transgressions by members against the property rights of other members of the band have not been recorded, although the stealing of goods possessed by other groups, such as the French, are known to have occurred after competitive conditions had been introduced.[56] Nevertheless the Montagnais were not thieves. "The doors of the French are open to them, because their hands can be trusted. . . ."[57] Whereas the execution of justice among the French was subject to centralized control by duly constituted officials, the behaviour of the Montagnais was controlled by public opinion, and justice was executed by means of the blood feud.[58] The Micmac band acted in judicial matters, not through a chief, but through a council of elders.[59]

Chieftainship was not a rigid office, nor were the duties of a leader of a definite or pronounced nature. A Montagnais chief's authority was all in his tongue's end, and he was not obeyed if he did not please the Indians.[60] The inheritance of chieftanship was practised, as it is today by the Timiskaming Algonkians,[61] but a talent for leadership was prerequisite,[62] and if a leader proved to be vicious he was despised by the Indians who said "that a man who cannot govern himself is not fit to govern others."[63] The status of chiefs among the Micmac was closely similar, and it is probable that the elaborate ceremonies and jurisdictions that appertain to the office today are the result of the political lesson which was learned from the Iroquois allies of the French in the eighteenth century, and which culminated in the Wabanaki confederacy.[64]

---

53. Jesuit Relations 30, 133.
54. Lahontan 2, 474.
55. MacLeod (2) and (3).
56. Jesuit Relations 32, 37; 36, 143.
57. Jesuit Relations 6, 249.
58. Jesuit Relations 12, 169.
59. LeClercq (2) 237.
60. Jesuit Relations 6, 243.
61. Speck (8) 5.
62. Jesuit Relations 16, 135.
63. Boucher 54.
64. Jesuit Relations 2, 73-75; Speck (1) 107-125; Speck (6).

Some of the stages in the transition to a less democratic form of society may be indicated. From being a leader in war and the hunt the Micmac chief became also a commercial representative of the band in its dealings with the French traders, taking their furs and giving them what they needed in return.[65] The temptation of the chief to assume a higher economic status than his fellows was inherent in this system. Denys records the case of an individual who aped the dignity of a French commandant, dwelt in a fort of stakes and bastions which was guarded by armed sentinels, and which visitors were forced to salute with a discharge of muskets. The Indians obeyed him through fear rather than friendship, and if they were delinquent in what he considered their duty he beat them.[66] Nevertheless if one possessed of European commodities disputed the chieftainship but failed in a hunting competition with the recognized chief he was forced to relinquish his claim.[67] On the other hand a definite change from liberality to selfishness was recognized by LeClercq:

> "It is true that this generous disposition is undergoing some alteration since the French, through the commerce which they have with them, have gradually accustomed them to traffic and not to give anything for nothing; . . ."[68]

Probably the change came more slowly among the relatively isolated Malecite, but among the Penobscot and the Abenaki a special phenomenon was to be observed. Here French officers assumed the role of war chiefs and led the bellicose border Indians against the English. In this way authority was wielded from beyond the confines of the group.[69] Sometimes priests would be acclaimed as chiefs, as in the case of Dreuillettes who enjoyed economic and ceremonial distinctions and who served as a diplomatic representative to the English on behalf of the Abenaki.[70]

North of the St. Lawrence the nature of political control was perhaps more sharply modified. At an election of chiefs at Sillery in 1640, which the Jesuits conducted by secret ballot, the Christians were found to have prevailed over the pagans. "The election over, they looked at one another in great astonishment, never having proceeded in this manner."[71] One who was already a chief by inheritance did not compete. One was made a captain of prayers; two, one Christian and one pagan, were to keep the young men dutiful, and elections were to be held yearly. The captain of prayers became a formidable personage. At Tadoussac he went armed with a "heavy whip of cords, with large knots, in order to beat those who should fail to be present at the prayers:"

> "He imagined that the tonsure that we have on our heads had a great influence in making the others pray to God and was necessary for those who undertake to teach. He had his head shaved like ours, and taking a whip or rope, he went through the cabins calling the others to prayers, and striking those who did not promptly obey."[73]

---

65. LeClercq (2) 234-235.
66. Denys 195-196.
67. LeClercq (2) 236.
68. LeClercq (2) 245.
69. Murdoch 1, 206.

70. Jesuit Relations 36, 79; 38, 33.
71. Jesuit Relations 18, 101-103.
72. Jesuit Relations 24, 127.
73. Jesuit Relations 26, 117.

Because the French were seen to render their officers respect and obedience the Indians did likewise.   At Tadoussac "they render the honours to their Captain which they see rendered to Monsieur the Governor."[74]

With the possible exception of Membertou the most outstanding of the eastern Algonkian chiefs on the seventeenth century was Noel Tecouerimat, who, on account of his high character, eloquence, and capacity for leadership, retained the esteem of his fellows at Sillery and at the same time remained a good friend to the French.   He was anxious that his people should take their place and share in the benefits of the new society, and for forty years he occupied the foremost place in the councils of Sillery.   When he died in 1666 he was left without a successor for several years "according to the custom of the Savages."[75]   A war chief of Tadoussac was named as his successor by his relatives, and was given the deceased's name in order to "resuscitate" him. At this election there were present French, Algonkins, Montagnais, Micmac, Abenaki, Etechemins, Atticamegs, Nipissings and Hurons.   These people who had formerly been separate entities organized on a kinship basis, now became a corporate body having a political existence based on a territorial tenure in the feudal system of New France.[76]   When the Abenaki migrated to Canada and succeeded the Montagnais and others as the proprietors of Sillery they became subject to similar conditions.

North of the St. Lawrence the conflict of the native and the European legal systems was inherent in the meeting of the two cultures, and it approached a crisis at an early date.   In 1616 two Montagnais, having been beaten by a Frenchman, and "through some jealousy", killed two of the French.   When the crime was discovered the French determined to seek retribution through judicial proceedings, and all the Montagnais withdrew from fear of vengeance. After the custom of the country they offered compensation in the form of a gift of peltries.   When the French demanded the delivery of the two malefactors in order that the affair might be investigated, the Indians "found this procedure and mode of justice very strange and very difficult, inasmuch as they have no established judicial procedure among them, but only vengeance or compensation by gifts."[77]   When they considered the possibility of war with the French they decided to comply with the requirements.   Champlain made them feel the enormity of the crime.   By French law the malefactors were punishable by death.   Punishment did not extend beyond the guilty parties, and under French law the group was not responsible for the actions of its members as it was among the Montagnais.   The Indians were forced to recognize the French as judges, and the killer, considering the welfare of his people above that of himself, begged to be put to death immediately.   The French decided to accept this offer as an honourable amends and judicial atonement for three reasons.   First, they feared the Montagnais who greatly outnumbered them. Second, they would be forced to continue to hold intercourse in a state of

74. Jesuit Relations 29, 127.
75. Jesuit Relations 50, 119; 52, 223.
76. Jesuit Relations 52, 227.
77. Champlain (1) 3, 191.

perpetual distrust.   And third, "trade might be injured and the king's service impeded. . . . . ."[78]

On account of differences of this kind between the French and the Algonkians a degree of incertitude characterized their relations for the next two decades.   Even in the early 'thirties the French experienced a sense of insecurity in living with the Indians,[79] since, due to the corporate nature of Indian custom any Frenchman might be attacked and killed for the crime of any other Frenchman, irrespective of his innocence.   An instance of the conflict of systems occurred between the French and the Iroquois in 1633.   When the latter, one of their number having been injured, demanded compensation by presents, the French refused, offering instead to punish the transgressor in the presence of the assembled Indians.[80]

Although many of the laws passed by the sovereign council were designed to control Indian behaviour, they also served to protect the Indians from the French.   When the council summoned the chiefs on 21st April, 1644, to inform them that the crimes of violence and murder should be subject to the penalties of French law, they also enacted that creditors would be hindered from pillaging the Indians when payments for debts were not forthcoming, since the Indians at this time were prevented from hunting by the continuous state of war with the Iroquois.[81]   Nevertheless in 1646 the Indians showed a disposition to take the law in their own hands:

> "The savages of Sillery killed a cow of monsieur Nicholas, which had been in the corn; she was valued at 75 livres. The savages were summoned by Monsieur the governor to do justice in this matter, and he ordered that they should pay 6 Beavers, which was done,—with the assurance that when they should complain, Justice would be done them for the damage which the cows might have wrought in their corn." [82]

At a later date Courcelles found it necessary to enact "qu'on n'usurpe point les terres sur lesquelles ils sont habituez soubs pretexte qu'elles sont meilleures ou plus convenables aus Francois."[83]

On the other hand it was "a prudent act to govern these peoples by the very persons who belong to their nation."[84]   The crimes resulting from excessive drunkenness forced the Governor and chiefs in 1648 to prohibit the sale, purchase, or excessive consumption of spirituous liquors.   It was said that the chief who spoke the law to his people knew that the Indians would not recognize French jurisdiction, so he assured them that all the chiefs spoke the law, and that they would be given over to the penalties of the French if they transgressed it.   At both Tadoussac and Three Rivers severe penalties for drunkenness were exacted throughout the period.[85]

---

78. Champlain (1) 3, 188-200.
79. Jesuit Relations 4, 217.
80. Jesuit Relations 5 219-221. The case in point was Sillery as late as 1652. See Jesuit Relations 37, 163-165.
81. Edits, ordnances 2, 16.
82. Jesuit Relations 28, 225.
83. Collection de manuscrits relatifs 1, 175.
84. Jesuit Relations 33, 49.
85. Jesuit Relations 35, 237, 269.

Among a people who were thrown suddenly and violently from a communal to a highly competitive society, in which disease and drunkenness contributed to the collapse of their morale, and in which their leaders became, as time went on, mere agents for the enforcement of foreign and ill-understood laws, the failure of many individuals to adapt themselves to the changed conditions was bound to occur, and the recklessness of a few who found a desperate relief in drunkenness, murder and rape,[86] was offset by the melancholy and despair of the many who died for want of the will to live in a land which they could no longer call home.

---

86. Edits, ordnances 2, 111.

CHAPTER 9

SOCIAL DISINTEGRATION

1.

Issuing as a secondary set of characteristics from the Canadian fur-trade, closely interlocked with the economic disruption which followed the displacement of native materials by European, intimately related to the disintegrating factors consequent to the spread of drunkenness and disease, and inter-acting with the elements of political modification which were outlined in the preceding chapter, was the social disorder that existed in eastern Algonkian life which was especially conspicuous in the customs and manners appertaining to love and war. These apparently superficial changes in customs and manners testify to an internal psychological turmoil which resulted from divergent sets of social values within the colony, which dissolved the social solidarity of groups, and which dislocated the reproductive functions of formerly stablized communities, all of which were fraught with serious consequences for the survival capacity of the native peoples. These factors may be dealt with under three heads in an ascending order of importance as, modifications of a minor order, those relating to warfare, and those relating to the sexual life and its ramifications.

Those of a minor order may be grouped about the phenomenon of nervous control which underlay the phlegmatism that characterized Indian peoples when they were in the presence of cynical and self-superior Europeans. Generally speaking, this control did not pervade the lives of the people in their intercourse with each other, and the reserved and undemonstrative manner was a front which they assumed only in the presence of strangers. In their assemblies, however, the Indians allowed each other to speak without interruption, and they found it necessary to beg for silence in the presence of the French who were possessed of a tendency all to raise their voices in a disconcerting bedlam.[1] Moreover, the Indians expressed derision when the French lost their tempers and pointed to their own self-control by way of contrast.[2]

It was not long, however, before a change of behaviour occurred. In small communities such as those of the eastern Algonkians every person knew his allotted place, and custom had formulated the laws of behaviour with respect to address and etiquette in general, so that the actions of an individual were already there waiting for him when he became a member of society. The coming of the French introduced him to larger communities which were ordered on different lines, and the customary forms of behaviour were no longer opera-tive. Thus he lost his balance, and aspects of his temperament which had formerly been subject to a check became emphatic and demonstrative. The acquisition of swearing and blaspheming on the part of the Micmac was a

---

1. Jesuit Relations 5, 25.　　　　2. Jesuit Relations 6, 231.

symptom of this change.[3]   Under the influence of growing French immigration at Quebec and Tadoussac in the 'thirties and 'forties the Montagnais were subject to similar influences.[4]   The acquisition of European recreational pursuits,[5] and the sobriety of the religious ceremonies of the French cut across the formalities of social behaviour which were characteristic of eastern Algonkian society.

2.

More significant than the foregoing data were those relating to warfare. In primitive times wars were based primarily upon the blood feud.   When a man was killed it was the duty of his relatives to avenge his death, but with the competitive economic organization which was implicit in the fur-trade wars were waged increasingly to hold or capture markets.   Moreover, warfare in colonial times had a religious aspect which has generally been overlooked by historians who have treated of the native allies of the French.   The latter were slow to master the technique of bush fighting which was practised by the Indians to advantage.   The guerilla aspect of this technique which involved quick ambuscades and hasty retreats was looked upon as the dishonourable practice of desertion by the French.[6]   But it might have happened on occasion that a member of a war party had a dream in which he visited the land of the dead and learned from his relatives there, on whose behalf the war was waged, that success would not be forthcoming, in which case it would be well to desist.   It is possible[7] that more than one desertion might be attributed to that cause.

Possibly on account of their fear of supernatural beings which were known to haunt the forest fastnesses in the dark hours the Indians never attacked each other at night and the English established a tragic precedent when they fell upon and roasted alive a sleeping village of Pequots.[8]   The Montagnais practice of keeping no watchers about a sleeping camp was a marvel and a source of annoyance to Champlain, whose admonitions were of small avail, "and they used to say that we knew better than they did how to protect ourselves in every way, and that in time if we were to come and live in their country they would be able to learn these."[9]

Moreover, a certain consistency was to be observed in the Indian mind which tended to place a literal interpretation upon passages of scripture.   It was a well-known dictum of Christians that one should love one's enemies, and it was one of the consequences of the teachings of the missionaries that the warriorship of the Montagnais had begun to be undermined by 1646.[10]   A

---

3. LeClercq (2) 252.
4. Jesuit Relations 7, 255; 29, 129.
5. Culin 792.
6. Jesuit Relations 9, 235.
7. Jesuit Relations 32, 93.
8. Levy-Bruhl 326 draws attention to the fact that in some parts of the world the ghosts of dead ancestors act as sentinels at night.
9. Champlain (1) 51.
10. Jesuit Relations 29, 83.

similar tendency affected the Miscou Christians who were deterred from attacking their enemies "because they imagined, from their speech, that they prayed to God."[11]   This tendency had become so comprehensive by LeClercq's time that the Micmac seemed "to have lost entirely that warlike disposition through which their ancestors formerly conquered and triumphed gloriously over the most numerous peoples of New France."[12]   When wars were no longer waged to avenge the deaths of relatives the incentive to conquer was sensibly lessened.

It was an additional duty in wars in which ancestors were involved to torture and burn prisoners taken from the ranks of the enemy, a practice to which the French resorted on more than one occasion.   Nevertheless the missionaries were generally against what they deemed a barbarous custom, and the French could not discourage the Montagnais and Algonkins from torturing an Iroquois in 1636,[13] and again in 1642.[14]   Three years later the change was more pronounced when it was "perhaps fifty years since any Savage prisoner has been so gently treated".   The women and girls did not rush naked into the water to seize the prisoner's spoils.   "Such unseemly conduct is banished from the residence of St. Joseph."[15]   Although the burning of prisoners has been recorded after this date its occurrence had become sporadic,[16] and in 1663 the Sillery Algonkians, instead of torturing Iroquois prisoners, conducted them into the chapel, "invited them to prayers, urged them to receive baptism, and intoned Canticles of devotion in their presence. . . ."   Having been baptized "reasons of state condemned them to death, but Christian piety exempted them from the stake—two being despatched with the musket; . . ."[17]   The softening influence of Christianity broke down the fighting spirit of the Indians, and the same religion through other channels tended to obliterate the primitive motive for warfare on behalf of deceased relatives, and hastened the dissolution of the solidarity of the Algonkian bands.

3.

Just as in the customs relating to warfare, so in those which were set around the sexual life can a disintegration be discerned.   Of the sex customs that were introduced from Europe, the kiss is of especial interest because it seems to have had no counterpart in the aboriginal life.   Its motivation was varied and its spread was symbolic of the change, just as were the data of a minor order which have already been dealt with.   Finally, in some cases it represented a perversion of the normal sexual functions.

Although the kiss of salutation, the sexual kiss, and the religious kiss may be distinguished on the basis of motivation, reverence and respect may accompany all three; but especially present are these attitudes in the religious

11. Jesuit Relations 28, 35.
12. LeClercq (2) 266.   There were, of course, economic reasons for this change.
13. Jesuit Relations 9, 263.
14. Jesuit Relations 22, 55.
15. Jesuit Relations 27, 237.
16. Jesuit Relations 30, 193.
17. Jesuit Relations 48, 111.

kiss.   Early in the century the Montagnais learned to kiss the hands of those who baptized them, and sometimes intractable Indians were made to kiss the ground as a penance.[18]   On the other hand, the kissing of a crucifix by the converted Montagnais was an act which could be readily comprehended in terms of their own primitive category of mystical transference of power by contact:[19]

> "The Catholic Church enjoins the duty of kissing relics, the Gospels, the Cross, consecrated candles and palms, the hands of the clergy and the vestments and utensils of the liturgy. . . . The altar is regarded as typical of Christ, and as such is kissed by the celebrant." [20]

In the Roman Catholic custom of kissing relics and sacred objects Crawley saw some of the primitive sense of responsibility by contact which was rendered stronger by the invocation of the name of the deity.   What had possibly become a social atavism to the seventeenth century European was restored to its original value by the North American Indians.

Standing apart from the religious kiss, but displaying a reverence sometimes comparable to it, was the kiss of salutation which was not always separable from the sexual kiss.   We have seen that the kiss was introduced for the first time among the Micmac in the time of Lescarbot.   Although the Eskimo and the Blackfoot were said to have practised the olfactory kiss,[22] it is possible that that recorded among the Plains Indians in the nineteenth century was derived from European sources.   At any rate early in the seventeenth century kissing and bowing in the French fashion became common among the bands at Quebec and Tadoussac, who formerly had met and parted without gesture.[23]   Evidence as to how the Montagnais acquired the habit of kissing is at hand:

> "It is not the custom of the Savages to salute each other with a kiss; but as Madame de la Peltrie quite often embraces and kisses these poor girls on meeting them, these good creatures imagine . . . that they must imitate her in order to do right." [24]

So definite has this trait become among the Cree who dwell today to the northeast of lake Winnipeg that now it is a duty for every man to kiss every woman he meets on New Year's day.[25]

As Lescarbot has said, the sexual kiss became popular among the Micmac in his time.   He represents it as a refinement of civilization which the crude natives had not known before, nor were they known to caress each other in courtship.   Where the kiss remained an act of reverence for a loved one it might be said to have maintained its place as a legitimate function.   Even where it was used to stimulate action as a preliminary to the act of sex, as was often the case,[26] it can be regarded as having had social value.   But where it became an end in itself, a compensatory act induced by the repression of the normal functioning of sex, it assumed the proportion of a perversion that was

18. Jesuit Relations 9, 61; 24, 27.
19. Jesuit Relations 24, 59.
20. Crawley 133-134. Ellis, H. 4, 221.
22. Crawley 125.

23. Jesuit Relations 11, 227.
24. Jesuit Relations 20, 251; 16, 21.
25. Chamberlain (16) 182.
26. Jesuit Relations 8, 165.

scarcely inseparable from the imposed modesty and the segregation of the sexes in religious institutions that was attempted throughout the period.

Although in some cases the disposal of body excretions was not relegated to privacy,[27] in others it partook of the nature of a religious rite, the distinguishing feature of which was seclusion during the process. This especially applied to the period of menstruation in women, although it was extended to other functions.[28] But in general there were marked differences between European and Indian modesty, with respect to both motivation and manifestation. The Indians "allege that Nakednefs is no infraction upon the Meafures of Decency, any otherwife than that it is contrary to the Cuftom of the Europeans, and condemned by the notion that they have of it."[29] The difference in motivation may be summarized by saying that the Indians placed the highest value on the things of this world, namely, food and sex, which were the prerequisites of physical well-being; whereas the medieval church postulated the doctrine of original sin, which involved the belief that man's physical nature was fundamentally bad, that the suppression of the ecstacies of the flesh, with the mortification of the body, was the only sure way to the life of eternal salvation in the hereafter. But the garment of otherworldliness did not fit the figure of the Indian. Those who took part in a war feast at Three Rivers in 1644, which featured the dance of the naked girls, received corporal punishment from the governor. By methods such as this a new sense of sin seized the minds of the natives.[30] On one occasion—

> "A young Christian Savage, having awakened in the night, and seeing a woman immodestly covered in her sleep, was seized with fright, —Not knowing how to warn this woman, for fear of putting her to confusion, he bethought himself of roughly beating a dog, and making it yelp aloud, so that the woman on waking should again cover herself properly." [31]

The fear of damnation was most marked among those girls and women who were segregated in convents at Sillery, Quebec and elsewhere, by the Ursulines and others. The horror of unchastity as a means to Hell fire required protection in clothing and taboos of action. The sex life was denied and the impulse was sublimated into religious fervour, which, in itself, might assume sexual characteristics depending upon the circumstances of the case.[32] The condemnation of sexuality involved the glorification of the Virgin, and contempt was felt for those who exercised sexual functions.[33] Thus the chastity of the girls at Sillery was protected by an old woman, who acted in a semi-official capacity.

> "When the young men come back from the war, she carefully assembles all the girls and locks them in at night, or shuts them up in the houses that we have built for them in the manner of the French, or in the granaries where they keep their provisions." [34]

---

27. LeClercq (2) 253; Jesuit Relations 44, 297.
28. Denys 407-410 and 443-444.
29. Lahontan 2, 417.
30. Jesuit Relations 25, 189.
31. Jesuit Relations 20, 177.
32. Ellis, H. 1, 39.
33. Ellis, H. 3, 192.
34. Jesuit Relations 25, 183.

> "They are so modest that, if one of them has her throat even a little uncovered, the others tell her that she will drive away her good Angel. This is now so accepted among them that, to warn a girl to keep within the bounds of decorum, they say to her, "Be careful that your good Angel does not leave you;" and the girl to whom this remark is made looks herself over, to see that there is nothing unseemly." [35]

> "These children have such a regard for purity that, when they go out walking, they avoid meeting men, and they are so careful to cover themselves with decency, that their deportment is very different from the custom of the Savages." [36]

One wept when she was reproached after a Frenchman had led her by the hand, "being greatly afraid that it would prevent her from being a Virgin." Thus virginity became largely a mystical conception. Moreover, chastity became a bar to miscegenation between the two races:

> "Last night this crucifix saved my soul, which a Frenchman endeavoured to ruin by seeking to ravish my honour through his own unchasity. He took me by the hand, and, drawing me to one side, he made me enter a house; then, suddenly and violently, Threw me upon a bed." [37]

The woman accused the Frenchman of wanting to re-crucify Jesus, and warned him of eternal damnation until he desisted.

This new sense of sin manifested itself conspicuously in the mortification of the flesh by flagellation, which was a manifestation of the sex impulse only insofar as sex was a symbol of the flesh, against which the ascetic wrath was directed. It can by no means always be classed as a perversion,[38] but may be regarded as an expression of religious emotion which has sprung from the suppression of the sexual emotions.[39]   At Sillery the action was definitely associated with sex. The mere idea of changing his wife seemed so great a crime to an Indian of that settlement that he slipped into a room near the chapel, and with a rope he beat himself so hard over the body that the noise reached the ears of the priest who forbade him such a severe penance.[40]   At the last-mentioned place public beatings with a discipline of knots and cords occurred. The innocent shared with the guilty. Even the children, who had been exempt from chastisement in pre-European times, were made to approach the altar, their garments were removed and they were whipped. Mothers struck their children with rosaries while they were still at the breast, till the priest forced them to put an end to these excesses.[42]

We have, then, three stages in the adaptation of the inmates to their new cloistered environment. First, where the sexual emotions were sublimated into the religious and where hope was sustained by a belief in the life hereafter, complete adaptation may be said to have occurred. Second, where the revulsion of feeling against the flesh failed to be sublimated as in the first case those with a predisposition towards masochistic expression gave themselves up to flagellation, the will to live lapsed, and despair and untimely death

35. Jesuit Relations 19, 51.
36. Jesuit Relations 22, 185.
37. Jesuit Relations 43, 229.
38. Ellis, H. 3, 129, 136.

39. Ellis, H. 1, 325.
40. Jesuit Relations 22, 67.
42. Jesuit Relations 27, 193-201; 5, 197.

ensued. This may be looked upon as partial adaptation and was one of the causes of the declining birth rate and resulting depopulation. The third stage, that of complete inadaptation, was characterized by failure to integrate the personality with the new environment, and was more directly sexual in its expression. Such compensatory activities as masturbation and sodomy were probably not unknown,[43] and orgiastic outbreaks with a reversion to the primitive state may have occurred. Herein lay an additional cause of depopulation.

4.

The conflict between the eastern Algonkian and the European moral standards with respect to marriage was a conspicuous feature of the contact of the two peoples. The influence of the contact may be traced with respect to the pre-marital state, courtship, marriage, divorce, and polygymy. Champlain is authority for the statement that a degree of sexual promiscuity was customary between Montagnais adolescents, but in the light of recent researches it is possible that this may have been limited to cross-cousins. On the other hand the Micmac appear to have had a higher esteem for chastity than the Montagnais,[44] although it is probable that throughout the area adolescence was the period of greatest sexual licence. Not only was this custom taken advantage of by French traders, modifying their standards of living considerably, but the loose morals of the French served as a bad example to the Indians who were accustomed to daily condemnation of these practices by their missionaries.[45] The exemplary conduct of the priests, who were almost always men of austere morals, contrasted with that of the trading class, and exerted a profound influence upon the Indians throughout the period. Moral lapses on the part of priests were virtually unknown. Generally speaking the Indians appear to have been as strict in courtship as the French and did not indulge in the caresses which were customary among the latter. When a Christian girl at Sillery was reprimanded for having received the caresses of a pagan she replied, "I am not French; I have seen Frenchmen trifling with girls, caressing them, but this is not our custom, . . ."[47] On the other hand, drunkenness seems to have disposed the Indians to rape, the frequency of which called forth restrictive legislation on the part of the French, although in the eyes of the Indians intoxication automatically freed them from blame.[48] Drunkenness moreover was said to have accounted for an outbreak of indecent conduct at Tadoussac in 1643, and in order to eliminate secret immoral practices the neophytes called for a public confession on the part of all the inhabitants. The night visits which suitors were accustomed to make to their prospective

---

43. Pitt-Rivers 64. Though no cases of these perversions were reported among the eastern Algonkians in the 17th century, among the Illinois in the 17th century and the Nascopi in the 19th hermaphrodites were reported. There is, however, no reason to connect them with European influences.
44. LeClercq (2) 251.
45. Denys 450-451.
47. Jesuit Relations 18, 141.
48. Jesuit Relations 48, 227; Boucher 52.

brides came under the surveillance of the Jesuits who advised the Indians to substitute day visits and who constituted themselves as intermediaries in courtship.[49]   At Quebec the priest "heard on good authority that some shameless women, who had approached some men at night and solicited them to do evil in secret received for an answer only these words: 'I believe in God. . . . he forbids such actions. . . '"   When Island Algonkins solicited Christian girls they were referred to the Jesuit Fathers, and were told that "they could not expect to marry any Christian girl unless they were baptized . . . but unfortunately some of them, when far away from our settlements, marry at the solicitation of their relatives. . . We have confirmed some in their marriages since baptism."[50]   Thus baptism tended among the more sedentary Indians to displace skill in oratory, the hunt, war, and leadership, besides personal physical attraction, as a qualification for matrimony.   These night visits which were an essential feature of courtship were prevented at Tadoussac by the use of locks, door-bells, and sentinels to protect the segregated girls.[51]   At Quebec a young woman who talked with her suitor against her parents' wishes was condemned to be flogged by a family council.   This punishment was the first of its kind among the eastern Algonkians.   It occurred in 1642.   The suitor complained to his fellow pagans at Three Rivers of the ill-treatment which he had received, and they threatened to attack the Christian settlements.   Montmagny declared that those who attacked the Christian Indians also attacked him.   "Such a sermon preached in a Fort armed with canon had its effect."[52]   The influence upon marriage of the segregation of Indian girls in convents and homes was far-reaching.   In the first place, in a society in which cross-cousin marriage was operative, it restricted the number of potential brides, which must have provoked resentment and a feeling of direct loss on the part of the bridegrooms.   And in the second place, the resulting shortage of women placed a severe strain upon sexual morality.   Moreover, the new division between pagan and Christian cut across the old political divisions between the separate bands and tribes, and thus they were distinguished by divergent sets of social standards.

The Roman Catholic church of course never recognized the validity of the Indian marriages, and in their eyes it was necessary that their ceremony should be accreted to the simple Indian rite, the latter being worthless and contrary to the laws of God.[53]   The Catholic influence was to be discerned at Sillery in 1642 in the method of proposal which has both Christian and pagan elements.

> "They paint on a piece of bark a young man and a maiden, holding each other by the hand, in the position that they assume in church when they get married; and the swain sends this picture to his mistress by one of his friends." [54]

Among the Malecite in the last decade of the century it was necessary that a man should consult the Jesuit and the relations of the girl before he was

---

49. Jesuit Relations 24, 37-41.
50. Jesuit Relations 16, 63.
51. Jesuit Relations 22, 231-233.

52. Jesuit Relations 22, 125-127.
53. Rand XXXI.
54. Jesuit Relations 22, 71.

allowed to marry,[55] but it must be confessed that a long interval existed between the aboriginal and the Christian marriage ceremony among those bands who were accustomed to wander over their hunting territories for the greater part of the year and to appear at the settlements only during the summer season. The Micmac, who were married in their own fashion already, were forced to travel a long distance to be married by the curé at Port Royal, who moreover required an interpreter as he did not understand their language.[56]

It is interesting to note the statement of several missionaries to the effect that married couples lived for several months in a state of chastity after the ceremony and that they might separate if they were distasteful to each other.[57] It is not clear whether this referred to the married state or the period of service rendered by the suitor to his prospective father-in-law. This custom still prevailed among the Christian Montagnais at Quebec in 1647,[58] but Denys spoke as if it had fallen into disuse among the Micmac in his time.[59] Both economic and religious factors may have made it impracticable.

It was not so difficult for the missionaries to get the Indians to submit to Christian marriage rites as it was to make them understand that it was contrary to the law of God to dissolve the bond. To them marriage was not bound by an irrevocable decree, but the free and equal parties to the contract could dissolve it at will of either. ". . . if any natural antipathy exists between husband and wife . . they separate from one another, in order to seek elsewhere the peace and union which they cannot find together."[60] But in spite of the ease of divorce among the eastern Algonkians it was not as frequent an occurrence as might be supposed. Exchanges of gifts and the force of public opinion exercised a stabilizing influence.[61] The value of doweries was increased by the French since, as LeJeune said, "a husband will not so readily leave a wife who brings him a respectable dowery." In 1638 the Company gave four arpents of cleared land to two Indian girls who were to marry Christians.[62] On the other hand it was frequently found necessary to threaten women with prison if they should leave their husbands. Sometimes the women submitted, at others they preferred the degradation of imprisonment to the companionship of their former mates. On one occasion a woman was kept for twenty-four hours without fire or blanket, and with scarcely any food. On another a woman who fled from her husband was threatened with being chained by the foot for four days and nights without food.[63] There is no doubt that women occupied a more degraded position in the settlements of Christians than among the wandering pagans, where divorce was relatively easy. "When they are at a distance of two or three hundred leagues in the woods, resort to the Pastor is a very onerous condition."

Of all the Algonkian customs the missionaries found polygyny the

55. Gyles 44.
56. Diereville 82-83.
57. Jesuit Relations 19, 69; 37, 155.
58. Jesuit Relations 31, 169.
59. Denys 407.
60. LeClercq (2) 242.
61. Boucher 56-57.
62. Jesuit Relations 14, 263.
63. Jesuit Relations 18, 107; 22, 83; 24, 47-49; 28, 205.

most difficult to eradicate, and in spite of all their arguments against it,[65] the Indians could give reasons for the continuance of the practice.   As an Algonkian said in 1639 of the new marriage conditions:

> "I do not fear drunkenness, nor eat-all feasts, nor the consultation of demons, nor our songs, nor pride, nor theft, nor murder; but I do fear women. God commands us to marry but one wife, and, if she leaves us, not to take another; behold me, then, obliged to remain single, for our women have no sense. To live among us without a wife is to live without help, without home, and to be always wandering." [66]

Another declared that the commandments of the Christians conflicted with each other.   One stipulated that one must not kill, another that one must keep only one wife.   He loved one wife and had sent the others away but they continually returned, so that to kill them was the only way to get rid of them, he said.[67]   The strain on the husband in his attempt to conform to his own and the new morality at one and the same time with respect to polygyny was one of the greatest induced by the contact of the two races. Moreover, often one wife was not sufficient to shoulder the burden of work which fell to her lot, so that help-mates were highly esteemed.   On the other hand the more wives there were the more mouths there were to feed.   Nevertheless the custom was adhered to throughout the entire area during the greater part of the period.   Although those who had kept two wives, contrary to the vows made at their baptism, did not dare to appear at Tadoussac in 1670, sixteen years later the missionary could say that none of the regular visitors to that port had more than one wife, and all were regularly constituted church marriages.[68]   Nevertheless polygyny was reported among the Algonkins at Three Rivers in 1647, among the Atticamegs in 1651, the Porcupines and Abenaki in 1652, the Papinachois in 1667 although it was not recorded among those of Lake Manicougan three years earlier, and among the Miramichi Micmac in 1677.[69]   There is reason to believe that polygyny continued long after the Jesuits had left the mission field among the eastern Algonkians.

5.

Of major importance as a factor of disintegration, equal if not greater than the new social values which were made current among the Indians by the missionaries, was the sexual relation which developed between the Indians and the French.   It is commonly supposed, particularly among English-speaking critics, that the French Canadians inter-married freely with the Indians and that the former therefore bear a large infusion of Indian blood in their veins.   It is proposed to examine this belief somewhat closely in order to ascertain what degree of truth is inherent in it, insofar as it relates to the

---

65. See for example Jesuit Relations 11, 265.
66. Jesuit Relations 16, 161-163.
67. Jesuit Relations 11, 177.
68. Jesuit Relations 53, 85; 63, 249.
69. Jesuit Relations 49, 55; 51, 75; 38, 35 seq; 37, 215; 37, 59; 31, 257; LeClercq (2) 176.

eastern Algonkians.   It is also proposed to trace the disintegrating influence of miscegenation on the Indians themselves.

An examination of the sources readily shows that certain obstacles stood in the way of miscegenation between the French and the Indians.   First of all there was the linguistic barrier, which was more formidable to the rank and file than to the Jesuits.   But even they had difficulty in mastering the Indian languages.   LeJeune wrote in 1636: "It is my decisive opinion that for lack of a complete knowledge of the language we have not yet even begun to unfold the grandeurs of our belief."[70]   On the other hand some knowledge of the native languages was necessary to the trade, and it is interesting to note that the Indians of Quebec and Three Rivers were borrowing and corrupting French words in the fourth and fifth decades of the century.[71]   As a result of social intercourse "there is a certain jargon between the French and the Savages, which is neither French nor Savage; and yet when the French use it, they think they are using the Savage tongue, and the Savages, in using it, think they are using good French."[72]   But the Indians in general were slow to learn French.   As late as 1666 Talon wrote to Colbert recommending that they be taught French so that it would not be necessary to learn the native languages in order to communicate with the Indians.[73]   Sexual relations have a habit of transcending linguistic differences but nevertheless the linguistic factor is worthy of consideration.

More far-reaching as a barrier was the general cultural divergence between the two groups.   Here again, heterogeneity of manners and habits does not necessarily preclude relations of a sexual nature, but the theory is submitted that differences of this kind would make individuals belonging to divergent groups less attractive to each other and less capable of social intercourse on a basis of equality.   Shortly after the restoration of New France by the Treaty of St. Germain en Laye the Jesuits began their educational programme among the Montagnais whereby French and Indian children were mingled in the school in order that assimilation might be accelerated and Christianity inculcated.   It was felt necessary to teach the girls as well as the boys because the latter would ultimately marry the former and would lapse into barbarism if this were not undertaken.[74]   It is said that the Montagnais girls were fond of the French and took pride in imitating them.[75]   But the seminary for boys was abandoned after five years and the Jesuits concentrated their energy on the Sillery and Three Rivers segregations.   Although Eastman maintains that segregation was adopted because the French children were in danger of becoming perverted by the contact, Marie de l'Incarnation stated in 1644 that it was because the Indians were generally more devout than the French and that segregation was effected so that they would not imitate the morals of certain of the colonists.[76]

---

70. Jesuit Relations 9, 89.
71. Jesuit Relations 5, 59; 31, 265.
72. Jesuit Relations 5, 113-115.
73. Eastman 117.

74. Jesuit Relations 5, 145.
75. Jesuit Relations 11, 223.
76. Eastman 115; Marie de l'I. 35

This policy was continued until New France became a royal province in 1663 when the home government made it a point of colonial policy to assimilate the native peoples.   In 1666 Colbert wrote "to try to civilize the Algonquins . . . . and the other savages who have embraced Christianity, and dispose them to come and settle them in community with the French, live with them, and bring up their children in their manners and customs."[77]   He recommended that the French and the Indians should be made one people by means of intermarriages.[78]   In the following year he urged Talon to mingle the Christian Indians with the French "in order that, having but one law and one master, they may form only one people and one blood."[79]   Not only did the minister urge the intendant to adopt these measures but the king wrote to Laval deploring that so few of the Indians had adopted the French mode of living.   The children should be given a French Catholic education with the end that the two groups should be united into "one same people."[80]   Accordingly, Laval founded a seminary in 1668 in which the instructions of the king were to be carried out,[81] but although the modern Laval University grew out of this project, as far as the Indians were concerned the effort did not last a decade.[82]   In the same year in which the seminary was founded the Jesuits made concessions to the king's wishes.   "We have begun also to pay some attention to our Savages here. . . . "   Laval and the Jesuits had "already placed a number of little Savage boys in their Seminaries, to be brought up there with the French children."   Talon intended to send five Indian girls to the Seminary of the Ursulines.[83]

During Duchesneau's administration the king advised mixing the Indians among the French in small numbers to bring about "a single body of people", but existing missions were favoured.[84]   In writing to Colbert, November 2nd, 1672, Frontenac condemned the policy of the Jesuits in no uncertain terms.   In spite of the fact that the Indians about Quebec continually frequented the French settlements hardly one could speak French.   The Jesuits "devoient songer, en rendant les Sauvages sujets de Jesus-Christ, de les rendre aussy sujets du Roy".   The greater number of the missions were pure mockeries, and the Jesuits "songent autant à la conversion du castor qu'à celle des ames".[85]   Frontenac again reiterated his views to the king on November 6th, 1679.[86]   During the intendancy of De Meulles the most concrete effort to promote assimilation was made.   The Sulpicians and the nuns of Montreal were commended for their success in civilizing the Iroquois, and the Jesuits and Ursulines of Quebec incurred nothing but opprobrium. De Meulles wrote to the minister, November 12, 1682:

> "Il seroit encore fort à propos que le Roy se servest de la maison nomme les Islets proche des Recollects pour en faire une manufacture de fille sauvages, et au lieu de les faire instruire aux ursulines ou elles

77. Eastman 114.
78. Eastman 119.
79. Eastman 117.
80. Eastman 118.
81. Jesuit Relations 52, 47.
82. Barbeau (9) and (10).
83. Jesuit Relations 51, 173.
84. Eastman 173.
85. Decouverts et etablissements I, 247.
86. Collection de manuscrits relatifs 1, 268.

> n'aprennent qu'a prier Dieu et a parler francais, ce qu'elles ont oublié en si peu de temps que des lors qu'elles ont espouse quelques sauvages on les voit peu prier Dieu et jamais parler francais mais au lieu de les instruire d'une manière qui ne convient nullement aux sauvages il faudrait leur aprendre à vivre à la facon des villageoises de France, c'est a dire scavoir filler, coudre, tricotter, et avoir soin des Bestiau, et pour cette effet on en prendroit un certain nombre que l'on auroit soin d' instruire tous les jours a filler le file dont on se serviroit pour les toilles de la manufacture, coudre tout ce qui seroit necessaire a leurs usages, et d'autres a preparer la laine pour faire des estoffes, et on pourroit prendre deux ou trois tour à tour qui serviroient au fermier huit jours tous les mois a donner à manger à toutes sortes de bestiaux, tirer les vaches, et autres choses de la campagne, estant eslevez dans cet esprit, je ne doute point qu'estant marriez a des sauvages elles . . . . . . a leurs maris les engager a s'abiller, se nourrir, et vivre comme nous, pour leurs oster avec le temps cet esprit de sauvage, et lorsque l'on mariroit les d. filles en leur donnant une vache, un cochon, du bled, et un peu de grain de chanvre, ils se feroient une petite habitation dont ils pourroient subsister; en eslevant ces sauvagesses de cette manière on ne laisseroit pas encore de leur aprendre à lire à escrire et leur croyances il ne faudroit faire consister le revenue de la ferme qu'en nourriture de bestiaux le lieu estant fort propre pour en eslever dont on nourriroit les ouvriers, on pourroit faire aussy labourer quelques terres pour avoir du fourrage." [87]

From this recommendation three facts of some importance emerge. First, the French were more inspired with the idea of emulating supposed Spanish achievements in the Indies than with drafting their policy to meet local needs. Second, the recommendation may be taken as typical of the attitude of the home government, and indicates that no intelligent treatment of the native problem was to be forthcoming in the near future. For instance, in praising the successes of the Sulpicians among the Iroquoians in the neighborhood of Montreal, who were a sedentary people and whose social and political organization was highly complex, by its very nature facilitating adaptability, no allowance was made for the fact that the Jesuits were confronted with the infinitely more difficult task of bringing the Algonkian bands all the way from a wandering and hunting economy to a sedentary and agricultural mode of life. Third, the recommendation to set up manufactories in which the Indians should be employed indicates that among them the fur-trade had ceased to be a prime concern of their economic life, and that now, with the depletion of the beaver and other means of sustenance, they were to become wards of the king at a minimum cost to the home government.

The ministry concorded with the view of De Meulles and two years later proceeded to act upon his recommendations to aid the Montreal missions. On the 10th April, 1684, the minister wrote:

> "Sa Mejeste a accorde 500 livres pour les Sauvagesses de la Montagne de Montreal. Elle ne veut pas qu'il les soient mises aux Ursulines et elle a donné ordre de faire passer trois femmes pour leur apprendre à tricoter et trois autres pour leur apprendre à filer et à faire de la dentelle afin de pouvoir introduire ces manufactures dans le pais qui seront avantageuses à la colonie." [88]

---

87. C11A 6 DeMeulles 12th November 1682.
88. Collection Moreau de St. Mery 4 April 10th 1684.

Although Denonville was not in accord with De Meulles' proposals his own recommendations were only partially sound. In 1685 he wrote to the minister:

> "Ces dereglemens . . . se trouvent bien plusgrands dans les familles de ceux qui sont Gentilshommes, ou qui se sont mis sur le pied de le vouloir estre par faineantise ou par vanite n'ayans aucune resource pour subsister q' les bois, car n'estans pas acoutumez a tenir la charrue, la pioche et la hache, toute leur resource n'estant que le fuzil, il faut qu'ils passent leurs vies dans les bois. . . . L'on a creu bien longtemps que l'aproche des sauvages de nos habitations estoit un bien tres considerable pour acoutumer ces peuples a vivre comme nous et a s'instruire de notre relligion, je m'apercoy . . . que tout le contraire en est arrivé car au lieu de les acoutumer a nos Loys, je vous assure qu'ils nous communiquent fort tout ce qu'ils ont de plus mechant, et ne prennent aux mesmes q.'ce qu'il y a de mauvais et de vitieux en Nous. . . .
>
> Je trouve tout ce que nous avons de sauvages establis dans des bourgades comme a Sillery, Lorette, au sault de la prairie, a la Montagne de Montreal, tout cela Monseigneur est en verité tenu dans une discipline et, une regle a faire plaisir a voir. Il n'y a pas asseeurement de ville et de village en France si bien regle, qu'en tous ces lieux la; tant qu'il n'y a pas d'ivrognes qui arivent de nos habitations; Mais . . . a l'egard des autres sauvages qui sont vagabonds et errans autour des Seigneuries particuliers sans estre rassemblez en bourgades comme les autres, vous ne scauriez croire Monseigneur le tort que cela fait à la dissipline de la colonie, car non seulement les enfants des Seigneurs l'acoutument à vivre en libertinage comme eux, mais mesme abusent des filles et femmes sauvagesses qu'il entretienent avec eux, et menent a leurs chasses dans les bois, ou souvent ils souffrent la faim jusques à manger leurs chiens." [89]

Thus, he opposed assimilation on the ground that the two races adopted the worse aspects of each other's culture. Those who roamed over the seigniories were given to excessive drunkenness and the sons of seigneurs imitated their nomadic life and debauched the Indian women. He made no distinction whatever between the Iroquoian and Algonkian villages and seems to have assumed that the teaching of music, trades, and agriculture, including the care of pigs and poultry, all of which were conspicuous features of the former, also obtained among the Algonkians.[90] The Abenaki alone succeeded in adapting themselves to the new method of living.[91] Among the Micmac the seeds sown by the Jesuits in the seventeenth century were still bearing fruit in the segregations of the nineteenth century.[92] The conclusion is that the missionaries failed to assimilate the eastern Algonkians to French civilization and that the cultural divergence continued throughout the period to be a barrier of some importance to recognized marriage between individuals of the two races. On the other hand it may have been that the cultural barrier to marriages which were recognized by the French fostered relations of an illicit nature, although this casual relationship cannot be postulated with a great degree of certainty. Besides linguistic and general cultural differences, a third factor, which may have varied in time and place between promoting and hindering miscegenation, was that of physical differences. That European immigrants have found native women

89. CllA 7 Denonville to the minister 1685.
90. Eastman 241. Author does not draw attention to these distinctions.
91. Lahontan 1, 48-49.
92. Rand XIII.

often pleasing and sometimes beautiful may be ascribed in a large part to the absence of women of their own kind in the new country,[93] and with the growth of settlement the native woman has generally become a receding factor. Considering the shortage of French women in the seventeenth century, the attractiveness of these to the Indian men need not detain us at length. In spite of punitive laws which might indicate frequency, the actual instances of Indians raping French women are rare in the records of the time, and so far as the area under consideration is concerned there is little ground for the belief held by Ellis that the most intelligent of the natives preferred European women to their own.[94]   On the other hand, in spite of the fact that sometimes Indian girls preferred their own kind to French mates,[95] Lahontan stated that they preferred the French on account of the virility of the latter.[96]   The comparitive sexual periodicity between Europeans and non-Europeans constitutes a problem which might well repay further study.   The need for further co-ordination between the historical data and research into the question of the relative periodicity of Indian men and women is evident.   All that can be said at present is that Lahontan's statement was probably in the main correct, and is partly substantiated by the fact that the Indians, in order to compete successfully in courtship with their French rivals "pull their beards out in order to be more agreeable to the women.   I have seen," said a missionary in 1627, "only three or four who had not done so, and this but recently in imitation of the French. . . ."[97]   Physical differences then were not, in the light of factors determining the contrary, a barrier of major importance to the miscegenation of the two races.

A fourth obstacle to miscegenation between the French and the Indians lay in the new sense of sin which had a special application to sexuality, which was inculcated by the missionaries, and which has already been dealt with in another connection.   The women of Tadoussac in 1686 successfully resisted certain French libertines although they were offered brandy as an inducement.[98] Of the Indians in general who frequented the French settlements Lahontan remarked:

> "Tis true the French, being uncapable to diftinguifh between the Married and Unmarried Women, fometimes make their addrefs to the former, when they find them alone in the woods, or when they walk out into the Fields; but upon such occafions they always receive Anfwer; 'The Fiend which is before mine Eyes hinders me to fee thee'." [99]

On the other hand there were certain factors of a circumstancial nature which induced favourable conditions for intermarriage and miscegenation between members of the two races. First, financial outlay, designed to favour intermarriage, was not unknown. At Quebec in 1639 a worthy and pious person

---

93. Ellis, H. 4, 151-153.
94. Ellis, H. 4, 153.
95. Mary de l'I. 24; Jesuit Relations 30, 157.
96. Lahontan 2, 455. He says elsewhere, 2, 416, that the Indian women did not usually tempt the French.
97. Jesuit Relations 4, 205.
98. Jesuit Relations 63, 251.
99. Lahontan 2, 461.

gave a hundred écus "for the wedding of a young Savage girl sought in marriage by a young Frenchman of very good character".[100] Second, the French men greatly exceeded in number the women throughout the period and probably throughout the whole area under consideration. Even in the settled area on the St. Lawrence there were relatively few women as late as 1653 when a shipload arrived in the colony. Most of these were married soon after their arrival, and it was felt that this would add to the stability and strengthen the morale of the colony.[101] But anything like an equality of the sexes did not obtain until Talon imported "His Majesty's Maidens" after 1665. Moreover, it is probable that even in the settled area the great toll taken in war left many Indian women at Sillery and elsewhere without mates. For Acadia, which was less thickly settled than the St. Lawrence valley, the census of 1685 is suggestive:[102]

> **French:** Men 1791, women 1672. Difference 119. Adolescent boys 1522, adolescent girls 988. Difference 534. Total of males not provided for, 653.
>
> **Indians:** Men 230, women 425. Difference 195. Adolescent boys 113, adolescent girls 90. Difference 23. Total of females not provided for 172.

Thus, it is seen that in the case of the French there was a surplus of males, and in the case of the Indians there was a surplus of females. Although statistics taken at that time may have been far from accurate, the above figures may serve as circumstancial evidence that a degree of miscegenation occurred in Acadia in the seventeenth century. Moreover, it must not be forgotten that the French, largely on account of the relationship between their material culture and that of the Indian, were regarded as superior beings by the latter. For this reason it is not improbable that Europeans were desired by the Indian women, as was the case in Mexico; and conversely, the Indians having been inferior in the eyes of the French, the latter would have had few, if any, qualms about seducing their women.

Let us now proceed to summarize the documentary evidence at hand in order that the number of actual marriages may be ascertained. First, one meets with surprise the statement that at Quebec between the years 1608 and 1667 only three marriages were recorded between French and Indians, since this was the very period in which French women were most scarce. Moreover, Roy has found the record of only one inter-racial marriage at Three Rivers.[103] The first marriage between a French man and a Montagnais at Quebec occurred in 1644, and two French married two Huron girls somewhat later in the century.[104] It is not certain that these were the same as those mentioned by Roy.

At Tadoussac intermarriage appears to have been somewhat more extensive, but negligible when the total population is considered. It did not, however, commence early, for in 1636 the French there were not allied to

---

100. Jesuit Relations 16, 35.
101. Jesuit Relations 41, 185.
102. Collection de manuscrits relatifs 1, 350-351.
103. Roy, P.G. 56-58.
104. Jesuit Relations 5, 288; 47, 289.

In Three Rivers church records
1648 Pierre Boucher married an algonkian
1657 Pierre Coue dit Lafleur married an algonkian
1683 Louis Coue dit Montour married a Sokoki
among others

the Montagnais by any marriages.   The chief of the port complained that although the missionaries took their children from them to be educated he did not know of any family that kept a French man with it.[105]   On the other hand it was recorded in 1660 that Albanel had married a Frenchman to a Christian Montagnais girl without publishing the bans, and the recording of the incident implies that if the proceeding had been regular it would not have been mentioned.[106]   In 1671 Frontenac wrote that the contraction of marriages between the traders and the Indians at Tadoussac was not conducive to the well-being of the trade.[107]   When in 1686 Crepieul drew up rules to be followed by missionaries among the Montagnais he implied that all was not running smoothly with those which had already occurred.   He wrote: "Let him not marry with the rites of the Church any Frenchman to a Savage woman, without the consent of the parents, and without Monsieur's approval.[108]   Another indication that marriages were by no means infrequent at Tadoussac emerges from the fact that an additional irregularity was brought to the attention of the sovereign council which took it upon itself to appoint a guardian for the Indian woman in the case.[109]

Although church marriages appear to have been exceptional in the St. Lawrence valley illicit sexual relations were probably very frequent, how frequent it is impossible to say since anything like statistical evidence is entirely lacking.   At the western posts miscegenation between the coureurs de bois and the Indian women was the rule rather than the exception.[110]   But even in the settlements, "In the Night time, all of them, barring the Jefuits, roll from Houfe to Houfe to debauch the Women Savages."[111]   A recent study of the physical characteristics of the Indians of Labrador indicates that sexual relations between the French and the natives were not uncommon in the past.[112]

In Acadia the French had been encouraged to intermarry freely with the Micmac by the home government in order that the new land might be peopled without draining France of its inhabitants.   In the eighteenth century in Nova Scotia the English wished to emulate the policy of the French by offering bounties on intermarriage.[113] But conditions in seventeenth century Acadia made official interference unnecessary.   As early as the time of Poutrincourt "La plupart se marierent a des sauvagesses, et passerent le reste de leurs jours avec les sauvages adoptant leur manière de vivre".[114]   Maurault believed that marriages with Indians were so frequent in the years from 1607 to 1675 when European women were scarce that there were few Acadian families with no Indian blood in their veins.[115]   Under the distinguished leadership of the Baron de St. Castin intermarriage between traders and Indian women was

---

105.   Jesuit Relations 9, 233.
106.   Jesuit Relations 45, 149.
107.   C11A 7, 1683; Memoir important sur la traitte de Tadoussac.
108.   Jesuit Relations 63, 267.
109.   Jugements et deliberations January 11th, 1694, 3, 819.
110.   Carver 349.
111.   Lahontan 2, 444.
112.   Hallowell (2).
113.   Brebner 36.
114.   Maurault 84.
115.   Maurault 75.
116.   C11D 2-(1) de Menneval, 10th September 1688; Collection de manuscrits relatifs 2, 134; Murdoch 1, 141.

particularly frequent in the Penobscot valley,[116] and the St. John river and the Gaspé coast were not without their metis population.[117]

Illicit relations, moreover, were frequent in Acadia. Sometimes these were recognized as valid by the Indians but not by the missionaries. Sometimes they were carried on outside the usage and sanction of either culture, as in the settlements along the St. John river.[118] Conditions in this respect were particularly bad in Gaspé where many fishermen kept Micmac girls as concubines. The custom was to sell liquor to these girls, not only to get them drunk for nefarious purposes, but to make them debtors and, therefore, dependents. If they attempted to escape they were offered violence. Some Jesuits who touched in at Gaspé in 1676, at a time when the missions had been abandoned on account of the excessive drunkenness, thought it best to "meddle not in this business."[119]

Let us now return to the allegation which was mentioned at the beginning of this section; namely, that the French-Canadian population of today bears a large infusion of Indian blood. Although marriages were frequent in Acadia and to some extent on the Saguenay, they were rare in the settled area of New France. Miscegenation was general in settlement and hinterland, but, as far as the French were concerned, the movement was centrifugal. It must be remembered that Indian men did not mix with French women, but that French men held intercourse with Indian women. The important point here is that the children followed the mother, that is, became identified as Indian rather than French. Their descendants today are to be found on the edges of settlement and in the northern interior upon which it borders. The main body of the French Canadian people possess a negligible quantity of Indian blood, but what little there is, is probably widely disseminated.[120] Indeed, it seems not impossible that, considering the social consolidation of the French Canadians within the last hundred years which has saved them to some extent from the melting pot in which the English settlers have become immersed, the French Canadians may possess the purest blood of any large social group in North America.

6.

Miscegenation and the conflict in sex mores between the French and the Indians exerted a modifying influence upon the institutions of the latter. We have already seen that in ancient times the Algonkian bands, which were composed of groups of related families, divided into families which hunted during the winter on the lands temporarily allotted to them, and moved down to the coast or to lakes and rivers in the summer to fish. It was perhaps during the latter period, when families were reunited that courtship and marriage were most frequent. It is not improbable that cross-cousin marriage, traces of which have been detected among the Ojibwa, Ottawa and Algonkins north

---

117. Denys 219. Editor's Note; Gyles 17.
118. Murdoch 1, 215, 224.
119. Jesuit Relations 60, 125-127.
120. These statements do not apply outside of Quebec, for instance in Manitoba.

of the Great Lakes, [121] was at one time practised by the eastern Algonkians as well, although evidence seems at present to be lacking.[122]   Cross-cousin marriage, that is, the usage by which the children of biological brothers and sisters[123] were prospective mates, was affected by European immigration in two ways.   First, since the French brought few women with them the surplus of males which resulted was bound to exert a disintegrating influence upon a formerly stabilized community.   The French cut into this cross-cousin relationship and left male Indians without mates, although the high mortality of men in warfare partly accounted for the difference.   The French were often successful in this project for reasons which have already been described. Second, the marriage of cousins was not tolerated by the Roman Catholic church, and with the spread of Christianity the custom would naturally have broken down.[124]   Today among the St. Francis Abenaki cross-cousins and parallel cousins are grouped together.[125]

On the other hand the levirate among the Abenaki, that is, the moral obligation of a man to marry or at least care for his brother's widow and children appears to have survived the conflict.[126]   A similar custom was noted among the Misstassini Cree in 1672 but how it has since been modified is not clear.[127]   It appears, however, to have been related to a custom which occurred among the Montagnais in 1646 according to which a man, not necessarily a brother, took the name of the deceased, perhaps receiving his personality therewith, married the widow and cared for the deceased's children.   The Jesuits strongly objected to this custom, and there is some reason to believe that it fell into disuse among those bands who were most closely associated with the French.[128]   Besides the levirate the sorrorate may have existed anciently among the Abenaki, but as polygyny was discouraged by the missionaries no traces of it are found today, although it is said to occur among the Nascopi.[129]   Of all the eastern Algonkian peoples the Abenaki of St. Francis have adapted themselves the best to European conditions.   This may have been in part due to their composite origin.[130]

7.

The failure of the eastern Algonkians to adapt themselves to the changed social conditions which were inherent in the migration of a people of French Catholic culture into the New World resulted in the depopulation of many of the native bands.   The influence of the accessories of the new culture, as they diffused along the routes of the fur-trade in the seventeenth

---

121. Hallowell (4).
122. Rand (4) 223-224.
123. In many communities the brother-sister terminology is not confined to the biological relationship.
124. Hallowell (4) 543.
125. Hallowell (3) 135-140.
126. Hallowell (3) 138.
127. Jesuit Relations 56, 215.
128. Jesuit Relations 29, 215-217.
129. Hallowell (3) 138.
130. Hallowell (3) 143-144.

century, has already been dealt with.   The expansion of the European nations into the western hemisphere was essentially economic in motive, so that all other factors, including the establishment of the Kingdom Terrestrial, were subsidiary to this one drive.   From this point of view the depopulation of the new area was the result of an economic cause.   It would be different, however, to maintain that displacement of native by imported materials, with the ensuing disruption resulting from this factor alone, was of greater import than the factors of drunkenness and disease which were also consequent to the economic expansion of Europe.   And although Mr. Pitt-Rivers has found it to be so in the Pacific Islands, it would seem to be manifestly untrue to say that the factors of drunkenness and disease were of less import than those of a political and social nature which have been considered in this and the preceding chapter.   All were interwoven inextricably in one complex which must be treated as an organic situation.

The social factors which have been dealt with above, however, were deep and far-reaching in their effects.   We have seen that the imposition of alien sex mores, involving in some cases the subordination of free contracting parties to external control and in others the segregation of the sexes in convent institutions resulted in a loss of the will to live.   Marie de l'Incarnation herself recognized and understood that if the Indians did not escape to roam in the woods with their relatives, if they continued in the institution in which they were placed, the constraint made them melancholy and they became ill.   She declared that it was impossible to civilize more than one in a hundred.[131] Moreover, sensitivity to affronts on the part of the intruders caused despair and sometimes ended in suicide.[132]   Added to this was the despair which ensued from a high infant mortality among a people who loved their children and whose medicine men were powerless to stem the strange diseases.   Not only, moreover, were more children dying, but less children were being born due to the mental depression of the women, which resulted from the other factors above enumerated.   The mental depression disturbed the tumescence which favoured, if it was not essential to, fertilization.[134]

On the other hand such persistency as there has been may have been due to the fact that the Indians assimilated a degree of white blood.[135]   It is said that a hybrid stock is more fertile than the pure, and that mixture produces a type which is superior in fertility, vitality, and cultural worth than either of the parent stocks.   Certain influences, however, would counteract this result; namely, when marriages are limited to the poorer social and physical types in the community.[136]   Contrarily it has been maintained that miscegenation does not necessarily give rise to a new middle type, but that the offspring tend to revert to the paternal or the maternal stock.   Reversion has been found to be usually towards the more primitive or less specialized stock which is less

131.   Eastman 118.
132.   LeClercq (2) 247.
134.   Pitt-Rivers 143-146.
135.   Smith, N. G.
136.   Kroeber and Waterman, Chapter 20, p. 204; Chapter 21.

adaptable to the changed living conditions.[137]   If this were so the offspring
of French and Indian intermarriage would not gain much in adaptability over
their pure Indian brethren.   If, however, the hybrid is more adaptible to
changed conditions he is by the same token less adaptible to the constant
factor.   Thus, those who were of mixed blood tended to cluster around the
edges of settlement and lost the capacity to carry on the pristine hunting economy.[138]   It has been found that those of pure blood are far less adaptable to
great changes in cultural forms than has generally been supposed.   The data
which have been considered in this chapter testify to the truth of this contention.

A pattern of intermarriage in Pacific Islands,
and the conclusions Bailey draws from it, are
neither true nor relevant in French Canada where there
was far more intermarriage than Bailey is aware of —
and the children scattered across the continent
actively engaged in the fur Trade. A descendant of
Pierre Couc, Nicholas Montour, returned to buy a
seigneury at Three Rivers when he retired from a
partnership in the Northwest Fur Trading Company. French-
Indian settlements sprang up in the Ohio, Mississippi,
Missouri, Saskatchewan and other river areas of the west;
and many of the "French" were part algonkian or Huron from
Quebec intermarriages. There were several settlements
of free French and French-Indian mix in early Pennsylvania,
co-existing with the English.

---

137. Pitt-Rivers 18.
138. Pitt-Rivers 15.

CHAPTER 10

THE EFFECT OF CONTACT ON THE FRENCH

1.

The influence of the Indians on the French in the sixteenth century was briefly summarized at the end of the chapter on the clash in Acadia at the turn of the century. In the preceding chapters on the seventeenth, much of incidental import has been dealt with. It is proposed herein to gather together the strands, and to estimate the nature and the extent of the modifications in French culture both in the old and the new worlds. Since the immigrants from the old world left much of their culture behind them they were naturally dependent to some extent upon that which they found in their new environment. Besides such household effects which they could bring with them, which were necessarily limited in quantity, they were dependent upon the resources of the country for sustenance. Lacking the special knowledge which was required to exploit the resources of a changed environment, they were compelled to seek support from the indigenous population.[1]

On the material level, the French were dependent upon the native food supply, especially game, in the pursuit of which they were novices. Another salient feature was in French dependence upon the Algonkian means of transportation. Not only was the cooperation of the Indian essential to travel along the tortuous and difficult forest ways, but the methods which he had worked out, through centuries of adaptation, were indispensible to the immigrant. In summer the canoe furnished the means for river travel as no other vehicle could. Its lightness enabled it to be carried easily over the portages from one stream to the next, and its shallow draft and quick response to the move of the paddle made it of paramount importance for traversing shallows and rapids. Denys says of the St. John, "Boats cannot go up this river higher than eighteen to twenty leagues because of the falls and of rocks which are scattered there, thus compelling a resort to canoes."[2] In the time of Lahontan the character of canoes was somewhat modified by the use of oars and sails for travel on the larger lakes, and on the Saguenay the "north shore canoe", which was a combination of the French boat and the Montagnais canoe, was evolved; but in general the canoe was taken over by the French without modification, except that the need for transporting large cargoes affected its size.[3]

It was, however, useless in the winter when the rivers were frozen, at which time it was replaced by the toboggan and the sledge. Moreover, ". . . . it is the custom in this country to walk on snow shoes during the winter, for fear of sinking into the snow, in imitation of the Savages; who

---

1. Innis 386 (1).
2. Denys 119; Innis (1) 393.

3. Lahontan í, 62-65.

never go otherwise to hunt the moose."[4]   The use of the snowshoe necessitated the wearing of moccasins.   In 1633 the Jesuits had no French leather, but they desired it because ". . . the shoes of the Savages take water like a sponge, and those leathers from France would keep the feet dry."[5] Even with adequate material equipment the French generally experienced difficulty in forest travel when unaccompanied by Indian guides[6].

The difficulty in transporting large quantities of fresh meat and vegetables over the long sea route from the old world made the French dependent to a great extent upon the native food supply.   In 1613 when Argall destroyed the French establishments in Acadia, Biencourt and Charles de la Tour sought refuge among the Micmacs whose means of sustenance kept them alive until relief came from the mother country.[7]   But although a distinction must frequently be made between life in the hinterland and in the settlements, Quebec was dependent almost entirely upon Indian hunting for its fresh meat supply as late as 1643.[8]   Although they later became somewhat accustomed to it, the French did not relish the smoked meat of the Indians any more than the Indians liked the salted food of the French.[9]

Besides the moose, beaver and other animals, the fauna of the St. Lawrence and some of its tidal tributaries contributed to the food supply of the French.   After several years in proximity with the Montagnais at Quebec they became expert wielders of the harpoon in catching eels,[10] and in 1636 they learned pike-fishing from the Indians at Three Rivers.[11]   By 1652 the French had become so experienced as to be able to take five or six thousand eels in one night.   At this time the season for eels lasted for two months, and enough were taken and dried to supply the colony for a whole year.[12]   By 1684, the Sillery Montagnais having been exterminated or dispersed, the French had completely taken over their eel fishery between Quebec and Three Rivers.[13]   In fact, under the guidance of the Indians, the Frenchmen took over the technique of fishing, hunting, canoeing and other forest pursuits which in time transformed the settled European peasant into as expert a *coureur de bois* as was his dusky fellow savage.

Meat and fish were supplemented by the use of various vegetable products, the chief of which was the wild berry, particularly the blueberry, which grew in abundance along the rocky ridges and valleys of the Canadian shield. Moreover, maple sap was "the drink of the Indians and even of the French, who are fond of it."[14]   The greater dependence was had on berries and maple sap, since fruits natural to France, with the exception of some varieties of apples, did not succeed in Canada, and had gained little ground by 1720.[15] These products combined with cider and the judicious use of wine to preserve the health of the colonists against scurvy and other afflictions.   Moreover, the corn, beans, pumpkin and squash of the agricultural Iroquoians, and the

4. Jesuit Relations 4, 193.
5. Jesuit Relations 5, 127.
6. LeClercq (2) 169.
7. Murdoch 1, 73.
8. Jesuit Relations 24, 177.
9. Jesuit Relations 5, 61.

10. Jesuit Relations 6, 311.
11. Jesuit Relations 9, 167.
12. Jesuit Relations 40, 215.
13. Lahontan 1, 50.
14. Denys 381.
15. Charlevoix 1, 239.

wild rice of the Ojibwa of the Great Lakes region, gave the French a source of food which was adequate to the long journeys that were of necessity made to the interior in search of furs.   Certain Indian methods of preparing food were adopted by the Europeans, as is evidenced by the occurrence of such words as hominy and sagamite in both the French and the English of this continent.[16] The constant engrossment of many of the able-bodied French Canadians in the business of trading in furs seriously injured their own agricultural development in the settled region of the St. Lawrence valley and threw some of the burden upon Indian agricultural products.[17]

Besides foodstuffs the French who dwelt far from the settled areas around Quebec were often forced to rely upon Indian implements and utensils since the difficulty of obtaining an adequate supply in remote places was sometimes great.   Bark containers were in frequent and widespread use at Tadoussac,[19] and in Acadia they were used even as brandy casks, although they proved to be a highly perishable material.[20] Besides the canoe and snowshoe industries which were developed by such peoples as the Abenaki, Huron, and Micmac, an export trade in curios, ornamented canoes, and such trinkets sprang up in Acadia in the time of LeClercq.[21]   And in this connection Lahontan says: "There are fome little Baskets made of the young Birches, that are much efteemed in France; and Books may be made of 'em, the leaves of which will be as fine as Paper. . . . .   I have frequently made ufe of 'em for want of Paper, in writing the Journal of my Voyages."[22]   But these industries were infinitesimal in comparison with the main occupation of securing furs.

The clothing of the French who remained in the settlements in summer was not much modified by Indian influence, but "During the snows we all, French and Savages, make use of this kind of foot-gear (moccasins) in order to walk upon our Snowshoes; when the Winter had passed, we resumed our French shoes, and the Savages went barefooted."[23]   As the winters were long, moccasins were worn for a good part of the time. Although the poorer French were known to clothe themselves in blankets in the Indian fashion, it was, with the exception of skin caps, really only while the French were travelling in the hinterland that they adopted the more suitable Indian costume.[24]   The figure of the coureur de bois, with his skin cap, his sash, his deerskin leggings, and his moccasins and snowshoes, is so well-known that there is no need to enlarge upon it.

Sometimes the native architecture was found to be expedient by the French, even in the settled areas. At Quebec in 1640 "The hall of the Hospital being too small, it was necessary to erect some cabins, fashioned like those of

16. LeClercq (2) 108. For many words of Indian origin in French Canadian see Dionne (2). Also Chamberlain (17).
17. Innis (1) 395; C11A 10 August 10th 1688. See also Innis (2) p. 295 on the contribution of the Hurons to French agriculture in the period before French agricultural development.
19. Jesuit Relations 26, 113.
20. LeClercq (2) 165.
21. LeClercq (2) 96.
22. Lahontan 1, 370.
23. Jesuit Relations 7, 17; Marie de l'I. 33; Massicotte (2) on bottes sauvages, an Indian industry which was later taken over by the French.
24. Jesuit Relations 32, 47.

the Savages, in their gardens."[25]   As late as 1647 glass was so scarce in the colony that the missionaries were compelled to use linen for their church at Sillery, and one may well imagine that skins were sometimes used for this purpose.   In the back districts architecture was almost uniformly native.   The Abenaki built Dreuillettes a chapel of boards in their manner in 1647, and the Europeans frequently adopted the Indian lean-to as a woodland shelter.[26]   At first, as when LeJeune wintered among the Montagnais shortly after his arrival in the colony, Europeans found living conditions in the Indians' cabins insufferable, but those who frequented them for any length of time found it difficult to get used to their own on their return to civilization.   The Relation of 1658 states:

> "I have known Fathers who could not take their sleep on a bed, because they had become accustomed to sleep like the Savages. If they were given, on returning from their Missions, a pallet or mattress, they were obliged, until they had regained their former habits, to pass a portion of the night upon the paved floor of the room, in order to sleep for a little while more at their ease." [27]

On the other hand it is improbable that the palisades which surrounded some of the early settlements were copied from those of the Indians.   Since Stadacona was probably not a stockaded village Cartier's men would probably have had no example before their eyes.   And although Chauvin's house at Tadoussac in 1600 "was surrounded by hurdles . . . and a small ditch dug in the sand", he could not have learned this from the Montagnais who dwelt at that point, since they lived in open villages.[28]   Wooden stockades were not unknown in Europe as late as the end of the fifteenth century.

In treating of the influence of European diseases upon the Indians it was mentioned that the Indians were possessed of a variety of medicinal herbs which was as great as that of contemporary Europeans and which the latter adopted to an extent which has not yet been fully estimated.   "They have simples in use among them that are very good for curing wounds, particularly gun shot ones."[29]   It is noteworthy that the Micmac were alleged to have possessed a cure for epilepsy.   A soldier of fort St. John, who had been afflicted for fifteen or twenty years and who had fits almost every day, was cured by herbs employed by an Indian woman.   Shortly afterwards, however, she decamped and her remedy remained unknown.[30]   But at another time Marie de l'Incarnation took the trouble to get a "pied d'elan" for an Ursuline of Tours who suffered from epilepsy,[31] and Lahontan records the hearsay that "the far hind Foot of the Female kind, is a cure for the Falling-Sickness; . . ."[32] Another remedy to which he refers was the maidenhair fern of which a syrup was made which was exported in large quantities to Paris, Rouen and other

25. Jesuit Relations 19, 9.
26. Jesuit Relations 31, 189; LeClercq (2) 165.
27. Jesuit Relations 44, 281.
28. Champlain (2) 1, 49.
29. Boucher 64.
30. Dièreville 109.
31. Marie de l'I. 26. Editor says belief in remedy still exists.
32. Lahontan 1, 104.

cities.[33]   Many of the folk medicines which are current in the province of Quebec at the present time have their origin in the indigenous culture,[34] and even such a distinguished doctor of the seventeenth century as Dr. Sarrazin did not scorn to make ample use of Indian remedies.[35]   Moreover, recourse to Indian surgery was not unknown, as when a priest in 1645, who suffered from smoke-blindness, was cured by a Montagnais woman who, "armed with a bit of knife blade, or of rusty iron, scraped his eyes till a little humour flowed from them."[36]   But above all, the sweat house of the native came into general use among the colonists.   "The sweat-house. . . . is the great remedy of the Gaspesians; and it can be stated as a fact that a number of the French have also found therein a cure for chronic inflammations and sufferings which seem incurable in France."[37]   And to this Denys adds the testimony that "Our Frenchmen make themselves sweat like them, and throw themselves into the water similarly, and are never incommoded thereby."[38]

But even more insidious and more far-reaching were the influences of the Indians upon the French character as revealed in the manners and morals of the period.   It does not seem possible to determine the extent to which ignorance of the native languages was a barrier to social intercourse in the seventeenth century, but it is probable that the more experienced traders were conversant with several, and many would necessarily have had a smattering of at least one; it was always a prerequisite of the successful missionary.   In 1699 the wife of one of the officers who was stationed on the St. John river spoke Micmac as well as she spoke French,[39] and the native metaphor was generally adopted in the political speeches to the Indians.[40]   In Acadia, at least, where French settlement was sparse, Micmac and Malecite must have been the common vehicle of communication.[41] It is evident from a perusal of N. E. Dionne's dictionary that the native dialects have exerted a considerable influence upon Canadian French.

The dress, tatoo marks, and ornaments, of Indian origin which were worn by the French are indicative of some modification in the colonial mentality.[42]   It was recognized by the Jesuits that without schooling in reading, writing, plain-chant, and the fear of God, "our French would become Savages, and have less instruction than the Savages themselves."[43]   To the child of the colonist the indulgence in Indian games was a pleasant and necessary pastime,[44] and the frequent sight of his father, uncles and brothers, taking part in the ceremonial dances of the Iroquois and the Algonkians must have awakened

33. Lahontan I, 372.
34. LeClercq (2) 96; Massicotte (1) 176.
35. Vallée 59-60.
36. Jesuit Relations 27, 217.
37. LeClercq (2) 297.
38. Denys 417.
39. Diereville 86.
40. Jesuit Relations 22, 237.
41. Murdoch 1, 96.
42. Diereville 98. Although body painting was widespread among eastern Algonkians tatooing may not have occurred. See Sinclair 370, 393.
43. Jesuit Relations 36, 175.
44. Boucher 57 refers to jack-straws. Culin, 729, records only among Eskimo and Haida, but from Boucher's remarks it must be concluded that it was known in the eastern woodlands.

an exotic emotion in his breast.[45]   On the other hand, as is usual with the music of vastly different cultures, that of the Indian seems to have exerted no influence upon that of the colonists.   Even references to the Indian in French-Canadian folk songs are rare, although there is one which commences "C'était un vieux sauvage;" and "Marlbrouk s'en va-t-en guerre" contains the lines "four old Indians and two old squaws".[46]

Perhaps the most conspicuous change of custom on the part of the French was in their methods of carrying on warfare.   To the Indians' habit of stealth in moving through the forest and his skill in ambuscade they added what would seem ferocious cruelty to the humanitarian minds of the early twentieth century.   A like manifestation was to be observed in New England during and after King Philip's war, and the harshness and cruelty of the Thirty Years' War in Europe undoubtedly had repercussions in the colony. Champlain's horror at the burning of Iroquois prisoners was an unusual sentiment at that time.   The French, like other Europeans, were inured to cruelty. In the colony, as in Europe, it was a case of measure for measure.   At Quebec in 1647 the governor ordered the Sillery Indians not to torture an Iroquois prisoner as long as was customary "or reduce him to filthy nakedness, or make quarry of him like dogs."[47]   Later the Jesuits connived at the burnings. ". . . . we have scarcely ever seen an Iroquois burned without regarding him as on the way to Paradise; nor have we considered a single one as certainly on that road whom we have not seen pass through this torture."[48]

In the clash of cultures, even when one group is far superior to the other in most ways, both generally undergo considerable modification, and it is seldom, if ever, entirely beneficial.   With the rise of that figure in New France which was known as the coureur de bois, life in the colony underwent a marked change.   In the first place "He brought back with him, among his own people, the polygamous conjugal standards of the wilderness."[49]   In which connection Lahontan says.

> "You would be amaz'd if you faw how lewd thefe Pedlers are when they return; how they Feaft and Game, and how prodigal they are, not only in their Cloaths, but upon Women. Such of 'em as are married, have the wifdom to retire to their own Houfes; but the Batchelors act juft as our East-India-Men, and Pirates are wont to do; for they Lavifh, Eat, Drink and Play all away as long as the Goods hold out; and when thefe are gone, they e'en fell their Embroidery, their Lace, and their Cloaths. This done, they are forc'd to go upon a new Voyage for Subfiftance." [50]

Moreover, in other spheres than that of sex morals the contact is seen to have been detrimental.   Corruption at the trading posts, particularly those of the pays d'en haut, was the rule rather than the exception.   And from cheating the Indian it was a short step to cheating his fellow Frenchman and the gov-

---

45. Jesuit Relations 8, 29; 27, 289.
46. Chamberlain (12) 107-116.
47. Jesuit Relations 32, 23.
48. Jesuit Relations 46, 85, 95. See also Halkett for prejudiced account, Chapter 3.
49. Munro (2) 203.
50. Lahontan 1, 54.

ernment. The corruption and the weakening of the colony in its last days
may be traceable to the lowering of standards which resulted from the French
woodsmen having shaken off the shackles of their own society, and from social
and commercial intercourse with a people of vastly different culture.[51]   In
speaking of the French Canadian character as a whole Charlevoix is less con-
demnatory. He acknowledges that "the example and frequent intercourse with
its natural inhabitants are more than sufficient to constitute this character".
Moreover, "there is some room to imagine that they commonly undertake
such painful and dangerous journeys out of a taste they have contracted for
them. They love to breathe a free air, they are early accustomed to a wandering
life; . . ."[52]   They lacked discipline and made poor servants due to their
great haughtiness of spirit.   Their unbounded confidence in their own ability
was the result of a life of self-reliance spent in a wilderness infested with
enemies, both natural and human.   By those who fail to discern a continuity
in Canadian mental life no connection will be made between the independent
French-Canadian fur-trader, with his scorn for imperial edicts of outlawry,
and the French-Canadian rebels of 1837 and the Quebec nationalists of the
mid-nineteenth century.   Surely it is significant that the frequent excommuni-
cations of the Bishop of Petrea against those who were engaged in selling
liquor to the Indians were set at naught by the coureurs de bois and the settlers
whose orthodoxy must have been shaken by their contact with religions other
than Christianity, although Charlevoix declared that the French-Canadian
generally had a great fund of piety and religion.   Certainly he was as super-
stitious as western European peasants of that date were.   It was, therefore, not
astonishing that many of the beliefs which were current in the colony were
adopted by him.   It was held by the Algonkins that a throbbing of the breast
heralded the arrival of a visitor.

> "One of our Frenchmen, who has long associated with these Bar-
> barians, has assured me that he has frequently found out by experience
> the truth of these pretended prophecies; and lately, said he, a certain
> Savage woman, feeling her breast throb, said to her mother and the
> others who were in the Cabin, 'The French will soon come here,' which
> was true; he was one of those who appeared." [53]

The Micmacs believed that a fire would seize the privy parts of anyone who
should set foot upon a certain island near Lunenburg harbour.   Razilly, on
one occasion, invited a Capuchin priest to land upon the island in order to
disabuse the people of their superstition, but he refused.[54]   At the end of the
eighteenth century a starving Cree hunter went to David Thompson to ask
him for a wind, but he was told that the Great Spirit was the master of the
winds.   "Ah", he said, "that is always your way of talking to us, when you
will not hear us, then you talk to us of the Great Spirit. . . . I told him the
Good Spirit alone could cause the winds to blow, and my French Canadians
were as foolish as the poor Indian; saying to one another, it would be a good
thing and well done if he got a wind; we should get meat to eat."   Later

---

51. Munro (2) 203.
52. Charlevoix 1, 247-249.

53. Jesuit Relations 9, 117-119.
54. Denys 153.

Thompson's men, while at the trading house, "related how I had raised a storm of wind for the Indian, but had made it so strong that for two days they had got no fish from the nets, adding, they thought I would take better care next time.   In these distant solitudes Men's minds seem to partake of the wildness of the country they live in."[55]   And even a Seigneur d'Haberville could pin his faith upon an Indian superstition.[56]

But another tendency which was contrary in its ultimate influence was discernable.   The medieval belief that the nature of man is fundamentally bad which is inherent in the doctrine of original sin, and the belief in a universal and absolute ethic, began to give way at the time of the Renaissance to a consciousness that there were other codes of manners and morals than the European which were not only equally valid but perhaps even more so.   This relativity in ethics was due in no small measure to the contact of Europeans with exotic cultures in the period of overseas exploration.   Even LeJeune could write in 1633, "Some place beauty where others see nothing but ugliness. The most beautiful teeth in France are the whitest; in the Maldive Islands whiteness of teeth is considered a deformity, they paint them red to be beautiful; and in Cochin China, . . they paint them black. Which is right?"[57] But one would scarcely accuse a Jesuit of subscribing to a relativity in ethics.

From the doctrine of original sin it was natural for the opponents of ecclesiastical and political despotism and corruption to swing to the theory that man was fundamentally good; that at some time in the dim past he had been a noble creature; and that if the shackles of civilization could be cast aside he might again enter a golden age.   In the American Indian the French philosopher found a "bon sauvage" living in a state of nature which came to be the summum bonum of human attainment.   This idea was partly the result of the Jesuit Relations which were read widely in France by all classes of people, who must have listened to the strange tales of the western continent with a wrapped attention which was not unmingled with awe, and who must have yearned for the pristine simplicity and virtue, which, magnified by their romantic minds, never could have existed on land or sea.   An early description of the noble savage exists in the Relation of 1648 and refers to the Atticameg Montagnais.

> "It seems as if innocence, banished from the majority of the Empires and Kingdoms of the World, had withdrawn into these great forests where these people dwell. Their nature has something, I know not what, of the goodness of the Terrestrial Paradise before sin had entered it. Their practices manifest none of the luxury, the ambition, the avarice, or the pleasures that corrupt our cities."[58]

This concept reached its most characteristic and exalted form in the writings of Lahontan, who was a man of wit and sensibility, and who was highly conscious of much of the meanness of contemporary European life.   Of his work R. G. Thwaites says,

---

55. Thompson, D. 122-124.
56. Aubert de Gaspé 256.

57. Jesuit Relations 5, 107.
58. Jesuit Relations 32, 283.

"In the pages of Lahontan the child of nature was depicted as a creature of rare beauty of form, a rational being thinking deep thoughts on great subjects, but freed from the trammels and frets of civilization, bound by none of its restrictions, obedient only to the will and caprice of his own nature. In this American Arcady were no courts, laws, police, ministers of state, or other hampering paraphernalia of government, each man was a law unto himself, and did what seemed good in his own eyes. Here were no monks and priests, with their strictures and asceticisms, but a natural, sweetly-reasonable religion. Here no vulgar love of money pursued the peaceful native in his leafy home; without distinction of property the rich man was he who might give most generously. Aboriginal marriage was no fettering life-covenant, but an arrangement pleasing the convenience of the contracting parties. Man, innocent and unadorned, passed his life in the pleasures of the chase, warring only in the cause of the nation, scorning the supposititious benefits of civilization, and free from its diseases, misery, sycophancy, and oppression. . . ."

Of the man himself he says,

"In his hatred and scorn of the current ecclesiasticism and despotism, he anticipated Rousseau; his cynical criticism of existing institutions foreshadowed Voltaire; his exaltation of the virtues and blessings of the savage state, preluded the Encyclopedists. In the Discours sur l'Origine et les Fondemants de l'Inegalité parmi les ommes, Rousseau apparently borrowed many ideas from Lahontan's Dialogue; Chateaubriand's gentle barbarian Atala is brother to the astute and charming Adario." [59]

In the chapter on the collision of French and Micmac cultures in Acadia the link between the American Indian, Montaigne and Rousseau, was noted. Here is another link between the Indian and the French Revolution.

The influence of the French on the Indians, and of the Indians on the French, resulted from a contact which was implicit in the fur-trade in New France. As the fur-trade has been dealt with adequately and in detail elsewhere there is no need to summarize its history here.[60] Dr. Innis has shown its basic importance to Canadian development and its far-reaching effects both in the new and the old world. Not only did it stimulate existing and give rise to new industries in France,[61] but it was the coat and currency of the French-Canadian for more than a century.[62] Moreover, it formed the framework for the other industries and for the political institutions of New France by forcing a policy of centralization upon its participants.[63] Not only for its economic but also for its political existence was the colony dependent upon its native allies. Charlevoix speaks of the Abenaki in the eighteenth century, "who, though far from being numerous, have been during the last two wars the chief bulwark of New France against New England."[64] The French and the Abenaki had common economic interests. The fur-trade was the raison d'etre of the colony, and the Indian was a factor without which there would have been no fur-trade. "We have not yet realized that the Indian and his culture were fundamental to the growth of Canadian institutions."[65]

---

59. Lahontan 1., Introduction by R. G. Thwaites.
60. Innis (1).
61. Innis (1) 388.
62. Wampum was secondary as a medium of exchange. See Jesuit Relations 9, 173-175.
63. Innis (1) 117, 120.
64. Charlevoix 1, 133.
65. Innis (1) 397.

CHAPTER 11

RELIGION

1.

The assertion that the Indians were without religion occurs with startling frequency throughout the earlier accounts of exploration and travel relating to North America. Where there were no priests, temples, images, or other visible signs of worship, it was blandly assumed that the cult of the supernatural was lacking. It was with the feeling that the minds of the Indians were almost completely blank tablets that the Jesuits hopefully began to impart Christian doctrine with a view to speedy and widespread proselytization. We have already seen them at their work in Acadia at the turn of the century. After Biard and his fellows were expelled in 1613 missionary endeavour became intermittent in this area and Quebec supplanted Port Royal as the chief centre of diffusion. The early Recollet missions were without widespread effect, and the capture of Quebec by the Kirkes put a temporary stop to French expansion, so that it was not until the sixteen-thirties that Christianization was begun in earnest.

Although the life of the wilderness was one of extreme hardship, Le-Jeune was able to state that whereas he had had only two pupils in 1632 these had increased to twenty by the following year. It was necessary for him to coin words in order to translate the story of the creation, the Pater, the Ave, the Credo, the mysteries of the Holy Trinity, and the Incarnation into the Montagnais tongue.[1] In 1635 twenty-two Montagnais and other Indians were baptized in and about Quebec, but he says "We do not yet trust baptism to any except those whom we see in danger of death, or to children who are assured to us; for not yet being able to instruct these Barbarians, they would soon show a contempt for our Holy Mysteries, if they had only a slight knowledge of them."[2] Although only the sick and dying were baptized these were plentiful enough on account of the new imported diseases which were at this time making their presence felt. Greater progress was made in 1636 when fifteen children were baptized with the consent of the parents who also were giving a keen ear to the new faith. This attention resulted from the consummate fear that seized their hearts at the words of the missionaries who did not hesitate to paint the frightful torments of Hell in glowing terms.[3] In all a hundred were baptized in 1636 and the number was trebled in the following year.[4] Eat-all feasts, the consultation of shamans in illness, and the belief in dreams were renounced by the new Christians of Quebec although contig-

1. Jesuit Relations 5, 117, 187; 11, 149-167.
2. Jesuit Relations 7, 275.
3. Jesuit Relations 8, 247; 11, 89.
4. Jesuit Relations 11, 81.

uous bands were not yet influenced to any extent.   By the end of the decade twelve hundred, including Hurons, were baptizd at Quebec, Sillery, and Three Rivers.   Many of these were adults in good health.   Most of the Quebec band were now nominally Christian so that the record of baptisms fell off during the 'forties, but it is more than probable that much of the old religions continued beneath the veneer of Christianity.   The raids of the Iroquois kept more isolated peoples from coming to the settlement.   Those who were able went to Sillery for protection and speedily became Christian since apostates and pagans were not allowed there.   In this way the Iroquois were a factor in the spread of Christianity.   Whenever paganism is recorded at Sillery in the 'fifties it is probable that reference is made to recent arrivals from the interior.[5]

Although the Tadoussac band was perhaps the earliest of all the Montagnais to trade with the French it was comparatively late in receiving missionaries.   The manner in which they were first approached was stated in the Relation for 1641:

> "Although the Savages of Tadoussac are almost the first ones that our vessels met, yet the good news of the Gospel was carried to them only after it had been taken to many others . . . it was not we who won them, but our . . . new Christians of the residence of St. Joseph." [6]

Fourteen or fifteen were baptized in June, 1640, and several families became Christian.   At Sillery Indians spoke against their brutal manners, their superstitions, and their drums so "that all those who had these went immediately for them, and broke them into a thousand pieces."   Eat-all feasts, chants, body-painting, and the use of tobacco were given up by several, but the Montagnais deemed it necessary to guard the Jesuit with a pistol against certain Malecite and other unfriendly Indians.[7]   "Not long ago the Savages were still ashamed to pray to God in public; now they are not ashamed to kneel down, to clasp their hands, and to pray aloud".[8]   By 1643 many of the northern interior bands were becoming aware of the alien faith, and some were not averse to listening to the sermons of the Jesuit.[9]   In order to aid the excellent memories that characterized an illiterate people, who were able to learn long prayers with the utmost ease, the misionary gave five sticks for the guidance of the interior bands; a black stick, for horror of their former superstitions; a white for prayers; a red for the ritual to be observed on Sundays and feast days; one wound with ropes, that delinquents might be corrected with love and charity; and one notched with various marks, as a guide to conduct in dearth and plenty.[10]   One hundred adults were baptised at Tadoussac in 1643, forty in 1644, and sixty from a single band of two hundred in 1646. "The savages who appear the most zealous are those of the north shore, of which the mission is at Tadoussac."   They were at this time economically

---

5. Jesuit Relations 43, 227.
6. Jesuit Relations 21, 81.
7. Jesuit Relations 20, 187, 191; 21, 105.
8. Jesuit Relations 22, 223.
9. Jesuit Relations 24, 155 for list of bands.
10. Jesuit Relations 29, 137, 141.

dependent upon the French; and, moreover, they were made to fear the wrath to come, for those of Tadoussac used a picture of a damned soul to frighten remote bands into acceptance of Christianity.   It portrayed an Indian sorcerer, a beater of drums, who was now burning in the rage and fury of Hell.   Given the sympathetic complex, the picture was an earthly replica of an actual fact, and it was, therefore, a fearful sight to the natives, whose own religious experiences were vivid in the extreme.   Moreover, the immigrants were regarded as superior by the Indians and were, therefore, revered and imitated on that account. Lastly, conversion was promoted by the fact that the success of a group was attributed by the group to its gods.   Hence, since the Europeans were indubitably successful, their gods must have been more potent than their own. That conversion, however, did not necessarily involve disbelief in their own gods is evident from the fact that many non-Christian beliefs are current among the eastern Algonkians at the present time.

During the 'fifties a vast concourse of Indians made Tadoussac their rendezvous, but when Iroquois raids made the journey dangerous they preferred to remain in their own isolated territories.   In 1653 the mission was extended to lake St. John where one hundred were baptized, and in 1659 it was decided to keep a permanent priest at Tadoussac to afford a base at the foot of the trade route.   In the 'sixties priests and Iroquois penetrated the interior where the efforts of the former suffered shattering blows at the hands of the latter who dispersed many of the interior bands. from their ancient haunts and scattered them in small groups in inaccessible places.   Nevertheless, eight or ten bands met at Necouba in 1661, some of whom had never before seen the French nor heard of the new faith.   Some, however, had been baptized by de Quen at Tadoussac and lake St. John in 1647.   When peace was made with the Iroquois in 1668 four hundred Indians were able to gather at Tadoussac, of whom one hundred and forty-nine received confirmation at the hands of Laval. "God reserved for this mission the conversion of some unbelieving Savages who had lived a long time among Christians, with an astonishing aversion for Christianity."[12]   Although conversion now appeared to be becoming general in the St. Lawrence watershed, superficially at least, it was not until 1672 that Albanel was able to bring some of the Misstassini Cree within the fold, in the course of his dual mission to the shores of Hudson bay.   In the account of Crepeuil's sojourn among the Montagnais in 1671-72 no mention was made of conjuring, invoking the manitou, polygyny, or any aboriginal custom which had formerly been frowned upon.   The letter implied that all with whom he had wintered were firm Christians.

Missionary effort on the part of the French was infrequent among the bands who lived on the north shore of the St. Lawrence below Tadoussac. Nevertheless, the Tadoussac Christians themselves became cross-bearers.   In 1652 they preached to the Betsiamites band, exhorting them to renounce their drums, conjurors' lodges, eat-all feasts, and polygyny.   They were not to kill, commit adultery, steal nor lie.   Although at this time a score were baptized

---

12.   Jesuit Relations 51, 281.

they were isolated from the main lines of trade and doubtless in subsequent years they reverted to their former state, since it is expressly stated that the great earthquake of 1663 scared the Indians of the north shore into more rigid observance of the rites of the church.[13]   In the following year the Jesuit Nouvel visited the Papinachois at Escoumains and Sault au Moutons and was conducted by them to lake Manicouagan "where never before had a European made his appearance", although the Indians of this region were armed with muskets.[14]   This lake was the meeting place of the band known as Ouchestigouet, of whom eighty were baptized.[15]   Proselytization continued through 1666[16] to 1670 when the Oumamiois Montagnais were visited at Godbout. It is said that polygyny and sorcery were not conspicuous there, and that forty-five children and adults were baptized.   One who had been baptized sixteen years before had retained and taught others the principles which he had learned.

The influence which Sillery exerted as a centre of diffusion for Christianity among the bands below Tadoussac was also extended to the peoples of the St. Maurice above Three Rivers.   Notable among these were the Atticamegs who were the most amenable to the new religion although they had seldom visited the French in large numbers and had never been visited in their own country by the missionaries before 1644.   At this time the few Christians among them were greatly outnumbered by the pagans.   However, by 1647 five or six bands, including the Atticamegs, who frequented Three Rivers were said to have been mostly devout Christians.   Although they were first visited in their home country in 1651 by the Jesuit Buteux the Atticamegs had long since erected a large cross and a chapel for their devotions.   "It was a bark cabin with an arched roof, at the end of which was a sort of Altar, . . . the whole decorated with blue blankets, on which were fastened paper pictures and some small crucifixes."[17]   The children "all had their rosaries, and knew their prayers very well, for they had taught them to one another."[18]   Even the old people who had never seen Europeans were well disposed towards Christianity.   The Atticamegs were instrumental in carrying the faith and strengthening and extending the political alignment to the Cree and other central Algonkians until small-pox and Iroquois raids annihilated them as a cultural unit in 1660.[19]

As for the tribes south of the St. Lawrence we have already observed that the Micmacs were the first to be amenable to conversion at Port Royal at the turn of the century.   After the destruction of Port Royal a lapse of some years occurred in which no missionaries were present to the Micmac; and full accounts of the Recollets missions which lasted from 1619 to 1624 appear to be lacking.   When the Jesuits again found their way into Acadia it was to the shore of Bay Chaleur and the neighbouring gulf coast that they went instead of to the Bay of Fundy side.   The area had then become a centre of the dry-fishing industry.   Although a mission was established at Miscou

13. Jesuit Relations 48, 71.
14. Jesuit Relations 49, 43.
15. Jesuit Relations 49, 63, 73.
16. Jesuit Relations 50, 117.

17. Jesuit Relations 37, 39.
18. Jesuit Relations 37, 41.
19. Jesuit Relations 43, 53.

in 1635 it was not until 1645 that any headway was made. Fourteen were baptized in this year, including a family of eight, of whom six were on the point of death. Notwithstanding the small number of conversions the priest declared that he had never seen the Micmac better disposed.[20] Some credit for this amenability must be written to the account of the Montagnais of Tadoussac who expended much energy in attempting to effect the conversion of those Miscou Indians who were accustomed to come to Tadoussac to trade. But although Laval confirmed one hundred and forty Micmac at Gaspé in 1659, the mission was abandoned by the Jesuits in 1661 on account of the widespread drunkenness and debauchery, which has already been recorded. Later the Recollets carried on a more or less successful mission for some years but it is said that the French were expelled from this part of Acadia in 1692 by the natives.[21]

The latest of all the eastern Algonkian tribes to embrace Christianity in any numbers were the Malecite, owing to their position as an interior river-dwelling people. It is said that almost the first time they were approached for conversion was at the Good Shepherd mission of Rivière du Loup in 1677. The four or five hundred who comprised the floating population of this point included also Indians of the Passammaquoddy and Penobscot, besides those of the St. John. They were described at this late date as nomads "more than any other people in this country".[22] Although they had great contempt for prayer "The picture of a damned person, which I exhibited in the chapel did not fail to inspire them with salutary ideas".[23] Nevertheless, very few were baptized in this year, and it is probable that little more than the surface was scratched in the seventeenth century.

Southeast of the Penobscot the Abenaki of the Kennebec had come into contact early with Europeans, but neither the French nor the English hastened to send priests to them. It was not until 1644 that the Montagnais sent some of their own number to invite the Abenaki to embrace the faith. Not only did their visits to Quebec become more frequent, but the Capuchins and Jesuits made flying visits of good will to their territory. When Dreuillettes visited the Abenaki in 1647 only those on the point of death were baptized although "some sick people dragged themselves more than a league and a half in order to see him,"[24] After the blundering tactics of the English and the smooth diplomacy of Dreuillettes conversion became more frequent, and when King Philip's war was at its height large numbers of Abenaki flocked to Quebec to embrace Christianity. They "so soon imitate one another, that we have hardly any difficulty in making them acquire the most important sentiments of a true Christian".[25] It was these immigrants who survived as the largest Christian eastern Algonkian group, a fact which was perhaps due, as has been suggested elsewhere, to their composite origin. It was not until the end of

---

20. Jesuit Relations 28, 23.
21. Jesuit Relations 24, 310; LeClercq (2) 127.
22. Jesuit Relations 60, 263 seq.
23. Jesuit Relations 60, 265.
24. Jesuit Relations 31, 185.
25. Jesuit Relations 63, 33.

the century that those of the Abenaki towns in what is now Maine, who did not follow their fellows to Canada, received conversion to any appreciable extent.[26]

2.

It might be maintained, however, that the rapid spread of Christianity was more apparent than real. The glowing accounts of Indian piety with which the Jesuit Relations were liberally embellished, partly for reasons of propaganda, the vast outlay of men and resources which were put into the field, and the more than lip-service which was undoubtedly a fact in innummerable cases, might lead the observer of the present century to suppose that the Indian rites and superstitions were swept away by Christianity as before a great cataract. That this view would be entirely erroneous becomes more clear when the obstacles to the advance of Christianity are considered.

These may be grouped under ten heads. Initially, the linguistic barrier had to be overcome before the concepts of the new faith were imparted. Among the eastern Algonkians abstract terms were not very abundant and it was necessary for the missionaries to invent terms in order to impart the abstract concepts of Christianity. The arrière-pensées of the Christian concepts were, undoubtedly, very often missed by the Indians. Other barriers which were related to language were mentioned by LeJeune whose case may be taken as typical. The missionary's own memory was defective when trying to master the Indian languages. The jealousy of shamans and the hostility of disaffected apostates baulked tutorial aid. The inherent difficulty of Indian languages to a European, coupled to the adverse conditions which were induced by war and disease,were almost insuperable.[27]

Second, due to the isolation and the nomadic existence of the Indians the Jesuits had more trouble in keeping their Christians than in acquiring them.[28] "You will instruct them today, tomorrow hunger snatches your hearers away, forcing them to go and seek their food in the rivers and woods."[29] As late as the third quarter of the century few of the Papinachois had not some superstitions on account of the wandering life which kept them from the missionaries. Several of the Oumamiouek who had been baptized at Tadoussac were not confessed for seven years afterwards.[30] Of twenty-three Papinachois children at lake Manicougan in 1664, who had been baptized at Tadoussac * and Betsiamis some years previously, most had to be instructed again "having no knowledge of their blessedness".[31] When Albanel visited the Oumamiois at Godbout in 1670 they had not been visited by a priest for five years. The case is especially interesting of the Malecite who seem to have dwelt in a pocket which for long remained unpenetrated by European culture. Although their neighbours, the Micmac, were the earliest encountered, the two "do not love each other much, and have no close relations with each other", which accounts

26. Jesuit Relations 65, 87.
27. Jesuit Relations 7, 31-33.
28. Jesuit Relations 25, 113.

29. Jesuit Relations 6, 147.
30. Jesuit Relations 36, 225.
31. Jesuit Relations 49, 59.

in part for the lack of diffusion.   Even the Micmac, who, with the Malecite, thronged Rivière du Loup in 1677, retained little of their former Christian teaching, but adhered to many of their pagan practices.[32]   The Malecite do not seem to have acquired much Christianity from the Penobscot and Abenaki who were proselytized earlier.   Although the Recollets administered to the Malecite of the St. John after 1689, pagan beliefs and rites were in full swing in 1690, few having been converted to Catholicism.[33] The field work of Speck, Hallowell and others has brought to light a large amount of religious lore among the Montagnais-Nascopi and others within the present century, which makes it clear that Christianity and the native beliefs have often continued to exist side by side, the lack of system making it possible for diverse creeds to be held simultaneously.

The isolation of some of the eastern Algonkian peoples was partly due to the zeal of the church for new and farflung bands who were still active hunters, and with whom contact was highly lucrative to the traders.   It is true that no deliberate neglect of those broken and decimated people who were left behind as the fur frontier advanced was to be discerned on the part of the priests, but they were always keen about the peoples who were undecimated by war, disease, and the other consequences of the contact with European culture.   In this connection it is interesting to note that a woman who had been baptized by Biard at Port Royal some thirty years before was confessed for the first time at Miscou in 1643.[34]   Those of the Port Royal area complained that although they had "long frequented the French settlement on our shores" they had never been taught as were those at Miscou.   "We know not what it is to pray, at least in our own language; our children are not taught as you teach them here."[35]   Similarly, those of the Labrador coast were not made the objects of special endeavour, and it is probable that even the Tadoussac mission was discontinued in 1699 and was revived at only brief intervals.[36]

In the fourth place, since the missionaries were accustomed to go among those tribes with whom trade connections had just been established, and since these tribes were the special objects of Iroquois attacks and massacres, the spread of Christianity was retarded in consequence.   "As soon as any Father sows the seed of the faith in a new country, sickness and war at once follow him."[37] Moreover, they often reverted to the custom of consulting the manitou through fear of their implacable enemies, as in the case of the Papinachois in 1664 who were suffering from the Iroquois at this time.   Added to this, disease, which was considered in an earlier chapter, made less and less Indians available for conversion; not only by decimating their ranks in some cases almost to the extent of annihilization, but also by instilling them with the fear that baptism was the cause of their deaths on account of the frequency with which the two were associated.   Again, scurvy among the French sometimes broke up a mission as in the case of that at Seven Islands in 1674[38]   And fifth, we saw elsewhere

---

32. Jesuit Relations 60, 271.
33. Gyles 32-35.
34. Jesuit Relations 24, 147.
35. Jesuit Relations 28, 33-35.
36. Jesuit Relations 56, 302.
37. Jesuit Relations 37, 67.
38. Jesuit Relations 59, 53.

that drunkenness became so bad that it was given as the chief reason for the abandonment of the Micmac missions of Gaspé and Bay Chaleur, to say nothing here of kindred peoples.   Then, public ridicule of converts by their pagan fellows,[39] together with the rivalry between the priests and the native shamans were obstacles of considerable efficacy.[40]   To the latter will be extended more detailed treatment later.

In the eighth place, age was a factor of resistence to Christianity among the Algonkians.   On account of the close psychic connection between love and religion it is said that the majority of conversions occur during adolescence.[41]   Whereas the Montagnais children at Quebec in 1639 were amenable, "The only quite obstinate ones I have seen were a few old men, whose brains, dried up in their old maxims, had no longer any fluid in which to receive the impression of our doctrine."[42]   And the old men, as in many primitive communities, were not without prestige.

A ninth point was that, due to the political rivalry between church and state, as we have seen in the case of liquor control, and to some extent between the religious orders within the church itself, the efficacy of the missions was seriously impaired.   A united front might at least have liquidated drunkenness.   And lastly, the missionaries baptized their converts without complete cognisance of the fact that there was a deeply rooted body of religious belief, and righteous habits of mind which were the result of generations of adaptation to a highly specialized physical and social environment, of which willy-nilly they were more tenacious than life itself.   It is not improbable that this last factor was the most trenchant of all.   It, therefore, requires a more extended treatment.

3.

The Indians were, of course, unaware of the idea of natural causation which was the product of the nineteenth century science.   The distinction between natural and supernatural, between flesh and spirit, which was implicit in the doctrines of the medieval church, and of the Jesuits in New France, was not recognized by such primitive peoples as the eastern Algonkians.   Indeed, the terms "natural" and "supernatural" tend to become meaningless since the natural and the super natural were so closely inter-related.   The Indian

"peopled his world with numerous 'powers,' some great, mysterious, and awe-inspiring, some small and of little or no account . . . he . . . gave them such anthropomorphic traits as speech and knowledge, even ascribed to them human or partly human forms. So the 'power' of the cataract became its 'spirit'. . . . The 'power' of the cataract was only an attribute, but the 'spirit' was a separate existence. It carried the same name as the cataract, and the name heightened its individuality, giving it the status of a definite supernatural being. . . . Some

39. Jesuit Relations 16, 99.
40. Jesuit Relations 20, 265.
41. Ellis, H. 1, 310.
42. Jesuit Relations 16, 199.
     Jenness (1) See chapter on religion. See also Jones (1) 185.

spirits were vague and nameless, others as definite as the deities of ancient Greece and Rome. But ultimately they were no more than personifications of the mysterious forces which the Indians saw working in nature around them."

Besides these localized supernatural beings there was, in many of the north American Indian religions, a "personification of the mysterious powers or forces operating in man's environment, forces that were conceived as eminations from some higher force. The Algonkians called both this higher force and its individual manifestations 'manito' ". The belief in this "higher force," of which Jenness speaks, does not, so far as I am aware, appear in any of the explorers' accounts of the seventeenth century or in any reports of field work among the eastern Algonkians. Lahontan did not specify the people to whom he referred when he wrote:

> "The Existance of God being inseperable from his Essence, it contains everything, it appears everything, and gives motion to everything. In fine, all that you see, all that you conceive, is this Divinity which subsists without bounds or limits, and without Body; and ought not to be represented under the Figure of an old Man, nor of any other thing, let it be never so fine or extensive. For this Reason they Adore him in everything they see. When they see anything that's fine or curious, especially when they look upon the Sun or Stars, they cry out, O Great Spirit, we discern thee in everything. And in like manner when they reflect upon the meanest Trifles they acknowledge a Creator under the name of the Great Spirit or Master of Life." [43]
> "But if you ask them in particular why they Adore God in the Sun, rather than in a Tree or a Mountain; their Answer is, That they choose to admire the Deity in publick by pointing to the most glorious thing that Nature affords." [44]

It was said, however, that the Montagnais in 1627 thought of Jesus as the sun. It could not have been otherwise than that they should think of him as the most powerful particular object in nature which they knew. They "call the Sun Jesus, and it is believed that the Basques who formerly frequented these places, introduced this name. It thus happens that when we offer Prayers it seems to them that we address our Prayers to the Sun, as they do." [45] At the end of the century Diereville wrote that they had formerly thanked the sun for the good he had done them, and that they had supplicated the demon not to harm them, but that the missionaries had disabused them of these beliefs, and that if they had not renounced them in his day they had at least not increased their beliefs in their own religion. [46] The nature and the identity of the demon is not certain since Diereville regarded these powers in terms of his own theology.

It was the anthropomorphic supernatural beings rather than the higher force of which Jenness speaks which bulked large in the religion of the Algonkians. The nature and function of some of these were very vague. It is

43. Lahontan 2, 434.
44. Lahontan 2, 437. Thwaites is wrong in referring to the sun as a symbol. Manito or power was in trees, mountains and stones, and other natural phenomena as the author said (p. 435-436) but due to its commanding position, brilliance and beneficial power it was felt as the chief repository of manito, or the vehicle of the most powerful supernatural being in nature.
45. Jesuit Relations 4, 201-203.
46. Diereville 93; LeClercq (2) 144.
47. Masson 414.

said that the Nascopi at the end of the Eighteenth century recognized a spirit who was the creator of the earth and themselves, but it went unworshipped.[47] Among the Montagnais it was not anthropomorphic and it possessed no definite personality. Alexander identifies it with Atahocam who made the earth and sky,[48] but it was not certainly the creator since "... . they only spoke of Atahocam as one speaks of a thing so far distant that nothing sure can be known about it".[49]

Other beings were more active and more personalized, having the attributes of human beings both in appearance and in action. Of such a kind were the culture heroes, Gluskap of the Micmac, and Messou of the Montagnais. It was in terms of these that the Christian hierarchy was conceived. Sometimes Gluskap was confused with Noah, sending out a white dove which returned to him coloured black and became a raven.[50] At others he appears as the cause of the flood, but being a benevolent culture hero, he does not drown the Indians; he turns them into rattlesnakes with the genius of a trickster. In this tale the idea of punishment for evil appears.[51] In another tale he appears as the creator of men and the heavenly bodies. There was a period of the Law before the coming of Christ in which he had to be obeyed, and it is generally as an Old Testament figure that he appears in the adulterated tales,[52] although occasionally he may be seen as the successful rival of Christ.[53] In the tale of Gluskap's journey Hebrew and Micmac elements are well mingled. "Gluskap was the god of the Micmacs. The great deity, Ktcinisxam, made him out of earth and then breathed on him and he was made." Then he prophesied the coming of the Europeans and the baptism of the Micmacs. He had departed just before 1610, when the prophesy was fulfilled, "because he knew he had to make room for Christ, but he is the Micmac's god and will come to help them if they ever need him."[54] Although it was sometimes as a vague power, perhaps localized in the sun, that the Montagnais first apprehended Christ, at others he was doubtless thought of in terms of their own trickster hero. The magic performances of the latter were stepping-stones to the miracles of Jesus. Thus the central Algonkians could understand that the wafer became the body of Christ since Nanabozho had turned bits of his own or his wife's flesh into raccoons for food.[55]

No well defined dualism marked the Algonkian cosmogony, such as that which distinguished the Iroquoian of the nineteenth century. The latter, even, was doubtless accentuated and systematized by the Jesuit teaching of the opposing concepts of a beneficient God and a satanic power, of the duality of heaven and hell. With the Indians, spirits were beneficient or mischievous according to effect, not morally good or bad according to an absolute objective ethic. If a gun should burst and maim its owner, it was because an evil spirit was lodged within it. Conversely, the most useful article, sometimes the most mysterious, such as a solar quadrant, possessed a high degree of potency. As

48. Alexander 20.
49. Jesuit Relations 6, 157.
50. Leland (1) 26-27.
51. Leland (1) 110.
52. Parsons (1)* 88.
53. Speck (26) 60.
54. Speck (26) 59.
55. Leland (1) 338.

we have already pointed out in dealing with the displacement of materials, it was because of their superior potency that European implements were desired and cherished.[56] As was observed earlier, disease was the result of an anthropomorphic manito, the wife of one whose protection was sought in war, who wore a robe made from the hair of her victims, who might appear as fire, and who could be heard roaring as a flame.[57]   But Lahontan pointed out that "devil" was no translation of matchi manito, that the Indians did not think of the devil as having the figure of a man, with tail, horns, and claws; they thought of it as an evil force, signified more closely by misfortune, fate, or unfavourable destiny.[58]   It might, however, form a point of departure for the belief in Satan, coupled perhaps with the person of the malicious trickster.[59]

Of great moment in the lives of the eastern Algonkians was the belief in guardian spirits or departmental deities, which were not sharply distinguished from other manitos since any might become a guardian spirit on occasion. Notable among these were the elder brothers of the animals which were larger than the actual animals but which resembled them in every respect.   If an Indian should see "the elder of the Elks, he will take Elks, possessing the juniors through the favour of their senior whom he has seen in the dream".[60] Before a bear could be killed, its guardian spirit was subject to special rituals of propitiation on the part of the hunter.   A Montagnais of Tadoussac in 1652 prayed to God that he might kill a certain animal because God was "Lord of the Animals".[61]   Here perhaps God was fused with the culture hero to whom the guardian spirits were subordinate.[62]   Individual Indians might obtain personal guardian spirits through dreams, and it is not improbable that these, together with the elders of the animals may have furnished the Indians with a means of apprehending the Christian hierarchy of saints whose duties as guardians and whose functions as departmental experts were analagous. Mention of other manitos, some definitely and others vaguely anthropomorphic, will be reserved until a discussion of ceremonies of propitiation and coercion.

4.

Dreams, whose particular function as means of obtaining a guardian spirit has already been mentioned, played an integral and important part in eastern Algonkian religion.[63] Some were regarded as real and actual as the events of the waking life whereas others were considered as not true dreams.   How the two were distinguished is not certain.   The actions of the dream were regarded

56. Lahontan 2, 446.
57. Jesuit Relations 6, 175; see also Masson 414.
58. Lahontan 2, 448.
59. Passamaquoddy superstitions 229.
60. Jesuit Relations 6, 161; see Speck (3) 285.
61. Jesuit Relations 37, 195.
62. Jesuit Relations 6, 159.   "These elders of all the animals are the juniors of the Messou. Behold him well related, this worthy restorer of the Universe. He is elder brother to all the beasts." This passage seems to indicate a hierarchy. See also pp. 161-163 for other Montagnais beings.
63. See Johnson (1) 177 for custom amongst Golden Lake Algonkins.

as those of the soul or spiritual counterpart of the individual dreamer.   Not only were the actions a prediction of the future, but the true dreams exercised a control over coming events of which they demanded the fulfilment.   For instance, some Micmac in 1661 attacked and killed some Montagnais in fulfilment of a dream which exercised the responsibility of fulfilment over a whole group.[64]   The French in the early days were in frequent peril of their lives, since their lives were subject to the caprice of the dreams of their native allies. Dreams were considerd at first by the Jesuits as a great obstacle to the conversion of the Indians although they afterwards became the chief means by which this was achieved.

Although the French themselves believed in dreams, LeJeune ridiculed the Indians for the same belief.   The Quebec Montagnais in 1634 would not believe in God until they had seen him.   The European god had not come to their country so they did not believe.   ". . . . make me see him and I will believe in him."   When LeJeune explained that the soul as well as the body had eyes, a shaman answered, "I see nothing except with the eyes of the body, save in sleeping, and thou doest not approve our dreams."[66]   Even after conversion the Tadoussac Indians could not suppress their old beliefs and continued to dream that they should prepare eat-all feasts, that they should pray no more, and that sickness should be cured by putting eagle's feathers on the body.[67]

But when the images that were formed in the minds of the Indians as the result of the persistent teaching of the Jesuits began to recur in dreams a powerful means to the acceptance of Christianity was achieved, since they were still believed as true in spite of former Jesuit ridicule.   The priests themselves gave them more credence when they assumed a Christian character.[68]   In 1640 a certain Indian having had a dream, "publicly maintained before his nation that souls can go to Heaven, and that he would already be there if he had been baptized".   On another occasion the parents of dead children were visited by these in dreams and were told to embrace Christianity.[69]

The French were deliberate in their efforts to impress the minds of the Indians with the truths of their faith.   In 1640 they planned a drama in order to frighten the pagans into acceptance of Christianity.   The soul of an unbeliever was portrayed undergoing horrible torments and pursued by two demons, with the result that one of the spectators had a frightful dream of hell.[70]   On another occasion an Indian dreamed that he had been to heaven and had seen Jesus with his own eyes.   That mental saturation with Christian images was largely responsible for the dualism of later times may be gathered from the dream experiences of the seventeenth century, as exemplified by the following type:

"I saw myself surrounded by a great light. . . . I saw the house of that great Captian who has made all. . . . This suddenly disappear-

---

64. Jesuit Relations 47, 223 seq.
66. Jesuit Relations 7, 101.
67. Jesuit Relations 22, 227.

68. Jesuit Relations 48, 53.
69. Jesuit Relations 18, 199-201; 36, 25.
70. Jesuit Relations 18, 87.

ing. I lowered my eyes towards the earth, and saw a frightful gulf which paralyzed me with fear. . . . I was left . . . with a desire to believe and to obey God all my life. . ." [71]

Dreams never ceased to be significant features of Indian life,[72] and they continued to be a means of far-reaching import in the adaptation of the Indians to the conditions imposed by the new religion.

5.

To the eastern Algonkians the soul was vaguely conceived but its functions were very definite. It has been shown already how the events of dream were thought to be the real doings of the soul. If a Montagnais should cease to dream or to be moved by some great passion he would say that his soul had left him. It might, moreover, leave him while he yet lived, to go to his relatives in the land of the dead. This soul was thought of as the shadow replica of the man, or as a black image with human organs and needs, as among the Micmac.[73] A second soul was identified in some way with the body and was considered to go to the grave with it; and a third seems to have been identified with the intellectual faculty. This brain soul might be fed upon by an evil manito which was wont to put dried and withered leaves in its place, so that the person became "foolish and heedless".[74]

That soul which was associated with dream appears to have been peculiarly immortal. It was feared by the living who sought to prevent its return to this world by every means at their command. Supposing during the earthquake of 1663 "that the souls of the departed were striving to break through the gates of death and return into new bodies and reenter their former dwellings, they fired shots into the air . . . . believing that thus they were hindering the approach of the souls".[75] Those of their ancestors who had been killed in battle exercised a peculiar power over them, and it was necessary that they should avenge their deaths. We have already suggested this as the cause of feuds between groups of blood kindred. Ceremonial sallies, which were not unknown among the Montagnais may have served the same purpose.

Moreover, conflict with the missionaries arose from the fact that funeral rites had to be performed in the customary manner so that the soul of the departed would not be in want during and after his journey to the land of the dead. Awe of the soul was mingled with a very real affection for the dead relative. "A Savage coming to see the English Captain this winter, and seeing that everything was covered with snow, felt compassion for his brother who was buried near the French settlement. . ." so that it was necessary "to clear away the snow to satisfy him".[76] Not only did the necessities of this life, including air to breathe and freedom of passage, appertain to the other life, but this need extended to inanimate objects such as implements and utensils the

71. Jesuit Relations 14, 139.
72. Rand (2) 242.
73. LeClercq (2) 212-214.

74. Jesuit Relations 16, 191-193.
75. Jesuit Relations 48, 195.
76. Jesuit Relations 5, 55.

souls of which were indispensible to the welfare of the dead individual. Of the custom as it was practised in his day by the Micmac, Denys furnishes us with an apt description:

" 'But with respect to the kettle,' said he, 'they have need of it, since it is among us a utensil of new introduction, and with which the other world cannot yet be furnished. Do you not see,' said he, rapping again upon the kettle, 'that it has no longer any sound [77] and that it no longer says a word, because its spirit has abandoned it to go be of use in the other world to the dead man to whom we have given it. [78]. . .' At a time when they were not yet disabused of their errors, I have seen them give to the dead man, guns, axes, iron arrowheads, and kettles, for they held all these to be much more convenient for their use than would have been their kettles of wood, their axes of stone, and their knives of bone, for use in the other world. [79]

But since they cannot now obtain the things which come from us with such ease as they had in obtaining robes of Marten, of Otter, or of Beaver, bows and arrows, and since they have realized that guns and other things were not found in their woods or in their rivers, they have become less devout.

The Indians today practice still their ancient form of burial in every respect, except that they no longer place anything in their graves, for of this they are entirely disabused. [80]"

Besides the economic reasons here given for the disuse of the custom, imitation of French customs, the French being the dominant group, together with the teaching of the missionaries which in some cases led to conversion and the acceptance of a different world view, were not without weight.

At first the priests thought it expedient to allow the Montagnais to continue the custom of placing possessions in the grave for use in the land of the dead and to hold the feast which was the sine qua non of the funeral ceremony,[81] although they did what they could to discourage scaffold burial.[82]   It is, therefore, found that the graves and ceremonies of the second quarter of the century are marked by mingled Indian and Christian traits.   At Three Rivers in 1636 children were buried with French and Montagnais rites in the Christian cemetery.   The face was painted red and black, the body was wrapped in a strip of bark and covered with a white sheet which was obtained at the store, after which it was blessed by the priest and interred in holy ground.[83]   Among the Atticamegs scaffold burial continued during the 'fifties, together with the custom of placing weapons or household utensils on the grave, although the use of crosses in cemeteries was becoming general among the northern bands at this time.[84]   The new Christians were taught to bury their dead in such a way that they were facing eastward, but in the old pagan graves the body looked westward, the traditional direction of the land of the dead.[85]

As among all peoples who have conceived of personal immortality, the Algonkian land of the dead was merely an idealized representation of the world which they already knew: life was incomparably less irksome, food was

---

77. Having been buried for some time it was rusted and punctured and had lost its ring.
78. Denys 440.
79. Denys 439.
80. Denys 442.
81. Jesuit Relations 6, 129-133.
82. Jesuit Relations 9, 47.
83. Jesuit Relations 8, 259.
84. Jesuit Relations 37, 49, 215.
85. Jesuit Relations 44, 309.

plentiful, and the exercise of the senses was no doubt of a keener quality.   In the Montagnais resort, which abounded in blueberries, the dead were thought to occupy their time with continual feasts and dances.[86]   As it is probable that pain was unknown, they revolted violently against the Christian discrimination of souls into heaven and hell.   A sorcerer of Tadoussac "had seen the place where the souls of the baptized and of the unbaptized go, and that it is neither Heaven nor the pit, but a place toward the setting Sun, where they meet together."[87]   In spite of repeated remonstrance they continued to adhere to the belief of their ancestors.[88]   Baptized and unbaptized children were placed in the same grave since the Indians did not want to separate those who were fond of each other.   " 'Yet they are quite distant from each other,' said the Father; 'the one has been baptized and the other has not, and consequently the one is happy and the other groans in the flames.' "[89]   This belief had become current among the Micmac in LeClercq's time, who then recognized a dualism—an agreeable land for the good, and an unpleasant for the bad who sat eating the bark of rotten trees and who danced violently.[90]   Sometimes they tried to evade with a logic of their own the fate conjured up by the missionaries. "Perhaps . . . we people here have no souls, or perhaps they are not made like yours, or it may be that they do not go to the same place."[91]   It was a philosophy of despair, induced by cultural disintegration.   For to the eastern Algonkians the next world was an automatic sequence to this world, irrespective of individual action.   Thus they did not believe that one could be saved or damned on his own account.   There was no idea that the deeds of this life were expiated in the next.   The ethical control of the group to keep inviolate tabu and custom was maintained by public sentiment, or when this failed, by ceremonies to placate the supernatural force which had been offended. It was only when the native belief had been greatly modified that the conception of a Messiah, the key principle of the Christian ethic, became possible.[92] It was not till well into the eighteenth century that the Micmacs' belief in personal salvation gave birth to the idea of a saviour of their own people.[93]

6.

We have seen that the Indians believed that their souls possessed the capacity of predicting the future and of revealing the events of the future in true dreams.   And we have seen that, as they made a point of re-enacting the events of the dream in real life, the idea of prediction of the future merges or is one with that of control of the future.   Thus, an individual's soul revealed to him what had to be done.   The thought of the dream, the use of a word, and the enactment of a rite or ceremony, were all means to satisfy that universal craving of man to control his present and future environment so that

86. Jesuit Relations 16, 191.
87. Jesuit Relations 33, 24.
88. Jesuit Relations 8, 23.
89. Jesuit Relations 8, 255.

90. LeClercq (2) 212-214.
91. Jesuit Relations 7, 165-167.
92. Speck (23) 23.
93. Chamberlain A. F. (13).

it must react to his own advantage.   The relationship between magic and religion is the subject of much controversy and there is no need to enlarge upon it here.   Both systems have sprung from the same human impulse which is based upon the psychology of wish-fulfilment.   If magic is a means of coercing personal beings and impersonal powers either to benefit oneself or relatives, or to inflict injury upon an enemy, and if religion is the belief in personal supernatural beings who control departments of nature and who require to be supplicated in order that they might grant conditions favourable to life, then the two, magic and religion, appear to have existed side by side and to have supplemented each other in eastern Algonkian culture.   With the progress of missionary teaching it is possible that formerly benevolent manitos came to be regarded as evil, and it is possible that the supplication of their own supernatural beings was supplanted by coercive ceremonies.

Many of the old pagan customs were obliterated while others merged with and underlay what appeared superficially to be Christian ceremonies, just as the annual Micmac festival of St. Ann's Day, which was held throughout the nineteenth century, consisted partly of the ancient "wigubaltimk" and "neskouwadijik", and dances of the old time Indians.[94].   Many of the religious observances of both the Algonkians and the French, whether in the shape of rites or abstinences, related to the food supply.   With the Algonkians they were concerned largely with the propitiation of the guardian spirits of the game animals, particularly those of the bear and the beaver.   Bear ceremonialism, in various forms, occurred widely throughout the northern hemisphere.   Special honorific terms of appellation were employed by the Montagnais, the Têtes de Boule, the Penobscot, the Abenaki, and others, when they were approaching a bear with the intention of killing it; and among the Misstassini Cree a hunter was accustomed to nourish his "great man" or soul by drinking bear's grease.[95]   Rites were performed also at the cooking and eating of the bear.   The elder brothers of the beaver and certain fish and birds were the objects of certain rites among the Micmac of Port Royal at the end of the seventeenth century, in spite of missionary efforts to obliterate these superstitions:

> "That which remains to them of superstition is the pulling out of the eyes of fish, birds, and beasts and throwing them away, saying that without that they would be perceived by their counterpart, and could no longer approach them and they never burn the bones of them nor their remains. By a similar abuse they never singe the feet of . . . waterfowl, believing that those who remained living could [96] rest upon the sand and on account of that they could scarcely be caught by them."

But referring to the roasting of eels and the throwing of beaver bones to the dogs, Denys states that the Micmac of the gulf coast did not practice those rites in his day, since the French had disabused them of these beliefs.[97]   When LeJeune taunted the Montagnais for conserving animal bones, saying that the French and the Iroquois captured more game than they did and yet threw the

94. Rand (2) XXXI
95. Speck (18) 455; Hallowell (1) 43-45; Speck (11) 15-17.
96. Diereville 94.
97. Denys 430, 442.

bónes to the dogs, they answered that the French and the Iroquois cultivated the soil, that they were not dependent upon animals for food, and that their customs did not apply to themselves.[98]   When the Tadoussac Christians threw beaver bones to the dogs, their pagan fellows accused them of folly, saying that they would catch no more.[99]   It cannot be too often stressed that the breaking of ancient and hallowed tabus by newly converted Christians, who yet remained immune from any dire consequences, was one of the most salient factors in disintegrating the faith of those who had remained pagan.   Besides the guardian spirits, or elder brothers, there were other supernatural beings who were thought of as the personifications of special departments of nature. Communication with the "genii of light" enabled the shamans to divine the future;[100] exorcism was employed to drive out the evil manitou who caused disease; the protection of another was invoked in war,[101] and the seasons also were believed to be spirits, vaguely anthropomorphic, although unconcerned with human affairs.[102]   As among many other tribes, the thunder or wind bird was associated with the weather, and could be provoked by the breaking of a tabu.   The Montagnais complained to LeJeune that Father de Noüe would cause a heavy wind by working in the woods at an early hour in spite of the red sky.[103]   But superstitions of this kind were ridiculed to no purpose by the Jesuits, since they themselves believed in omens and second sight,[104] held public processions and prayers to end drought, and sprinkled holy water and rang bells to keep the blackbirds from eating the corn.[105]

It was, therefore, not strange that the priests did not always succeed in forcing the Indians to violate their own rites and abstinences;[106] they often carried them over into the fasts and food tabus of their own religion.   The Indians could comprehend the new by virtue of their own customs.   Thus, the Montagnais Christians of Sillery in 1639 voluntarily abstained from meat during Lent, while the pagan members of the families ate in abundance.   Even tobacco was not smoked on communion days "which is a rather difficult thing for a Savage, who prefers tobacco to food and drink".[107]   Crucifixes, tapers, rosaries, and paper calendars were taken by them on their winter hunts as reminders of fast days.   And the Miscou Micmac observed Sundays, Fridays, and other fast days during the winter hunt of 1645, even to the point of much suffering.   On the positive side, the Montagnais in 1636 wished to sacrifice tobacco to Jesus for success in the hunt.   "These are their tricks . . . . or devices they have retained from some of our French, who formerly deceived them under these fine pretences;" but in reality it was an old rite transferred to a new deity.[108]

Nevertheless there were sometimes serious obstacles to the observances of Christian abstinences.   The season of Lent, for example, was customarily observed by an agricultural people from time immemorial, among whom it

98. Jesuit Relations 6, 213.
99. Jesuit Relations 20, 199.
100. Jesuit Relations 6, 163.
101. Jesuit Relations 6, 175.
102. Jesuit Relations 6, 161.
103. Jesuit Relations 5, 151.

104. Jesuit Relations 46, 203.
105. Jesuit Relations 48, 161; Gyles 53-54.
106. LeClercq (2) 228.
107. Jesuit Relations 32, 229.
108. Jesuit Relations 9, 213.

corresponded to the period of scarcity towards the end of winter, when the supplies of the previous season of plenty were running low, and before the rebirth of the vegetable world at Easter or at kindred festivals.   On the other hand, among the Algonkians game was scarce in the inclement months of January, February and March before the opening of the rivers and the return of fish and fowl, whereas it could be easily tracked in the melting snow of spring and after game became abundant.   Thus, during Lent, having spent months on the verge of starvation, large supplies of fresh meat were again available.[109] For this reason the priests found it impossible to impose the incompatible custom upon a hunting people.   At Fort St. Joseph in 1688 the Jesuit Aveneau did not preach abstinence from meat in Lent after a winter of extreme shortage.[110]   And speaking of the beavers, otters, and seals, of Acadia, Lahontan wrote: "Thofe who love meat are indebted to the Doctors, who perfuaded the Popes to Metamorphofe thefe terreftial Animals into Fifh; for they are allowed to eat of 'em without fcruple in the time of Lent."[111]   Besides food, sexual abstinences were also observed in the Catholic church.   On one occasion an Indian wished to marry before proceeding to the spring hunt.   If he postponed it for forty days on account of Advent, who, he asked, would make his snowshoes?   If he should ask his betrothed he would be the laughing stock of his people.   Nevertheless the marriage was postponed at the will of the priest.[112]

Another set of phenomena was involved with the coercion or control of that impersonal manito to which frequent reference has already been made. Certain natural or artificial objects were thought to be the repositories of this manito, or were vaguely associated with the mysterious power.   They were localized in animal bones, peculiar stones, tufts of feathers, and kindred objects. Other objects were supposed to be evil, and were avoided.   Thus, on one occasion three pieces of curved iron were alleged to have caused the illness of an Algonkin, from whom they were extracted by a shaman.[113]   Generally the amulets or luck stones of the natives were the special objects of Jesuit wrath, but they were surreptitiously used at Sillery as late as 1642; and at Tadoussac "the charmed stones that make men lucky at play, or in the chase, are held in esteem only by some stubborn persons, who produce them in secret only, for fear of being jeered at by the faithful."[114]   Here also it was not long before crucifixes were being substituted for the old stones, as a priest wrote in 1676:

> "One must be provided in this country with medals, small crucifixes a finger in length, or smaller still, small brass crosses and brass rings, also some in which there is the figure of some saint, or the face of Jesus Christ or the Blessed Virgin; wooden rosaries, very black and very thick, which they wear hanging from the neck or about the head."[115]

109.   LeClercq (2) 110.
110.   Lahontan (1) XX.
111.   Lahontan 1, 326.
112.   Jesuit Relations 18, 229-231.
113.   Jesuit Relations 9, 85.
114.   Jesuit Relations 22, 73, 229; 24, 135; Amulets are still in use among the Montagnais and Misstassini in spite of early missionary efforts. See Speck and Heye (11).
115.   Jesuit Relations 60, 137.

The use of the cross soon became widespread throughout the whole area.[116] The Micmacs spoke of the God of the cross and the Atticamegs prayed before an embossed crucifix.[117] During the illness of a Micmac chief "the Savages bethought themselves to apply to his body some images, Rosaries, and Crosses; for they make great account of these, using them against the molestations of the Demons."[118] But the Indians did not have a monopoly of such beliefs, for the case is recorded of a Frenchwoman in New France who believed that illness could be cured by hanging keys about the neck;[119] and the Jesuits saved a Montagnais woman in child labour by placing a relic of St. Ignace about her neck. "Hardly had her . . . body touched the Reliquary, when she was delivered without difficulty and without pain,—to the astonishment of all the Savages; . . . ."[120]

Related to the use of amulets, or the mutilation of the image of one's enemy, was the belief, which was based upon the sympathetic complex, that the possession or knowledge of a name involved also the possession of the object or person named. Thus the magic word invoked the thing it signified. It was for this reason that the Indians could not at first endure the frequent reference to death on the part of the Jesuits; because they could see that it was making them die.[121] "Formerly if one spoke of death in their country, he became a criminal, and, as it were, a murderer. Now they have changed their style; . . ."[122] For the same reason an eastern Algonkian would never tell his real name to a stranger lest he put himself in his power.[123]. Sometimes names were changed at regular intervals from childhood to old age, or in sickness, the act of which was either symbolic or gave the individual "a new lease of life". In the same way a dead chief might be resuscitated by having another individual take his name.[124] How closely this rite approached to that of a reincarnation is not certain; but at any rate, it furnished the Indians with a means, additional to those which we have already enumerated, of comprehending the Christian resurrection:

> "The Indians of Quebec in 1647 were 'beginning to give quite a distinct character to the harmless usages that they have derived from their infidel ancestors . . . it was the custom of the Savages to bring back to life those among them who were persons of note, or who were greatly beloved. . . . This is still done, in order that the orphans may not be abandoned; for he to whom the name of their father is given takes charge of the children. . . .
>
> The officiator accompanied the rite with the declaration that '. . . inasmuch as life is taken away from us only to be again restored,— it is not a death, but an absence; and, consequently I take this resurrection of my nephew . . . as a symbol of the true resurrection to which we look forward.' "[125]

---

116. Jesuit Relations 22, 57; 32, 213.
117. Jesuit Relations 26, 77; LeClercq (2) 189. These cases may represent fetishism. See Haddon 66, 72-91 for fetishism; and 29 seq for distinctions between talismans, amulets, fetishes and idols.
118. Jesuit Relations 45, 63.
119. Jesuit Relations 16, 195.
120. Jesuit Relations 31, 151.
121. Jesuit Relations 9, 117.
122. Jesuit Relations 37, 47.
123. Jesuit Relations 5, 93; 44, 305.
124. Jesuit Relations 16, 203.
125. Jesuit Relations 32, 209. See Haddon 22 seq, 26, for the magic power of words.

We are now in a position to summarize some of the salient contributions of Christianity to eastern Algonkian religion.   By a process of blending, some of the Christian deities and sacred personages were identified or confused with Algonkian supernatural beings.   Possibly sometimes the local beings were supplanted or thrust into the background.   Thus, Jesus, a powerful deity of the Europeans was at first identified with the sun or the spirit that dwelt within it.   Gluskap played the part of Noah or of the instigator of the flood while at the same time retaining some of his own characteristics.   At other times he was the rival or the forerunner of Christ.   The guardian spirits and other supernatural beings were akin in function to the Christian saints.   In more than one case a malicious trickster no doubt degenerated into the person of Satan.   Dreams were extremely vivid forms of religious experience which at first hindered but eventually aided conversion after they had assumed a Christian character.   The material world tended to become "despiritualized" by the teaching of the missionaries, and material objects were no longer thought of as possessing souls which could pass to the land of the dead.   Thus the old forms of burial tended to fall into disuse.   But the idea of individual salvation or damnation came hard to a people who regarded the next world as an automatic sequence to this life.   Old rites and ceremonies continued to underlie those of a superficially Christian character.   Others which were unsuited to the native life, even in its altered circumstances, did not take root.   Algonkian amulets and luck-stones were discarded in favour of, or held their places beside those of a Christian character, as they do today.   And finally, the supplication and coercion of supernatural beings continued to survive beside, and not sharply distinguishable from, the supplication of Christian deities.

7.

In conclusion something should be said of the professional jealousy which arose between the Catholic priests and the Algonkian shamans, and which provided a powerful force of opposition to the spread of Christianity, since it was to the shamans that the people looked for an attitude towards, and an interpretation of, the new religion.   The shamans saw their opponents as greater magicians than themselves; they saw themselves confronted by a magic with which they could not cope, and they knew that their own prestige and power were in jeopardy.   And it was necessary that the Algonkians should recognize that the supernatural beings of the immigrants were more powerful and capable of protecting them from their own, before they would switch their allegiance.   On one occasion when the Montagnais were in deadly fear of an evil manito, LeJeune harangued it in their own language, challenging it to approach; and although they were impressed they did not fail to offer a sacrifice of eels.   But a retaliation was scored in 1634 when the Montagnais shaman invited LeJeune to enter the conjuring lodge so that he might see the manitos for himself.   Fearing, however, that the Indians would commit some outrage upon him the priest declined.[126]   He continued, nevertheless, to undermine the reputation of the shamans by ridiculing their pretensions and by exposing them to their own people as charletans.   In 1637 a crisis was reached when the shaman of the Quebec band wagered that his lodge should be shaken by the manitos although he himself would not touch it.   When LeJeune tripled the wager the people took sides and the betting became general, and when he promised them the bettings if he should win them, he won the majority to his side.   At this point the sorcerer lost confidence and asked for a postponement of the contest.   But instead of appearing at the appointed time the shaman went into the woods to hunt hares.   LeJeune gathered the people around him and dumbfounded them by performing a simple trick with a piece of magnetic metal.   From the embarrassing wiles of the shaman he had issued victorious.[127]   In the following year the shaman "burned all the utensils of his art, and has never again consented to tamper with it since then,—although he has been often secretly solicited to do so, and with valuable presents".[128] By 1638 LeJeune could write:

> "The Sorcerers and Jugglers have lost so much of their credit that they no longer blow upon any sick person, nor beat their drums, except perhaps at night, or in isolated places,—but no longer in our presence. No more eat-all feasts are seen, no more consultations of demons. . . . The other superstitions will be suppressed little by little. When any one of them does practise these, he does all he can to prevent our being informed of it, for fear of being reported." [129]

By 1647 it was said that the superstitions of the Quebec band were completely suppressed;[130] but by this time the band itself was at the point of extinction.

Although the native ceremonies had begun to lapse among the Tadoussac band by 1646, its members who had a particular flair for supernatural consultation, began without authority to assume the functions of priests.   One exercised the sacred ceremonies, while another constituted herself as confessor. This continued until it came to the ears of the priests.[131]   Among the Atticamegs sorcery still was practised in 1648, and among the Papinachois, sorcerers were still active opponents of the priests as late as 1663.   Among the Island Algonkians, where the power of the shamans was at its greatest, during the first quarter of the century, the priests were accused of the blackest of magic and were in hourly danger of their lives.[132]   Among the Abenaki Dreuillettes' strong personality forced the sorcerers to acknowledge their weakness and the power of Jesus, and their hostility was followed in some cases by a docile mind.   Desiring to enjoy the esteem rendered to the priests, inspired by the messianic role of saviours of their people, and taking advantage of the abandonment of the Acadian missions by the Jesuits, certain Micmac assumed a new dignity, heard confessions, and performed religious rites, which were comparable to those which have already been mentioned in connection with the Tadoussac Montagnais.   One of the Kennebec declared that he had received

---

126. Jesuit Relations 6, 169-173.
127   Jesuit Relations 11, 257-261.
128. Jesuit Relations 14, 133.
129. Jesuit Relations 14, 223.

130. Jesuit Relations 32, 253.
131. Jesuit Relations 29, 125.
132. Jesuit Relations 20, 250; 24, 209.

a gift from heaven which enabled him to perform the sacred mysteries. This was a picture which had been traded to him by the French. Women set up as religieuses leading secluded or monastic lives, and saying prayers to the sun in their own fashion. One of these had beads of jet which were the remains of a rosary, and which she regarded as her charm. They had come to her from heaven, and she could invoke them to cure the sick or to prophesy the approach of enemies. She was devoted also to a king of hearts from a pack of playing cards, the foot of a glass, and a medal, before which she prostrated herself as before divinity.[133]   These Micmac messiahs were not unknown in the nineteenth century.[134]

In such ways did the eastern Algonkians adapt themselves to the exactions of the new religion. Here, as in the economic and social spheres, many failed to make the adjustment and died, life having lost its meaning; or their halfbreed descendants were absorbed into the white tide that swept over the eastern woodlands in the romantic and chivalrous days of British and French colonial expansion. Happy were those whose territories lay beyond the hinterland of white settlement.[135]

---

133. LeClercq (2) 229-232.
134. Rand (2) 230
135. Speck. Since the chapters on Political Modification, Social Disintegration and Religion were written there has appeared Speck, F.G. "Ethical Attributes of the Labrador Indians" AA 35 No. 4 1933, p. 559. Dr. Speck has shown that the Montagnais and Nascopi, who today live on and beyond the fringe of white settlement, retain many of their pre-Columbian attributes; such as, no idea of reward and punishment in the future life; hospitality and consideration of the welfare of one's fellows; esteem for women and children; night visits of suitors; honesty, and almost total absence of thieving; veracity; and cooperation. Traits that would indicate certain changes which are touched upon in this thesis are also dealt with in the article.

CHAPTER 12

ART, PICTOGRAPHY AND MUSIC

1.

In 1914 the results of Dr. Speck's preliminary researches into the art of the northeast were published under the title of "The Double-curve Motive in Northeastern Algonkian Art". According to his view the motive consists of two opposed incurves as a foundation element, with embellishments modifying the enclosed space, and with variations in the shape and proportions of the whole.[1] Subordinate are the realistic floral patterns and the geometric designs; the former consisting of the three lobed figure, the blossom, bud, leaf, and tendril; the latter including the cross-hatched diamond, circle, zigzag, rectangle, and serrated border. From the Nascopi, where the primary curve is found almost exclusively, the floral elements grow in importance as one proceeds westward through the Montagnais to the Great Lakes where it tends to usurp the field. Thus the primary motive is most characteristic in the extreme northeast. Generally speaking the progression from curve to floral preponderance as one proceeds in a westerly direction occurs south of the St. Lawrence as it does in the north. Among the Penobscot the realistic floral figures may occur as separate design elements or they may merge with the double-curve, always, however, remaining secondary in importance. Among this tribe also the curves have served as political symbols of the Wabanaki confederacy which the author has attributed to Iroquoian influence. Throughout the northeast the motive was "a presumably indefinite plant or floral figure", constituting "an originally non-symbolic decorative element."[2] The author did not at this time suggest the possibility of European influence upon any aspect of northeastern Algonkian art.

After a more extended and detailed study of Penobscot art, Dr. Speck in 1927 re-affirmed his original position with respect to native versus European origin.[3] The curved designs are aboriginal, and correspond to painted designs on skin, beadwork and embroidery among the Montagnais and Nascopi. He believes that the double-curve figures were, if not actually derived from, at least historically related to the bitten patterns in birch-bark, which, although the biting of patterns is known only as a children's game among the Penobscot today, are still used by Montagnais, Nascopi, Cree and Ojibwa women to derive ideas for beadwork, silk embroidery and birch-bark etching. He observes elsewhere that certain Mohecan beadwork designs on birch-bark have probably succeeded porcupine quill work or etchings.[4] Among the Penobscot the double-curve is found carved in wood or incised in birch-bark, accom-

1. Speck (5) 1.
2. Speck (5) 17.
3. Speck (28) 31.
4. Speck (20) 9.

panied by geometrical figures, composites, and realistic animal likenesses.   In this field of ornamentation the realistic floral designs are generally lacking. The relation of later materials and methods would seem to indicate that the primary curve is of pre-historic origin.

Dr. Speck states that the geometrical figures, such as the zigzags and triangles are very old, and pre-European.   That an incized stone blade with linear patterns, similar to some in a Penobscot border series was discovered by Willoughby in a pre-historic burial place in Maine,[5] he takes as evidence for the pre-historic provenance of cross-hatched and zigzag designs.   Moreover, Dr. Speck maintains that the curve patterns were probably originally plant representations, and he adduces evidence to support the contention that plant representations were prophylactic fetishes "associated with the protective and curative properties of the medicinal herbs which are so important to these Indians in the treatment of disease."[6]   This may be taken as a further indication of a pre-historic origin. The same origin is held for the Penobscot realistic floral designs because they occur with the double-curve, although they have been greatly developed since European contact when they were separated from the curved figures and used as units.   Those which are to be found today "are clearly of modern origin, since they occur almost solely on objects made within the last fifty years".   Some stimulation of native productiveness is to have been expected from the introduction of European materials, such as that which popularized the ribbon applique and painted decorations of the Penobscot,[7] that which modified the totem poles of the northwest coast, and the wall paintings of certain South African peoples,[8] but the use of silk thread, cloth, beads, steel needles and knives does not appear to have stimulated the artists of the Têtes de Boule to finer efforts.[9]   As we know in our day, the quantity of production is by no means coordinated with a finer sense of artistry.

Diametrically opposed to the view that the basic motives of northeastern Algonkian art are of native origin is that held by Mr. Marius Barbeau, who ascribes them entirely to French influence, since none of the traditional garments of the Indians, on which these designs often occur, are pre-Columbian.   Rather they are the styles of the French renaissance and peasant art. According to this view the floral art, to which the double-curve has been intimately related, is derived from the rococo figures and ornaments of the period of Francis I.[10]   Mr. Barbeau, who has made extensive collections of early French Canadian eccelesiastical art, stresses the importance of the school of artisans founded by Laval at Cap Tourmente in 1669, the Ursuline school at Quebec, and others at Three Rivers, and Montreal, where the Indians were taught sewing and embroidery.   The French and the Indians were taught together for purposes of assimilation. Appliqué and embroidery on garments were

5.   Speck (28) 73; Mr. T. F. McIlwraith believes that it is unsafe to generalize from such scant evidence; since the incised blade might have belonged to some earlier culture which was entirely distinct from that which is considered here.
6.   Speck (28) 59.
7.   Speck (28) 53.
8.   Chamberlain (14) 208.
9.   Davidson (1) 116.
10.   Barbeau (10) 512.

derived by the natives from their teachers in these schools. The floral and geometric designs go back to colonial days when Eskimo, Algonkian and Iroquois girls made church ornaments for many years. Afterwards deer sinew, moose hair, and porcupine quills were substituted when silk was lacking. Beads (rassades) were supplied by the traders. ". . . . educators . . . . introduced a form of renaissance art among their early wards that has since been mistaken for one wholly their own."[11] Mr. Barbeau has suggested that in his opinion the double-curve may be the conventionalized segment of a Christian cross.

One would naturally look to the records of the seventeenth century to throw some light upon the problem These, however, are disappointingly meagre. We are told that Micmac dwellings were ornamented "with a thousand different pictures of birds, moose, otters and beavers, which the women sketch there themselves with their paints".[12] Moreover, they painted figures of animals, including birds, on their faces in red, white, black and yellow.[13] The tatooing of all sorts of figures, including crosses, flowers, and the name of Jesus was practised in 1699. At the same time Diereville observed that the manufacture of moccasins ornamented with porcupine quill designs were made only to sell "those who want to wear them to show them in their country. "[14] Whether this refers to the disuse of an old or the beginning of a new art technique is by no means certain.

Evidence from the tribes dwelling north of the St. Lawrence is generally not more explicit. In 1638 the Montagnais were observed to be wearing "painted and figured robes".[15] Beyond this meagre description the Jesuits do not seem to have been interested, although they actively discouraged body painting.[16] In the second quarter of the century porcupine quill work was practised by the Algonkins since a tobacco pouch embroidered with quills was noticed in their possession, which would strengthen the belief that the porcupine quill work among the Micmac, which was mentioned above, was an ancient art of these people.[17] Among the same people the dream origin of certain designs which were used for prophylactic purposes was mentioned by the Jesuits, and is comparable to that which has been recorded by Dr. Speck among the Penobscot, contrary to the general statement of Dr. Boas to the effect that protective motives are wanting in North America.[18] But the Jesuits recorded that the Algonkins cured a patient by making her lie on a sheep skin upon which were painted canoes, paddles, animals, and other figures, or upon a sheet decorated with the figures of men-singing and dancing. This cure had been revealed in a dream.[19]

Certainly the pictorial representations of individuals expiating their sins in eternal torment must have made a profound impression upon the minds of the Indians. At Sillery in 1681 "as soon as anyone arrives, they come to ask

11. Barbeau (1) See also Barbeau (9).
12. LeClercq (2) 100.
13. LeClercq (2) 95.
14. Diereville 97-99.
15. Jesuit Relations 14, 267.

16. Jesuit Relations 18, 153.
17. Jesuit Relations 25, 125.
18. Speck (28) 79.
19. Jesuit Relations 8, 261.

me for a picture of hell, to show it to him".[20]   And the growing importance
of European design and ornament could have been observed at the Abenaki
chapel of St. Francois de Sales in 1684.   Besides an image of St. Francis done
on satin, with a border of gold and silver fringe.

> "The whole Altar was covered with a great number of Collars,
> made in all sorts of designs; Bugle beads and strings of porcelain; and
> articles worked with glass Beads and porcupine quills."[21]

But the most illuminating piece of ·evidence concerning the modification of
northeastern Algonkian art by European influence was recorded at Tadoussac
in 1647, which may indicate that the art of the Montagnais was wholly
geometric, and that naturalistic representation, necessitating irregular curved lines,
was wholly lacking, although the tatooing of serpents, toads, squirrels and eagles
has been recorded among the Neutrals and Tobacco Nation.[23]   In 1647 the
missionary wrote:

> "We have furnished this year a little tapestry of drugget, to
> embellish the chapel of Tadoussac; . . . One of them remarked that
> this tapestry was made in a watered pattern, ran to his people: 'Be on
> your guard,—they have exposed the souls or figures of serpents and
> snakes in their house of prayers. Do not enter it, for it is all surround-
> ed with the robes and garments of Demons.'"[24]

The problem of European influence upon the art of these peoples may
never be satisfactorily solved. One fact, however, is worthy of note. Dr. Speck
states that the double-curve is the primary motive, and that the floral designs
are secondary and dependent upon it.   I wish to suggest the proposition that
the floral figures are not necessarily connected in origin with the double curve.
Their association in some cases may represent a fusion of the aboriginal double-
curve with the European floral elements which Mr. Barbeau believes to have
been derived from French renaissance art.   It is noteworthy that in the art
of the Nascopi, who have been the most far-removed from European influences
of all the Algonkian tribes, the double-curve appears to dominate the field, to
the almost total exclusion of floral figures.   Whereas the floral figures grow
in importance with every succeeding tribe as one moves westward from the
Montagnais to the central Algonkians of the Great Lakes.   The floral designs
preponderate along the line of what was the main route of the fur-trade in the
seventeenth century.

---

20. Jesuit Relations 62, 43.
21. Jesuit Relations 63, 27-31.

23. Sinclair 369.
24. Jesuit Relations 31, 247.

2.

A special interest has been attached to the occurence of the cross among the Micmac. Its use was first recorded by Lescarbot at the beginning of the century. He says:

> "Sagamos . . . eats nothing without lifting up his eyes to heaven, and making the sign of the cross, because he saw us do so; . . . and having seen a great cross planted near our fort, he has made the like at his house . . . saying, that he is no longer a savage. . . . And what I say of him, I may affirm of almost all the others." [25]

In 1612 Biard distributed crosses of brass to the Indians at Port Royal, [26] and in 1635 those of Cape Breton were said to have adopted it and painted it on their bodies. Emphasis should be laid on the fact that the use of the cross as a decoration among all of the eastern tribes was in imitation of the missionaries who sometimes did not travel to remote places as fast as their sacred symbol. [27] Frequent reference to the cross among the Micmac was made before LeClercq's time, and when he visited the Micmac he found it used for a variety of purposes.

> "They wear it pictured upon their clothes and upon their flesh; they hold it in their hands in all their voyages, . . . they place it both outside and inside their wigwams, as a mark of honour which distinguishes them from the other nations of Canada." [28]

Moreover, it was erected in the centre of band council assemblies when decisions of moment were made. It was hung around the head for protection and worn at night on the head to ward off evil spirits. Pregnant women wore crosses of wampum and beads over their wombs. Clothes, cradles, canoes, snowshoes and dwellings were adorned with it. [29] In the round it was used as a landmark for fishing and hunting places, sometimes with double and triple cross-pieces, and in the cemeteries to mark the graves of the dead, the latter being almost certainly of Christian derivation. [30] Its manifold functions appear to belie LeClercq's statement that it had fallen into disuse on account of war and disease.

LeClercq tried to make the Miramichi Micmac admit that the cross had been introduced by the first missionaries, and he rejected as impossible the statement that the cross had been in use before the arrival of the first ship, since no one then living could have remembered that event. It is now generally known that the cross was a widespread motive in pre-Columbian Indian art, [31] and it has even been used as an argument in favor of contact with the old world in ancient times. [32] Moreover, the Micmac explanation of the origin of the cross is probably correct. It was said to have appeared to an individual in a dream with the implication that it would cure an epidemic which was then killing the whole people. [33] They said that other Micmac bands had mission-

---

25. Lescarbot 3, 94.
26. Jesuit Relations 2, 101.
27. Jesuit Relations 8, 163; 37, 33; 31, 253.
28. LeClercq (2) 145.
29. LeClercq (2) 148-149.

30. LeClercq (2) 151.
31. Peet (2) Chapter 8; Saintyves 71.
32. LeClercq (2) 37-38 notes.
33. LeClercq (2) 146.

aries but that they did not have the cross, and that they themselves had been visited by the priests at a later date.   The exclusive use of the cross by one band may be explained on the ground that it was a group symbol which could be used only by the band whose member had dreamed about it.   Ownership of the symbol was collective with respect to the band.[34]   Dr. Ganong has suggested the possibility that the cross was a conventionalized representation of a bird in flight, since waterfowl were as characteristic of the Miramichi as the salmon was of the Restigouche, and the salmon is remembered as the symbol of the latter band to this day.   On the other hand the Miramichi band had as symbols the sturgeon, the beaver, and a man with a drawn bow.   But Dr. Ganong questions the latter as a basis for the cross, and suggests that LeClercq found the native cross modified by Christian influence, since it was customary to utilize the pagan symbol for Christian purposes.[35]   There is, of course, no reason to believe that the dream in which the cross appeared did not occur after the first contact and was not stimulated thereby, and its distinguishing character among the Miramichi might have been due to the fact that no member of another band had had that precise dream, which in itself, may definitely have marked ownership.   It is interesting to note that only among the Micmac is the double-curve characterized by a "horizontal bar in the centre of the enclosed area supported upon two out-curves from the bottom".[36]

3.

Broadly speaking, the exact relationship between the Algonkian art forms and their pictography has not been worked out, if indeed, it ever will, although Dr. Speck has in some instances connected pictographs with the double-curve.[37]   But it is probable that certain inscriptions having a curative and protective value may be closely related to or even classed as pictographs. Certainly the Malecite, Passamaquoddy, Penobscot and Micmac totems were represented in pictographs, in the latter case the symbol being two Indians paddling a canoe after a deer, though the manned canoe is said to be a modern addition.[38]   It is probable, moreover, that human, animal and plant forms were represented, though their extent and nature in prehistoric times is not certain.

LeClercq's tutorial efforts among the Micmac elaborated their pictography beyond that of neighbouring tribes.   He noticed that the children were accustomed to make marks on birch-bark with charcoal to aid their memory as they prayed,[39] which was a custom practised also among Montagnais bands, notably the Atticamegs.[40]   He determined to make use of existing symbols, to

---

34. LeClercq (2) 191.
35. LeClercq (2) 39-40.
36. Speck (5) 7.
37. Speck (28) 62.
38. Mallery 379. Could representations of the chase have resulted from scarcity of food due to fire-arms and fur-trade?
39. LeClercq (2) 24, 131.
40. Jesuit Relations 24, 83.

change them and to amplify their number so as to be able to express to his pupils certain unfamiliar Christian concepts such as the sacred mysteries of the Trinity, the Incarnation, baptism, the Penitence, and the Eucharist. Since these and kindred ideas were totally unknown he must have begun almost anew, and finally to have wrought an almost complete transformation of the native pictography.[41] Moreover, contact with a new culture, involving a displacement of materials, and the introduction of foreign customs and concepts, must have greatly amplified the Algonkian pictography, if it did not have the opposite effect of obliterating it by the spread of European literacy and by growth of the stigma that was attached to native traits.[42]

It is by no means certain whether the pictographs were the result of individual conception, their meaning not being clear to any one but the inventor, and requiring to be taught by him, or whether their meaning was generally recognizable throughout a given area. Maurault noticed in the nineteenth century that the Abenaki used very singular hieroglyphics which they traced on bark during explanations of the catechism and which they taught to others.[43] Moreover, this practice was found to be current in the seventeenth century:

> "Some would write their lessons after a fashion of their own, using a bit of charcoal for a pèn, and a piece of bark instead of paper. Their characters were new and so peculiar that one could not recognize or understand the writing of another,—that is to say, they used certain signs corresponding to their ideas; as it were, a local reminder, for recalling points and articles and maxims which they retained." [44]

On the other hand, when papers were presented to certain Micmac who had come from a long distance on purpose to be instructed, LeClercq found that they "could already decipher the characters with as much ease as if they had always lived among us."[45] LeClercq's system has existed among the Micmac, but not among neighbouring tribes down to the present day,[46] but so changed from definite Micmac symbols were those recorded by Kauder in 1866 that they cannot be considered as examples of genuine Indian pictography.[47]

Neither the native nor the elaborated pictographs ever approached the condition of true writing, for sometimes the ideogram represented mnemonically a single word, two words, a whole sentence, or even a verse.[48] Within more recent times few of the Micmac had any idea of the connection between the characters and the vocables of the language. They were not able to read since they could not detach the symbols from their places in a prayer and use them in a different context to represent the Micmac word or words which they were supposed to represent.[49] Thus the system was not elastic, and although it may have accelerated the growth of Christian knowledge in a limited way, it was destined by its inherent rigidity to remain a restrictive vehicle. And, moreover, where true writing was practised, as among some of the Atticamegs children in 1648, it is more than probable that the proverbial long and accurate memory

41. LeClercq (2) 24-25.
42. Lahontan 2, 512 seq.
43. Mallery 666.
44. Jesuit Relations 38, 27.
45. LeClercq (2) 130.

46. LeClercq (2) 25.
47. Mallery 669; LeClercq (2) 30.
48. Mallery 670.
49. LeClercq (2) 125-126.

of the native became shorter and more faulty.   In general, it appears that, although Montagnais girls at Quebec were able to write in their own language as early as 1640, literacy made slow progress, which was partly due to the unstable living conditions of the time.

4.

The nature and extent of European influence upon the music of the eastern Algonkians is subject to the same uncertainty as that which exists with respect to art and design, but realizing the close association of the two races, some modification is to have been expected.   Unlike the Puritans, who did not sanction the playing of a Jew's harp, the French Catholics maintained a close connection between music and church ritual, and the missionaries found that music was a quick means of attracting the attention of the Indians to the imported faith.[51]   The songs of both groups were mainly of a religious nature since the Indians were accustomed to sing songs to the various supernatural beings in order to secure guidance to the food supply, and those which were the occasion of marriage, war, and death were not without a close religious association.   If the testimony of the missionaries can be accepted the Indians showed a quick appreciation of European music and adapted themselves to it with facility.   The Montagnais showed a liking for French songs in 1634 and often asked LeJeune to sing to them.[52]   And on another occasion some Montagnais begged that "some of our young people should dance to the sound of a hurdy-gurdy, that a little Frenchman held".[53]   By 1645 the Sillery Indians had learned to sing very melodiously.[54]   In the same year the Micmacs of Miscou ". . . since we have set their prayers to music . . . take a remarkable pleasure in attending them, and pride themselves on singing very well".[55] That their pride was not unjustified is testified by LeClercq:

> "They have . . . rather good voices as a rule, and especially the women, who chant very pleasingly the spiritual canticles which are taught them, and in which they make a large part of their devotions consist. These women do not give the same pleasure when they sing in the manner of the Indians. . . ." [56]

The Jesuits found that the Abenaki at Sillery in 1681, who had fine voices, were keen students of the French songs and were impatient to teach them to each other.   These songs were not always equally pleasant and the priests did not hesitate to play upon the Indians' emotion of fear when converts were to be won.   At St. Francois de Sales in 1684 they gave

> "instructions on Hell by means of certain Mournful Songs and some spectacular representations, which have had considerable influence upon our savages. I have tried to express in those Mournful Songs, all that is best fitted, according to the Idea of the Savages, to

51. Spell 119-120.
52. Jesuit Relations 6, 183-185.
53. Jesuit Relations 9, 269.

54. Jesuit Relations 27, 117.
55. Jesuit Relations 28, 33.
56. LeClercq (2) 292.

torment one damned, and the vices which are the most common among them." [57]

Unlike the Spaniards in Mexico whose settled purpose it was to suppress the native arts, crafts and music, the French made use of native songs for purposes of proselytization. LeJeune was in the habit of concluding his school programmes with the singing of the Pater Noster translated into Algonkian rhythms, and it is probable that songs translated into Montagnais were set to native airs.[58]   Moreover, the Indian songs which are current in the province of Quebec at the present time are said to be adaptations of "les melodies gregoriennès" and "des airs de cantiques francais".[59]   It is probable, however, that the drum remained the chief musical instrument of the Indians, although the French had violins, flutes, and organs, at Quebec in the seventeenth century.[60] These were in use in the dramatic rituals of the church to which the Indians were often willing accessories, and which were the most important ceremonials of the colonists, although stage plays translated into native languages were not unknown.   Although it is the view of Mr. D. Jenness that the impact of civilization has exerted little effect on Indian music,[61] Spell has maintained that the music of the Indians which is studied today as their own differs from that of pre-European times on account of the French influence.[62]

---

57. Jesuit Relations 63, 671.
58. Spell 123; Jesuit Relations 22, 243.
59. Gagnons 183.

60. Spell 124-126.
61. Jenness (1) 108.
62. Spell 130.

CHAPTER 13

MYTHOLOGY

It is not generally admitted today that contact with the Norse colonies in Vinland has left any perceptible imprint upon aboriginal American culture.[1] Apart from claims made for the Norse influence on certain Eskimo traits, such as the igloo dome, and upon certain Indian bannerstones, gouges, and astronomical concepts,[2] the only attempt worthy of note here was made by Charles G. Leland to prove that the mythology of the Micmac and Wabanaki was in part or wholly derived from that of the Norse colonists. In default of concomitant characteristics in the spheres of material culture and social organization he was forced to rely entirely upon what internal evidence there might chance to be. He found that the mythology of the eastern Algonkians bore a closer relationship to that of the Northmen as it was portrayed in the Elder or Poetic Edda than it did to that of the central Algonkians. The bulk of his argument centred about the characteristics and actions of Gluskap, the culture-hero, and Laks, the trickster. To what extent is Leland's thesis tenable in the light of the wider knowledge of North American mythology that exists today? And to what extent was Leland justified in assuming a Norse influence from the material at hand in his day? He knew that the Northman and Wabanaki had come together, although he presumed upon the extent of their intercourse to an unwarranted degree. Also he knew that the mythology of the eastern group diverged widely from that of the other Algonkian tribes. It is true that the Montagnais-Nascopi show more resemblances to the eastern Algonkian with respect to tales lying outside the culture-hero type than within it, and that in the culture-hero cycle the similarities with the central Algonkian tales are more pronounced than they are with the Wabanaki cycle.[3] In the same way the strong numerical resemblances between the Ojibwa and Micmac mythologies lie wholly in the instances not relating to the culture-hero cycle, few of the latter being found alike in the two tribes.[4] In tales concerning the culture-hero which are not included in the cycle there is almost as little agreement between the eastern and central groups as in the connected cycle itself. Notable exceptions in which an agreement is found are in the tale of the "hood-winked dancers" which is widespread among North American tribes, and in the tale of "the rolling rock", the "visit to the culture-hero", and "the bungling host". It would seem, therefore, that the Gluskap cycle, with its attendant dualism, stands apart from the other Algonkian hero cycles to a marked degree. Gluskap is more benevolent than Nanabuju, and among the Micmac the more fiendish type of practical joke was attributed to the animal trickster who was known to Leland as Lox, and who appears sometimes as a badger and sometimes as a

---

1. Jenness (1) 219, Note 1.
2. MacLeod (1) 12.

3. Dixon (3) 5.
4. Dixon (3) 4.

wolverine. But must we seek for the origin of Gluskap in far Scandanavia when the Iroquois, who were on intimate terms of war with the Micmac for a long period, had evolved or borrowed from sources unknown an elaborate dualism involving a good and evil principle neither of which were directly identified with the benevolent culture-hero or the animal trickster which they also possessed. Several prominent attributes of the eastern culture-hero have been traced to Iroquoian types.[5] Likewise the Iroquoian flint man occurs among the eastern tribes.[6]

But apart from the hero cycles the Micmac and the central Algonkians had many common factors. The Micmac shared with the Ojibwa, "the bungling host," "cold dispersed by heat," "disobedience punished," "the obliging ferryman," "the freezing test," "the magic growth of attendant animals", and other motives. With the Fox they held in common, "the bungling host," "the heat test," "the rolling skull," "the shortened trail," "water from the belly," "the magic flight" and "symplegades".[7] Some of these motives are almost world-wide, and as they are not dependent upon the culture of any particular group they have diffused widely. On the other hand, the culture-hero is to some extent a demi-god who is concerned with the particular group ·to which he belongs, and about whose personality there clusters a body of associations that spring from the conservative tendencies of the particular group. This tends to explain the fact that the similarities between the tales of the eastern and central tribes lie outside the hero cycle. And when these similarities are coupled with the Iroquois and Micmac affinities it can be readily seen that the folk-tales of the eastern Algonkians do not require an immediate investigation outside of the eastern woodlands.

For a comparative study of folklore, as for that of other departments of human culture, certain rules of procedure must be laid down. The most important and comprehensive of these rules is to the effect that " . . .whenever a story which consists of the same combination of several elements is found in two regions, we must conclude that its occurrence in both is due to diffusion."[8] But when Leland proceeded from a general comparison which was based on personal impressions to a detailed analysis of Norse and Micmac mythologies, he postulated a common origin on the basis, not of the same combination of the several elements, but of the elements scattered haphazardly among other complexes, the general contexts of which are widely different. Compare, for instance, the Wabanaki myth that tells of the birth of Gluskap and of his evil twin Malsumsis in which the latter, in his impatience to be born in an unusual manner, bursts through his mother's side, killing her:

> "Now the great lord Glooskap, who was worshipped in after days by all the Wabanaki, or children of light, was a twin with a brother. As he was good, this brother, whose name was Malsumsis, or Wolf the younger, was bad. Before they were born, the babes consulted to consider how they had best enter the world. And Glooscap said, "I will be born as others are." But the evil Malsumsis thought

---

5. Dixon (3) 5.
6. Dixon (3) 8.

7. Dixon (3) 5.
8. Boas (3) 13.

himself too great to be brought forth in such a manner, and declared that he would burst through his mother's side. And as they planned it so it came to pass. Glooscap as first came quietly to light, while Malsumsis kept his word, killing his mother." [9]

Compare this passage with that in the Edda with which Leland seeks to find a parallel:

> "'Tis said that under the Frost-giant's arm
> Grew a boy and girl together;
> Foot with foot begot of that first wise giant,
> And a six-headed son was born." [10]

Here the Frost-giant is a male "who knew not joy of a giantess", whereas the parent of Gluskap and Malsumsis is a woman. The Micmac twins are both male, and the Norse are male and female. Moreover, they do not converse about the manner of their birth as in the Micmac version, and they do not burst through the side of their parent, causing death, as does the Micmac brother. Because a six-headed demon appears in Micmac mythology in a widely different context there is no reason whatsoever for associating it with this unnatural birth. Leland's thesis becomes less tenable when we find that the culture-hero of the Ojibwa, Nanabuju, argues with his brother as to who shall be born first, just as in the case of Gluskap and Malsumsis, and ". . . . they burst open their mother."[11] As the unnatural birth is Iroquoian, and as it occurs elsewhere, notably among the Armenian Christians and the Buddhists of India, there is no necessity to build up a case for its Norse origin.[12]

Much the same may be said for the motive involving the "deceitful confidence" according to which Malsumsis plots to kill Gluskap. Leland sees in this incident a resemblance with the murder of Balder by Loki, the bad-boy of the Scandanavian pantheon. The two brothers grew up together, each having a charmed life:

> ". . . the younger . . . asked the elder what would kill him . . . Glooscap, remembering how wantonly Malsumsis had slain their mother, thought it would be misplaced confidence to trust his life to one so fond of death, while it might prove to be well to know the bane of the other . . . Glooscap, to test his brother, told him that the only way in which he himself could be slain was by the stroke of an owl's feather (Rand has a cat-tail flag), though this was not true. And Malsumsis said, 'I can only die by a blow from a fern-root.' So . . . with . . . feathers he struck Glooscap while sleeping. Then he awoke in anger . . . said that it was . . . by a blow from a pine-root, that his life would end. Then the false man . . . smote him on the head with a pine-root. But Glooscap arose unharmed, drove Malsumsis away into the woods . . . and . . . said, 'Nothing but a flowering rush can kill me'. But the Beaver, who was hidden among the reeds, heard this, and hastening to Malsumsis told him the secret of his brother's life. . . . Therefore Glooscap arose in sorrow and in anger, took a fern-root, sought Malsumsis . . . and smote him so that he fell down dead." [13]

Apart from the fact that in both accounts death is caused by the appli-

---

9. Leland (1) 16.
10. The elder or poetic Edda 51.
11. Jones (2) 7.

12. Dixon (3) 6-7; Leland (1) 15.
13. Leland (1) 16-17.

cation or the thrust of a fragment of an organism, none of the incidents narrated in the Prose Edda corresponds in any way to those of the Indian tale just quoted. In one case the instrument of death is a twig of mistletoe, in the other it varies between an owl's feather, a cat-tail, a fern-root, and a pine-root. Moreover, Balder is not Odin, and it is the latter who figures in Leland's mind as the Norse counterpart of Gluskap. Malsumsis fails to kill Gluskap and is himself slain; whereas Loki, through the action of a third person, the blind god Hother, with whom there is no corresponding character in the American tale, actually succeeds in effecting Balder's death. And the general contexts have nothing in common. Balder is the son of Odin. The goddess, Frigg, dreaming that he would die, exacted an oath from all living things not to harm him. Discovering that the mistletoe has been neglected because it is "too young to swear", Loki induces Hother to throw it at Balder in the midst of the assembled gods.[14] Balder's elaborate funeral ceremony has no counterpart in the Wabanaki myth.

The opposition of the two brothers and the slaying of one by the other are Iroquoian motives, and are also found among the Ottawa and the Pottawatami.[15] When Nanabuju's brother desires to destroy him, the hero says, "If I should gently touch those cat-tails with my foot, then I should die".[16] And elsewhere, of only one thing is Nanabuju afraid, "It is the root of the apukwa (bulrush)."[17] Leland's contention, that the Ojibwa is derived from the Micmac version, lacks substantiation.[18]

That the story of the creation of man among the Micmacs is derived from Norse sources seems to be equally invalid. Among the North American Indians, with the exception of some Californian tribes, there are no true creation myths. But the mythology of all was concerned partly with the story of how the world was brought from a primeval mythological era to the state in which it exists today by the agency of a culture-hero. Into this category falls the story of the creation of man. In the Passamaquoddy tale Gluskap "took his bow and arrow and shot at trees, the basket-trees, the Ash. Then Indians came out of the bark of the Ash-trees".[19] In the Elder Edda we have:

> "Then came three gods of the Aesir kindred,
> Mighty and blessed towards their home.
> They found on the seashore, wanting power,
> With fate unwoven, an Ash and Elm.
>
> Spirit they had not and mind they owned not,—
> Blood, nor voice nor fair appearance.
> Spirit gave Odin, and mind gave Honir,
> Blood gave Lodur, and aspect fair." [20]

Here the creation results from the concerted efforts of three gods, Odin, Honir, and Lodur. In the Indian version Gluskap is the sole agent. Leland is authority for the statement that the basket-tree is the ash; but the elm, which

14. Leland (2) 223.
15. Dixon (3) 6-7.
16. Jones (2) 31.
17. Schoolcraft, Hiawatha 19.
18. Leland (1) 109.
19. Leland (1) 18.
20. The elder or poetic Edda 283.

is alleged to represent Eve, is lacking in the American tale.   Moreover, "embla" which is translated in the above excerpt as "elm" is declared to be of doubtful meaning.[21]   It is clear also that the method of bringing man into the world is different in the two cases.   Odin, Honir, and Lodur give spirit, mind, and blood, respectively.   The manner in which these qualities are transmitted is not stated.   Gluskap shoots arrows into the tree from which men spring as a result.   Now, the tradition of men having sprung from arrows occurred among the Beothuk, although here the arrows were shot into the ground.   It would seem, therefore, that the act of shooting arrows is the central element, and not the object, namely, the tree at which they are shot, which does not occur in the Beothuk account.   The fact that existing knowledge of Beothuk mythology is limited almost to this one incident does not necessarily detract from its significance.   One would have expected the Beothuks to have come within the sphere of Norse influence more than the Indians of Acadia, being, as they were, closer to Greenland and the North Atlantic sea-lanes, and more exposed in later times to foreign influences.

In spite of this Leland identifies the Wabanaki ash as the Norse tree of Yggdrasil, because Iduna, the goddess, is imprisoned in it as a punishment;[22] and because Gluskap transforms a man into a cedar, not an ash.   The tale tells that four men succeeded in reaching Gluskap's abode.   He who was ill-tempered desired to be pious, meek and holy; the poor man wished to be rich; the hated, loved and respected.   The last, desiring longevity, became a gnarled cedar.   Gluskap said, "The Great Spirit alone knows how long he will live."[23] Here we find several European decorations, but no analagous association of elements occurring in the Indian and the Norse save the isolated incident of the imprisonment of an individual in a tree.   Therefore, lacking that association of elements required by the principle enunciated above, we cannot assume that diffusion between the two peoples has taken place.

In Scandinavian mythology the controller of the winds is conceived as a giant clad in eagle's plumes, who sits at the end of the heavens.   Leland says, "no one who knows the Edda will deny that Wuchowsen, or the Wind-Blower, as he appears in the Passamaquoddy tale, is far more like the same bird of the Norsemen than the grotesque Thunder Bird of the Western tribes".[24] But surely there is a distinction between a giant clad in eagle's plumes and a giant bird which, at least in its physical characteristics, closely resembles the western thunder bird. And even if the creature were anthropomorphic we have a parallel close at hand in the Iroquois deity Ga-oh, the spirit of the winds, who is thought of as an old man sitting in solitary confinement, "surrounded by a tangle of discordant winds, and ever impatient of restraint".   His home is stationary in the western heavens.   When he is perfectly quiet the winds are at rest.   When he moves slightly he causes a breeze, and when he struggles in his restlessness and impatience he creates a hurricane.[25]   The abode of the

21. The elder or poetic Edda 283.
22. Leland (1) 103.
23. Rand (2) 253.

24. Leland (1) 113; (2) 227.
25. Morgan 1 151.

Norse giant is at the end of heaven; that of Wuchowsen is on a high rock at
the end of the sky; and that of Ga-oh is in the western heavens.   The descrip-
tions are not full, and there is little to choose between them.   Although wind
is caused in the three cases by the movement of the body or its appendages, the
context of the Passamaquoddy myth has no counterpart in the Edda.   The
Indians could not hunt the sea-fowl because a tempest was blowing.   When
Gluskap tied both wings of the bird all the waters became stagnant.   So he
loosened one of his wings and now only moderate winds are felt.[26]   These
incidents are typically American in their conception, and there seem to be no
Norse equivalents for them.

Several less striking motives involving the actions of Gluskap and his
associates are linked by Leland with the Scandinavian mythology.   The hero
engages in a freezing contest with a powerful magician, and something of the
kind occurs also among the Northmen.   It is, however, found also among the
Ojibwa.   Both Odin and Gluskap are said to possess two attendant wolves,
but actually one of Gluskap's attendants is a loon.[27]

Perhaps Leland's closest approach to a definite Norse analogy appears
in the tale of Gluskap's whale-hunting expedition and freezing competition
with Kitpooseagunow who was a giant born after his mother's death.   The
killing of the wife, the birth of the second son after death, the murder of the
father, the origin of flies from the old man's powdered bones, the origin of the
markings on birch-bark, the origin of the bullfrog's crumpled back, and a few
succeeding incidents, all of which occur in Rand's version, but not in Leland's,
are lacking in the Edda.[28]   But there are, undoubtedly, several resemblances
in the succeeding motives.   Kitpooseagunow said to Gluskap:

> " 'Let us go on the sea in a canoe and catch whales by torch-
> light;' to which Glooscap, nothing loath, consented, for he was a mighty
> fisherman. . . . Now when they came to the beach there were only
> great rocks lying here and there; but Kitpooseagunow, lifting the
> largest of these, put it on his head and it became a canoe. And pick-
> ing up another, it turned to a paddle, while a long splinter which he
> split from a ledge seemed to be a spear. Then Glooscap asked, 'Who
> shall sit in the stern and paddle and who shall take the spear.'
> Kitpooseagunow said 'That will I' . . . and soon the canoe passed over
> a mighty whale . . . but he who held the spear sent it like a thunder-
> bolt down into the waters . . . and the great fish was caught."

This incident is followed by the freezing contest.

> "The sky is red; we shall have a cold night;"

and Gluskap knew that his host would make it cold by magic.

> "And at midnight, when all was burnt out, Marten froze to
> death, and then the grandmother, but the two giants smoked on, and
> laughed and talked. Then the rocks out-of-doors split with the cold,
> the great trees in the forest split; . . ."[29]

In the Edda we have a not dissimilar sequence:

---

26.   Leland (1) 111; (2) 227.   28.   Rand (2) 62; Leland (1) 74.
27.   Leland (2) 224.   29.   Leland (1) 76.

"Thor went,
Grasped the prow,
Quickly with its hold-water,
Lifted the boat
Together with its oars
And scoop;

Wilt thou do
Half the work with me?
Either the whales
Home to the dwelling bear,
Or the boat fast bind?

The mighty Hymir,
He alone
Two whales drew
Up with his hook."

It is true that here there is no mention of rocks transformed into a canoe, a paddle, and a spear.   One is, of course, a canoe to be paddled and the other a boat to be rowed.   One employs a spear and catches one whale, the other uses a hook and catches two. But there are analogous associations, and each is succeeded by the freezing episode.   In the Edda

"The icebergs resounded
As the churl approached;
The thicket on his cheeks
Was frozen.
In shivers flew the pillers
At the Jotun's glance." [30]

As has already been mentioned, the freezing incident itself is a typical Indian motive which occurs, for example, among the Ojibwa.   It is probable that the whale-hunting expedition has analogies in other sections of the continent, although the Ojibwa tale in which Nanabuju is swallowed by a sunfish is by no means identical.   What is not so certain is that the association of the hunt with the freezing test occurs outside of the Wabanaki and Eddic myths.   The question, therefore, arises: is the association of such a nature as to preclude its independent origin and its evolution along convergent lines? Because one of the motives, and probably the other also, are both Indian, the similarity would appear to be accidental and the independent origin an easy possibility.   If there has been a diffusion of motives from Scandinavia to America, it would not be wise to forget the significant part played by Bering Strait as an orifice through which traits have flowed in both directions from the earliest times.

The last incident of the Gluskap cycle related to the final destruction of the world. Gluskap is making arrows and preparing for a great battle in which he will kill everybody and burn the world.   Although it is not recorded in the tale as related by a Passamaquoddy Indian, Leland appears to interpolate a host of details which he has gathered from the Norse and Wabanaki mythologies in general.[31]   The hero will kill the wolf-destroyer, or evil being, together with the stone and ice giants, the sorcerers, goblins, and elves.[32]   This

---

30. Leland (1) 80.
31. Leland (1) 130-133.

32. Leland (2) 227.

is likened to Ragnarok, the twilight of the gods, when Odin will fight the Fenris wolf and all will be consumed.   But against this argument stands the fact that the tale has been so adulterated with Christian ideas that the pre-Columbian residue is virtually inseparable.   The idea of Gluskap sitting in his wigwam making arrows might very easily be aboriginal, but the meagre description that follows concerning the final upheaval is as close to the Christian concepts of Armaggedon and the Day of Judgment as it is to Ragnarok. In the final section the narrator says that, "Me hear how some say world all burn up some day, water all boil all fire; some good ones be taken up in good heavens, but me dunno,—me just hear that.   Only hear so."[33]   Leland declares that the Indians always distinguished between their own traditions and those of the Whites by employing the device "I heard", and no doubt they did when they were aware of the distinction, but it is well known that they could not always distinguish between the two.   Therefore, the device cannot be relied upon in the absence of concomitant traits.

It is scarcely necessary to mention, however, that the final destruction of the world is an almost universal belief.   Like Gluskap, Quetzalcoatl, King Arthur, and Nanabuju, to select only a few from many possible examples, are expected to return and exercise an important function in the final disposition of the human race.   "I foresaw", said Netzahualcoyotl, the Mexican prince, "that our rule began to be destroyed. . . . The darkness of the sepulchre is but a strengthening couch for the glorious sun. . ."[34]   Periods of cataclysm followed by eras in which civilization was reborn were the essence of Mexican ideology, which were symbolized elsewhere in the mutations of the phoenix. It is possible that the concept grew out of a recognition of the rhythm of the seasons as expressed in the Easter festival among the Christians and in the ceremony of the White Dog among the Iroquois.   It is most likely, therefore, that the Micmac concept originated independently of the Norse.

Many of the objections applicable to Leland's treatment of Gluskap hold also for the adventures of the animal trickster Laks or Lox.   In view of the concepts of a devil formed in later times from the teachings of the missionaries it is misleading to term Laks an "Indian Devil".   One cannot help feeling that in comparing Laks with the Norse Loki, Leland has been misled by the superficial and incomplete resemblance of the names.   The name Laks or Lox is said to be not Indian, and might easily be a corruption of the English word "lynx", if it is remembered that the character is as often a wolverine as a raccoon.[35]   Occasionally adventures are attributed to Fisher that are elsewhere ascribed to Laks,[36] and it would, therefore, seem that Leland has employed the blanket term Lox to cover a variety of animal tricksters to whom were ascribed the same general characteristics by the Indians.   Although Leland endeavours to find analogies between the tricks of Laks and Loki, he discovers the real resemblance in their characters, but unfortunately the same argument would apply equally well to Nanabuju and other mythical beings.   Loki was the

---

33. Leland (1) 131.
34. Brenner.

35. Leland (2) 227.
36. Mechling (1) 64-65.

father of the wolves, and certainly Malsumsis was identified as a wolf, both among the Micmac and the Menomini,[37] but I do not find it anywhere stated that Laks was associated with the wolves. When Laks tells a lie his feet cry out and expose him. There is no suggestion in the tale that the feet are male and female, but Leland presumes this because a certain giant in the Edda is said to have given birth to a six-headed son who was conceived by the feet of a boy and girl who were inside him. This is the same incident which is related elsewhere to the birth of Gluskap. Moreover, in the Passamaquoddy tale the phallos exposes Laks when the feet· have been cut off.[38] But here we have a motive not unlike that of the talking vagina among the Malecite, which has been attributed to late European influence.[39]. Leland asserts frequently that Laks is a fire spirit, because "when he had jumped twenty or thirty times more, there arose a little smoke, and having his heart cheered by this he kept on jumping . . . then Lox jumped again, and this time the Indian Devil came up within him, and he swore by it that he would jump till it blazed or burst . . . . . and being at last aweary he fell down in a swoon, and so froze to death".[40] Loki is a fire spirit and here Laks dies from want of fire, but the motive might easily be a perversion of "cold driven away by heat" which the Micmacs shared with the Ojibwa. In another tale Laks is prickled by thorns and stung by ants, and ". . . . . the constant appearance of thorn-hedges, pricking with a sleep-thorn in German and Norse legends, is a mythical way of expressing the idea of the funeral fire".[41] There is indeed a certain resemblance here but the analogy is not of the strongest. It would be necessary, however, to plot the distribution of the motive among many North American tribes before any definite statement could be made. It would also be necessary to compare the context of the Indian tale with that in which the same motive occurs in Scandinavia in order to determine the extent of the analogy.

Leland treads on less certain ground when he attempts to base his theory on the fact that Laks and Loki both had the power to change themselves into women. Moreover, he sees in this power to change sex the identification of the twins who, as "boy and girl together" enabled the giant in the Edda to give birth to a six-headed son, forgetting for the time that Gluskap and Malsumis are both males and possess an entirely separate identity from Laks.[42] When the Wabanaki and Norse myths are compared it is found that there are no points in common save the isolated occurrence of a change in sex. In the Indian tale it is Badger who, aided by his little brother, deceitfully kills the wild fowl, gives a feast, overhears a conversation and

". . . having got them to show him the way, he sometime after turned himself into a young woman of great beauty, or at least disguised himself like one, and going to the village married the young chief. . . . And then she—he announced that a child would soon be born. And when the day came Badger handed out a bundle, and said that the babe was in it. . . . But when the chief opened it what he found

---

37. Dixon (3) 6-7.
38. Leland (1) 206; (2) 224.
39. Mechling (1) 86.

40. Leland (1) 173-174.
41. Leland (1) 178.
42. Leland (1) 27.

therein was the dried, withered embryo of a moose calf. In a great rage he flung it into the fire, and all rushed . . . to catch **Badger.**" [43]

As we proceed it becomes clearer that the Indians of Acadia possessed tales of several animal tricksters to whom were attributed the same general characteristics. In the above tale it is badger; in others the rabbit, the raccoon, the wolverines, or the lynx who play the role of tricksters. Laks is only one, and not the most important of these creatures. The name is translated as "loup cervier" or Indian devil, and the Micmac word for wolverine is variously translated as panther, lucifee, lox, and Indian devil. Laks, therefore, belongs to the feline tribe, and Leland errs in identifying him also with badger, rabbit, and raccoon, who are in themselves separate entities. [44] Compare the above excerpt which recounts an adventure of badger with that passage in the Elder Edda in which Loki's change of sex is mentioned. Aegir, the god of the sea, has invited the other gods to partake of a banquet in his coral caves at the bottom of the sea. Loki breaks in upon the feast, kills a servant, taunts the gods for their shortcomings and derides them for their mistakes. [45] Odin retorts with the words.

> ". . . eight winters wert thou below in the earth
> like a maiden, milking kine,
> and there thou gavest birth to bairns,—
> which I weened was a woman's lot." [46]

The situation here is in no way akin to that in the Indian tale; in the one Loki gives birth to bairns and in the other badger presents her husband with a bogus child. In the former the birth is a biological function; in the latter it is the culmination of an elaborate deception. Neglecting for a moment the argument as already advanced, it is not inconceivable that the changing of sex should have originated independently among the eastern Algonkians since changes of sex actually occurred among several Indian tribes. Hermaphrodites among the Nascopi and the Illinois Indians were observed to assume the social and possibly the physical aspects of women. And, moreover, among the Chukchee of northeastern Siberia, who dwelt midway between Scandinavia and Acadia, shamanistic changes of sex on the part of both men and women were by no means uncommon, and these were sometimes physical as much as mental in their manifestation. [47]

In the Kalevala, but not in the Eddas, a stag, when bounding by a hut belonging to a Lapp family, kicks over a kettle and blinds two old women. This act is attributed to racoon among the Micmac. [48] Fisher is the principle in the Malecite version. Two old women, recognizing him as the individual who caused the children to drown, determine to kill him. One of them ". . . . took her little axe and killed him, skinned him, and put him into a pot to boil. While he was cooking, one woman was seated on each side of the fire sewing. After a while Fisher jumped up and splashed the boiling water over both." [49]

---

43. Rand (2) 263; Leland (1) 89.
44. Mechling (1) 81-82.
45. Guerber 225.
46. The elder or poetic Edda 255.

47. Bogoras 448-460.
48. Leland (1) 176.
49. Mechling (1) 64.

If this motive was diffused from northern Asia to Acadia it is probable that it travelled by way of Bering Strait which divides the sub-arctic Mongoloid belt into two parts.   Leland admits that the parallel is not close.[50]

Laks is treated as a derivitive of Loki in several less important respects. In a Passamaquoddy tale an unnamed Indian surreptitiously cuts off the hair of a mermaid, and in the Edda Loki steals the hair of a goddess.   In both cases the thieves are forced to make restitution.[51]   Elsewhere Loki is chased by a stone giant, called Thiassi.   This is unsuccessfully related to the Micmac story in which the trickster races with a stone giant, the latter being a typical Indian motive.[52]   There are some points of similarity between the tale in which Laks is carried into the air by a bird known as the culloo and that in which Loki is caught up into the sky, but the resemblances are not so striking as to preclude the probability of independent origin.[53]

The final episode in the career of Loki is essentially stark tragedy.   The humourous quality that is so characteristic of the Micmac trickster's adventures is entirely lacking in the account of the death of Balder at the banquet of the gods, the venemous slander that follows, and the final flight of the renegade. "Then Loki went forth and hid himself in Franang's stream in the form of a salmon, when the gods caught him and bound him. . . . Skadi took a poison-ous snake and fastened it up over Loki, so that poison dripped from it upon his face.   Sigyn . . . held a basin under the drops."[54]   Compare this with:

> "Kusk . . . thought he would go and get a dinner from Lox. Lox served him . . . in a broad, flat platter. Poor Kusk could hardly get a mouthful. . . . Soon after, Kusk made a fine soup, and invited Lox to dinner. This he served in a jug . . . none of it had Lox. . . . Blue Jay . . . ran out on a bough of a tree which spread over a river, and in a minute fished out a large salmon. 'Truly,' thought Lox, 'that is easy to do, and I can do it'. . . . Then he, too, ran down to the river and out on a tree, and, seeing a fine salmon, caught at it with his claws. But he had not learned the art, and so fell into the river, and was swept away by the rushing current." [55]

In the one case Loki dies disguised as a salmon; in the other Laks drowns trying to catch a salmon, so that there are really no points in common between the two tales. Leland knew that the Indian story was an Aesop's fable and is somewhat inconsistent in supporting his theory by the comparison.

Although Leland weaves the bulk of his argument around the persons of Gluskap and Laks, there are many elements not bearing directly on the hero or the trickster which he fits into his scheme.   One of these is concerned with giants who are endowed with supernatural power and who live in the North. Now the belief in giants may depend partly upon what has been called the psychic unity of mankind.   To the nature of people, who are alien enough to call forth speculation on the part of the more imaginative individuals in a given group, is added a grotesquery which has its roots in vague fear and im-poverished curiosity.   The size of the alien people is altered and their charac-

50. Leland (2) 228.
51. Leland (1) 270.
52. Leland (2) 228.

53. Leland (1) 157; Guerber 104.
54. The elder or poetic Edda 269.
55. Leland (1) 195.

teristics are accentuated and distorted. Hence we have bipeds with stone cheeks, half-flint men, unipeds, and giants with icy hearts. The Micmac and Wabanaki variety had special characteristics.   In one Micmac tale they are liver-coloured and are associated with the coming of the white people.   If Rand is correct in assuming that their huge canoes and their war-whoops are European ships and fire-arms, then these two elements are excellent examples of a complete fusion of traits.[56]   The power of the Chenoo to see great distances is elsewhere attributed to European spy-glasses.   Certainly these tales often bear a strong infusion of European elements as in the story in which the chenoo became converted to the Roman Catholic faith.[57]   An Indian might be transformed into a chenoo against his will.   Six Micmacs were hunting on the Saguenay. One became sick and surly and ordered the others away so that he would not kill them for he knew that he was turning into a Chenoo.   They did not at first know what ailed him.   They tracked him into the north.[58]   In order to kill a chenoo effectively it was necessary to burn every part of his body.[59]   The circumstances that surrounded the transformation of an ordinary individual into a chenoo led Rand to believe that the chenoo was a lunatic and that the tales were told to explain loss of sanity.   If this is so, then his other contention that the cannibal chenoos are involved in the coming of Europeans must be false because lunacy in pre-Columbian times must have occurred, although possibly with less frequency than in the Euro-American period.   Not only does Leland not mention lunacy as a possible explanation, but he rejects the notion that the creature has a post-European origin.   Although in one chenoo story guns are mentioned Leland takes the liberty of replacing them with arrows because "the chenoo stories are evidently very ancient, and refer to terrors of the olden time."[60]   In spite of this he gives a tale in which a chenoo is regenerated by swallowing tallow, and suggests that it might relate to final christianization.   The chenoo "was dying.   This was after the white men had come.   They sent for a priest.. . . . . At first he would repel the father in anger.   Then he listened and learned the truth.   So the old heathen's heart was changed. . . Here he is softened by kindness and his "heart" is changed. The motive may have originated in that of the Malecite tale in which the giant reciprocates kind treatment.   When he is given medicine he vomits a big piece of ice.   "The Indian kicked it into the fire in spite of the protestations of the giant. . . . . . When he vomited the third time he stopped the Indian from kicking the ice into the fire.   If the Indian had kicked it into the fire he would have died."[62]   If the ice was a necessity of life it is probable that it was the heart of the chenoo which was "of ice in the human figure".[63]   The icy heart and the association of the chenoo with the north might lead one to suppose that

---

56. Rand (2) 142.
57. Rand (2) 198.
58. Rand (2) 250.
59. Rand (2) 246.
60. Leland (1) 253. A possible basis for the chenoo story may be in the occurrence among the Montagnais north of Lake St. John of a disease, the symptoms of which were lunacy, hypochondria, frenzy, and a ravening for human flesh. It was necessary to kill the victims to stay their madness. See Jesuit Relations 46, 263-265.
62. Mechling (1) 76.
63. Leland (2) 249.

the creaure was an anthropomorphization of cold weather. If this were so the Micmac version in which the chenoo vomits all sorts of filth would be a degeneration.[64]

Leland suggests a Norse origin for the chenoo, because

"When the heart of a woman—home of love—
he Loki ate half-burned with linden wood, ..."[65]

Elsewhere "heart" is translated as "thought-stone".[66] The heart is burned, but the ice melts when it is kicked into the fire. There is no suggestion that the thought-stone is ice. Moreover, the chenoo does not seem to have been a stone giant like Hrugnir "that hard-hearted giant whose head was rock-hewn".[67] If the chenoo were stone a parallel could be found in the stone giants of the Iroquois. Leland parallels the Norse Jotunheim, which was alleged to be in the North Atlantic, with the abode of the chenoo in the north country. The river Ifing is identified with the subterranean river in the Micmac tale.[68]

If Norse culture did not influence that of the Eskimo with which it was in contact for a long period, how much less must it have affected the Indian. Leland considered the possibility that the Norse influence on the Indian was transmitted by the Eskimo as an intermediary group, but there are very few similarities between the Algonkian and the Eskimo tales, there being only two Eskimo motives in Leland's collection of Algonkian tales, and these are widespread elsewhere.[69] Likewise the bear ceremonials which occur in the Kalevala and also in Micmac lore are characteristic of all Mongoloid peoples from Finland to Bering strait and from Bering strait to Nova Scotia and they cannot be used as evidence to support the Norse theory.[70] Only in one instance does Leland's thesis seem to fulfil the requirements commended in the principle that when the same combination of elements is found in two regions diffusion is the most plausible explanation and the burden of proof must rest with the advocate of independent origin; that is the instance already mentioned in which the whale hunting expedition is followed by the freezing test. But in this instance the thesis is partly invalidated by the fact that the freezing test is a North American motive, the spread of which throughout the continent is inconceivable from a Norse source. Ample evidence has been given to show that certain Indian elements are present in the Norse mythology in different combinations, but according to the principle this is no proof of diffusion. It results rather from the fact that, although the variations in combinations of traits are infinite in number, the possible number of traits themselves is restricted and determined by the limited range of human thought which possesses a unity couched in basic and inherent tendencies.

---

64. Mechling (1) 76.
65. The elder or poetic Edda 221.
66. Leland (2) 229.
67. The elder or poetic Edda 187; Leland (2) 226.
68. The elder or poetic Edda 45; Leland (1) 281-290.
69. Boas (3) 17.
70. Leland (2) 231.

MOTIVES AND DECORATIONS

Heretofore we have been concerned almost exclusively with that type of folk-tale which is known as a myth and which refers to the period of the world's history when creatures had not assumed their present form. The above survey of Norse and Wabanaki mythologies has shown that myths are concerned chiefly with supernatural beings. The rocks and trees were different. Cape Blomidon and the reversible falls at Saint John had not yet undergone transformation. Distinct from the myth is the simple folk-tale which is of an historical or quasi-historical nature, in which the principal characters are human, and which refers to the present dispensation of the world.[71] With respect to Indian folk-tales it is extremely difficult to distinguish between the two types of tale. For example, we have seen that the chenoo, whatever his origin, was a mythical being who was associated with the wonders of the olden time. But many of the tales in which the chenoo is the central figure are clearly concerned with the post-European epoch and often involve white people. Although the Indians themselves distinguished theoretically between myths, traditions, and folk-tales, the classification is of little value and will not be emphasized here.

A study of European elements in Indian folk-tales is of particular value, not only because it reveals an important aspect of the growth of Euro-American civilization, but because it may throw some light upon the method by which the body of pre-Columbian folk-tales was built up. Folklore was as capable of modification in former times as it is today. Although the unfused European and Indian tales are sharply distinctive, this is not always known to the Indian narrator. Sometimes tales which have been borrowed by the Indians from the whites have undergone no changes whatever with respect to the substitution of Indian elements for European. Sometimes so little of the European elements remain intact that a tale may be mistaken for an aboriginal. In Latin America the native tales have almost been obliterated in the deluge of European tales that followed in the wake of the Spanish and Portugese conquests.[72] In Acadia the fusion of Indian and French tales was so great that it is sometimes with the greatest difficulty that the elements may be separated. It is far from feasible to effect an accurate chronology on the basis of the material at hand, but it is nevertheless desirable that the time and circumstances in which the fusion of a particular tale or group of tales occurred, should be ascertained in order that a complete picture of the contact of Indian and European peoples may be painted, and in order that the principles governing the clash and fusion of cultures may be induced.

Far more than that of any other people, the folklore of the French has influenced that of the eastern Algonkians, both in Acadia and through the frequent contacts made in Canada. Not only were the French the first to establish social communication with the Indians of Acadia and to leave a lasting imprint on their culture, but that communication was of a nature that has never been attained by emigrants from the British Isles. It was characterized by as

---

71. Jenness (1) 186.   72. Boas (5) 386.

complete a show of equality on both sides as is ever likely to occur between people whose traditions and general cultures are so widely divergent. Although the fusion of French and Indian tales is probably taking place at the present time, in a very limited way, considering modern conditions by and large and although extensive transfusion occurred in the eighteenth and nineteenth centuries, it is possible that the seventeenth century witnessed the high point of the process. Although there are noteworthy exceptions, the bulk of French folklore was introduced into New France before 1673 when immigration on a large scale ceased by order of the king.[73] It does not follow, however, that the fusion with the Indian tales was necessarily confined to the seventeenth century. It is possible that certain tales of the one group may have existed side by side with tales of the other group which would make fusion feasible. It is possible, on the other hand, that when an indigenous tale had marked resemblances to one of foreign origin an immediate fusion took place. In order to date the fusion with any degree of certainty it is necessary to consider carefully the nature and combination of the fused elements.

The elements of which folk-tales are composed are of two kinds, and may be designated as motives and decorations. By the term "motive" is intended the exterior action by which a tale progresses from the beginning, through the climax, to the conclusion; but one tale may include a number of motives in sequence. The characteristics of the actors being stereotyped, there is no unfolding or development of the character, and there are no emotional or intellectual conflicts. The actors appear fully equipped at the outset of the tale and they continue to act in mechanical accord with their predetermined equipment. Unlike the negroes of west Africa who ascribed to animal actors all the characteristics and emotions proper to man, the Indians generally made of each animal a type.[74] The jay is inquisitive.[75] The tortoise is ugly and decrepit. And the crow peeps, spies, begs, pilfers, and tells tales.[76] We have seen already that Laks, the wolverine, is greedy and treacherous. Into the fabric of the motive is woven an aggregate of decorative units which lend the tale form and colour. They are comprised of the food, clothing, dwellings, means of transportation, implements, weapons, and stylistic devices, that appear in the tale and add a special quality to the time-sequence of the motive. It is in terms of motives and decorations that the nature of the European influence on the folk-tales of the eastern Algonkians will be gauged.

As motives and decorations were influenced unevenly it is necessary to consider the following combinations which are arbitrary but useful: Indian motives with Indian and European decorations; Indian motives with European decorations; European motives having Indian decorations; European motives having European and Indian decorations; European motives and European decorations; blended European and Indian motives with Indian decorations; blended motives with Indian and European decorations; blended motives with European decorations; and lastly, new motives which developed

73. Barbeau (7) 191.
74. Jenness (1) 188.

75. Rand (2) 270.
76. Leland (1) 59.

from, and were dependent upon, the situation of the Indians in Euro-American times, the decorations of which reflect the Euro-American environment of the eastern Algonkians in the colonial era.

It is possible to say with some degree of certainty that tales having Indian motives and decorations are pre-Columbian, since any tales acquired by the group within recent times would be most likely to bear the stamp of European or Euro-American elements. Likewise, it is probable that tales which have been recorded among the Indians and which possess European motives and decorations, to the exclusion of all Indian elements, belong to the late eighteenth or nineteenth centuries when the aboriginal culture had been so wasted away as to lack the intensity required to imprint itself upon the oral literature. But in the other types of combination in which perhaps as much of the indigenous as of the alien is found, the greatest period of fusion was perhaps the seventeenth century, at the time before the expulsion of the Acadians when the French element was at its strongest, and before the immaterial aspects of the native culture became overwhelmed in the flood of recent Euro-American times.

It must not be thought, however, that when two tales were fused, either with respect to motives, decorations, or both, that the fusion occurred at one definite time, that the tale became a static property, and that it underwent no further changes between the time of the initial fusion and the time when the tale was recorded in writing. But it is probable that the process was characterized by periods of relative movement and rest rather than by one of continuous change. The cause of movement lies in the fluidity or plastic quality of the folk-tale; the cause of rest or static property lies in the conservative quality of resistence to change. Without cognizance of the psychological mechanism which acts in the diffusion of culture from one group to another it may not be possible to account fully for the causes of movement and rest, but certainly the ethnological or historical aspect of the process of substitution, addition and subtraction of elements in a tale is noteworthy. With respect to decorations it may be said that, although they frequently become archaic, they tend to remain embedded in the texture of the tale until the culture of the group to which they refer has become so changed that they are no longer comprehensible, at which time they are dropped or replaced by familiar elements. The positive and negative accelerations of change with respect to motives are so closely bound up with psychological laws that we will defer the discussion of them until after we have reviewed the ethnological evidence.

A considerable number of tales which are evidently of pre-Columbian origin have what seem to be Indian motives together with decorations which have been derived from both America and Europe. In some of them the European decorations are almost negligible, but the fact that they occur at all raises important problems involving the folk-tale. In the tale in which Gluskap is deserted by his comrades certain well-known American motives occur and it is probable that the entire tale is pre-Columbian with respect to both classes of elements. For instance, the motive involving the vermin-infested head of the hag, and the freezing test to which allusion has already been made, are both Indian.[90]   The same may be said of the decorations.   We have, however, a magic belt by which an individual who is old and decrepit is rendered young and handsome.   It is quite conceivable that a belt having this particular function is aboriginal, but, like many decorations the origin cannot be asserted with any degree of finality until a comprehensive survey of the occurrence of magic belts in America is made.   Like the head of the hag, the study of folk-lore is infested with problems of this kind which are of little significance in themselves, but which in the aggregate might serve to swing a theory from its supposed base in fact.   In the same way the tale of the partridge and his won-derful wigwam seems undoubtedly to be Indian in motive and decoration, and, if it has not been subject to interpolations, entirely a pre-European tale.   But the man who bears "on his head a house, or a large birch wigwam of many rooms,"[91] may be a European conceit, or it may be an aboriginal amplification. Likewise, in the tale of the dance of old age, Mitche-hant, or the devil, may have been interpolated by Leland, it may be a fusion of the Christian devil and an Indian evil spirit, or it may simply be the Indian spirit in its original form.[92]   Although there is an element of doubt in the above instances, there can be none when we find silver brooches occurring as decorations in the tale that tells of the origin of the black snakes.   Folk-tales may seldom be primar-ily aetiological.   This element may have entered the tale at a late stage in its development or it may sometimes have been added in the telling of the tale to a white audience.   But here the origin of the black snakes seems closely con-nected with the main motive, and it is probable that it is pre-European.   But the Passamaquoddys, of course, had no knowledge of silver until the Jesuits worked silver brooches and spread them among the Indians for religious pur-poses.[93]   It is probable that the silver brooch supplanted some similar abori-ginal element at some time during the eighteenth century.   Perhaps if more material decorations had been mentioned in the tale there would be more evi-dence of a substitution of elements.   As it is we can learn little from this ex-ample.   In one of the tales of the Laks cycle cloth is mentioned, and as cloth was one of the first articles traded with the Indians, it could easily have been substituted for skins at an early date.[94]   In the Passamaquoddy tale of the woman who married the thunder a "beautiful girl dressed in silver and gold" appears.[95]   Although Leland says that these metals were known in pre-Colum-bian days it is improbable that they were used to any appreciable extent and as decorations they can safely be classed as European.   It may be allowed, how-ever, that they might not be present in the tale at all, but may have been added at the time of the recording of the story in English for the edification of the collector.   More easily recognizable as European is the key that occurs in the

---

90. Rand (2) 270 seq.
91. Leland (1) 291.
92. Leland (1) 327 seq.
93. Parker (1) (4) Silver ornaments became common among the Iroquois during the French and Indian wars in the eighteenth century. Probably there were none among the Passamaquoddy prior to 1700.
94. Leland (1) 184.
95. Leland (1) 266.

story of how one of the partridge's wives became a sheldrake duck.[96] Not only is the locked box European, but it is doubtful whether the elf in the box is not the same as the one occurring in the Petit Jean tales of the French Canadians. The Blue Beard motive is immediately apparent. The wife pries into the husband's secret against his orders. Whenever she touches the elf her hands become red, and she cannot erase the stain. The aetiological element is Indian, but the origin of the motive is uncertain. In the tale of the man who married among the giants we have an Indian motive and Indian decorations, all except the mention of the socks worn by the men and the use of the stylistic device "I guess she is going yet" which are probably European elements.[97] Likewise, in the story of Wejiboquet we find a completely native motive with decorations the majority of which are also native. But the cooking of meat in kettles is clearly European, and the custom of kissing was unknown among the Micmac, or indeed any Indians, until it was introduced by the French in Lescarbot's time at Port Royal. Again we find the device, "I guess he is going yet."[98] The fusion may have occurred in the middle of the seventeenth century. In the "Travels of Gloskap" steel traps are mentioned.[99] In all these tales there is no decoration that can safely be used to delimit the time of fusion. In the tale of Gugus' duel the likening of the chenoo's face to that of a monkey is, of course, a very recent addition.[100] Otherwise the tale is completely aboriginal. When we turn from these Indian tales which have decorations of doubtful origin to some of the adventures of Mahtigwess, the rabbit, we are confronted with frequent European decorations which are interspersed among the aboriginal and which have the appearance of having superceded others. The rabbit had magical powers and sought to elude Loup Cervier thereby. When the latter came to a fine wigwam "all he saw was an old man......whose hair was gray, and whose.......appearance was heightened by a pair of long and venerable ears."[101] When he awoke he found himself on the open heath almost starved. So far the tale seems to be entirely Indian. Then he came to a large Indian village. "The first building he saw was a church, in which service was being held. And he, entering, said hastily to the first person he saw, 'ha! ho! have you seen a rabbit running by here?'......'You must wait till meeting is over before asking such questions. Then a young man beckoned to him to come in, and he listened till the end to a long sermon on the wickedness of being vindictive and rapacious: and the preacher was a gray ancient, and his ears stood up over his little cap like the two handles-of a pitcher......" Having been entertained on what seemed to be wine and biscuits he awoke as before to find himself in a rabbit warren, and the food, some of which he had eaten, was then found to be excrement. In the last incident Loup Cervier came to a ship "with sails spread......and the captain stood so stately on the deck, with folded arms, and ..... a cocked hat, the two points of which were like two grand and stately horns." Loup Cervier was repelled by a volley of musquetry and "if he is not

---

96. Leland (1) 300.
97. Michelson 35.
98. Michelson 41.

99. Michelson 51.
100. Parsons (1) 59.
101. Leland (2) 213.

dead, he is running still." In the original Passamaquoddy tale the first incident may have been repeated mechanically, and the church and the ship of the other incidents may have superceded these. Or it is possible that the ship supplanted a canoe in the original. Although the sympathies of the Indians were undoubtedly with the rabbit, something of their point of view is reflected when the wild cat is forced to listen to a long and boring sermon on Christian vices. Large towns and churches would not have been common among the Passamaquoddys until the end of the eighteenth century and it may be that the fusion occurred at a fairly late date. The final device "he is running still" or "il court encore" is derived from the French Canadians.

Into the class of tales which have Indian motives and Indian and European decorations fall the historical traditions of wars with the Mohawks, which predated the advent of the French in the sixteenth century and which have continued almost to the present time, having reached their high point perhaps at the time of the Seven Years' War. Two of these traditions, for example, show no European tinctures. One of these is the adventure of Noojebokwajeejit.[102] The Mohawks were at this time in Canada. A Micmac who was born among them seeks to escape to his own country and is pursued. Magic is pitted against magic, and in the battle we have a good example of the pre-Columbian psychology and lore of the Micmacs. The escape is followed by a courting and a marriage which are achieved in the ancient Indian manner. In the other the abduction of the chief's wife is followed by the attainment of revenge.[103] She lures her enemies over a falls on the St. John river. She herself succeeds in swimming ashore, "leaving the raft.....to go over the falls, and be dashed to pieces and destroyed." In another incident of the Kwedech or Mohawk war only two European elements may have been introduced in the early days of the colony. There are no fire-arms used. Rand says that seven was a potent number among the Indians and that they had a mighty medicine composed of seven barks, roots, and herbs, but in reality they were accustomed to think in fours rather than in the threes and sevens of Europeans. In the tradition of Ababejit we have what is doubtless a tale of pre-Columbian origin unless the use of fire-arms proclaims it of early Acadian date. It is possible, however, that guns may have supplanted bows and arrows in the tale at a later time.[105] But the origin of some of the traditions is not so uncertain. We find that, in an incident of the war with the Kenebek Indians, "they had a small vessel lying inside the long bar that makes out at Merrigomish; this was immediately emptied of its ballast, drawn across into the sea, filled with men, arms, and ammunition (for it was since the advent of the French), and immediately run up to the Kenebec ports..... "[106] After the war peace was made and games were played. "There was one more game mentioned; it was pitching quoits,—the name of which, soopalaooltijik, is so clearly Micmackified French (jouer palet) that the origin of the play, so far as our Indian friends are concerned, is clearly marked and stamped upon the language."[107] The hostility between the Micmacs and the

---

102. Rand (2) 169.
103. Rand (2) 137.
104. Rand (2) 207.

105. Rand (2) 126.
106. Rand (2) 179.
107. Rand (2) 181.

catholic Iroquois of the Lake of Two Mountains was still felt at the end of the eighteenth century.[108]   A Micmac was stolen by these Indians.   He grew up to be able to speak English and French, besides several Indian languages.   Having returned to his native land, one day he surprised a party of scouts.   "....they all seized their bows and arrows, as they had no guns, and stood on the defensive," but found that they were old friends.   Now although guns were generally used by the Indians in colonial times they could be purchased by them only in furs.   When the frontiers of the fur-trade had been flung well out onto the central plains, as they had by this time, the eastern Indians who did not follow the fur frontier were left without purchasing power and were frequently forced to revert to the bow and arrow.   If there had not been concomitant European elements it might easily have been supposed that the tradition was pre-historic on this account.

From the above review of tales that have Indian motives and a combination of Indian and European decorations it cannot be said that the fusions occurred in every case at the same time.   On the other hand it appears that the introduction of elements has occurred as early as the seventeenth century in some cases, and as late as the nineteenth in others.   The European decorations in some of the tales give no clue whatsoever as to the time of their introduction.   For others only tentative limits, within which the fusion occurred, can be set.

Let us now consider the group of tales which have European motives and Indian decorations.   As Gluskap plays an important part in three of these it might with reason be contended that they are typical Indian tales which lack any evidence of European influence.   It will be seen later, however, that Gluskap and other mythical beings are involved, in a number of tales, with the encroachments of Europeans.   It is, therefore, possible that deeds which were formerly ascribed to, let us say, Petit Jean, are now attributed to Gluskap.   On the other hand the resemblance between the motives may be superficial.   In the story of the beautiful bride, for instance, the characters are certainly all Indian.[109]   A man is aided by Gluskap, a Megumuwesu, a very strong man, a very swift man whose leg is tied close to his body, and an individual who restrains the whirlwind in his stuffed nostrils.   These compete successfully for the bride in athletic feats.   Although there are no European elements in this tale, these three helpers, strength, swiftness, and whirlwind, occur elsewhere in Rand in a tale having many European decorations.[110]   It may, however, as the informant believed, be a tale of ancient times.   In another story which has a similar motive Gluskap contributes a magic string in order to insure a successful issue.   The tasks imposed on the suitor are not unlike those which confronted Petit Jean on the many occasions in which he went in search of a bride.   He must slide down a mountain on a hand sled in competition with wizards.   On the return journey the chief unsuccessfully attempts to hinder the bride and groom by magic.[111]   Whereas these two tales require special in-

---

108. Rand (2) 223.
109. Rand (2) 185.

110. Leland (1) 13.
111. Rand (2) 23.

vestigation, that in which Gluskap creates the water creatures may be dismissed summarily.   The tale has at some time undergone modifications so that the original Indian has been replaced by what seems to be a European motive.   It is true that the drought, which Gluskap breaks by thrusting the spear into the frog monster so that "there gushed forth a mighty river," is aboriginal, as is the transformation of the Indians into crabs, leeches, and fish.   But the motive by which they are transformed seems to be more like that of certain European fairy tales.   The Indians said to each other, " 'Suppose you had all the nice cold, fresh, sparkling, delicious water there is in the world what would you do?'   And one said that he would live in the soft mud, and always be wet and cool.   And another that he would plunge from the rocks.....And the third, that he would be washed up and down with the rippling waves[112].....Now it chanced that these things were said in the hour which, when it passes over the world, all the wishes uttered by men are granted.   And so it was with these Indians."[113]   In the Micmac version the motive of the hoarding of water is followed by the freezing episode, and there is no mention of the magic time when all wishes are granted.[114]   There seems to be little doubt that the latter is a European motive.   It is not unlike that relating to midsummer night about which Sir James Barrie wrote "Dear Brutus," and Leland likens it to Rabelais' story of the golden hatchet.   It is far less certain that the Kookwes, a mythological giant of the Micmacs, has in any way been influenced by European conceptions, although he is stupid like those in "Jack the giant killer."

Of the other examples which seem to have French motives and complete, or almost complete, Indian decorations, two involve serpents, two have rabbits for their leading characters, and two centre about creatures who are called "partridge."   In one of the serpent tales a woman's sixth husband finds her in the act of love with a snake.   She had killed his predecessors by communicating the venom to them on their marriage bed.   He refuses to sleep with her and the venom kills her.[117]   Leland rejects the possibility that this is a European tale.   It occurs among all the Wabanaki, the Indians of Guiana, and above all among the Eskimo in the tale of the faithless wife, although in the latter case no serpent is mentioned.[118]   If it is aboriginal, which seems likely, then the aetological element attributed to it by Leland is recent.   He supposes it to account for the origin of "a certain disease," which, however, is generally conceded to have been introduced by the white people into the eastern woodland.   The story in which two girls are transformed into water snakes may be that of Melusina and may be derived from a French Canadian source.[119]   In the first of the rabbit stories several motives are discernible.   The first which resembles the tale of Andromeda is probably European.   With the aid of a rabbit the hero saves the chief's daughter from a cannibal giant.   This motive is followed by that of the obliging ferryman.   It is a widespread aboriginal motive in North America.   Two of the jealous suitors, having failed to drown

112. Leland (1) 118.
113. Leland (1) 118-119.
114. Rand (2) 68-73.
115. Leland (1) 120.

116. Rand (2) 183.
117. Leland (1) 273.
118. Rink 143.
119. Leland (1) 268.

the hero, are changed by him, one into a porcupine and the other into a hog. The transformation may or may not be European, but the hog certainly is a decoration derived from across the sea.[120] The second rabbit story has for its motive the imitating host which is widespread in both Europe and North America. Rabbit tries to imitate his host, Kingfisher; finally he kills the young fishers and is pursued. It may be derived from the Lafontaine fables through the French Canadians or it may be pre-Columbian. The decorations are inconclusive.[121] In the Malecite tale of partridge several motives occur. The first is European with Indian characters and decorations and is exemplified by a quarrel over the division of a moose. This is followed by the Indian motive of dancing a tree down, and the final motive seems to have arisen out of the Indians' Euro-American environment. So often were the Indians made drunk and cheated of their belongings.

> "Kiwakw [122] saw that he would have to use strategy, so he invited Partridge into his wigwam. There were three rooms in this wigwam and in the second many bottles were stored. Kiwakw took down a few bottles and mixed Partridge some medicine. He told Partridge to drink it, for it would do him good. . . . When Partridge had finished his third portion, he asked Kiwakw if he would give the bottles with the wigwam if they traded houses. . . . By this time Partridge was fairly drunk and soon went fast asleep. When he awoke it was morning and he found himself in a snow drift instead of in the wigwam. He flew up into a tree and began to eat the birch buds. So partridges do to this day, and even to this day, if a dog eats partridge guts, he gets drunk."

Whatever the original pre-Columbian motive was like, it certainly underwent an important change to suit the experience of the Malecite in his new and not altogether satisfactory Euro-American environment.

"The mournful mystery of the partridge witch" as it appears in Leland is curiously un-Indian.[123] The decorations are entirely Algonkian, with the single exception of "addio" which has obviously been derived from the French salutation "adieu," but it is unlike other Algonkian tales in one respect. It has already been observed that in Indian folk-tales, and, indeed, in those of many other peoples, the characteristics of the actors are stereotyped; the action is external and no emotional or intellectual conflicts are portrayed. Therefore, there is no development or unfolding of the character who, moreover, appears at the outset fully equipped with automatic responses to typical and recurrent situations. In this tale, however, there is a definite progression in which the hero steels himself to meet a situation which he cannot control and which he finally accepts with the equanimity of one who has mastered a conflict within himself. This growth of character and fatalistic nature of the motive are what distinguishes it from the rank and file of Indian folk-tales. It is true that there are stock Indian motives within the main theme. Two brothers are hunting in the woods. They complain that there is no woman to care for the camp in their absence. One day the younger came home and found that "garments

---

120. Leland (1) 227.
121. Mechling (1) 77.
122. Mechling (1) 78. Kiwakw is here misnamed. See Note 2.
123. Leland (1) 295.

had been mended, the place cleaned and swept, a fire built, and the pot was boiling." Without telling his brother, one day the younger came home early and surprised a beautiful girl, busy with the housekeeping. She lived with the brothers all winter but would not return to their village in the spring. The younger told his father the story of the girl, but the father was angry and ordered the girl to be slain for a witch. When the elder brother shot at her she flew away as a partridge. When the younger met her in the woods she said,

> "Do not marry anyone else. For your father wishes you to do so, and he will speak of it to you, and that soon. Yet it is for your sake only that I say this. . . . And he grew brave and bold, and then he was above all things. And when she told him that if he should marry another he would surely die, it was as nothing to him. Then returning, the first thing his father said was, 'My son, I have provided a wife for you' . . . And he said, 'It is well. Let it be so.' Then the bride came . . . four days they feasted. But on the last day he said, 'This is the end of it all . . .' and a great sickness came upon him, and when they brought the bride to him he was dead."

The motive of De La Motte Fouqué's "Undine" is curiously similar in many respects to that of the Partridge Witch, although in the Undine there is no birth of resolution by which the hero steels himself against inexorable fate. But, to confine ourselves exclusively to the external action, a knight falls in love with a water nymph, marries her in the forest, and lives happily with her for a time.[124] But when they removed to castle Ringstetten the knight gradually transfers his affections to Bertalda. By his perverse temper the knight forces Undine to return to her own people in the streams and waters of the earth. But before she goes she says,

> "Alas, sweet friend, alas! farewell! They (her people) shall do you no harm; **only remain true**, so that I may be able to keep them from you. I must, alas, go away. . . . Oh woe, woe! what have you done."[125]

When the knight has resolved to marry Bertalda, he dreams that Kuhleborn, the spirit of the river, says to Undine, "......let only a few days pass, and the priest will have given the nuptial blessing, and then you will have to go upon earth to accomplish the death of him who has taken another to wife."[126] When the priest says that marrying and mourning are not so unlike, the knight "placed various strange constructions upon these words, and upon his dream, but it is very difficult to break off a thing which a man has once regarded as certain," so the knight is married, and because he is married he dies.[127]

It is not improbable that the Undine and the Partridge Witch have a common origin. The artist, Fouqué, has embellished the tale with the romantic chiaroscuro of his own imagination, and he gives a wealth of detail which is not present in the Indian version. But Fouqué used as a groundwork an old European tale which may well have been transmitted to the Wabanaki by the early French settlers and fur-traders.

In some of the other European tales the decorations are more equally

---

124. Dela Motte Fouqué, Undine 45-50.   126. Ibid. 97.
125. Ibid. 91.   127. Ibid. 103.

divided.   The Micmac story of the three strong men is an Aryan tale which has been transmitted directly by the French Canadians.   The central features are the fight with an elf who had previously devoured all food, the lapse of memory resulting from the lick of a black whelp.[128]   In the Penobscot version the strong man conquers a goblin by seizing his red cap.   He fights also copper, silver, and gold demons, and swords are used in the tale.   As the Indian informant said, respecting this account, "When Indians in it, as they do in many others, speak of kings and queens or ships and ivory, I think they got it all from Europe."[129]   "The origin of corn," on the other hand, is referred to as a story of the olden times, but it is evidently adulterated with European elements.   An Indian's golden-haired wife says to him before she dies,

> " 'Then tie my hands together with cedar bark and drag me seven times around this clearing; but no matter what happens don't look back.' After he had felled all the trees and burned them, the clearing was dotted with charred stumps of the burnt timber. So he dragged her around seven times. . . . It was in the spring when he left; but when the autumn came . . . The place was no longer black with the charred stumps; it was beautiful with the yellow waving corn. The yellow tassels reminded him of his wife's golden hair." [130]

From tales having European motives and European and Indian decorations we proceed logically, to those which reveal European motives and European decorations, some of which have been subject to no perceptible alterations in the process of borrowing, and in others of which the tincture of Algonkian culture is negligible.   Not the least important in this group is the series of tales relating to Petit Jean.   It is impossible to say whether this character is culture hero, trickster, or noodle; whether he was laughed with, or laughed at, but it is certain that his droll exploits have afforded unbounded amusement to the Indians, for the tales have been borrowed by them in large numbers, have been spread widely by them throughout America, and have contributed to the Paul Bunyon cycle of the Maine lumberjacks to an as yet unestimated extent:[131] Among the Micmac some of these stories have suffered slightly in the transfusion, and may even have collected some Indian elements, but these are not readily perceptible.   In "the magic coat, shoes, and sword," a brother seeks his sisters who have been sold by their father for liquor.   Having found them he goes in search of a wife.   He comes to a city where brides are invariably stolen by an ogre on their wedding night.   When the king promises the hand of his daughter to the man who will kill the ogre, the daughter in turn is whisked away.   By the aid of a magic coat, shoes, and sword, which were obtained by a ruse from three stupid robbers, the hero finds out where the ogre's soul is kept and destroys him.   He returns the brides to their husbands and takes his own.   The hero is a prince.   Towns, intoxicating liquors, soldiers, sentinels, horses, chariots, and money, all testify to the fact that the tale was borrowed by the Indians at a comparatively late date in the period of European

---

128.   Leland (1) 311.
129.   Ibid. 322-323.
130.   Mechling (1) 87.   See also Leland (1) 225 how master rabbit gave himself airs.
131.   Statement of Mr. Marius Barbeau.

contact when they had lost so much of their culture that it has left no mark on the decorations.[132] Although Petit Jean is not mentioned by name the motive seems to be characteristic of this cycle, as it does also in "the magic food, belt, and flute," in which a booby, having been sent to market to sell a cow, is forced to exchange it for (1) food that will not diminish, (2) a belt that binds, and (3) a flute that causes the audience to dance and is attended by invisible hornets. With the aid of these he forces the landlord to forswear the rent due him. The booby then seeks the daughter of the king of a neighbouring town and wins her by means of his magic agents. When the king, being unreconciled to his ugliness, casts him into a den of wild beasts, he binds them with his magic belt, and the two substitute suitors are attacked by the invisible hornets. Finally the king yields, ugly Jack becomes handsome, and succeeds to the throne.[133] In the Malecite tale of Strong John the hero again aspires to the hand of a princess. His encounter with a monster, whom he is sent to kill, is reminiscent of a Micmac battle between two chenoos, and the manner in which he plays one giant off on another is elsewhere attributed to Lox. By these and other feats of skill he obtained his princess.

> "John's good fortune was now complete . . . one day the giant who was now serving him . . . noticed that he took something out of his pocket and talked to it. . . . He determined to secure this thing. . . . Early one morning the giant rushed in and said, 'Master, there are many ducks on the lake this morning' . . . John picked up his gun and ran down to the lake, forgetting in his hurry to put on his vest. The giant . . . put on the vest, drew the box from the pocket, and opened it, when . . . he saw the little man dancing. [134] This little man . . . asked him what he wished for. 'I want this house and all the inmates transported to a lonely island in the sea', said the giant. . . . When John looked around . . . the palace . . . had vanished . . . he again met the old man who had given him the box . . . said the old man . . . 'there is but little I can do for you; but I will give you power to change yourself into a fox. You will have to call a large bird . . . to take you over to the island. . . . When he the giant chases you, lead him through the woods, and then double on your tracks and return to the house. Get your vest and the little man'. . . . John easily secured his vest and the box . . . the little man stopped dancing and said, 'What do you want, master?' 'I want this house and everything in it transported back to its original place,' John replied, 'and I want the giant chained inside.' When John got back to his old home, he hitched horses to the giant's limbs and had him torn to pieces." [135]

The Micmac variant of this tale must have been borrowed at a very much earlier date than that of the Malecite, because much of the aboriginal environment and social heritage of the Micmacs has been fused into it.[136] The characters are Indians, who wear moccasins and live in wigwams in the forest. The hero's escape by means of magic arrows is a variant of the widespread American motive of the magic flight. When he arrives at an Indian village to sue for the hand of the chief's daughter, he is not told to kill a monster, obtain the tongues of three giants, or to collect a debt from a neighbouring king as in

---

132. Rand (2) 14.
133. Rand (2) 34.
134. Box and dancing man occur in several Wabanaki tales.
135. Mechling (2) 229.
136. Rand (2) 7.

the Malecite version; he is told to remove a mountain, and to vanquish the chief's enemies in battle.   Having secured his bride, the theft of the dancing man follows, as in the Malecite tale, though in the Micmac the conditions are Indian:

> "This servant manages to steal the 'household god', and to run away with it,—wife, wigwam, and all. . . . One day the master of the house went out a hunting. . . . Now it so happened that his servant had often been led to inquire in his own mind what could be the secret of his master's wonderful prowess. Seeing the coat . . . he takes it up and slips it on . . . he feels the box . . . his eyes rest on the dancing image. The little fellow stops his dancing, suddenly looks up, and exclaims. . . . 'What do you want of me?' . . . 'I want', says he, 'this wigwam with all its contents removed to some spot where it cannot be discovered.' . . . The original owner comes home, and finds himself minus wife, wigwam, magic box, and all. But he still has his magical bow and arrow; and shooting his arrow and giving chase, he is soon at the secluded wigwam . . . he looks in and sees the perfidious servant asleep with the coat under his head. He then slips it on, opens the box, and wishes himself back, wigwam, wife, servant, and all, to their original home . . . the faithless servant is in his hands . . . he is killed, flayed, and a door blanket is made of his skin."

To this tale is appended an incident which does not appear in the Malecite version.   It is distinctly Indian in character and reflects the pre-Columbian environment.   The horned serpent and the concept of the external soul are both aboriginal;

> "The old chief himself is a great boooin (medicine man . . .) whose tutelar deity is a chepechcalm (. . . horned serpent . . .) He is chagrined to find himself outdone by his son-in-law. . . . He says quietly to him one day, 'I want you to bring me the head of a chepechcalm for my dinner.' 'I will do so', he replies. The dancing doll is commanded to bring one of these frightful monsters to the village . . . the fight is long and fearful, but finally . . . he severs the dragon's head from his trunk. . . . He finds the chief alone, weak and exhausted, and sitting bent nearly double; he walks up to him and pounds him on the head with the dragon's head. The old necromancer's magic is gone; his teomul, his medicine . . . is destroyed, and he falls and dies." [137]

In the Malecite version Strong John decides to seek service under the king.   He pretends that he is a great warrior and writes on a piece of paper that he has killed a hundred and fifty people with his right hand and a hundred with his left.   He pins the paper on his back and sets out for the palace:

> "When he arrived there, he lay down and feigned sleep. one of the guards happened to pass by, and, reading the notice on his back, reported the circumstances to the king, who ordered John brought to his presence. The guard took a long pole and nudged him with it. John awoke with a curse, and demanded why he had been awakened, for he was having a fine time dreaming of battle. The guard said that the king wanted to see him.
> 'If the king wants to see me', John replied, 'he can come to me.'
> Now, the king had among his subjects a giant whom he feared, and was anxious to be rid of. Thinking that in John he had found an instrument for his purpose, he condescended to go and see him, and he promised the young man a large sum of money if he entered his service." [138]

---

137. Rand (2) 12.   138. Mechling (2) 229.

This incident links the Petit Jean cycle with the European Penobscot tale of the old drunkard who became the king's general:

> "There was once an old Indian who spent most of his time drinking. One day when he awoke from a drunken night's sleep, he found himself lying in his vomit, and swarms of flies crawling over him. When he got up to go about his business, he encountered a friend, who saw the flies covering his bare back. His friend slapped his back, smearing the dead flies in blotches. . . . Pretty soon he began telling people that the spots on his back stood for the number of enemies he had killed, he was so brave a man. [139] So he got the name of being a terrible warrior as he went on. By and by he came to the king's (Kindjames) [140] country, where a great war was being fought between the king's soldiers and the enemies, who were trying to take the land. When the king heard that such a great man was in his country, he sent for him."

Compare this incident with the corresponding incident in the French tale:

> "Un jour, un tailleur mangeait dans la rue une tartine de fromage blanc. Voyant des mouches contre un mur, il donna un grand coup de poing dessus et en tua douze. Aussitot il courut chez un peintre et lui dit d'ecrire sur son chapeau: J'EN TUE DOUZE D'UN COUP, puis il se mit en compagne." [141]

Or the Spanish version which has been recorded in Chile:

> "Haz de saber para contar y entender para saber que este era un pobre zapatero llamado Juan Bolondron. Un dia que estaba sentado en su banco tomando un plato de leche, como cayesen algunas gotas de leche en el banco, se agruparon muchas moscas, y el les pego una palmada, y mato siete. Entonces se puso a gritar:
> —i Soy muy valiente, y en adelanteme he de llamar Don Juan Bolondron Mata-siete-de-un-trompon." [142]

The Indian version differs from either the French or the Spanish in that drunkenness, which was the curse of the native in the Euro-American milieu, is represented with its attendant squalor.   Moreover, subsequent incidents in the French version are not found in the Penobscot tale.   The purely fictional competition with a giant for the hand of a princess is replaced in the Indian by what might very easily have represented Indian experience in the turbulent European scene in the seventeenth century.   When the old Indian had had his audience with the king

> ". . . the old man became very much frightened when he found that the king thought he was so brave. . . . But the king would not hear of his backing down. . . . So the king had the old man put upon a big white horse, and sent some soldiers with him to show him where the fighting was going on . . . the old man got more and more frightened. Pretty soon the big white horse took fright and began tearing toward the battle. . . . Now as they swept along, they dashed right through a burying-ground with the big wooden crosses, like trees, among the graves. As the big horse dashed beneath the arms of one of these crosses, the old man grabbed at it to get off the horse. But the old cross was rotten underneath, and it broke off at the ground . . . and

---

139. Speck (7) 83. "The Penobscots used to paint emblems representing exploits on their backs".
140. Term for "king" derived from James I of England.
141. Cosquin 350.
142. Biblioteca de las tradiciones populares Espanolas tomo I, p. 121.

> there he was tearing toward the battle . . . carrying the big cross in his arms . . . when the enemy saw the big white horse and the man with the cross coming against them, they fell upon their knees and gave up. So the king's soldiers won the battle, and the old man was made the king's great general for his bravery." [143]

As the complete tale bears a slightly closer resemblance to the Irish version it is not improbable that it travelled from the British Isles to the Penobscot country by way of New England.[144]   These people, unlike the other Wabanaki, came early under the influence of the English as much, perhaps, as under that of the French, since their territory bordered upon both New England and New France.   It is interesting to note that with the Russian version there is still greater agreement.   In the Mongol version the incident of killing enemies with a tree snatched while on the back of a run-away horse appears, but the fly-swatting incident does not.[145]   This, however, occurs in India.   The Spanish tale, as a whole, bears a closer relation to the French than it does to the Indian, the latter being the only version in which the hero is a drunkard.

The colonial environment of the Indian is reflected also in "The disobedient boy who became a prince."[146]   A young man was told by his father never to cross a certain mountain, but he disobeyed.   There he met a caribou who said, "If you shoot me some day you will kill your father."   But he shot. Here in this tale is the Indian idea of the external soul that occurs in so many of the Indian tales, and the European motive is given an Indian setting which is dependent upon hypothetical Indian experience in the Euro-American world. In the French Canadian version, from which the main incidents in the tale are doubtless derived, the hero is a prince, who, after being cast on the Isle of Orleans to be devoured by wild beasts, arrives at the chateau of a king.[147]

The horse that defecates gold coins is not found in the French Canadian version.   It occurs, however, among the Malecite.[148]   And the trick of curing the king's blindness which occurs in the French Canadian tale is absent in both the Malecite and Penobscot variants.   It is found, however, among the Micmac in a different context.[149]   The Malecite tale does not show the marked Indian influences that are found in the Penobscot account.   It may scarcely be adequate to say that this is due to the fact that the Malecite were closer to the French Canadian centre of diffusion than were the Penobscot, and that they were less of a seafaring people than the latter.

Besides these secular tales there is a group which is tinged with the monastic and miraculous concepts of the medieval church, and which has doubtless depended upon the teachings of the missionaries for its successful diffusion among the Indians.   Although "The boy that was transformed into a horse" has certain Indian elements, such as the symplegades, it belongs properly to this group.[150]   An angel aids a boy to save his brother who has been trans-

---

143. Speck (7) 83.
144. Cosquin 351-352.
145. Ibid. 352.
146. Speck (7) 81.
147. Barbeau and Bolduc (4) Le petit jardinier, pp. 97-101.
148. Mechling (2) 219.
149. Rand (2) 123.
150. Rand (2) 30.

formed into a horse, and teaches them their prayers from a prayer book. After the evil father, who had sold his son for liquor, is consigned to the Devil, the angel takes the boys away, presumably to Heaven. In "The solitary maiden" the atmosphere of the nunnery is portrayed. A lost princess dwells in a lonely house for seven years. She dreams that she must cut certain flowers before a man arrives. The man parades as a prince but in reality he is an evil spirit who is attempting to destroy her soul. She prays to God and is lifted up to Heaven before the mischief is wrought. Rand suspected this to be the story of some saint, that the white lilies symbolize moral purity, and that the moral is one of self-denial, prayer, and faith.[151] Different in context from either of these, but springing from the same medieval world-view, is the Micmac tradition of a chapel to St. Ann which was built by a miracle near Quebec. The tale tells how the crew of a vessel were caught in a great storm in the St. Lawrence river.[152] "The captain read from the prayer book . . . hatchway was now removed, and to their surprise, no water was to be seen; but they were close to a forest by the side of a highway, and near at hand was a large stone chapel with a cross on the top of the steeple. . . After the country passed into the hands of the English heretics, they made an audacious attempt to burn this chapel. . . ." The Micmac sympathies are here shown to be with the French Catholics rather than with the English heretics.[153]

The eastern Algonkian mind became partly submerged in the new French rather than the new English culture, both of which began to flood the eastern seaboard in the early days of the seventeenth century. But the reactions of the Wabanaki varied in different places and at different times. These reactions are transfigured in the folk-tales, sometimes as adjustments, sometimes as maladjustments, to the culture of the intruders. At first the white man was invested with a supernatural aura as a result of his exotic and not readily comprehensible qualities. The thing of wonder has received a post mortem expression in a widespread pseudo-historical tale which doubtless refers to no particular event, but rather represents an accretion of various perceptions:

> ". . . a young woman had a singular dream . . . that a small island came floating in towards the land, with tall trees on it, and living beings . . . the wise men . . . pondered over the girl's dream but could make nothing of it. . . . Getting up in the morning, what should they see but a singular little island. . . . There were trees on it . . . on which a number of bears, as they supposed, were crawling about. They all seized their bows . . . intending to shoot the bears; what was their surprise to find that these supposed bears were men. . . . Among them was a man dressed in white . . . who came towards them making signs of friendship. . .
> . . . the necromancers were displeased; they did not like it that the coming of these foreigners should have been intimated to this young girl. . . . Had an enemy . . . been about to make a descent upon them, they could have foreseen and foretold it by the power of their magic; but of the coming of this teacher of a new religion they could know nothing." [154]

---

151. Rand (2) 150.
152. Rand (2) 282.
153. For additional tales with European motives and decorations see Parsons (1) 102-133. No. 44 has negro elements.
154. Rand (2) 225.

Here we have the first bewilderment of the native mind. Elsewhere the note struck is one of timidity. An Indian town had for some time remained isolated from other Indian towns. "When any white people came to the shore they ran away afraid."[155] But they soon learned that there were material benefits to be obtained from the strangers, and their culture hero, Gluskap, was invested with the boldness that they themselves lacked. The hero here becomes the creation of their repressed natures:

> "They saw a man-of-war. Gloskap and Amkotpigtu went along side the warship. They begged for their grandmother a pair of scissors, a knife and fork, some thread, some clothes, and some provisions. The boss of the man-of-war had to give what they asked or they would have destroyed them."[156]

But Gluskap did not take kindly to the encroachments of the whites. The king foolishly tried to take him prisoner and, of course, failed. His servant, Little Martin, was decoyed before the mouth of a cannon and shot at. When the smoke cleared he was found to be sitting unhurt astride the cannon, to the astonishment of the bystanders. Enraged at white treachery, Gluskap abandoned the country.[157] Somewhat akin, but of a less mythical nature, is the story of an Indian chief's visit to France. Soon after the discovery he is taken as a curiosity to demonstrate the Indian method of killing and curing game. To revenge himself for being made into an exhibition "he went into a corner of the yard and eased himself before them all".[158] Here is the defense-mechanism of brazenness that hardened about the submissive tendency of the Indian in contact with the materially dominant European. In the Passamaquoddy version it was Gluskap who first discovered Europe. "Glooskap discovered England, and told them about it." When he went to France they fired at him but could not hurt him. He did not come to see the king but to have his mother baptized as a Catholic.[159]

When Gluskap, the protector, had departed in anger the Indians fared ill. They were powerless against the aggressive avarice of the whites. "The first white man who came to the country went up to an Indian's wigwam in front of which there stood a bench. The white man took a seat on it, beside the Indian, who then moved a little farther off to give him plenty of room. The white man then took the place which he had left. This continued until the Indian had to leave the bench, there being no room left for him."[160] So the Indian lost his birthright and became a mere instrument in the great imperialistic wars of the French and English in the eighteenth century. But the eastern Algonkians became instruments in the hands of the French because the French tried to assimilate them and sometimes to meet them more than half way, and not to segregate them and thrust them aside after the manner of the hide-bound and insular English. But the instrument was by no means passive in the eighteenth century wars:

"... there was a battle at Annapolis Royal, between French and English

---

155. Parsons (1) 72.
156. Michelson 54.
157. Rand (2) XLV.
158. Rand (2) 279.
159. Leland (1) 127.
160. Jack (2) 102.

and Indians. Of course this French people pretty well cleaned out. Then they told the Indians, 'Can't you help out?' **Of course the Indians didn't know anything about war. They was hardly civilized**. . . . Every chance they git the English would clean the Indian settlers out . . . Baryo, from Yarmout', an' his brother-in-law from Port Lawrence, fought a lot till they got tired. Then they got surrounded. Put locks an' chains on 'em. Goin' to get hanged in a few days. Baryo said, 'Well, we're here now, but I'm goin' home today. . . . Baryo breaks the bonds . . . Then they . . . got passed the guards. . . . They came after him, but he cleaned up hundreds of them. . . . A Frenchman saw him. He was glad to see the Indian. The Frenchman made a big brush pile . . . He fix bed an' a quilt in there. Kep' him there . . . till after a while his foot got all right.

". . . he went home . . . there was a lot of soldiers in the barracks there. . . . He had nothing but the butcher knife. He went in an' sat by the stove. . . . There was a lot of high bugs there. Then somebody said, 'There's an Indian man right there. . . . You just stay there till I get my supper, 'cause you might make stink.' Baryo say, 'I don't know who make stink first,' an' he ups an' stabs the man to death. . . Then he put the lights out. He started strikin' with his tomahawk. He got in the door an' chipped them as they come out. . . . He give the Indian war whoop. The English gets scared an' think there a lot of Indians there. . . . After a while the battle stopped. Then he took a light an' lit it. He saw three or four Englishmen standin' there. He killed them an' went home." [161]

The external conditions of the new life together with the teachings of the missionaries wrought a profound change in the Micmac religious mind. A pseudomorphosis resulted from the acculturation of the two creeds and the mythical characters of pre-Columbian times became greatly confused with the Biblical.   Gluskap's position in the new hierarchy varies in several of the tales belonging to this group.   At times he becomes a forerunner of Christ, a sort of Hebrew prophet, being more in keeping with Jewish concepts as portrayed in the Old Testament than with the dispensation of the New, but at the same time he retains something of his position of culture hero:

"Gluskap was the god of the Micmacs. The great deity, Ktcinisxam, made him out of earth and then breathed on him, and he was made. . . . Then he prophesied the coming of the Europeans and the baptism of the Micmacs. . . . As he prophesied it came true, for in 1610 the first Micmacs were baptized and became Christians. Gluskap had departed just a little before them, because he knew he had to make room for Christ; but he is the Micmac's god, and will come to help them if they ever need him. When Peary discovered the North Pole, he saw Gluskap sitting at the top of the pole, and spoke to him." [162]

In another tale Christ appears as the creator of the world and of Gluskap. Then he creates the second man, Hadam, who is white and who carries a sack with papers in it. Gluskap walks on the water but when Hadam tries to follow he sinks.   So Gluskap says, "You will have to go back now.   From the people who come from you, sin will come."   Then Gluskap gave rules to the people, which were the rules to be observed by Indian children at the missionary schools.   ". . . girls must go out one door, and boys out the other door. . . . No courting then. . . . . At that time they were good people.   They obeyed their father and mother.   If people didn't follow Gluskap's rules, they would kill them, and burn them. . . . We believe he is living yet in this world. . . . .

---

161. Fauset 307.   162. Speck (26) 59.

The last people he lived with he told he was not going back to rule them.   He told them that some time they would get religion."[163]

Sometimes he is confused with Noah, but it is he who causes the flood, and not God. Although he was angry he did not drown the people but changed them into rattlesnakes, because the Micmac culture hero was more benevolent than Jehovah.[164]   Sometimes he competes with Christ in the same way that he competed with the evil magicians of mythological days:

> "One time when Gluskap had become the Indian's god, Christ wanted to try him to see if he was fit: so he took Gluskap to the ocean, and told him to close his eyes. 'Then Christ moved close to the shore an island which lay far out to sea. When Gluskap opened his eyes, he saw it. Christ asked him if he could do as much as that. Then Gluskap told Christ to close his eyes a while. When Christ opened his eyes, he found that Gluskap had moved it back to its place again." [165]

The salient features of the ethnological evidence have now been reviewed.   It is found that tales having exclusive Indian elements are pre-Columbian, whereas those having exclusive European elements are of comparatively recent diffusion among the Indians.   The other classes do not fall into any definite sequence; that is for example, tales having Indian motives and Indian and European decorations do not necessarily precede those having Indian motives and complete or almost complete European decorations, although this would tend to be the case.   The chronological sequence depends not on the combinations of decorations so much as upon the nature of the decorations themselves. Each tale presents a separate problem and must be judged according to the nature of its constituents.   It is, however, possible to say in certain instances that a European tale which occurs in one tribe with its pristine European decorations intact is of later diffusion than that in another tribe the decorations of which have been displayed by Indian elements.   The Malecite and Micmac versions of a Petit Jean tale present a case in point.   The Micmac tale was evidently received at a time when the material culture of that tribe was still integral enough to impose itself upon the decorations.   The Malecite version was doubtless received by that people when their material culture had been almost entirely displaced by the materials of Europe.

Most of the tales studied fall into four categories.   The first has purely Indian elements.   The second shows Indian motives together with mixed decorations.   The third has purely European constituents.   And the fourth gives evidence of having arisen from the contact of Europeans and Indians in the Euro-American environment.   Tales having blended European and Indian motives have not been found, unless "The invisible boy" is a solitary example.[167]   In this Cinderella tale the hero is an Indian and all the decorations are also native. The hero, however, is invisible, and invisibility may be invariably European.[168]   The greater part of the tale is not dependent upon the Cinderella

---

163.   Parsons (1) 88.
164.   Leland (1) 110.
165.   Speck (26) 60.
167.   Rand (2) 101.
168.   Suggestion of Mr. W. J. Wintemburg.

motive and is entirely Indian in conception since it revolves about the Indian idea of the external soul, or more exactly in this case, the guardian spirit.   But is the Cinderella motive European or Indian?   The motive appears to Mechling to have been aboriginal among the Wabanaki.[169]   With respect to Europe it may have been "An adaptation of a familiar medieval novel; starting, as it would seem, less than four centuries ago" and "received with enthusiasm .. by the Indians of America."[170]   Leland contended, not without reason, that the tale represents an acculturation of an aboriginal solar myth to the French Canadian Cinderella.[171]

But must a motive be either European or Indian?   May it not be a fusion in some cases from both sources?   It may not at present be possible to answer these questions conclusively.   The term "motive" requires more precise definition than has been accorded it by ethnologists so far.   Are motives and decorations entirely separate entities, or are they aspects of some integer?   And if so, what is the relationship between them?   Neglecting stylistic devices, decorations are objects with a spacial significance, that is, they are tri-dimensional.   But whether static or dynamic in their properties, they are impossible to conceive apart from the concept of duration; and energy in all of the tales studied so far is of the kinetic variety, so that we have not only duration but also change.   Now change itself is impossible to conceive apart from objects having a spacial significance, any more than the connotation of a verb is possible apart from that of at least one accompanying noun.   So we are forced to the conclusion that decorations and motives are ultimately aspects of an integer. But how are these aspects related?   In the Micmac Cinderella tale the ugly (seemingly inferior) sister succeeds in winning the hero whereas the tolerably good-looking (seemingly superior) sisters fail.   Reducing this to its lowest terms we have success of inferior, with failure of superior as a corollary.   Now the inferior one is a character, and the character is made up of characteristics which are decorations.   The significant decoration here is ugliness.   So that the Cinderella motive is not the Cinderella motive merely by virtue of success, but also by the fact that it is ugliness that is succeeding.   So that it takes the verb "to succeed" plus the noun "ugliness" to integrate into the resultant motive "Cinderella".   It must be confessed, however, that reasoning of this kind leads no where.   In the last analysis, a motive is of an organic nature and thereby renders definition difficult.   But before it can be accurately determined whether the Micmac tale is aboriginal or derived from European sources it is necessary to study all available versions both in America and Europe with respect to the constancy of the verbal aspect in its particular relation to the variability of the significant decorations of the characters.   The motive doubtless springs from the same psychological source as that which has given rise to the motive of littleness overcoming size and strength which occurs so frequently in eastern Algonkian folk-tales.

---

169. Mechling (2) 55.
170. Newell 15.
171. Leland (1) 308.

PSYCHOLOGICAL FACTORS

No study of foreign influences on the folklore of any given ethnic group would be adequate without some recognition of the operation of psychological factors in psychological terms. F. C. Bartlett has made inroads into this almost virgin field in his work, "Psychology and primitive culture". Whatever criticism might be leveled at his adherence to the theories of MacDougall by the behaviourist psychologists of America, and elsewhere, does not affect us here. for we are not so much concerned with the environmental or hereditary origin of instinctive tendencies as we are with the way in which these tendencies affect the data of folk-tales.

Now, cultural elements find a footing within an alien society by being attached to tendencies which are already operative within that society. The prevailing tendency between the two groups may be one of comradeship, or it may be one of dominance and acceptance. Moreover, the Indian group itself might be a comradeship group or one in which dominant and submissive factions are contained. There is a close relationship between the conservative tendencies of the group and its tendency towards primitive comradeship. The latter prevails with respect to modes of thought, feeling, and action, all of which grow familiar through repetition and result in a crystallization of existing forms, which leads to conservation.[172] This conservation, being selective, favours the replacement of detail by detail to form distinctive patterns which are, in turn, a proof of the opposite tendency of constructiveness. The basis of selection lies in what Bartlett calls group difference tendencies.[173] They are closely related to the culture or social heritage of the group, and reflect the material environment, games, war, social organization, ceremony, magic, and religion. Although the group difference tendencies determine the direction of themes, the predominant instincts of the group determine the themes themselves. If a certain instinct is dominant in a group it will be reflected in the tales. Thus, as Petit Jean is very often concerned with securing a bride it might be taken that the sexual element has had a very strong appeal for the French settlers and traders. As hunger frequently went unsatisfied in the tight economic conditions of the northern forest world, the search for food often serves as a theme in the Wabanaki tales.

The group difference tendencies may become disintegrated under certain conditions of relationship with the incoming people. For instance when the immigrants achieve dominance by force of arms the native traits will tend to become extinct and be replaced by those of the aggressive culture. When the immigrants dominate on account of their possession of a superior culture the new elements may mix with the old to form a complex of unreconciled traits. When the incoming group achieves dominance by virtue of superior culture as well as by force of arms then violent social reversions may prove that there has been an underground persistence of the old ways. This is occasional

---

172. Bartlett 65.
173. Bartlett 159.

among the eastern Algonkians in the fields of both mythology and religion. Occasionally, tales of fraud replace tales of superiority when the native group loses its dominance.   Several cases of this occur in the Micmac collections.   On the other hand a true blend of elements results from contact in which the participants are aware of a measure of comradeship.   If the tales studied are any criterion this appears to have been the prevailing condition in Acadia in the colonial period.

NOTE.   The materials of the above chapter have been gathered from the collections gleaned from and relating to the eastern Algonkian tribes who dwelt south of the St. Lawrence.   But whereas a large body of material is now available for the latter, that which relates to the Montagnais and the Nascopi north of the St. Lawrence is extremely meagre.[174]   As field work progresses among these Indians it is to be hoped that a sufficiently large number of folktales will become available to warrant a study of the influences which have resulted from the contact with European culture.

---

174. A beginning has been made by Speck (19) (27); Turner L. M.; and Strong 285-286.

BIBLIOGRAPHY

Abbreviations

A. A.—American Anthropologist.
B. A. E.   —Bureau of American Ethnology
J. A. F. L.—Journal of American Folklore
R. S. C.   —Royal Society of Canada.

Note. All the printed material, including anthropological literature, and primary and secondary historical sources, has been run together alphabetically since the notes and references to each chapter are coordinated with the bibliography The reason for the disregard of a topical bibliography will become obvious to the reader who makes use of the references. The manuscript sources are given separately.

Manuscript Sources

Public Archives of Canada,
Series C.11.A.
      "   C.11.B.
      "   C.11.C.
      "   C.11.D.
Collection Moreau St. Mery

Anthropological literature, primary and secondary historical sources

Abbott, M. E., History of Medicine in the Province of Quebec. Toronto 1931.

Adams, J. T., (1) The Epic of America.   (2) The founding of New England. Boston 1921.

Akagi, R. H., The town proprietors of the New England colonies.   Philadelphia 1924.

Albert, T., Histoire du Madawaska; d'apres les recherches historiques de P. Therriault, etc.   Quebec 1920.

Alexander, H. R., North America, Volume 10.   The mythology of all races.   Boston 1916.

Alger, A. L., In Indian tents.   Penobscot, Passamaquoddy and Micmac. Boston 1897.

Anderson, W. P., Micmac place names in the Maritime provinces and the Gaspe peninsula, recorded between 1852 and 1890 by the Reverend S. T. Rand.   Geographic Board of Canada, Ottawa 1919.

Atkinson, G., (1) The extraordinary voyage in French literature before 1700.   (2) Relations de voyages, etc.

Aubert, de Gaspé, P.   The Canadians of old, trans. by C. G. D. Roberts, New York 1890.

Babcock, W. H. (1) Certain pre-Columbian notices of the American aborigines. A. A. 18 N. S. 1916. (2) Legendary islands of the Atlantic. Study in medieval geography. Am. Geog. Soc., Research Series 8. N. Y. 1922.

Bailey, A. G., The significance of the identity and disappearance of the Laurentian Iroquois. Trans. R. S. C. Third Series, Section 2, Vol. 27, 1933.

Bancroft, H. H., The works of. History of Mexico, 1883.

Barbeau, C. M. (1) America's oldest school of arts. M. S. (2) Anecdotes populaire du Canada. J. A. F. L. Vol. 33. (3) Asiatic migrations into America. Can. His. Rev. Vol. 13, 1932. (4) With E. Bolduc and M. Tremblay. Contes Populaires Canadiens (3iemme Serie) J. A. F. L. Vol. 32. (5) Contes populaires Canadiens. J. A. F. L. Vol. 29. (6) Contes populaires Canadiens. J. A. F. L. Vol. 30. (7) The field of European folklore in America. J. A. F. L. Vol. 32. (8) The native races of Canada. Trans R. S. C. 3rd Series, Sec. 2, Vol. 21, 1927. (9) Nos. anciens artisans. Rev. trimestrielle Canadienne Sept. 1933, No. 75. (10) The origin of floral and other designs among the Canadian and neighbouring Indians. Int. Cong. Am. proc. 1930.

Bartlett, F. C., Psychology and primitive culture. Cambridge 1923.

Baxter, J. P., A memoir of Jacques Cartier, Sieur de Limoilou, his voyages to the St. Lawrence. N. Y. 1906.

Beard, C. A. and M. R., The rise of American civilization. N. Y. 1927.

Beauchamp, W. M. (1) Lapse of time theme. J. A. F. L. Vol. 10. (2) Metallic implements of the New York Indians. N. Y. State, Mus. Bull. 55. (3) Metallic ornaments of the New York Indians. A. A. Vol. 6, N. S.

Beauvois, M. E., (1) La grande terre de l'ouest dans les documents Celtiques du moyen age. Int. Cong. Am. Madrid 1882. (2) La Normambegue, avec de preuves de son origine scandinave fourni par la langue, les institutions, et les croyances des indigenes de l'acadie. Int. Cong. Am. Section 3, Vol. 1.

Beazley, C. R., The dawn of modern geography. 2 volumes, 1897 and 1901.

Belleforest, F. de, L'histoire universelle du monde. Paris 1570.

Benedict, R. F., The concept of the guardian spirit in North America. Mems. 29-33. Am. Anthrop. Assoc. Menasa, Wisconsin, 1923.

Bergen, F. D., Popular American plant names. Jour. Am. Folk-Lore, vol. v., 1892, pp. 89-106; vol. vi., 1893, pp. 135-142.

Bibaud, F. M., Biographie des Sagamos illustres de l'Amerique septentrionale, etc. Montreal 1848.

Biblioteca de tradiciones populares de Espana.

Biggar, H. P., (1) The early trading companies of New France, etc. Toronto 1901. (2) The precursors of Jacques Cartier, 1497-1534. Canadian Archives Pubs. 5 Ottawa 1911. (3) The voyages of Jacques Cartier published from the originals with translations, notes and appendices. Can. Archives Pub. 11, 1924.

Birkett, H. S., A brief account of the history of medicine in the Province of Quebec. 1535-1838, N. Y. 1908.

Boas, F., (1) America and the old world. Int. Cong. Am. 21, 1924. (2) Anthropology. Encyclopedia of the social sciences. (3) Dissemination of tales among the natives of North America. J. A. F. L. Vol. 4. Pages 13-20 (4) Migrations of Asiatic races and cultures to North America. Science Monthly, Feb. 1929, pp. 110-117. (5) Mythology and folk-tales of the North American Indians. J. A. F. L. 27, pp. 374-410. (6) Religion. Handbook of American Indians, etc. Bul. 30, B. A. E.

Boucher, P., True and genuine description of New France, etc. Ed. E. L. Montizambert, Montreal, 1883.

Bourinot, J. G., Historical and descriptive account of the island of Cape Breton, and of its memorials of the French regime, etc. Montreal 1892.

Bourne, E. G., Spain in America, 1450-1580. Vol. 3 of the American Nation: a history, ed. A. B. Hart.

Breard, C. & P. Documents relatifs a la marine normande, et a ses armements aux XVI. et XVII. siecles pour le Canada. Rouen 1889.

Brebner, J. B., Subsidized inter-marriage with the Indians. An incident in British colonial policy. Can. Hist. Rev. Vol. 6, p. 33.

Brenner, A., Idols behind altars. N. Y. 1929.

Brinton, D. D., The myths of the new world, etc. Philadelphia 1896.

Brown, W. W., (1) Chief making among the Passamaquoddy Indians. J. A. F. L. 5, pp. 57-59. (2) Some indoor and outdoor games of the Wabanaki Indians. Trans. R. S. C. sec. 2, 1888. (3) Wa-Ba-Ba-Nal, or northern lights, J. A. F. L. 3, p. 213.

Bryce, J., The relations of the advanced and the backward races of mankind. Oxford 1903.

Burns, H. A., Tuberculosis in the Indian. The American Review of tuberculosis. Vol. 26, 1932.

Bushnell, D. I. Jr., Native villages and village sites east of the Mississippi. B. A. E. Bull. 69, 1919.

Carpenter, J. E., Comparative religion. London.

Carver, J., Travels through the interior part of North America, in the years 1766, 1767 and 1768. London 1778.

Casgrain, H. R., Histoire de l'hotel dieu de Quebec. Quebec 1878.

Chamberlain, A. F., (1) The acquisition of a written language by primitive peoples. Am. Journ. Psych. 17, 1906, pp. 69-80. (2) The Algonkian Indians of Baptiste lake. Can. Inst. An. Rep. 1890-91, pp. 83-89. (3) Algonkian words in American English. J. A. F. L. 15, 1902, pp. 240-267. (4) The Aryan element in Indian dialects.

Can. Ind. Owen Sound, 1891. Vol. 1, pp. 148-153. (5) The Beothuks of Newfoundland. An. Archeol. Rep. 1905. Toronto 1906. pp. 117-122. (6) Contribution of the American Indian to human civilization. Proceedings of the Amer. Antiq. Soc. 1903. New Series 15. pp. 91-126. (7) The Indians of the eastern provinces of Canada. An. Arch. Rep. for Ont. 1905. (8) The influence of Algonquin language on English speech in America. Sec. H. p. 503. Proc. of the Am. Assoc. for the Adv'ment of Science, 1903. (9) The influence of European contact on aboriginal institutions. Sec. H. p. 528. Proc. of the Am. Assoc. for the Adv'ment of Science, 1905. (10) The maple amongst the Algonquin tribes. A. A. 1891. Vol. 4, pp. 39-45. (11) Maple sugar and the Indians. A. A. 1891, pp. 381-383. (12) Memorials of the Indian. J. A. F. L. 15. pp. 107-116. (13) New religions among the North American Indians, etc. Journal of Religious Psychology, Vol. 4, pp. 1-49. Worcester, Mass. 1913. (14) Some influences of race contact upon the art of primitive peoples. Journal of Race Development, vol. 2, 1912, pp. 206-209. (15) Some interesting phases of the contact of races individually and en masse. Open Court, Chicago, 1913. Vol. 27 pp. 25-38. (16) Variations in early human culture. J. A. F. L. 19, 1906. pp. 177-190. (17) The vocabulary of Canadian French. Int. Cong. Am. Sec. 15, pp. 21-30.

Chamberlain, M. (1) The Indians in New Brunswick in Champlain's time. Acadiensis, vol. 4, p. 280. (2) On the relation of tribes in Acadia. N. B. Mag. vol. 1, p. 41. (3) The origin of the Maliseets, N. B. Mag. vol. 1, 1898.

Champlain, S. de, (1) Works, 6 volumes. Champlain Soc. Toronto. Ed. H. P. Biggar. (2) The voyages and explorations of, 1604-1616, etc., together with the voyage of 1603. Ed. E. G. Bourne, N. Y. 1906, 2 vols. (3) Voyages of, 1604-1618. Ed. W. L. Grant. N. Y. 1907, in The Original Narratives of early American history. Gen. Ed. J. F. Jameson.

Charlevoix, F. X. de, Journal of a voyage to North Amercia. 2 vols. Chicago 1923.

Clark, J. T., Rand and the Micmacs. Charlottetown, 1899.

Coleman, T. D., Tuberculosis. N. Y. 1909.

Collections de manuscrits, contenant lettres, memoires, et autres documents historiques relatifs a la nouvelle France, etc., Quebec 1883.

Cooney, R., A compendious history of the northern part of the Province of New Brunswick and of the district of Gaspe in lower Canada. Halifax 1832.

Cooper, J. M., Field notes on northern Algonkian magic. Int. Cong. Am. 1928, pp. 512-518.

Corti, Count E. C., A history of smoking. London 1931.

Cosquin, E., Le tailleur et le jeant. Roumania, vol. 5. 1876, p. 350.

Crane, T. F., The diffusion of popular tales. J. A. F. L. vol. 1, 1888, p. 8.

Crawley, A. E., Studies of savages and sex. London 1929.

Davidson, D. S., (1) Decorative art of the Tetes de Boule. of Quebec. Ind. Notes and Mons. 10, No. 9. (2) The family hunting territories of the Grand Lake Victoria Indians. Int. Cong. Am. 22. Rouen 1926. (3) The family hunting territories of the Waswanipi Indians of Quebec. Ind. Notes, Vol. 5, January 1928, No. 1, p. 42. (4) Folk-tales from Grand Lake Victoria. J. A. F. L. 41, p. 275. (5) Notes on the Tetes-de-Boule ethnology. AA. New series 30, p. 18. (6) Some Tetes de Boule tales. J. A. F. L. 41, p. 262.

Dawson, Sir J. W., Fossil men and their Modern Representatives. London, 1888.

de Costa, B. F., The northmen in Maine. Albany 1870.

Decouvertes et etablissements des francais dans l'ouest et dans le sud de l'amerique septentrionale, Vol. 1, 1614-98. Memoires et documents inedits...par Pierre Margry.

Denys, N., ed. W. F. Ganong. The description and natural history of the coast of North America (Acadia). Champlain Society, Toronto, 1908.

Diereville, (1) Relation du voyages du Port Royal de l'Acadie, ou la nouvelle France. Amsterdam 1710. (2) ed. Dr. J. C. Webster. Champlain Society, 1934.

Dionne, N. E., (1) La nouvelle France de Cartier a Champlain 1540-1603. Quebec 1891. (2) Le parler populaire des Canadiens—Francais ou lexique des Canadianismes, Acadianismes, Anglicismes, Americanismes, mots anglais les plus en usages au sein des familles Canadiennes et Acadiennes francaises, comprevant environ 15,000 mots et expression. Preface par M. Raoul de la Grasserie, Que. 1909. pp. XXXIV, 671.

Dixon, R. B., (1) The building of cultures, 1928. (2) The early migrations of the Indians of New England and the Maritime provinces. Am. Ant. Soc. New Series, Vol. 24, 1914, Part 1, pp. 65-76. (3) The mythology of the central and eastern Algonkins. J. A. F. L. 22, pp. 1-10. (4) Racial history of man. 1923.

Documents relating to the colonial history of New York.

Drake, S. G., The old Indian chronicle, etc. Boston 1867.

Druilettes, R. P., Rapport de; envoye en deputation a la nouvelle angle terre....... 1651. Le Canada Francais. Quebec, Vol. 20, No. 10, 1933, pp. 941-949.

Earle, A. M., Customs and fashions in old New England. 1916.

Eastman, M., Church and state in early Canada. Edinburgh, 1915.

Edits, ordonnances royaux, declarations et arrets du conseil d'etat du roi, concernant le Canada. 3 volumes, Quebec 1854.

Elder, W., The aborignees of Nova Scotia. N. A. Rev. 1871.

The elder or poetic Edda commonly known as Saemund's Edda, Part 1, mythological poems, ed. O. Vray, London, 1908.

Elliott, A. M., On Indian words in French Canadian. Am. Journ. of Phil. Vol. 8, pp. 145-151; pp. 338-340.

Ellis, G. E., (1) The red man and the white man, 1882. (2) With Morris, J. E., King Philip's war. 1906.

Ellis, H., Studies in the psychology of sex, six volumes, 1913-1928. Philadelphia.

Emerson, E. R., Indian myths,........America compared with........other countries. Boston 1884.

Faillon, l'Abbé, Histoire de la colonie francaise en Canada.   Villemarie 1865.

Farrand, L., The basis of American history.   In the American Nation: a history. Ed. A. B. Hart.

Faulkner, H. V., American economic history, 1925.

Fauset, A. H., Folklore from the half-breeds in Nova Scotia.   J. A. F. L.   38, p. 300.

Fewkes, F. W., A contribution to Passamaquoddy folklore.   J. A. F. L. 3, pp. 257-280.

Frost, H. K., Two Abnaki legends.   J. A. F. L. 25, 1912, p. 188.

Fraser, Sir J., (1) The golden bough.   (2) Totemism and exogamy.   London 1910.

Gaffarel, M., Basques, Bretons, et Normands sur les cotes de l'amerique du nord pendant les premieres années du XVI siecle.   Int. Cong. Am. Sec. 7, 1888, pp. 57-68.

Gagnon, E., Les sauvages de l'amerique et l'art musical.   Int. Cong. Am. Sess. 15, pp. 179-188.

Ganong, C. K., The early economic history of the Maritime provinces (Acadia) 1497-1607.   Thesis.   University of Toronto Library.

Ganong, W. F., (1) The economic mollusca of Acadia.   Wampum among the New Brunswick Indians.   Bulletin of the Natural History Soc. of New Brunswick.   No. 8, 1889, pp. 3-116.   (2) Historic sites in the province of New Brunswick.   T. R. S. C. 1899, Sec. 2, p. 213.   (3) The identity of the animals and plants mentioned by the early voyagers to eastern Canada and Newfoundland.   Trans.   R. S. C. Series 3, section 2, 1909, p. 197.   (4) The origin of settlement in New Brunswick.   Trans. R. S. C. 1904.   2nd Series XV. Sec. 2, p. 3.   (5) Upon aboriginal pictographs reported from New Brunswick.   N. B. Natural History Soc.

Gathorne-Hardy, G. M., The Norse discoverers of America.   Oxford 1921.

Genet, J., Esquisse d'une civilization oubliée.   Paris 1927.

Gilpin, J. B., Indians of Nova Scotia.   Transactions of Nova Scotia Inst. of Nat. Science, 1878, pp. 260-281.

Goddard, P. E., Facts and theories concerning Pleistocene man in America. A. A. 29, 1927, p. 262.

Goldenweiser, A. A. (1) The social organization of the Indians of North America. J. A. F. L. 27, pp. 411-436.   (2) Totemism.   An Analytical study.   J. A. F. L. 23, 1916.

Greene, E. B., The foundations of American nationality, 1922.

Grinnell, G. B., Tenure of land among the Indians. A. A. 9 N. S. p. 1.

Guerber, H. A., Myths of the Norsemen. London 1909.

Gyles, J., Memoirs of odd adventures, strange deliverances, etc., in the captivity of, etc. Cincinnati 1869.

Haddon, A. C., Magic and fetishism. London 1906.

Hagar, S., (1) The celestial bear. J. A. F. L. vol. 13, 1900, pp. 92-103. (2) Micmac customs and traditions. A. A. 8, 1895, pp. 31-42. (3) Micmac magic and medicine. J. A. F. L. 9, 1896, pp. 170-177. (4) Weather and the seasons in Micmac mythology. J. A. F. L. 10, pp. 101-105.

Hakluyt, R., (1) Discourse on western planting. 1584. Collections of the Maine Hist. Soc. Series 2, Vol. 2, 1877. (2) Diverse voyages touching the discovery of America. London 1850. Ed. J. W. Jones.

Halkett, J., Historical notes respecting the Indians of North America, with remarks on the attemps to convert and civilize them. London 1825.

Hallowell, A. I., (1) Bear ceremonialism in the northern hemisphere. A. A. 28. N. S. p. 1. (2) The physical characteristics of the Indians of Labrador. Soc. des Am. de Paris, 1929, N. S. 21, p. 337. (3) Recent changes in the kinship terminology of the St. Francis Abenaki. Int. Cong. Am. Rouen Sept. 1926, Vol. 2, pp. 97-145. (4) Was cross-cousin marriage practised by the north central Algonkians? Int. Cong. Am. 1930, pp. 519-544.

Hamilton, J. C., The Algonquin Manabozho and Hiawatha. J. A. F. L. 16, pp. 229-233.

Handbook of the Indians of Canada appendixed to the Tenth Report of the Geographic Board of Canada. Ed. J. White, Ottawa 1913.

Harrington, M. R., Iroquois silver work. The Anthropological Papers of the Am. Mus. Nat. Hist. vol. 1, part 6, pp. 351-371.

Harrisse, H., Decouverte et evolution cartographique de Terre-Neuve, etc. 1900.

Hart, A. V., American history told by contemporaries. Era of colonization. 1492-1689, N. Y. 1898.

Heagerty, J. J., Four centuries of medical history in Canada, 2v. Toronto, 1928.

Henshaw, H. W., Indian origin of maple sugar, A. A. Oct. 1890, p. 341.

Hewitt, J. N. V., Orenda and a definition of religion, A. A. n. s. 4, 1902, p. 33-46.

Hirsch, A., Handbook of geographical and historical pathology, 3 v. London, 1883.

Hoffman, On native Indian pictography, Cath. Univ. Bull., Washington, April, 1897.

Holder, A. V., Gynecic notes among the American Indians. Am. J. of Obstetrics, 1892, No. 1, p. 752.

Holmes, W. H., Art in shell of the ancient Americans, B. A. E. rep. 1880-1881, pp. 234-255.

Howley, J. P., The Beothucks or Red Indians; the aboriginal inhabitants of New-foundland, 1915.

Hrdlicka, A., Migrations from Asia to America and their traces. Int. Cong. Am. Proc. 33, N. Y. 1930, p. 44.

Innis, H. A., (1) The fur-trade in Canada; an introduction to Canadian economic history, 1930.   (2) Select documents in Canadian economic history, 1497-1783, Toronto, 1929.

Jack, E., (1) The Abenaki of the St. John River, Trans. of the Can. Inst. Toronto, 1891-1892. v. 3, pp. 195-205.   (2) Maliseet legends, J. A. F. L. No. 8, pp. 193-208.

Jameson, J. F., Original narratives of Early American history.   (a) Bradford's history of Plymouth plantation.   (b) Indian wars, 1913.   (c) Johnson's wonderworking providence, 1910.   (d) Winthrop's journal (History of New England), 2 v. 1908.

Jenness, D., (1) Indians of Canada, Dept. of Mines, Canada, Nat. Mus. of Can. Bull. 65.   Ottawa, 1932. (2) Notes on the Beothuk Indians of Newfoundland, Dept. of Mines, Canada, Nat. Mus. of Can. Ann. rep. 1927. Bull. 56, 1929, pp. 36-39.

Jesuit Relations and allied documents. Ed. R. G. Thwaites, Cleveland, 1897.

Johnson, F., (1) The Algonquin at Golden Lake, Ontario, Ind. notes, v. 5, 1928, p. 173.   (2) Notes on the Ojibwa and Potawatomi of the Parry Is. reservation, Ontario, Ind. notes, v. 6, July, 1929. No. 3, p. 193.

Jones, P., History of the Ojibway Indians with especial reference to their conversion to Christianity, London, 1861.

Jones, W., (1) The Algonkin Manitou, J. A. F. L. 18, 1906, 183-190.   (2) Ojibwa texts, v. 7, pt. 1, 1917; pt. 1919, Pubs. A. Ethnol. Socy.

Jussereau, F., Histoire de l'Hotel Dieu de Quebec, 1751.

Jugements et deliberations du conseil souverain de la nouvelle France, 6 v. Quebec, 1885, seq.

Knott, J., The origin of Syphilis, N. Y. Med. J. Oct. 31, 1908. p. 817.

Kohl, J. G., A history of the discovery of the east coast of N. America. Coll. of the Maine Hist. Socy. ser. 2. Doc. hist. of the State of Maine, v. 1, 1869.

Kroeber, A. L. (1) Catchwords in Amer. mythology, J. A. F. L. 21, 222-227.   (2) & Waterman, T. T. Source book in anthropology, chap. 20, The type of the half-breed Indian.

Lanctot, G., (1) Contes populaires canadiens, J. A. F. L. 36, p. 205.   (2) Contes populaires; contes de Quebec, J. A. F. L. 39, p. 371.

Lang, A., (1) The making of religion, London, 1898.   (2) Myth, ritual and religion, v. 2, 1913.

La Roncière, C. de, Histoire de la marine francaise, v. 2, Paris, 1900, v. 3, 1906.

Lahontan, Baron de, New voyages to N. America, ed. R. G. Thwaites, 2 v. Chicago. 1905.

Le Clercq, C. (1) First establishment of the faith, ed. J. G. Shea. (2) New relation of Gaspesia, with the customs and religion of the Gaspesians Indians, ed. W. F. Ganong, Champlain Socy. 1910.

Lee, F. E. The influence of the Jesuits on the social organization of the N. American Indians, doctoral dissertation, Yale, 1916.

Lefranc, A. Les navigations de Pentagruel, Paris, 1905.

Leland, C. G. (1) The Algonquin legends of New England, or Myths and folklore of the Micmac, Passamaquoddy and Penobscot tribes, Boston, 1884. (2) The Edda among the Algonquin Indians, Atlantic Monthly, Aug. 1884. (3) & Prince, J. D. Kuloskap, the master, and other Algonkian poems, N. Y. 1902.

Lescarbot, M. History of New France, ed. W. L. Grant, Champlain Socy. 1907, 1911 and 1914.

Levy-Bruhl, L. Primitive mentality, 1922.

Lighthall, W. D. (1) The false plan of Hochelaga, Trans. Roy. Soc. Can., sect. 2, series 3, May, 1932, 181-192. (2) Hochelagans and Mohawks; a link in Iroquois history, Trans. Roy. Soc. Can., series 2, v. 5, sect. 2, p. 199, 1899.

Lowie, R. H. (1) Primitive society. (2) The test theme in North American mythology, J. A. F. L. 21, p. 97.

McGuire, J. (1) Anthropological information in early American writings, Int. Cong. Am. Sess. 13, 1902, p. 17-26. (2) Ethnology in the Jesuit relations, A. A. n. s. 3, pp. 257-269.

McIlwraith, T. F. Ethnology, anthropology and archaeology, C. H. R. Dec. 1930, March, 1932, 1933.

MacIntosh, W. Aboriginal pottery of New Brunswick, N. B. Nat. Hist. Socy. 1909.

Macleod, W. C. (1) The American Indian frontier, London, 1928. (2) Debtor and chattel slavery in aboriginal North America, A. A. 27, n. s. p. 70. (3) Economic aspects of indigenous American slavery, A. A. n. s. 30, p. 632. (4) On the significance of matrilineal chiefship, A. A. n. s. 25, p. 495. (5) Trade restrictions in early society, A. A. 29. n. s. p. 271.

Magoffin, R. B. D. & Davis, E. C. Magic spades. The romance of archaeology, N. Y. 1929.

Maher, S. J. Tuberculosis among the American Indians, Am. Rev. of tub. 19, 1929, p. 407.

Mallery, G. Picture writing of the American Indians B. A. E., 10th ann. rep. pp. 378-379.

Mandements......des eveques de Quebec, v. 1 Quebec, 1887.

Marie l'Incarnation. Lettres historiques sur le Canada, ed. B. Sulte, Quebec, 1927.

Marret, R. R. The threshold of religion.

Massicott, E. Z. (1) Les remedes d'autrefois, J. A. F. L. 32, p. 176. (2) Souliers sauvages et souliers de boeuf, Bull. des rech. hist. November, 1924, p. 379-382.

Masson, L. F. R. Les bourgeois de la campagnie du nord-ouest, Recits de voyages, lettres,......Quebec 1889-90.

Masta, H. L. Abenaki Indian legends, grammar and place-names, Odenak, P. Q. 1932.

Mathew, G. F. (1) Discoveries at a village of the Stone Age, at Bocabec, N. B. Bull. of the Nat. Hist. Socy. of N. B. 3, 1884. (2) & Kain, S. W. On an earthenware pot of the Stone Age found at Maquapit Lake, N. B. Nat. Hist. Socy. 1905.

Maureault, J. A. Histoire des Abenakis depuis 1605 jusqu'a nos jours, Sorel, 1886.

Mechling, W. H. (1) Malecite tales, Can. Dept. of Mines, Geol. Surv. Mem. 49, Anth. series. (2) Maliseet tales, J. A. F. L. 26, 219-258.

Michelson, T. Micmac tales, J. A. F. L. 38. p. 33.

Moloney, F. X. The fur-trade in New England, Cambridge 1931.

Moore, C. V. Sheet copper from the mounds is not necessarily of European origin, A. A. n. s. 5, p. 27.

Moorhead, W. K. (1) Are the Hopewell copper objects prehistoric? A. A. n. s. 5, p. 50. (2) The red paint people of Maine, A. A. 15, n. s. p. 33.

Morgan, L. H. League of the Ho-De-No-sau-nee or Iroquois, N. Y. 1922; v. 2, N. Y. 1901.

Morice, A. G. (1) Disparus et survivants, Algonquins du Canada v. 21, No. 5, p. 277, Bull de la Societe de geographie de Quebec. (2) The fur-trader in anthropology, A. A. n. s. 30. p. 60.

Munro, W. B. (1) The Brandy Parliament of 1678. C. H. R. 2, p. 172. (2) The coureurs de bois, Proc. of the Mass. Hist. Socy. 57, 1923-4, p. 192.

Muntz, E. E. Race contact, N. Y. 1927.

Murdoch, B. History of Nova Scotia or Acadie, v. 1, Halifax 1866.

Murray, J. E. Study of the native peoples who dwelt in the St. Lawrence region at the time of its discovery and earliest exploration, Thesis Univ. of Toronto, 1921.

Newell, W. W. Theories of diffusion of folk tales, J. A. F. L. 8, 1895, p. 7.

Nordenskiold, A. E. Periplus. An essay on the early history of charts and sailing vessels, Stockholm, 1897.

Oesterley, W. O. E. The evolution of the Messianic idea, Study in comparative religion, London, 1908.

Old South Leaflets, Boston.

Orchard, W. C. Notes on Penobscot houses, A. A. n. s. 11, p. 601.

Osgood, H. L. The American colonies in the 17th century, v. 1. N. Y.   1904.

Pacifique, R. P. Quelques traits characteristiques de la tribu des Micmacs.   Int. Cong. Am. sess. 15, v. 1, p. 315.

Parker, A. C. (1) Additional notes on Iroquois silver-smithing, A. A. n.s. 13, p. 283. (2) The code of Handsome Lake, the Seneca prophet. N. Y. Educ. Dept. Bull. 530, 1913.   (3) The origin of the Iroquois as suggested by their archaeology, A. A. n.s. 18, 1916.   (4) The origin of Iroquois silver-smithing, A. A. 12, n.s. p. 349.

Parrington, V. L. The colonial mind, v. 1 of Main Currents in American thought, N. Y. 1927.

Parsons, E. C. (1) Micmac folklore, J. A. F. L. 38, p. 55.   (2) Micmac notes, J. A. F. L. 39, p. 460.   (3) Passamaquoddy superstitions, J. A. F. L. 2, p. 229.

Peet, S. D. (1) The cross in America, Am. Ant. & Or. J. v. x, no. 5.   (2) Myths and symbols or aboriginal religions in America. Chic. 1905.

Pennell, E. R. Charles Godfrey Leland, biography, 2 v. 1906.

Peterson, M. S. Some Scandinavian elements in a Micmac swan maiden story; Scandinavian studies and notes, 11 (4) Nov. 1930, p. 139.

Piers, H. Brief account of the Micmac Indians of Nova Scotia and their remains. Trans N. S. Inst. of Sci. v. 13, 1910-1914, p. 99.

Pitt-Rivers, G. H. L-F. The clash of culture, and the contact of races, 1927.

Plattard, J. L'Amerique dans l'oeuvre de Montaigne, Revue des cours et conferences, Paris, 1933. Dec. 15.

Pitts, J. D. (1) The differentiation between the Penobscot and the Canadian Abenaki dialects, A. A. n. s. 4, p. 17.   (2) Penobscot language of Maine, A. A. n. s. 12, 1910.

Putnam, F. W. Conventionalism is ancient American art, Bull. of the Essex Inst. v. 17, 1887.

Radin, P.   (1) Literary aspects of North American mythology, Can. Dept. Mines, June 15, 19. 5. Anthrop. series 6, Geol. surv. (2) Primitive man as philosopher, 1927. (3) Religion of the North American Indians, J. A. F. L. 27, 1914.

Rand, S. T.   (1) Dictionary of the language of the Micmac Indians, Halifax, 1888. (2) Legends of the Micmacs, Lond. 1894.   (3) A short history of facts relating to the history.....of the Micmac tribe etc. Halifax, 1850.   (4) Terms of relationship of the Micmac and Etchemin or Maliseet. A chapter in Morgan, L. H., Systems of consanguinity and affinity, Smithsonian contributions to knowledge 1870, v. 17, Smiths, pubs. 218.

Raymond, W. O.   The river St. John, St. John, 1910.

Reichard, G. A.   Form and interpretation in American art, Int. Cong. Am. 23, N. Y. 1930.

Reuter, E. V.   Race mixture; studies in inter-marriage and miscegenation, N. Y. 1930.

Rink, H.   Tales and traditions of the Eskimo, 1875.

Rivers, W. H. R.   Contact of peoples in Essays and Studies presented to W. Ridgway Camb. 1914.

Rousseau, P.   Les Hochelagas, Int. Cong. Am. 15, p. 280.

Roi, A.   Les sauvagesses de Chateaubriand et leur realité historique, Dec. 30, 1931, Rev. des cours et conferences.

Roi, J. E.   Principes de gouvernement chez les Indiens du Canada, Int. Cong. Am. 15, 161.

Roi, P. G.   Les petites choses de notre histoire, 6 v. 1919-1931.

Royce, C. C.   Indian land cessions in the United States, B. A. E. rep. 18, pt. 2, p. 527.

Sagard, Theodat, G.   Le grand voyage du pays des Hurons, Paris, 1865.

Saint-Valier, Mgr. de.   Etat present de l'eglise et de la colonie francaise dans la Nouvelle-France, Paris 1688.

Saint-Yves, P.   Le culte de la croix chez les Indiens de l'Amerique du Nord, Rev. de l'histoire des religions, v. 74, No. 1, 1916, p. 64.

Sawyer, C. W.   Fire-arms in American history, 1600-1800, Boston, 1910.

Schmitt, J.   Chasses des sauvages a l'ile d'Anticosti, Int. Cong. Am. p. 213.

Schneider, H. W.   The Puritan mind, N. Y.   1930.

Satchell, W. A.   Aboriginal tobaccos, A. A. n. s. 23, p. 397.

Shortt, A. Documents relating to Canadian currency, exchange and finance during the French period, Can. archives, 1925.

Sinclair, A. T. Tatooing of the North American Indians, A. A. n. s. 11, p. 362.

Skinner, A. Some aspects of the folklore of the central Algonkin, J. A. F. L. 27, p. 97.

Smith, G. E. & Malinowski, Spinden and Goldenweiser, Culture, the diffusion controversy, N. Y. 1927.

Smith, N. G. Notes on the depopulation of aboriginal America. A. A. n. s. 30, p. 669.

Speck, F. G. (1) Beothuk and Micmac, Indian notes and monographs, No. 22. (2) Boundaries and hunting groups of the River Desert Algonquin, Indian notes, v. 6, No. 2, April 1929, p. 97. (3) Culture problem in north-eastern North America, Am. Phil, Socy. Proc. v. 65, 1926. (4) Divination by scapulimancy among the Algonquin of River Desert, Quebec. Indian notes, 5, 1928, p. 167. (5) The double curve motive in north-eastern Algonkian art, Can. geol. surv. mem. 42, v. 17, 1914. (6) The eastern Algonkian Wabanaki confederacy, A. A. n. s. 17, p. 492. (7) European folk tales among the Penobscot, J. A. F. L. 26, p. 81. (8) Family hunting territories and social life of various Algonkian bands of the Ottawa valley, Mem. 70, Geol. surv. of Can. 1915, no. 8, Anthrop. series. Myths and folk lore of the Timiskaming Algonquin and Timagami Ojibwa, No. 9. (9) Family hunting bands as the basis of Algonquin social organization. A. A. n. s. 17, p. 289. (10) The function of wampum among the Eastern Algonkian. Mem. of the Am. Anthrop. Assn. 6, 1919, p. 3. (11) Game totems of the north-eastern Algonquin, A. A. 19. & Heye, G. G. Hunting charms of the Montagnais and the Misstassini, Mus. Am. Indians, Heye Foundation, N. Y. 1921, p. 19. (12) Huron hunting territories in Quebec, Indian notes 4, Jan. 1927, No. 1, p. 1. (13) Kinship terms and the family band among the north-eastern Algonkian, A. A. n. s. 20, p. 143. (14) Land ownership among hunting peoples in Primitive America and the world's marginal areas, Int. Cong. Am. (15) Malecite tales, J. A. F. L. 30, p. 479. (16) Medicine practices of the north-eastern Algonkian, Int. Cong. Am. 19. p. 303. (17) Micmac slate image, Ind. notes, 1, 1924, p. 153. (18) Mistassini hunting territories in the Labrador peninsula, A. A. n. s. 25, p. 452. (19) Montagnais and Naskapi tales, Tales from the Labrador peninsula, J. A. F. L. 38, 1925. (20) Northern elements in New England and Iroquois art, Ind. notes 2, Jan. 1925, No. 1, p. 1 (21) Penobscot tales, J. A. F. L. 28, p. 52. (22) Penobscot shaminism, Memoirs of the Am. Anthrop. Assn. 6, No. 3, 1919. (23) Primitive religion in "Religions of the past and present." Ed. J. A. Montgomery, 1918. (24) Reptile lore of the northern Indians J. A. F. L. 36, p. 273. (25) River Desert Indians of Quebec, Ind. notes 4, No. 3, July 1927, p. 241. (26) Some Micmac tales from Cape Breton Island, J. A. F. L. 28, p. 59. (27) Some Nascapi myths from Little Whale River, J. A. F. L. 28, p. 70. (28) Symbolism in Penobscot art, Anthrop. Papers of the Am. Mus. of Nat. Hist. v. 30, pt. 2, 1927. (29) Territorial subdivisions and boundaries of the Wampanoag, Massachusett and Nauset Indians, Ind. notes and monographs N. Y. 1928.

Spell, L. Music in New France in the Seventeenth Century, C. H. R. 8, pp. 119-131.

Squair, J. The Indian tribes on the St. Lawrence at the time of the arrival of the French. Ann. Archael. Rep. Ont. 1923, pp. 82-88.

Stamp, H. A Malecite tale: Adventures of Bukschinskmesk (Paktcinkures) J. A. F. L. 28, pp. 243-248.

Strong, W. D. (1) Cross-cousin Marriage and the culture of the North-eastern Algonquin. A. A. 31, p. 277, n. s. (2) Barren ground, white whale and Ungava religion, p. 285, Nascopi Mythology, p. 286.

Sulte, B. Histoire des Canadiens francais, 1608-1880, 8 v. Montreal, 1882.

Tanghe, R. Geographie humaine de Montreal, Montreal, 1928.

Thomas, C. Ethnology of Canada and Newfoundland, An. Arch. Rep. Ont. 1905.

Thompson, David. Narrative of his exploration in Western America, 1784-1812, ed. J. B. Tyrrell, Champlain Socy. Toronto, 1916.

Thompson, S. (1) European tales among the North American Indians, Col. College Pub., Gen. ser. Nos. 100 & 101, Language ser. v. 2, No. 34, Colorado Springs, Colorado. (2) Tales of the North American Indians, Harvard Univ. Press, 1929.

Trumbull, H. History of the discovery of America, etc. Engagements with the Indians, 1828.

Turner, F. J. The frontier in American history.

Turner L. M. Ethnology of the Ungava district, Rep. B. Amer. Eth. 11 pp. 167-349. Naskape p. 267 et seq.

Tyler, L. G. England in America, 1580-1652, The American Nation, ed. A. B. Hart, 1904.

Tylor, E. B. Researches into the early history of mankind and the development of civilization, Lond. 1878.

Unwin, G. Industrial organization in the 16th and 17th centuries, Oxford, 1922.

Vallée, A. Michel Sarrazin, Quebec, 1927.

Vetromile, E. (1) The Abenaki Indians, Coll. of the Maine Hist. Socy., v. 6, p. 203, 1859. (2) The Abnakis and their history or historical notes on the aborigines of Acadia, N. Y., 1866. (3) Acadia and its aborigines, Coll. of the Maine Hist. Socy., v. 7, p. 337, 1876.

Voorhis, E. Historic forts and trading posts of the French regime and of the English fur-trading companies, 1930. Dept. of Interior, Ottawa, MS.

Wallace, R. C. Cooperation in the natural and human sciences, C. H. R. 14, Dec. 1933, p. 371.

Waterman, T. T. The explanatory element in the folk tales of the North American Indians, J. A. F. L. 27, 1914.

Watson, L. W. The origin of the Melicites, J. A. F. L. 20, 1907, p. 160.

Weedon, W. B. Indian money as a factor in New England civilization. Johns Hopkins studies in hist. and pol. sci., series 2, v. 8-9, Balt. 1884.

Wendell, B. Cotton Mather, The Puritan priest, Camb. Mass. 1926.

Wertenbaker, T. J. The first Americans, 1607-1690, N. Y. 1927 v. 2 of A history of American life, eds. A. M. Schlesinger & D. R. Fox.

Williams, H. U., F. L. and others, The American origin of syphilis with citations from early Spanish authors, Archives of Dermatology and Syphilology, Dec. 1927, v. 16, No. 6, pp. 63-697.

Willoughby, C. C. (1) The adze and the ungrooved axe of the New England Indians, A. A. n. s. 9, p. 296. (2) Dress and ornaments of the New England Indians, A. A. n. s. 7, p. 499. (3) Houses and gardens of the New England Indians, A. A. n. s. 8, p. 115. (4) Primitive metal working, A. A. n. s. 5, p. 55. (5) Textile fabrics of the New England Indians, A. A. n. s. 7, p. 85. (6) Wooden bowls of the Algonquin Indians, A. A. n. s. 10, p. 423.

Wilson, Sir Daniel, Canada, a typical race of American aborigines, Trans. Roy. Soc. Can. 1884, ser. 2. sect. 2, pp. 55-106.

Winsor, J. (1) Anticipations of Cartier's voyages, 1492-1534, Proc. Mass. Histor. Socy. Ser. 2, v. 8, 1894, p. 67. (2) The results in Europe of Cartier's explorations, 1542-1603, Proc. Mass. Histor. Socy. v. 7, 1892, p. 298.

Wintemburg, W. J. Was Hochelaga destroyed or abandoned? A. A. n. s. 9, p. 251.

Wissler, C. The American Indian, 1922.

Woodbury, C. L. The relation of the fisheries to the discovery and settlement of North America, Boston, 1880.

Woodward, A. The Indian use of the silver gorget, Ind. notes 3, 1926, p. 233.

Wrong, G. M. The rise and fall of New France, 2 v. Toronto, 1928.

Index

Ababejit, folk tale concerning, 175

Abenaki (Wabenaki, Canibas): seek refuge in Canada, 3, 72, 91, 93; French and English attempt to secure goodwill of, 26–34; and Christianity, 40, 61, 120, 130–1, 132; religion, 47, 114, 141, 146; warfare, 48; and trade, 50, 62, 119; use of firearms, 51; and agriculture, 57, 88–9, 109; use of maple sugar, 58; drunkenness among, 72; and disease, 75, 76, 78, 82, 83; allow French to serve as war chiefs, 92; polygyny among, 105; common economic interest with French, 125; art, 148, 151; use of pictographs, 153; music, 155; mythology, 157, 158, 163, 165, 169, 179, 184, 185, 189, 190; folk tales, 177, 179, 184, 185, 189, 190

Aboriginal materials and effects of their displacement, 10–13, 46–65

Acadia, 48, 66, 121, 170; French-Indian relations in, 5, 8–25, 26, 125; struggle for supremacy in, 27, 30, 31–4, 50, 118; trade in, 40, 54, 119; use of European materials in, 54, 59; disease in, 79; settlement in, retarded, 88, 121; census of 1685, 111; intermarriage encouraged in, 112–13; Christianity in, 126, 129, 130

Aegir (Norse god), 166

Agriculture: Indian knowledge of, 3, 13, 44; French attempts to introduce, 11, 31, 56, 57–8

Albanel, Father Charles, 38–9, 52, 112, 128, 131

Alexander, H. R., 135

Alfonse, Jean, 25

Algonkian: as distinct from Algonkin, 2

Algonkian language changes, 19

Algonkians, 2, 4, 9, 25, 29, 38, 72; effects of European culture upon, 6, 34, 35, 36, 46–65, 91, 94; and agriculture, 13; their relations with French, 15; and Christianity, 16, 21, 90, 98, 108, 109, 133, 145–7; rallying ground at Three Rivers, 40–1; superseded as middlemen in fur trade, 44; use of firearms, 52; dependence upon Europeans for supplies, 56, 78; drunken-

ness among, 68, 70, 73; and disease, 76, 78, 81; concept of ownership, 86; polygyny among, 105, 180; and assimilation, 107; composition of bands, 113; causes of depopulation, 114–15; influence upon French, 23–5, 123–5; religion, 134–5; art, 148–151; pictographs, 153–5; music, 155–6; mythology, 157–69. See also Central Algonkians; Eastern Algonkians

Allumette Island, 2

Amulets, 143, 144, 145

Andros, Sir Edmund, 32

Argall, Sir Samuel, 26, 118

Armouchiquois, 3, 10, 11, 12, 13

Art: decline of Indian handicrafts, 46–7; elements of Indian, 148–51; place of cross in Indian, 152–3; relationship with pictographs, 153–5; double-curve motive, 148–51

Asia, 1, 2, 77, 167

Assimilation: French attempts at, 106–9

Atlantic Ocean, 23

Atticamegs or Whitefish, 3, 36, 55, 93, 154; description of, 41–2; extermination of, 42; and Christianity, 52, 85, 89, 90, 129; and disease, 76, 78, 83; polygyny among, 105; the Noble Savage, 124; religion, 139, 144, 146; art, 153

Aubert, Thomas, 5

Augusta, Maine, 29

Aveneau, Father Claude, 143

Badger (animal trickster), 165–6

Bailloquet, Father Pierre, 37

Balder (Norse god), 159, 160, 167

Bands: composition and changes, 84–90; solidarity destroyed, 88

Baptism: effect on Indians, 22–3, 103; alleged cause of disease or death, 80, 81–2, 132

Barbeau, C. M.: theory of Algonkian art, 149–51

Barrie, Sir James, 177

Bartlett, F. C., 190

Basques, 5, 18, 19, 66, 81, 134

DATE DUE / DATE DE RETOUR

DEC 0 4 1994

DEC 0 8 1994

DEC 1 3 1995 NOV 2 9 1995

JAN 1 0 1996

DEC 1 3 1995

DEC 1 2 1997 NOV 1 7 1997

DEC 2 2 1997

FEB 0 2 1999

FEB 0 5 1999

CARR M^CLEAN

38-297